Utility, Publicity, and Law

Utility, Publicity, and Law

Essays on Bentham's Moral and Legal Philosophy

GERALD J. POSTEMA

OXFORD
UNIVERSITY PRESS

OXFORD
UNIVERSITY PRESS

Great Clarendon Street, Oxford, OX2 6DP,
United Kingdom

Oxford University Press is a department of the University of Oxford.
It furthers the University's objective of excellence in research, scholarship,
and education by publishing worldwide. Oxford is a registered trade mark of
Oxford University Press in the UK and in certain other countries

First Edition published in 2019

Impression: 1

Published in the United States of America by Oxford University Press
198 Madison Avenue, New York, NY 10016, United States of America

British Library Cataloguing in Publication Data
Data available

Library of Congress Control Number: 2019937065

ISBN 978–0–19–879317–5

Printed and bound by
CPI Group (UK) Ltd, Croydon, CR0 4YY

Preface

The essays in this volume and its companion, *Bentham and the Common Law Tradition* (2nd edition, 2019), offer a reassessment of Jeremy Bentham's strikingly original legal philosophy. The task is, as David Lieberman put it, an "interpretive rescue operation,"[1] seeking to rescue Bentham's work from received interpretations of his utilitarian moral philosophy and positivist legal theory. The demand for this reassessment arose from an increasing appreciation amongst Bentham scholars of the vast scope of his writings, and the relations among them, made possible by the excellent work of the Bentham Project. Since the early 1970s the Project has been publishing in carefully edited critical editions many of his writings that had been unpublished prior to their efforts.

The singular aim of Bentham's work over his more than sixty-year career was to "rear the fabric of felicity with the hands of reason and law" (IPML 11). He claimed "the globe" as the domain of his aspiration (UC 25.26). The only limits on his thought and ambition that he recognized were "the limits of the earth and human kind" (B xi. 72). Striding boldly across conventional disciplinary boundaries, he followed his inquiries into nearly every corner of human experience and thought. Early on, he discovered his "genius for legislation" (B x. 27) and he brought to bear on his legislative efforts inquiries from metaphysics and meta-ethics to psychology, from the philosophy of language to economics, from international relations to the architecture of prisons. As he deployed it, reason enlisted all willing participants in his endeavor, looking for "mutual assistance" from all cognate sciences (UC 69.190, 193). Moreover, "legislation" for Bentham included not only lawmaking and code writing, but also political and social institution building and engineering of public spaces for effective control of the exercise of political power. In his more general philosophical work, Bentham sought to articulate a public philosophy to guide and direct all these "legislative" efforts.

Bentham's public philosophy included a new model of law for jurisprudence (*Corr.* I, 368) that, in his view, departed from the model used by natural law theorists like Grotius, Pufendorf, and Barbyrac and common-law jurists like Coke, Hale, and Blackstone. He elaborated this model in a theory of civil and penal law, a detailed constitutional code, a carefully worked out theory of adjudication, and a limited sketch of a plan for international law. We can fully appreciate the originality of Bentham's understanding of the nature of law and his core normative

[1] David Lieberman, "Economy and Polity in Bentham's Science of Legislation," in Stefan Collini, Richard Whatmore, and Brian Young, eds. *Economics, Polity, and Society: British Intellectual History 1750–1950* (Cambridge: Cambridge University Press, 2000), 107.

principle, the principle of utility, only when we see them as elaborated in the products of this life-long legislative project. The essays here collected seek such an appreciation. Emerging from this study is a positivist legal theory and a utilitarian moral–political philosophy that challenge in fundamental ways contemporary understandings of those doctrines.

Part II of this collection explores details of Bentham's new model of law and his elaboration of it, while Part I explores the philosophical foundations of his public philosophy. Three foundational philosophical doctrines anchor Bentham's jurisprudential theories: his theory of meaning and framework for analysis and definition of key concepts, his theory of individual and social psychology, and his utilitarian theory of value. Chapter 1 offers a quasi-pragmatist reading of the Bentham's views on language, epistemology, and ontology. It argues that Bentham devised a theory of meaning and the technology of thought that gave language the room it must have for the mind to do its essential work, while controlling its excesses and abuses. Chapter 2 sets out Bentham's "practicable" psychology, that is, his understanding of the principles of human psychology needed for his practical, institution-building, and moral advising projects. Bentham argued that, while self-regarding interests are always powerful, social motives play an important role in individual and social life. Human motivations, rooted in a complex constitution of human affections, are plastic, capable of responding to social circumstances and education. Thus, he insisted, it is possible to construct institutions to cultivate socially oriented motives, even extensive benevolence, to counter self-regarding interests.

The remaining four chapters of Part I discuss key aspects of Bentham's normative theory, focusing primarily on his utilitarian theory of value. Chapter 3 outlines the expressivist meta-ethics in terms of which Bentham cast his theory of value. From the meta-ethical requirement of publicity of moral judgment, Bentham constructed an important argument for the principle of utility. Chapter 4 argues that, although Bentham embraced a version of ethical hedonism, insisting that pleasure and pain are the ultimate bearers of value, nevertheless his respect for the demands of publicity on moral judgments led him to treat the language of interests, rather than the "felicific calculus," as the lingua franca of his moral, political, and legal theory. Bentham insisted that advancement of the universal interest is the ultimate end of government and the aim of all morality. Chapter 5 argues that equality lies at the heart of Bentham's theory of value. Equality was not merely an *ad hoc* and ill-fitting addition to his principle of utility, but rather was, as Mill said, "involved in the very meaning" of utility. In Bentham's understanding it reflects a person-regarding conception of value that recognizes the equal claim that each person's well-being has on our moral attention. Chapter 6 explores Bentham's notion of universal interest and its role in his moral and political theory. Social institutions designed to serve the universal interest are likely to call for the sacrifice of personal interests, he conceded, but they also make pursuit of such personal interests possible, and always include each member in the benefits resulting from the realization of the universal interest.

Part II explores core themes in Bentham's jurisprudence. Chapter 7 looks at some features of Bentham's theory of judicial reasoning. Although *Bentham and the Common Law Tradition* (including the Afterword of its second edition) develops this theme in detail, Chapter 7 sets the stage for that discussion by considering Bentham's earliest writings on the subject. These are of special interest because they announce the basic principles that guided Bentham's construction of adjudicative institutions in his later constitutional writings. Chapter 8 sets Bentham's favored command model of law in its historical context, highlighting his refinements of the model that dramatically transform the model. Chapter 10 offers a critical assessment of Bentham's scathing critique of natural rights and the attempts to embed them in the constitutional law of the new American and French republics. Bentham argued that the indeterminacy of broad constitutional rights threatens the necessary publicity of law, because the language of rights provides no public standards for assessing assertions of rights. In defense of constitutional rights jurisprudence, this chapter sketches an alternative conception of public justification and argues that indeterminacy does not threaten public justification understood in this way.

Chapters 9 and 11 study rarely discussed aspects of Bentham's jurisprudence. Drawing on the first chapter's quasi-pragmatist interpretation of his "theory of fictitious entities," Chapter 9 outlines his analysis of statements of probability and the probative force of evidence in law. Chapter 11 sketches his views on the nature and place of law in the global order. This study sheds further light on his understanding of the principle of utility and the institutionalization of the fundamental demand of publicity. Bentham's extended discussion of securities against misrule, outlined in Chapter 12, offers a sustained exploration of the necessary infrastructure of the rule of law. Bentham analyzed the background conditions and engineered the supporting institutions needed for a comprehensive and effective architecture of accountability. Publicity is a pervasive theme running through all of his moral, political, and legal theory. Chapter 13 brings together the most important occurrences of the idea of publicity in previous chapters. It documents Bentham's reliance on publicity throughout his career and demonstrates its centrality to his moral, legal, and political thought.

Acknowledgments

With one exception (portions of Chapter 7), essays brought together in this volume have been written since the original publication of *Bentham and the Common Law Tradition* (Oxford: Clarendon Press, 1986). I have substantially revised and expanded several of them—especially Chapters 1, 2, 3, and 4—other chapters combine portions of previously published work or revises to some extent previously published. Chapter 11 has not been previously published. This volume is intended as a companion to a second edition of *Bentham and the Common Law Tradition*, which includes an Afterword in which some of the main challenges to that work are addressed.

Chapter 1 is largely newly written, but it draws on section II of "Facts, Fictions and Law: Bentham on the Foundations of the Law of Evidence," *Archiv für Rechts- und Sozialphilosophie*, Beiheft 16 (1983), 45–54.

Chapter 2 draws on "Introduction," *Jeremy Bentham, volume 1: Moral and Political Philosophy*, G.J. Postema, ed. (Aldershot, England: Dartmouth Publishing Co., 2002), ix–xxxiii and portions of "Bentham's Utilitarianism" in *A Guide to Mill's Utilitarianism*, H.R. West, ed. (Malden, MA: Blackwell Publishers, 2006), 26–44.

Chapter 3 draws on portions of "Bentham's Utilitarianism" in *A Guide to Mill's Utilitarianism*, H.R. West, ed. (London: Blackwell Publishers, 2006), 26–44.

Chapter 4 draws on portions of "Bentham's Utilitarianism" in *A Guide to Mill's Utilitarianism*, H.R. West, ed. (London: Blackwell Publishers, 2006), 26–44.

Chapter 5 revises somewhat "Bentham's Equality-Sensitive Utilitarianism," *Utilitas* 10 (1998), 144–58.

Chapter 6 revises somewhat "Interests, Universal and Particular: Bentham's Utilitarian Theory of Value," *Utilitas* 18 (2006), 109–33.

Chapter 7 draws on "Bentham's Early Reflections on Law, Justice and Adjudication," *Revue Internationale de Philosophie* No. 141 (1982), 219–41.

Chapter 8 brings together "Legal Positivism—Early Foundations," *Routledge Companion to the Philosophy of Law*, Andrei Marmor, ed. (NY: Routledge, 2012), 31–47 and "Law as Command: The Model of Command in Modern Jurisprudence," *Philosophical Issues* (Supplement to *Noûs*) vol. 11 (2001), 470–501.

Chapter 9 revises sections I, II, and IV of "Facts, Fictions, and Law: Bentham on the Foundation of Evidence," *Archives for Legal and Social Philosophy*, Beiheft No. 16 (1983), 37–64.

Chapter 10 revises slightly "In Defense of 'French Nonsense': Fundamental Rights in Constitutional Jurisprudence," in *Enlightenment, Rights, and Revolution*,

N. MacCormick and Z. Bankowski, eds. (Aberdeen: Aberdeen University Press, 1989), 107–33.

Chapter 11 is newly written for this volume.

Chapter 12 slightly revises "The Soul of Justice: Bentham on Publicity, Law and the Rule of Law," in *Bentham's Theory of Law and Public Opinion*, Xiaobo Zhai and Michael Quinn, eds. (Cambridge: Cambridge University Press, 2014).

Chapter 13 slightly revises "Jeremy Bentham, Theorist of Publicity" in *Public Reason in the History of Political Philosophy: Classical Sources and Contemporary Commentaries*, Gerald Gaus and Piers Turner, eds. (London: Routledge, 2017), 354–74.

For research assistance, I am grateful to Kyle Driggers, Alfredo Watkins, and Michaela Tiller. I am grateful to Xiaobo Zhai for organizing a working session of the International Society of Utilitarian Studies in Karlsruhe, July 2018, on the essays included in this collection and to the following colleagues who commented on them: Francesco Ferraro, Michael Lobban, Michihiro Kaino, Daniel Priel, Simon Palmer, and Xiaobo Zhai. I am also grateful to Philip Schofield for help on multiple occasions throughout the years and for editorial work on the Bentham papers of the highest quality.

Table of Contents

Abbreviations

Works of Bentham

Article	Jeremy Bentham, "Article on Utilitarianism" in Jeremy Bentham, *Deontology together with A Table of the Springs of Action, and Article on Utilitarianism*, Amnon Goldworth, ed. (CW) (Oxford: Oxford University Press, 1983), 283–328.
B	Jeremy Bentham, *Works of Jeremy Bentham* (11 vols.), John Bowring, ed. (Edinburgh, 1838–43). Reprinted New York, 1962.
BCLT	Gerald J. Postema, *Bentham and the Common Law Tradition* (Oxford: Clarendon Press, 1986/1989) [Second edition 2019].
BL Add MSS	British Library, Additional Manuscripts.
CC (B)	Jeremy Bentham, *Constitutional Code* in B ix.
CC (CW) vol. 1	Jeremy Bentham, *Constitutional Code Vol. 1* (CW), Fred Rosen and J.H. Burns, eds. (Oxford: Clarendon Press, 1983).
Chrest.	Jeremy Bentham, *Chrestomathia* (CW), M.J. Smith and W.H. Burston, eds. (Oxford: Oxford University Press, 1983).
Civ. Code	Jeremy Bentham, *Principles of the Civil Code* in B i. 297–364.
Corr.	Jeremy Bentham, *Correspondence* (CW), 12 volumes (Oxford: Oxford University Press, 1968–2006).
Col.	Jeremy Bentham, *Colonies, Commerce and Constitutional Law—Rid Yourselves of Ultramaria* (CW), Philip Schofield, ed. (Oxford: Oxford University Press, 1995).
Com.	Jeremy Bentham, *A Comment on the Commentaries* in *A Comment on the Commentaries and A Fragment on Government*, J.H. Burns and H.L.A. Hart, eds. (London: Athlone Press, 1977).
CW	*Bentham: Collected Works* (Oxford).
Deont.	Jeremy Bentham, *Deontology together with A Table of the Springs of Action and Article on Utilitarianism* (CW), Amnon Goldworth, ed. (Oxford: Oxford University Press, 1983).
DO	Jeremy Bentham, *De l'ontologie et autres textes sure les fictions*, Philip Schofield, ed. (text), Jean-Piere Cléro and Cristian Laval, trs. and commentary (Paris: Éditions du Seuil, 1997)
FG	Jeremy Bentham, *Fragment on Government* in *A Comment on the Commentaries and A Fragment on Government*, J.H. Burns and H.L.A. Hart, eds. (London: Athlone Press, 1977).
FPP	Jeremy Bentham, *First Principles Preparatory to Constitutional Code* (CW), Philip Schofield, ed. (Oxford: Oxford University Press, 1989).
Gen. View	Jeremy Bentham, *General View of a Complete Code of Laws*, in B iii. 156–210.
IL (1827)	Jeremy Bentham, MSS on International Law dated June 1827, BL Add. MSS 33,551.120–125.
Influence	Jeremy Bentham, *The Influence of Natural Religion on the Temporal Happiness of Mankind* (published by Bentham in 1822, under the

	pseudonym, Philip Beauchamp), introduction by Delos McKown (New York: Prometheus Books, 2003).
IPML	Jeremy Bentham, *Introduction to the Principles of Morals and Legislation* (CW), Fred Rosen, ed. (Oxford: Oxford University Press, 1996). Revised edition of J.H. Burns and H.L.A. Hart, eds. (London, Athlone Press, 1970).
IRE	Jeremy Bentham, *Introductory View of the Rationale of Evidence* in B vi.
Limits	Jeremy Bentham, *Of the Limits of the Penal Branch of Jurisprudence* (CW), Philip Schofield, ed. (Oxford: Oxford University Press, 2010).
LW	Jeremy Bentham, *Legislator of the World: Writings on Codification, Law, and Education* (CW), Philip Schofield and James Harris, eds. (Oxford: Oxford University Press, 1998).
NS	Jeremy Bentham, *Nonsense upon Stilts* in *Rights, Representation, and Reform—Nonsense upon Stilts and Other Writings on the French Revolution* (CW), Philip Schofield, Catherine Pease-Watkin, and Cyprian Blamires, eds. (Oxford: Oxford University Press, Oxford, 2002).
OLG	Jeremy Bentham, *Of Laws in General*, H.L.A. Hart, ed. (London: Athlone Press, 1970) (largely superseded by *Limits*).
PF	Jeremy Bentham, *Pannomial Fragments*, in B iii. 211–30.
PIL	Jeremy Bentham, "The Principles of International Law," B ii. 537–60.
PT	Jeremy Bentham, *Political Tactics* (CW), M. James, Cyprian Blamires, and Catherine Pease-Watkin, eds. (Oxford: Clarendon Press, 1999).
Representation	Jeremy Bentham, "Essay on Representation," Appendix D in Mary P. Mack, *Jeremy Bentham: An Odyssey of Ideas* (New York: Columbia University Press, 1963).
RRR	Jeremy Bentham, *Rights, Representation, and Reform: Nonsense upon Stilts and Other Writings on the French Revolution* (CW), Philip Schofield, Catherine Pease-Watkin, and Cyprian Blamires, eds. (Oxford: Clarendon Press, 2002).
RJE	Jeremy Bentham, *Rational of Judicial Evidence* in *Works of Jeremy Bentham*, B vi and vii.
Stark	*Jeremy Bentham's Economic Writings*, Werner Stark, ed. (London: George Allen & Unwin, 1952), three volumes.
SM	Jeremy Bentham, *Securities against Misrule and Other Constitutional Writings for Tripoli and Greece* (CW), Philip Schofield, ed. (Oxford: Oxford University Press, 1990).
OAM	Jeremy Bentham, *Official Aptitude Maximized, Expense Minimized* (CW), Philip Schofield, ed. (Oxford: Oxford University Press, 1993).
TSA	Jeremy Bentham, *A Table of the Springs of Action*, in *Deontology together with A Table of the Springs of Action and Article on Utilitarianism* (CW), Amnon Goldworth, ed. (Oxford: Oxford University Press, 1983).
UC	Bentham MSS, University College London (reference to box, folio number).

Works of Other Authors

Aquinas	Aquinas, *Political Writings*, R.W. Dyson, ed. and tr. (Cambridge: Cambridge University Press, 2002).

Bs Com	William Blackstone, *Commentaries on the Laws of England*, 4 vols. (Oxford, 1765–69).
DC	Thomas Hobbes, *On the Citizen* [*De Cive*], Richard Tuck and Michael Silverthorne, eds. and trs. (Cambridge: Cambridge University Press, 1998).
Defender	Marsilius of Padua, *The Defender of the Peace,* Annabel Brett, ed. and tr. (Cambridge: Cambridge University Press, 2005).
Dialogue	Thomas Hobbes, *Dialogue between a Philosopher and a Student of the Common Law*, Alan Cromartie, ed. (Oxford: Clarendon Press, 2005).
DMC	Samuel Pufendorf, *On the Duty of Man and Citizen* (1673), James Tully, ed., Michael Silverthorne, tr. (Cambridge: Cambridge University Press, 1991).
EUJ	Samuel Pufendorf, *Elements of Universal Jurisprudence*, in *The Political Writings of Samuel Pufendorf*, C.L. Carr, ed., M.J. Seidler, tr. (Oxford: Oxford University Press, 1994).
Lev	Thomas Hobbes, *Leviathan*, Richard Tuck, ed. (Cambridge: Cambridge University Press, 1991).
OL	Francisco Suarez, *On Laws and God the Lawgiver* (1612), G.L. Williams, A. Brown, J. Waldron, trs. (Oxford: Oxford University Press, 1944).
OLN	*On the Law of Nature and of Nations* (1672), in *The Political Writings of Samuel Pufendorf*, C.L. Carr, ed., M.J. Seidler, tr. (Oxford: Oxford University Press, 1994).
THN	David Hume, *A Treatise of Human Nature*, David F. Norton and Mary J. Norton, eds. (Oxford: Oxford University Press, 2000).
Utilitarianism	J.S. Mill, *Utilitarianism* in Mill, *Collected Works*, J. Robson, ed., 33 vols. (Toronto: University of Toronto Press, 1961–91), vol. X.

PART I
FOUNDATIONS

1

Meaning, Analysis, and Exposition

The Technology of Thought

In the second decade of the nineteenth century, when he was well into his sixties, Bentham turned his attention to articulating in detail the theoretical infrastructure of his studies of political and legal philosophy and practice. One main component was his theory of language and its implicit ontology—his theory of real and fictitious entities. The other main component was his theory of human psychology. In both cases, these relatively late efforts did not substantially revise, but only elaborated, the ideas that had underwritten his work from the beginning of his career. In this chapter, we explore the theories of language and meaning, and the accompanying epistemological and metaphysical views, that lie at the foundations of his thought. In 1813–15,[1] he codified themes and arguments about language, meaning, ontology, and "logic" that he first sketched at the dawn of his career in the early 1770s.[2] Reflecting on language and its relation to thought and reality, he produced sophisticated theories of meaning and the technology of thought—the techniques and principles by which the active mind orders the domain of thought.

First and foremost a social and legal reformer, Bentham undertook philosophical reflection on the nature, use, and abuse of language in an effort to understand and improve the world. His intellectual energy was trained primarily on law and political ordering, but he looked to every mode of inquiry ("science") available for analytic and normative tools with which to "rear the fabric of felicity" (IPML I.1). He adopted, adapted, and elaborated some from other thinkers (e.g., his basic normative principle, the Greatest Happiness Principle), but others he invented himself. The most important of his theoretical innovations, in his view, was his theory of meaning, the heart of which was his analysis of language in terms of "real" and "fictitious" entities (BL Add MSS 33,550.4).[3] This theory mapped the relations between the domain of thought and physical reality and devised a method of analysis—definition by "paraphrasis"—that enabled systematic ordering of

[1] This work can be found in *Chrestomathia* and his essays on logic, ontology and language in B viii.

[2] Preliminary sketches of Bentham's basic position can be found in his earliest work, e.g., UC 169, 50–66; UC 27.3–5, 25, 53; UC 135.1–69 *passim.*; UC 106.2–3; UC 69.52–3, and the PPI manuscripts, UC 69.77–241 *passim.*, especially 140–1, 219–20, 227–8. The results of this work can be seen, for example, in his early writings on law and politics, for example, FG, Chapter V.

[3] This theory is conventionally referred to as Bentham's "theory of fictions," but this name is misleading. (See Philip Schofield, "Jeremy Bentham on Utility and Truth," *History of European Ideas* 41 (2015), 1125–42.) Bentham carefully distinguished between "fictions" and "fictitious entities," and he did so with principles set out in his theory of meaning.

Utility, Publicity, and Law: Essays on Bentham's Moral and Legal Philosophy. Gerald J. Postema.

thought. With this technology, Bentham sought to discipline potentially wayward language and thereby to deprive arbitrary power of one of its favorite weapons.

LANGUAGE

Bentham observed that language is an instrument of power, a device by which the arbitrary exercise of power can be masked and mystified. Even when it is not used to advance the ends of power, he observed, it can be deceptive, generating confusion and corrupting practical reasoning. He undertook to "pluck the mask of mystery" not only from jurisprudence (FG 410), but also from language itself; he sought to demystify it and discipline its use.

Locke held that language is a collection of signs of thoughts in the mind[4] and thus is a medium by which such thoughts are conveyed—communicated—from one mind to another. Bentham accepted this view, but he modified it in an important way. He recognized that language plays a significant role in interpersonal communication; he called this the "transitive" use of language. "Designation," the naming of objects, is a key operation of language in discourse.[5] But he insisted that in addition, and more fundamentally, language is necessary to the formation and ordering of thought. "By its intransitive use it is an instrument employed in the creation and fixation of thought itself" (UC 101.423; but see B viii. 320).

Language is "an instrument not only of *discourse*, but of *thought* itself," he wrote, "an instrument, by which not only are perceptions and ideas *communicated*, but ideas *formed*."[6] Through their senses, all sentient creatures interact with the world in which they live. The senses deliver "impressions" to the mind. These impressions are momentary ("flitting") and "indeterminate" (UC 101.332). Language enables human beings to give determinate shape and stability to these impressions and to endow them with a degree of permanency. "Unclothed as yet in words, or stript of them, thoughts are but dreams: as the clouds in the sky, they float in the mind one moment and vanish out of it the next." (UC 101.423; see UC 69.153). Moreover, language provides the technology by which the mental operations of abstraction, analysis, concept-formation, and inference can work on the contents of experience delivered to the mind by the senses. Thus, language makes possible every art and science, even the most primitive (UC 101.423). Indeed, human well-being is entirely dependent on language (UC 102.401), Bentham insisted. Without language human thought would be reduced almost to nothing, human experience would

[4] "Words, in their primary or immediate signification, stand for nothing but the ideas in the mind of him that uses them." John Locke, *Essay Concerning Human Understanding*, P.H. Nidditch, ed. (Oxford: Oxford University Press, 1975), III, 2, 2.

[5] Philip Schofield, *Utility and Democracy: The Political Thought of Jeremy Bentham* (Oxford: Oxford University Press, 2006), 12.

[6] UC 101.144n9, author's emphasis. "Language is not merely the instrument of discourse, it is moreover the instrument of thought. By language it is that a man not only discourses but thinks." UC 102.401. See also UC 101.423 and B viii, 119, 129, 174, 198, 219, 231, 320–3, and 331.

be virtually empty, and human existence would be diminished to that of animals. Language is "an instrument without the aid of which a man would not have any more ideas to communicate than those possessed by animals" (UC 101.145; UC 102.22). Without language all but the most primitive of thoughts would not just be incommunicable, they would be unthinkable. Human experience would be unavailable to thought, discourse, and action. However, this is not to say that communication is unimportant or secondary to the internal, intransitive use of language. On the contrary, Bentham believed that it is the need to communicate and the demands of making one's experience public that motivates the intransitive use of language and defines an important criterion of its success.

Yet, language can be misleading and mystifying. The imagination or fancy—sometimes innocent, sometimes sinister—is inclined to create ideas of *fabulous entities* and *fictions* (ghosts, witches, and chimeras; angels, demons, and gods; golden mountains and unicorns; common-law rules and original social contracts).[7] Indeed, some fictions are adopted for the explicit purpose of deceiving ("willful falsehoods").[8] However, we cannot banish all fictitious reference from our language, because language itself forces us to posit *fictitious entities*. Inevitably, we speak of qualities and modes of physical things, abstract entities and numbers, rights, and duties, and the like, as if they populated our physical world in just the way rocks, apples, dogs, and human bodies do. And this language, although in this respect deceptive, is necessary for thought and discourse (UC 101.322; 102.23 (DO 84)). Fictitious entities are a "necessity to which we are subjected by the imperfection of the instrument for the purposes of discourse, the necessity of mixing falsehood with truth, on pain of being without ideas, as well as without conversation" (*Chrest.* 277n.a).[9]

Without use of (names of) fictitious entities, no thought beyond that of the most primitive and non-human would be possible. Why is this so? Because, on Bentham's hypothesis, language was formed in the human species at a time when we were most directly engaged with concrete physical entities in our world. Our language was, and continues to be, inevitably concrete, forced to refer to physical substances. "A material image is the only instrument by which, the only medium through which, conceptions can be conveyed from mind to mind." Bentham wrote in his commonplace book, "Wherever there is a word, there is a thing; so says the common notion—the result of the association of ideas. Wherever there is a

[7] UC 102.23–24 (DO 84–6); B viii, 126, 199, 262; UC 101.342; UC 69, 52, 221; FG 509–11.

[8] UC 102.23 (DO 84); FG 410–11, 439–41.

[9] In a MS dating from the time of the writing of *Limits*, Bentham wrote, "wherever the thing which a man is said to have for his property is either less or more than one entire single and determinate corporeal object a fictitious entity is created as it were for the purpose and spoken of as being the object of a man's property." But, he adds, "It is not necessary upon the present occasion to enter into the examination of the necessity there may be for setting up this fiction: it is sufficient that it be actually and universally set up, and that it is so firmly engrafted into every language that it is now impossible to carry on discourse without it." Bentham, *Of Laws in General*, App. B, Part II, H.L.A. Hart, ed. (London: Athlone Press, 1970), 285. See also, B vi. 7; PF B iii, 218; B viii. 327.

word, there is a thing; hence the almost universal practice of confounding *fictitious* entities with *real* ones—corresponding names of fictitious entities with real ones" (B xi. 73).

Which entities are "real" and which "fictitious" and how can we tell the difference? How can we distinguish linguistically necessary "fictitious entities" from "fictions" and "fabulous entities"? More generally, how can we discipline the use of language not to lead us into confusion, deception, and falsehood? These are the questions Bentham's theory of meaning was designed to answer. He began with an inventory of the basic ontology of our world and our access to that world.

ONTOLOGICAL BASICS

Bentham's ontology is inseparable from his epistemology. They proceed in tandem, each dependent on and reflecting the other. This makes it difficult to set out the philosophical foundations of this thought in a straightforward, linear way. I begin with a sketch of the concepts Bentham typically used to explicate the ontological commitments of ordinary language. This will lead us to look to the warrant he offers for his scheme in his epistemology. The epistemology, however, will call for a refinement of his initial ontological scheme. Bentham maintained that, because of the essential role of noun substantives in language, we tend to think in terms of objects or entities, even though the most basic experiences from which language emerges and in which it is rooted is populated, rather, by states of affairs and events that these objects or entities participate in. The surface ontology of ordinary language, we shall see, is itself, in one important sense, "figurative."

To begin, Bentham held that inevitably we talk about and refer to entities. We talk of all of them *as if* they were real, but some are *real*, and some are *unreal*.[10] *Unreal* entities are either *non-entities* ("fabulous entities" or "fictions") or "fictitious entities." (These categories are meant to be exclusive.) Fictions or fabulous entities are not only not real, they lack linguistic legitimacy; they must not be accorded proper linguistic existence. Although they richly populate our daily conversations, they can and ought to be avoided. They play no proper role in thought. However, this is not the case for "fictitious entities." Although, properly speaking, they are not of the nature of real entities, they have a proper, indeed indispensable, role in thought. Therefore, they cannot be eliminated from language, without incapacitating thought. Frequently, Bentham spoke of the "impossible, yet indispensable existence" of fictitious entities (e.g., UC 102. 23 (DO 84)). They have this essential place by virtue of the relationship they bear to real entities and their participation in the world that they populate—a role determined by the universal need of human beings to understand their world and survive and flourish in it.

[10] In an unsent letter to d'Alembert, Bentham distinguished between "correct substantives" (*substantifs propres*) and "incorrect" (*impropres*) ones (UC 169.55).

The category of *real* entities, according to Bentham, comprises two exclusive groups: the mental and the substantial.[11] The category of *substances*, includes both *corporeal* (physical bodies) and *incorporeal* (spiritual bodies).[12] Because he thought the evidence for the existence of incorporeal substances is very weak, Bentham was inclined for most purposes to ignore that sub-category and focused exclusively on material or strictly physical substances. So, typically, he divided the category of real entities into *mental* and *material*, or *psychical* and *physical*, entities. The class of mental or psychical entities includes *sensations* (e.g., pleasure and pain) and *perceptions* (UC 106.2; TSA 77), which, again, include *impressions* and *ideas*. Following Hume, Bentham understood impressions to be the immediate deliverances of our senses, while ideas are in some ways derived from them.[13]

The psychical and physical seem to differ in their fundamental metaphysical natures, but Bentham distinguished them in terms of the mode of our epistemic access to them. Psychical entities are immediately "perceptible"; we have direct access to them. Their existence is known—"persuasion of them is produced"—by sense without reasoning (UC 102.13). In contrast, physical entities are "inferential": we know them by reasoning from evidence presented to our senses. We "perceive" material objects, but "of the supposed source of the perceptions that are experienced, the existence is, strictly speaking, rather a subject of inference than of perception" (UC 102.118).[14] While the existence of corporeal entities is inferred from evidence presented to the senses, incorporeal entities are inferred by reasoning alone. Among incorporeal entities, Bentham located God and the human soul. It appears that Bentham included the subcategory of incorporeal entities in the category of substances largely as a place-holder for conceptually possible entities. Whether there are any such entities to populate this subcategory, he believed, depends entirely on the strength of the arguments that can be made for their existence. Bentham was generally skeptical, and he concluded that those who are correctly unconvinced by the reasoning offered for the existence of incorporeal substances, may legitimately consign such entities to the category of non-entities (UC 102.11). Thus, so far as we can know them, real entities are either psychical or physical.

[11] Bentham's usage was not always consistent; sometimes he included the mental in the category of substances. In an early MS he wrote, "The only objects that really exist are *substances*. They are the only real entities. To convey any notion by words which are the names of any objects [other] than substances, we are obliged to attribute to such objects what in truth is attributable only to substances: in a word we are obliged to feign them to be substances. Those others in short are only fictitious entities" (UC 69.241). Bentham never denied that mental entities are real (indeed, he thought them to be the "most real"), so it appears that here he includes the mental in the category of substances.

[12] UC 102.8, 102.19 (DO 168); UC 101.337; UC 169.55; UC 69.227, 240.

[13] *Chrest.* 271n; UC 101.347, 417; UC 106.2. Bentham was much influenced by Hume's doctrines and liberally borrowed Hume's terminology, often without embracing the associated Humean understanding of it. Regarding his use of the term "impression," for example, he says, "I may be permitted to borrow the nomenclature of that subtle and elegant philosopher in this instance without adopting many of his opinions" (UC 70(a). 52).

[14] Bentham sometimes spoke of physical bodies as "perceptible" (e.g., UC 102.8, 14 (DO 168, 170–2)), but clearly, he means "indirectly perceptible" (see UC 101.118).

Consider the class of psychical entities. Bentham held that sensations are immediate mental experiences. They may have causes outside the mind, but they do not have what philosophers now call intentional objects. Impressions are presented to us by our senses—the immediate deposit of our sensory apparatus. They are utterly particular, undifferentiated and momentary. Along with sensations (e.g., particular pain sensations, or kinesthetic sensations), impressions are the primitive constituents of human experience. Ideas, in contrast, are of several kinds. Some, as Hume taught (THN I, III, vii), are copies of impressions, recovered from memory (*Chrest.* 271n; UC 101.347, 417). As such, they are particular and undifferentiated, like that which they copy. However, the mind is also populated with other ideas that are produced by the mind working on or with impressions—for example, mental images of concrete entities (RJE vi. 254), abstract ideas, especially those signified by common names (*Chrest.* 265–6n), and mathematical propositions, including idealizations.[15]

Unlike sensations (e.g., experiences of pain), perceptions have intentional objects. The immediate impression is given shape by judgment, which points beyond the immediate impression to a reality independent of it (RJE vi. 254–5; UC 69.133). Thus, as Bentham understood them, perceptions, even the simplest and most primitive, take themselves to be about something outside of themselves. However, Bentham insisted that, while apprehension of the idea is always veridical, the judgment regarding its intentional object may not be. On this insight, Bentham built a misleading doctrine of double reference of language.[16] In his view, utterances in ordinary language simultaneously refer to the ideas (thoughts or beliefs) of the speaker and to the objects of those ideas or thoughts (UC 102.459–61; B viii. 321; 330–1, 336). The *immediate* subject of communication, he maintained, is some belief, conviction, attitude, feeling, or other "thought" of the speaker (B viii. 330). The indirect or *ulterior* subject typically is some event, state of affairs, or real entity in the world beyond the mind. Although his terminology is unapt, it is meant to capture the difference between *signifying* some constituent of the mind and *referring to* some object or event in the world. To signify some content in the speaker's mind is not to denote, but rather to express, it—literally, to press it out (B viii. 227)—and thereby to convey the thought to others.

Ideas, impressions, and sensations are real entities, on Bentham's scheme, but they are not substances: they are psychical, not physical entities. Yet, he often

[15] "Mathematical propositions have no other certainty than what belongs to the conclusions of sense: for they are themselves derived from these conclusions: the only advantage they have is that the Ideas which form the terms of which they consist ... are taken from those objects of sense which can afford conclusions, and these [are] taken under circumstances in which they are least liable to occur. A mathematician takes his abstract idea of a line and a circle from the most perfect right line and circle he ever saw, and those placed at [such] distances from his eyes at which he is least liable to be mistaken in their figure: and if in these he [sees] any defects, any parts tending to curvature in the right line or to straightness or a different curvature in the circle he may make his idea of line and circle from even these imperfections ... by resolving not to suppose them to exist" (UC 96.118). See also UC 135.56; UC 69.219.

[16] See Chapter 9, 211-13.

insisted that "in the one there is just as much reality as in the other" (*Chrest.* 265n). "Material substances and perceptions [are] substantive and independent" (UC 46.20); and "if it can be alone, it exists [i.e., is real]; If not, it does not exist" (UC 169.55). Indeed, of the existence of the impressions or ideas (including abstract ideas) there is greater probative force, namely, immediate awareness, while the existence of a physical entity can only be inferred from perceptual evidence (*ibid.*). Impressions, Bentham maintained, are "the immediate object and subject" of perception, but the body that caused the impression "is but in a secondary and comparatively remote way the object and subject of the perception" (UC 101.118). This led Bentham sometimes to say that, in virtue of our direct access to them, psychical entities have the "better title to reality" (UC 102.14 (DO 174)).

EPISTEMOLOGY

It should be evident from the above that Bentham's ontology and his epistemology are intertwined.[17] This will become even clearer as we set out the epistemological foundations of his thought.

Primaeval Logical Analysis

Bentham's epistemology begins with the familiar empiricist axiom that all knowledge has its source in human experience. "Experience is the foundation of all our knowledge, of all our reasoning, the sole guide of our conduct" (RJE vi. 241). And, human experience, at its root, is sense experience: "sense is the foundation from which all ideas take their rise" (UC 101.332).[18] Perceptible objects present themselves to our senses; receiving an impression, we perceive the object.

However, according to Bentham, this simple retelling of the story of sensory experience conceals its complexity and the extensive role of the mind in the process. First, as we have seen, he held that perception always involves ("is accompanied by") judgment (UC 101.119). In the simplest case of perception one judges that the object exists. Perception engenders belief and belief points beyond the impression and the mind entertaining it. The mind takes the impression as evidence of something that obtains independent of it.[19] Second, the judgment that an object exists

[17] Piero Tarantino offers a realist interpretation of Bentham's theory of meaning in his recent work, *Philosophy, Obligation, and Law: Bentham's Ontology of Normativity* (New York: Routledge, 2018), esp. Chapters 1–2. His reading contrasts sharply with the quasi-pragmatist reading offered in this chapter largely because he does not appreciate, as I believe we must, the interdependence of Bentham's ontology and his epistemology and, hence, the important role of the active powers of the mind in shaping the world of experience.

[18] UC 101.332; see UC 69.219; UC 46.18; UC 135. 304–5, 311; B viii. 238.

[19] Bentham rejected the Humean doctrine (THN, I.3.7) that belief is merely an especially lively idea, because, he argued, increased liveliness cannot explain this essential role of judgment of pointing to a reality beyond itself (RJE vi. 254–5).

in the world beyond impressions and ideas presupposes a further engagement of what earlier philosophers called "the active powers of the mind." In *Chrestomathia*, Bentham tells a tale of naïve perception and the role of the mind in it (*Chrest.* 262–5). A farmer's daughter receiving a constant stream of momentary, undifferentiated impressions attends to one of them. Holding it in her attention, she focuses on a part of it, a plant; she then mentally separates the flower from the rest of the plant and then attends separately to its shape, color, and fragrance, elements of what she now takes to be the composite impression. She gives it a (proper) name, "flower." In doing this, the daughter engages in what Bentham called "primaeval analysis," singling out from the initial impression, various properties of an object. Later, receiving impressions that strike her as similar, she applies the same sound to objects that she isolates in them. Recalling these experiences, she relates them to each other and comes to form an idea that encompasses all of them, and uses "flower" (now using it as a common name) to signify that idea and the objects and their impressions from which it was derived. The daughter, Bentham maintained, engages in a form of analysis, an activity of the mind, which, at this point, is primitive and has "no science yet in it" (*Chrest.* 266), although sophisticated versions of the activity develop later.

Earlier in the same work, Bentham described this activity in detail:

> No portion of matter ever presents itself to sense, without presenting, at one and the same time, a multitude of simple ideas, of all which taken together, the concrete one, in a state more or less correct and complete, is composed. At the same time, though naturally all these ideas present themselves together, the mind has it in its power to detach … any one or more of them from the rest, and either keep it in view in this detached state, or make it up into a compound with other simple ideas, detached in like manner from other sources. But, for the making of this separation—this abstraction, as it is called—more trouble, a stronger force of attention, is necessary, than for the taking them up, in a promiscuous bundle, as it were; in the bundle in which they have been tied together by the hand of Nature: that is, than for the consideration of the object in its concrete state (*Chrest.* 58, author's emphasis omitted).

The picture Bentham paints for us here has the mind engaged at the beginning in "decomposing" the initially received impressions, isolating some elements from the background, ignoring others, and combining the selected items again into a construction of an object and its properties.

Bentham's language at the end of this passage might suggest a different picture: the mind receives a large number of simple ideas, produced by bits of extra-mental reality, which are then bundled together, albeit "promiscuously," by nature. However, I believe this language misleads us regarding Bentham's considered view. For on that view the items in the bundle, indeed the sense that what the perceiver attends to is a composite, are consequences of the activity of the perceiver's mind, rather than something given to by "nature." Bentham made clear that the activity—the "operation"—of constructing abstract ideas (e.g., of certain colors, shapes, fragrances, and the like) presupposes and uses the materials provided by the more primitive "logical analysis"; and logical analysis is performed on "physical wholes . . . which are in immediate contact with individuals," that is, with individual minds via their senses (*Chrest.* 261, 262, 268). It is only *after* this analysis or partitioning of primitive sensory experience, and its subsequent synthesis, that the images yielded by events can be regarded as bundles of determinate, assignable simple ideas. Simple ideas are not the work of nature, passively received by the mind, but rather the artificial products of an active and sophisticated human mind, seeking to satisfy its needs and pursue its interests. For Bentham, simplicity is not a sign of an idea's being primitive or basic; on the contrary, it is a sign of the idea's being the product of an intellectual process engaged in by an active mind.

This understanding of the epistemology of real and fictitious entities is echoed in Bentham's theory of language. The proposition is the basic unit of analysis, he maintained. "Nothing less than the import of an entire proposition [is] sufficient for the giving full expression to any the most simple thought" (B viii. 322). No word alone—of itself—signifies anything that exists (UC 169.56). We can capture in language the real existence of a particular object only by means of a complete proposition.[20] Thus, "every man who speaks, speaks in propositions, the rudest savage, not less than the most polished orator"; thus, "terms taken by themselves are the work of abstraction, the produce of a refined analysis" (B viii. 321; see 102.413–14). Animals speak solely in *propositions*, Bentham asserted (B viii. 322), but it is "by the faculty of *abstraction* man has learned to resolve propositions into *words*" (UC 102.81; author's emphasis). In the beginning was the proposition, not the word. "The truth is that in the first place came propositions, and that out of propositions, by abstraction and analysis, terms possessed each of them, of an independent import, were framed" (B viii. 322). Since "nothing less than the import of an entire proposition be sufficient for the giving full expression to any the most simple thought, it follows that no word, being anything more than a fragment of a proposition, no word is of itself the complete sign of any thought" (*ibid.*). Just as words are products of analysis of more primitive, whole-propositional utterances, so simple ideas, the building blocks of our complex modes of thought by which we come to understand the world, are products of an active mind. Qualities, for example, are only fragments of integral ideas: of qualities, "the expression is incomplete . . . the idea presented by it is but, as it were, the fragment of an idea" (B viii. 326). Moreover, the ideas associated with names of fictitious entities are the products of analysis: "it is by an operation of the nature of analysis, primaeval

[20] See Ross Harrison, *Bentham* (London: Routledge & Kegan Paul, 1984), 65–7.

analysis, that the ideas designated by the several names of fictitious entities have been formed" (*Chrest.* 272n). Thus, *both* the abstract ideas of color, figure, etc., *and* the particular simple ideas from which these ideas of qualities are derived, are fictitious entities.

Physical Base and the World of Human Experience

Against this background, it is possible to understand Bentham's otherwise paradoxical claim that "A body (real entity) is an aggregate of fictitious entities."[21] This is not to say, that real entities do not exist, that all our talk of a reality external to the senses is a fiction.[22] To say that would be nonsense in Bentham's view for two reasons. First, his entire discussion of the epistemology of fictitious entities was designed to explain and ground discussion of the difference between real and fictitious entities, not to explain it away. Second, Bentham repeatedly and very clearly rejected anything that approximated philosophical idealism or phenomenalism (B viii. 189, 197; UC 46.20). As we have seen, he sometimes maintained that psychical entities have the better title to existence in virtue of our direct access to them; nevertheless, he never doubted that the inferences by which we confirm the existence of the external world are reliable. He embraced an ontology that has a physical base that exists entirely independent of mind, although our access to that physical reality is only through mind-dependent impressions shaped into ideas and thoughts.

What could Bentham have meant by saying that a real body is an aggregate of fictitious entities? He means, I think, that the distinction between a body and its properties is the product of analysis, that not only are the properties and modes of a physical object fictitious entities, but so too is the body if it is considered apart from these properties and modes. Real entities present themselves to the human senses; the sensory product of that encounter is then subjected to analysis and reconstruction—matter is distinguished from form and figure, qualities are noted and distinguished, the body is distinguished from its motion, etc. (B viii. 201; UC 101.124). Talk of material bodies in motion expresses the product of the mind's analysis of immediate experience (and the strange proclivity of language to conceive of events in spatial terms: objects *in* motion). The sensory manifold is

[21] UC 135.69. The passage continues: "Bodies (Real Entities) are distinguishable by the fictitious entities (properties) they are known to be made up of (to contain) and again by the degrees of them they contain."

[22] Michael Quinn worried that my earlier reading (in Postema, "Fact, Fictions and the Law: Bentham on the Foundations of the Law of Evidence," *Archiv für Rechts- und Sozialphilosophie* Beiheft 16 (1983), 51) of Bentham's startling claim implied that Bentham thought that the mind's operations "prejudices the reality of real entities." See Michael Quinn, "Which Comes First, Bentham's Chicken of Utility, or his Egg of Truth?" *Journal of Bentham Studies* 14 (2012), 34. I did not mean to suggest any such conclusion and I wish here to forestall any such suggestion.

"decomposed" into many notable fictitious entities. Hence, the real, concrete object is, from the point of view of the active mind, an aggregate of fictitious entities, a "bundle of simple ideas determinate and assignable."

This does not entail the non-reality of the physical base which, according to Bentham's story, initially gives rise to the impressions on which the mind works. But it does strongly suggest that Bentham's fundamental ontology is not an ontology of objects or entities, but rather one of states of affairs ("situations") and events. The base-level events in the material world are ontologically particular bodies moving at an instant of time in portion of space; more properly expressed: they are material movings indexed to time and place—*this-moving-now-here* and *this-resting-here-now*. Bentham put his root understanding this way: "everything which can happen to a corporeal subject is resolvable into this, viz. the having been, during the length of time in question, either in a state of motion or in a state of rest" (UC 102.492 (B viii. 337)).

In his letter to d'Alembert, Bentham made the same point in epistemological terms. He wrote that a body can manifest itself, impress itself upon the human senses, only at a time and a place. And so, time and place are inseparable from perception. A perception of something is not fully expressed unless it is related to a time and a place.[23] His view was that this physical reality—these particular time-space physical events—interacts with human senses to produce undifferentiated impressions. Perceptions of the physical world have as their *sources* and their *objects* "states of things, which are either positions, that is, situations, or events, the results of motions" (UC 101.416).

Thus, it becomes clear also that, in Bentham's view, the constituents of psychical reality, while we may be inclined to speak of them as objects or entities, actually have the same ontological structure as the basic constituents of physical reality. Mind is a fiction, so mental acts are fictitious too, but sensations and impressions are mental particulars, temporally, albeit not spatially, located. They, too, are events rather than objects (UC 101.417); they are *feeling-pain-now* and *sensing-this-now*. (One might be tempted to use the sense-data theorist's *being-appeared-to-redly*, except that the typical, unanalyzed impression likely would not be limited to color-sensing events.)

This is the raw material, as it were, on which the active mind operates. Relative to this physical base, all the rest of the physical world and world of experiences is populated by fictitious entities—this includes motion, time, space form, and matter; secondary qualities, dispositions, mental acts, and minds; human relationships, customs, and rules; standards of good and evil, right and wrong, obligations, rights, and liberties. Our

[23] "Un corps ne sauroit se manifester {à nos sens} ni en mouvement ni en repos, sans se manifester en quelque tems & en quelque lieu. C'est pourquoi le tems & le lieu sont des objets considérations êtres inséparables de toute perception & par conséquence de toute perception qu'on éprouve et qu'on a occasion d'énoncer. La perception n'a pas été complettement énoncée, elle n'a pas été énoncée telle qu'elle a été jusqu'à ce que ces deux circonstances ayent été ënnoncées {mises devant nos yeux}" (UC 169.62).

minds have constructed these fictitious entities over time to understand and manage our interactions with the world in which we live, a world that it planted firmly in the physical and psychical base.

Fictitious entities "reside in or about real entities" (UC 46.21). They fall into groups that do, or can be arranged to, fall heuristically into a pattern of concentric circles progressing outward from real entities.[24] First-order (sometimes he calls them "semi-real") fictions include motion and rest, matter, form and figure, space, time, and (sometimes) relations. Second-order fictions include qualities and collective entities (e.g., genera, species, and collections of events, like war), which are aggregates of real entities or events all of which share some common properties. Higher orders of fictions include psychological entities like the will and normative entities like rights, duties, and liberty, virtue, and vice. Note that any "explication" of higher-order fictitious entities will be worked out in terms of lower-level fictitious entities. If a connection is to be made all the way to the physical base, it will have to be through a chain of such explications.

The physical base Bentham identified is, ontologically speaking, very thin and with respect to meaningfulness, impoverished. Yet, out of it, he believed, the human mind has constructed a thick, multi-textured, multi-layered physical as well as personal, interpersonal, and social world: a world of concrete material objects interacting according to causal laws—a world of apples and tables, of tigers and lambs—but also a world of persons and projects, of groups and communities, of states and their laws. The world of human experience, impersonal and personal, physical and psychical, rests on, but is not in any way restricted, or reducible, to this thin physical base. Neither does it "mirror" or seek to "correspond" to it. The world of human experience—the world populated by vast numbers, kinds and arrangements of fictitious entities—is a world in which mind is active, enabled and assisted by language. It begins with and is in important ways answerable to physical (and psychical) reality, but it is a separate domain, tethered to but not reducible to the base. We live, feel, think, choose, and act in this world; it is our world of meaningful experience, no less existing, and no less real, than the physical base in which it rests.

THE TECHNOLOGY OF THOUGHT

What, if anything, guides or directs the operations of these very active minds? And what keeps them honest? To answer these questions, let us return to Bentham's tale of the farmer's daughter.

[24] See, e.g., UC 106.2–3; UC 46.21; UC 102.16–17; UC 102.35–50, 78–9 (DO 88–110, 158–60); UC 101.322–9, 340–3 (B viii. 262–4); UC 102.434–4 (B viii. 325–7).

Interest and the Operations of the Mind

According to Bentham's story, "nature" itself did not direct the primitive activities of analysis, synthesis, and aggregation in which the daughter engaged (*Chrest.* 268n–9n). She might have formed her ideas well or poorly, but the standard of assessment is not conformity to nature. What, then, motivated her and by what standard should her performance be judged? "Interest" was Bentham's short answer; for "interest" is "in some shape or other the source of every thought as well as the cause of every action," even in the activities of singling out qualities and modes of things that human beings encounter in the world (UC 102.42 (DO 98)). Attention, the very first activity or "operation" of the mind employed by the farmer's daughter, is "an act of will ... applied to the direction or observation of an experience" (UC 101.414).[25] And this operation, along with primaeval analysis and synthesis and all other operations of the mind, are "appetitive faculties," that is, "faculties in which desire ... has place" (UC 101.409). Pleasure and pain, Bentham maintained, is the "bond of union and the channel of communication" between the perceptive faculty which apprehends the pleasure or pain and the desires of the appetitive faculty produced by the pleasure or pain (UC 101.412). Like her father's physical "analysis" (chopping the plant and burning it because he judged it to be an invasive weed), the daughter's mental activity was motivated by her curiosity, her wish to turn the flower to her purposes and her wish to engage others in that enterprise. It is the objects "before our eyes" that interest us, Bentham observed, "the things of which we must speak" and "must explain without ceasing ... to the mind."[26]

Interest directed the daughter's attention to the flower, held it there to enable her to look more closely, and engaged it again later. Interest guided her isolation of parts of the experience, noticing and delighting in the shape, color, and fragrance of the flower. Interest led her to engage her brother in conversation about the flower and to bring him to see it. Interest motivated her gathering instances into a "logical whole" to which she gave a common name. Such objects or properties "were at the same time most easily observable, most steady in their union, and most interesting to [her], whether in the way of use or harm" and names were given to them "for the purpose of putting to use their useful properties, or excluding the

[25] The whole passage reads as follows: "Attention is the result of an act of the *will*: of an exercise of the volitional branch of the appetitive faculty. In so far as attention has place—in so far as attention is applied to the *direction* or to the *observation* of an *experience*, the experience is converted into an *operation*, or, at any rate, in the field of thought—in the mental field—that place, which would otherwise have been the field of an experience and nothing more, becomes now the field of an experience and of a correspondent operation at the same time—an operation having for its subject the object which was the source or seat of the experience" (UC 101.414, author's emphasis).

[26] "Les objets réels et les objets fictifs sont des classes d'objets tout à fait disparates, qui ne s'allient ni se subordonnent d'aucune manière. Banissons donc ces derniers : les véritables objets qui nous intéressent, les objets que nous avons sous les yeux, & sur quoi nous avons à nous expliquer sans cesse, les choses s'entend, les personnes & les faits, voilà ce qu'il faut présenter à l'esprit, voilà ce qu'il faut arranger, & non pas des chimères" (UC 169.59).

operation of their pernicious properties" (*Chrest.* 269–70). Interest determines that about which we must communicate to others and must explain to ourselves and others (UC 169.59).

The role of interest was not limited, in Bentham's view, to primitive exercises of the mind. Logic, the most general "art" of the mind, giving direction to all the operations of the mind (UC 101.117; UC 101.92), has one "ultimate object," namely, well-being (UC 101.107). And interest underwrites our conviction that there is a physical world beyond our immediate experience. We have direct access only to our sensations, impressions, and ideas; nevertheless, we are convinced that our experience is anchored in a physical world independent of our minds. What warrant do we have for this conviction? Bentham's answer is simple: "because in point of practice, no bad consequences can, as everyone is ready to acknowledge, possibly arise from supposing it to be true; and the worst consequences cannot but arise from supposing it to be false" (UC 69.52; see B viii. 189n; UC 102.15 (DO 182)). That is, assuming a material world independent of our minds *works*. It enables us better to survive and flourish; and if I draw inferences from the contrary assumption, "I starve" (*ibid.*).[27]

Thus, in Bentham's view, the world of human experience, the world of fictitious entities, is constructed by an active mind, rooted in an independently existing material world, but that construction is directed not by *a priori* principles or categories, as Kant argued, but by human interest. Bentham's philosophical foundations are clearly empiricist, but they are not phenomenalist; rather, they are the product of an unusual combination of empiricist, realist, and quasi-pragmatist elements: we have sensory access to the external world, but the structure of reality as we know it is artificial, the product of the active human mind. Human experience, as ordered by our language-enabled active minds, is anchored to the physical base which gives rise to it—the physical base provides the inputs for the ordering of human experience—but the world of human experience does not mirror or map the structure of that physical base. It cannot do so, without emptying experience of all its rich, complex human texture. The physical base is, after all, only instantaneous moving matter, in Bentham's view, and the world of human experience is populated with colors and sounds, qualities and relations, apples and trees, interests and aims, relationships and communities, obligations and rights, and an uncountable number of other things—or rather an uncountable number of elements of experience we cannot help thinking of as things. The conceptual apparatus at

[27] Harrison observed that Bentham began his metaphysical inquiries "at much greater speed than Descartes or Locke. He immediately supposes that he himself, his pen, and indeed the whole material world exist" since nothing bad can come from supposing it true. Harrison adds, "A little tincture of utility dissolves these fundamental problems" (*Bentham*, 54). Harrison suggests that Bentham was not philosophically as careful as Descartes and Locke; however, I am inclined to think that his appeals to utility or interest was not a philosophical short-cut but rather indicates a foundational element of his philosophical orientation. It is a (quasi) pragmatist orientation, rather than a realism without adequate philosophical foundations.

our disposal has been determined not by *a priori* principles but by the needs, interests, and purposes of human beings and the strategies they develop to meet their needs and advance their purposes. Language does not provide us with a picture of mind-independent reality, but with tools needed to grasp and manipulate reality to our purposes. For Bentham, language, as Ogden noted, "is essentially a technological apparatus for dealing with the world of things in space."[28]

Directing and Disciplining the Mind

However, the physical base does not merely provide the raw material for the pragmatic ordering of our human world, according to Bentham; it also funds a critical component of the technology of thought.

Bentham's writings, early and late, contain frequent discussions of the operations of the mind and the apparatus by which they are directed to good purpose.[29] Division, exposition, definition, systematic arrangement, and "methodization" are explored at length, and more often deployed extensively in his discussions of ethics, law, and politics as well as language, grammar, and ontology. The master art, encompassing and guiding all the others, is logic (UC 101.96). Viewed narrowly, logic is the art of disputation (UC 69.153; UC 101.98), but taken in its widest and proper sense, it is indistinguishable from "metaphysics," which Bentham denominated the "art of making one's self understood" (UC 69.118, 153; UC 101.101). The business of metaphysics, so construed, is to examine, organize and assess the ideas belonging to the terms we use in ordinary language and in each of the sciences (UC 69.152). Metaphysics is "that common chamber of conference at which all sciences meet" (UC 69.207). Sometimes it works as "scavenger," clearing away conceptual and linguistic rubbish;[30] sometimes it works as "architect," building up "a suite of terms and expressions to lodge separately those meanings" that as yet have no secure or stable dwelling (UC 69.182).[31]

Logic-cum-metaphysics is, in Bentham's view, an *art* and as such it has an *end* (UC 101.92, 107). Aristotelians understood this end to be the acquisition and securing of knowledge, regarding knowledge as in itself more valuable even than human well-being. This is a mistake, Bentham argued, for well-being or happiness is the ultimate value; hence, human well-being is the proper ultimate end of logic (UC 101.156, 158, 107). Yes, the pursuit of well-being is "the province of ethics," which gives direction to

[28] C.K. Ogden, *Bentham's Theory of Fictions* (London: Routledge & Kegan Paul, 1932), xlvi.

[29] For his discussions in the 1770s see UC 69. 111, 125, 152–5, 182, 207, 216 and PPI *passim*. For later (1814) discussion see his writings on logic, language, and ontology in UC 101 and 102, being prepared for *Collected Works* by Philip Schofield.

[30] Bentham singled out Locke as especially effective in this enterprise, because he freed natural philosophy from "heavy congeries of obscure and useless nomenclature" (UC 69.182).

[31] It is this constructive activity that is most needed by jurisprudence, according to Bentham (UC 69.182).

human conduct, but "in that same pursuit it is the province of logic to take command and give direction to the course of ethics itself" (UC 101.108).[32]

The basic tool of logic is *definition* and the systematic arrangement of terms or concepts so defined. Metaphysics is "the science of definition," Bentham wrote early in his career (UC 69.155). "Exposition" of terms—that is, of names of fictitious entities—aims at clarifying and securing language, "fixing" terms plagued by ambiguity, and explaining them to obviate obscurity (B viii. 593). Bentham distinguished two types of definitional activity. The most familiar type is definition *per genus et differentiam*. This technique clarifies terms and refines and disciplines their use by locating some genus of which the term is a species and articulating the properties that distinguish it from other species of the genus. This is suitable for many terms or concepts of ordinary language and the sciences, but, Bentham argued, it is not available for many of the most important terms, especially those naming basic fictitious entities, because there may not be any larger genus of which they can properly be regarded as species. For exposition of terms signifying fictitious entities it is necessary to uncover the roots of fictitious entities in (relatively) real entities.[33] The techniques of *paraphrasis* and its junior partner, *archetypation*, alone can be used for this purpose.

Much of language is inevitably "figurative," Bentham observed. Fictitious language is unavoidable even if it can be misleading and even mischievous. It is possible, and sometimes illuminating, to identify the image or figure, inevitably drawn from the concrete physical domain, that underlies or informs the use of the fictitious name. His favorite example is that of "obligation" which, he surmised, summons the image of a man pressed down by a weighty object, or chain that binds a person to some action (*Chrest.* 272n; UC 101.218). This technique, which he calls "archetypation," may alert us to the historical origin of its use, but cannot by itself uncover the root of the idea typically signified by the word (*Chrest.* 272n). For this more important task Bentham invented another definitional device, which he called "paraphrasis."

In his *Treatise*, Hume wrote, "'Tis impossible to reason justly, without understanding perfectly the idea concerning which we reason; and 'tis impossible perfectly to understand any idea, without tracing it up to its origin, and examining that primary impression from which it arises. Examination of the impression bestows a clearness on the idea; and the examination of the idea bestows a like clearness on all our reasoning" (THN I.3.2). Without citing Hume, Bentham used nearly the same language, to describe his method of paraphrastic definition: "If it be true that our ideas are derived all of them from our senses, and that the only way of

[32] "Logic, like every other branch of art and science ... is not otherwise nor any farther deserving of regard, than in so far as it is, or is capable of being, of use ... [that is] capable of being conducive to the diminution of pain in some shape or other or to the increase of pleasure" (UC 101.108). Public welfare, Bentham wrote in *Chrestomathia*, is "the great and universal end to which all *art*, all *science*, all *language*, is, or ought to be directed" (*Chrest.* 120, author's emphasis).

[33] See p. 14, Bentham's notion of the levels or orders of entities.

rendering any of our ideas clear and determinate is to trace it up to the sensible objects in which it originates, the only method that can be taken for explaining them to the purpose is the method I have just been taking here" (*Limits* 317).

The task of paraphrasis is to explain the nature and origin of the fictitious idea, that is, "to show the *genealogy*, or (to borrow an expression from the mathematicians,) the *genesis* of the fictitious entity" (*Chrest.* 271n, author's emphasis). By "genesis" Bentham did not mean the historical origin of a word; for that origin is, for almost all fictitious entities, lost in the mists of history.[34] Moreover, paraphrasis is not designed to engage in such historical speculation. Rather, like the search for title of a piece of real property, it is the search for the *warrant* of the use of the fictitious term.

Bentham described the activity of paraphrastic definition as follows:

> To give the [name of a fictitious entity] a determinate meaning ... it will be necessary to make up this word, together with other words, into a phrase and thereupon show the equivalence ... as between the phrase in which this name of a fictitious entity is the principal word and the phrase containing the name of some corresponding real entity.[35]

The exposition of the term is achieved, according to Bentham, by "transmuting" or "translating" a proposition having a fictitious entity for its subject into one having a real entity for its subject. (UC 101.217(B viii. 246); TSA 75). The exposition proceeds in two stages. First, having selected the name of a (suspected) fictitious entity for exposition, one must "complete" it by putting it into a meaningful sentence (B viii. 247; TSA 74). Bentham labelled this stage "phraseoplerosis"—the activity of filling out the phrase. This sub-technique of paraphrastic definition is a direct expression of Bentham's core doctrine of meaning: the proposition is the basic unit of meaning. No single word has meaning except as part of a meaningful and truth-expressive, or at least truth-apt, proposition or sentence (B viii. 322 and UC 169.56).

The second stage, paraphrasis proper, involves translating the sentence containing the name of a fictitious entity for its subject into a sentence that contains a real-entity (or real entities) as its subject. This "translation" must meet the following three conditions: (1) the expounding sentence must use names of real entities in the subject position—or in the case of a series or chain of such definitions, it must

[34] Harrison, *Bentham*, 61–2.

[35] BL Add MSS 29,809.9. He defined the process in closely similar terms in early and late work. For example, in his early "Preparatory Principles Inserenda," he wrote, "To express an improper substantive by Paraphrasis is to compleat it into a sentence, and for that sentence to find an equivalent sentence consisting of words significative of real entities" (UC 69.221). In 1814 in *Chrestomathia*, he wrote, "the *paraphrasis* consists in taking the word that requires to be expounded—viz. the name of a *fictitious* entity—and, after making it up into a *phrase*, applying to it another phrase, which, being of the same import, shall have for its principal and characteristic word the name of the corresponding *real* entity" (272n). See also UC 101.217–24; B iii. 593–4n; TSA 74–5.

bottom out in a sentence using names of real entities; (2) the expounding sentence must be "an exact equivalent" of the expounded sentence (BL Add MSS 29, 809.9; see UC 69.221), they must "express the same import" (B iii. 594n); and (3) the real entity selected for this purpose must be that one "which alone" when embedded in a proposition of equivalent import, "is suited to the purpose" (TSA 74). Bentham did not explain or elaborate this last condition. He may mean only that it serves the purpose of providing an exact equivalent (in which case the third condition collapses into the second). Or he might mean that it serves the purpose of fully explicating, rendering clear to view, the meaning and significance of the expounded sentence. Or, again, he could mean that it serves some further purpose determined by the needs or interests of those providing or using the definition, or more likely, the purposes for which the figurative language was deployed. It is not clear which of these he had in mind.

When the proposition or sentence meeting the three conditions is found and laid alongside the sentence needing exposition, "by being *seen* to express the same import, it shall explain and make clear the import" of the latter (B iii. 594n, emphasis added)—the sentence using names of fictitious entities is understood by displaying the relationship that its import bears to the import of the sentence using names of real entities in place of names of fictitious ones (TSA 74). If the attempted translation proves unsuccessful, that is, if no singularly appropriate translation can be made, then we must conclude that what we took to be a legitimate albeit misleading use of a fictitious term has been shown to be a fraud, to be empty of meaning and hence, properly speaking, a *fiction* or the name of a *fabulous entity.* Fictitious entities for which successful paraphrastic definitions can be given are thereby vindicated, their use is warranted, and their misleading implicit reference to fictional entities is removed or at least rendered harmless (*Chrest.* 258; PF 218n).

Note, then, that this activity is founded on an assumption and begins with a hypothesis: the assumption is that fictitious language in general figures in meaningful, potentially truth-expressive thoughts and propositions, and the specific hypothesis is that the particular bit of fictitious language under investigation does so. The explicator's task is to find meaningful, potentially truth-expressive propositions in which the fictitious terms are typically used. The hypothesis in some cases may be disconfirmed, but definitions succeed precisely when they preserve this meaning and truth and thereby make it evident and secure. Thus, to speak of fictitious language or fictitious entities is in no way meant to deny the meaningfulness of such language or the ontological (let alone linguistic) validity of speaking of such entities (TSA 75). The aim of this elaborate form of definition is not to eliminate names of fictitious entities from our discourse, but to render their legitimacy and truth-preserving character manifest. "Let it not for a moment so much as be supposed that ... the reality of the [fictitious] object is meant to be denied," Bentham insisted (*Chrest.* 271a). Fictitious entities—space and time, colors and sounds, relations and properties, persons and minds, duties and rights—all *exist*; they are fictitious only in the sense that they do not exist *as physical entities*.[36] The mistake we make about fictitious entities is not the mistake of attributing existence to them, but rather of thinking that we can confirm their existence by just looking.[37] Their ontological status is different from physical objects (or rather space-time material movings). Moreover, their ontological legitimacy, and their meaningfulness (in propositions), is made manifest through skillful deployment of the technology of paraphrastic definition.

But, we might ask, why must we engage in the process of paraphrastic definition? Why is it important to trace the use of fictitious language to some base in physical reality? Bentham's initial answer is simply that paraphrasis provides the best way to explain the import or meaning of unavoidable figurative language, making it intelligible and improving our understanding. "It is only by means of the real that we can understand the nature of such as are fictitious," he wrote (UC 46.19; see TSA 74). In this respect, paraphrasis has the same "office," it performs the same function, as definition *per genus et differentiam* (UC 101.219). Yet Bentham assigned a more significant role for paraphrasis in human thought. When it comes to fictitious terms, understanding involves more than using them correctly, knowing how to construct meaningful thoughts with them. To understand them is, Bentham maintained, to know how to translate them using the technique of paraphrasis,[38] and understanding in this sense involves knowing that the term has "a determinate meaning" (BL Add MSS 29,809.9). "The names of these fictitious entities represent nothing in themselves until the phrases are related to or translated into other phrases, names of real things" (UC 169.60). However, the aim is not to *render* the language meaningful, that is, to make meaningful language that is without meaning,[39] but rather to make its meaning *manifest* and to *secure* it. Paraphrasis is designed to *fix the reference* of a term.[40] This is important because, untethered to reality outside the mind, the only import of fictitious language is "falsehood ... or nonsense" (TSA 75). Some fictitious entities are mere chimeras, creatures of imagination only (UC 102.75 (DO 154)). Language deploying such fictions is vulnerable to mischief and manipulation. Paraphrasis enables us to separate necessary fictitious entities, and meaningful language deploying them, from pernicious or at least useless fictions, securing the former in something real beyond mere fancy.

Thus, paraphrasis was one of Bentham's instruments (perhaps the most important one) for disciplining the exercise of the active powers of the mind. He does

[36] Space and time may, "in one sense indeed ... be said not to exist," Bentham wrote, "but this is only as much as to say that they are not material bodies" (UC 106.3).

[37] Harrison, *Bentham*, 61.

[38] "To understand abstract terms is to know how to translate figurative language into language without figure" (B iii, 181; see also TSA 75).

[39] As Philip Schofield suggested in *Utility and Democracy*, 34.

[40] For terms not capable of definition *per genus et differentiam*, paraphrasis is "the only form of exposition by which the import attached to is [them] capable of being fixt and at the same [time] placed in a clear and determinate point of view" (BL Add MSS 33,550.5).

not propose *reduction and elimination* of fictitious language and the patterns of thought it makes possible. He could not do so without utterly disabling thought and making it impossible for human beings rationally and prudently to interact with and manage their world. Bentham did not deny the reality of fictitious entities, but he did deny the reality of those supposed entities names of which cannot in principle be tethered to reality in the way paraphrasis makes possible.[41] It is fictitious language cut off from all such links that "has neither truth nor meaning" (TSA 74).[42] However, Bentham understood that imagination needs a governor, that the operations of the mind need control and direction. Requiring thought to be tethered, or at least in principle tetherable, to a reality outside of imagination, was one such governor.

It must be confessed, however, that is difficult to say less metaphorically and more precisely what this "tethering" consists in, in Bentham's view. I was once inclined to explain it by analogy to the gold standard for monetary currency: a given sum of pounds or dollars could in principle be exchanged for the sum's equivalent of gold, thereby securing its value for many economic transactions. But, we might think, it would be impossible—that is, the exchange economy would collapse—if everyone demanded the gold equivalent of the pounds or dollars they currently hold. Likewise, we secure the validity of the use of a given name of a fictitious entity by the technique of paraphrasis, and continue to use the name, rather than the real entity-definiendum; demanding the use of only the real-entity definiendum would bring in its wake the collapse of the discourse economy. This image may be useful in capturing Bentham's meaning, but it leaves idea of "tethering" still at the level of metaphor. More promising, perhaps, is to take a typical pragmatist line and explain the proper paraphrastic "tethering" in terms of successful practical use of the fictitious terms enabling successful interactions with others and our common physical, social, and normative world.

Paraphrasis represents for Bentham a key tool of thought. The world of human experience is not identical with the world outside of that experience, nor is it a mirror or model of that world, but neither is it an arbitrary fantasy world floating from the "real," that is, physical, world in which human experience is embedded. Human imagination can create fantasy worlds, but it is able to distinguish them from a reality-based world, in part, by using the fundamental techniques of logic, specifically paraphrasis, to tether its constructions to this reality base.

[41] Bentham attacked political and legal fictions, for example, rules of English Common Law, as proper *fictions*, i.e., as pure "falsehood" (FG 509; FPP 267). He argued that they, unlike names of fictitious entities, cannot pass the paraphrasis test.

[42] However, Bentham did not recommend rejecting all fictions. Some fictions still prove useful or even indispensable (B viii. 331). He observed that Newton's method of fluxion employs such fictions. "A point, or a line, or a surface, is said to have kept flowing where in truth there has been no flowing in the case" (*Chrest.* 371). But this explicit "falsehood" is nevertheless useful and necessary to the purpose of expanding knowledge. It is "not that no such fictions ought to be employed, but that to the purpose and on the occasion of instruction, whenever they are employed, the necessity and use of them should be made known" (*ibid.*).

LANGUAGE, REALITY, AND TRUTH

We can now sketch the main outlines of Bentham's theory of meaning. Driving Bentham's recourse to philosophical foundations of his thought was his concern about confusions in thought and practical reasoning exploited by those who exercise power over others. To control power, he thought, it was necessary to get control of thought, and to regiment thought it was necessary to regiment language. Language is in very large part "figurative," populating the world of thought with fictions and fictitious entities. To regiment language and discipline thought, it is necessary, he thought, to understand and manage this misleading and potentially mischievous use of figurative language.

Bentham's empiricist epistemology led him to adopt a sparse base ontology, a dualism of strictly particular physical and psychical events. That which exists fundamentally, on his view, is that which is presented to the mind, either directly (sensations and impressions) or indirectly by way of inferences from impressions taken as evidence of something that exists independently of mind. However, this dualist ontology does not exhaust or strictly determine the domain of truths that can be expressed. Bentham privileged the base physical and psychical events by denominating them "real," but the domain of truth in and of human experience includes both the real and the fictitious. The fictitious is that part of the domain of human experience in the construction, the constitution, and the ordering of which the human mind and human language play an essential role.

The domain of the fictitious includes most of the lived world of human beings. The line dividing "real" from "unreal" does not separate the empirical from the evaluative or normative. Rather, the domain of the fictitious includes the whole of the empirical world *as meaningfully experienced* by human beings and the personal world of dispositions and perceptions, aims and ambitions, expectations and disappointments. It also includes the interpersonal, social and cultural world, and the normative world, moral, legal and political. That is to say, the domain of human experience, ordered and rendered meaningful by thought, is far richer and more complex than the ontological base of lived experience.

The domain of fictitious entities does not mirror or correspond to the world of the physical base, so its truth is not determined by such correspondence. The surface ontology of the domain may be regarded as false, but it is false only to the extent that we take its entities literally as physical substances. It would be a mistake, on Bentham's account, to think that every proposition deploying fictitious language expresses a falsehood. The language the import of which is strictly false is language for which a paraphrastic link to the real base is not even in principle available. Truth in the domain populated by fictitious entities is not some different or inferior kind of truth, or truth in scare quotes. Although existence is a fictitious entity, it is true, and not just "true," that things exist. It is true, and not just "true," that objects move, that apples are red, that it takes time for the second hand to make a full circuit around the face of a clock, that individuals have a duty not gratuitously to harm others, and that an owner has a legal right to the return of property taken without her permission. These are truths which language forces us to express in a way that can be misleading, in ways that might suggest to the naïve listener or user that there are objects out there like motions, colors, times, duties, and rights. But to avoid being misled by our language we do not need to think of the domain of human experience as "fictional" or "untrue."

This domain is rendered meaningful through the efforts of thought and language working in partnership. But this constructive work is not arbitrary. Efforts can be more or less adequate or successful. They are undertaken with the technology of thought, governed by standards with a distinctively practical shape. They are tethered to the ontological base, but directed by practical needs, interests and aims that must be realized in the physical world. It is interest that directs the attention of mind to certain aspects of experience and seeks to understand and manage its components. Interest, Bentham maintained, directs us to that which we must understand, that which we must explain and that about which we must communicate with others.

Although this domain of the fictitious does not mirror or correspond to the world of the physical base, it is necessarily, practically connected to it. The physical base provides essential input to human experience—there is no thought, Bentham insisted, without impressions. It is also in that physical world that human beings formulate aims and expectations and seek to realize them; it is through interactions in and with that world that human beings must struggle for survival and flourishing. That world also funds an important constraining discipline on the activities of the mind as it orders human experience. It is to this physical base that the mind's constructive activities are ultimately answerable.

Bentham devised one way, indispensable in his view, to discipline the analytical and generative activities of the mind: the technique of paraphrastic definition. To show that some substantial part of discourse is fundamentally mendacious (his favorite examples are natural-law and common-law discourse) it is not sufficient to show that it relies on language deploying names of fictitious entities, but rather to show that its ontological commitments cannot be tethered at least in principle to the ontological base, that its alleged truths cannot be captured by means of paraphrastic translation.

The key elements of the paraphrastic technology reveal a good deal about the mode of analysis and argument that Bentham deployed in his moral, legal, and political philosophy. The task requires, first, that the key terms or ideas of the discourse be isolated and located in a context of (what is believed to be) meaningful use. This requires of the analyst a good faith effort to discern the truths meant to be expressed when the fictitious language is typically used. (Although Bentham said little about this activity, a good example of his use of the technique can be found in his analysis of customary social rules (BCLT ch. 7.1).) Second, the analyst must construct a paraphrastic equivalent which itself, or as part of a chain of such definitions, lays bare the relationship of the import of the fictitious language to the physical or psychical base. It is important to note that the translation succeeds in Bentham's view only if (a) a root in the ontological base is identified and (b) the meaningfulness, truth and suitability to purpose of the translated proposition is preserved. It seeks explication, we might say, *salva veritatis et utilitatis*. This condition requires that the analyst keep in mind the practical aim of the relevant portion of the fictitious discourse under consideration and this in turn requires awareness of and fidelity to principles and aims specific to that domain.

This technology, then, is not simply a conceptual or metaphysical (and thus practice- or evaluation-neutral) exercise. For the translation to be eligible, and its results credible, domain-specific norms and practical aims must be explored and skillfully deployed. Bentham insisted that this theoretical (he calls it "metaphysical") work of laying clear the basic ideas of a given domain of thought ("science") and subjecting it to his exacting discipline engages not only the scavenger but also the architect—it involves not only clearing away the rubbish, but also building a secure and properly functioning conceptual framework. The techniques suitable for this constructive purpose include paraphrasis, definition *per genus et differentiam*, and especially "methodization" and systematic arrangement. The conceptual architect seeks to order the domain by some rational and practically suitable principles, and to arrange its concepts and terms in a way that makes manifest the relations among the key elements of the domain and the truths meant to be captured by those terms. This, too, requires that the analyst grasp the practical aims of the domain and the expectations of those likely to use the discourse.

In conclusion, it is fair to say that Bentham's ultimate concern was not ontology, but language; he sought to understand the way our language facilitates and misleads thought, reasoning, deliberation, and action. He devised a theory of meaning and the technology of thought in order to allow language the room it needs to do its essential work, while controlling its excesses, especially the misuse and abuse of language by which some seek to exercise power over others.

2
Human Psychology, Individual and Social

In addition to his work on the epistemological and metaphysical foundations of his thought articulated in the second decade of the nineteenth century, Bentham also undertook to articulate more systematically the second pillar of his thought, his theory of human psychology.* His relatively late efforts, in both cases, did not substantially revise, but only elaborated, themes that had underwritten his work from the beginning of his career. We looked at Bentham's theory of the technology of thought in the previous chapter; in this chapter, we explore his understanding of human psychology and in particular his theory of motivation.

PLEASURE, MOTIVES, AND THE SELF

Psychology pursued as a purely speculative endeavor, Bentham opined, is "no better than push-pin," but if pursued as "practically applicable," it is of great value (TSA 71). It furnishes necessary materials and instruments for theoretical inquiries into law, politics, and morality. It explores the phenomena that the enterprise of eudaimonics (the art of ordering life to the maximization of well-being) deals with (*Deont.* 331). For Bentham, eudaimonics is not an *a priori* exercise. It does not merely apply derivatively to human nature and the dynamics of social relations; rather, it is *designed* precisely for human beings in their natural social habitat. As we shall see in later chapters, even Bentham's normative first principle, the principle of utility, takes its distinctive shape from needs of human beings (and, later, sovereign states), engaged in distinctive kinds of interactions. With these needs and interactions in mind, it seeks a sound basis for directing their human actions and structuring their lives.

In the opening paragraph of his *Introduction to the Principles of Morals and Legislation*, Bentham announced in dramatic fashion the intimate relationship between psychology and eudaimonics. In this unduly famous passage, Bentham wrote,

> Nature has placed mankind under the governance of two sovereign masters, *pain* and *pleasure*. It is for them alone to point out what we ought to do, as well as to

* This chapter has been adapted from G.J. Postema, "Bentham's Utilitarianism" in *The Blackwell Guide to Mill's Utilitarianism*, H. West, ed. (Malden, MA.: Blackwell Publishers, 2006). Copyright © 2008, John Wiley & Sons.

> determine what we shall do. On the one hand the standard of right and wrong, on the other the chain of causes and effects, are fastened to their throne. They govern us in all we do, in all we say, in all we think ... The *principle of utility* recognizes this subjection, and assumes it for the foundation of that system (IPML I.1, original emphasis).

This passage has caused much confusion amongst readers. Aware of this danger, Bentham wrote, immediately at the close of this passage, "enough of metaphor and declamation." Recent commentators have observed that this passage, announces not a general thesis, but rather Bentham's basic twofold strategy of theoretical enquiry.[1] His psychological enquiries were not ancillary to his normative work; they lay the core.

Yet, despite its key role in his theoretical work, Bentham's psychological theory is perhaps the least satisfactory part of his work. Although he was obsessed with conceptual precision, Bentham could not avoid linguistic confusions and conceptual entanglements regarding these issues. He adopted, without reservation, the familiar eighteenth-century conceptual frame dominated by the language of hedonism and egoism.[2] It did not serve his purposes well, as we shall see, but he never abandoned it. This forced him to articulate his views in ways that are often quite misleading. We can hope to appreciate these views and their role in his larger theory only if we look beyond the labels and slogans (which Bentham was not above using for rhetorical effect) to uncover his nuanced understanding of human affections, interests, and motives.

Psychological Hedonism

Bentham assumed, without argument, that the root terms of his ontology—the names of "real entities" to which all other language must be anchored—must also be the primitive terms of explanation of human behavior. He recognized only two basic constituents of reality: physical and psychical or mental states. Some mental states do not involve pleasure or pain; he called them "apathematic." But the mental states relevant to human behavior are sentiments with a hedonic dimension; they are "pathematic." The motivation-generating mental states, he insisted, are *pleasure* and *pain*. His project was to explain appetites, desires, motives and interests—all "fictitious entities"—"by connecting them to pleasures and pains" (BL Add MS 33,550.022).

[1] John Dinwiddy, *Bentham* (Oxford: Oxford University Press, 1989), 20; Ross Harrison, *Bentham* (London: Routledge & Kegan Paul, 1984), 108–12.

[2] Hume also inherited the psychological hedonism common in British moral philosophy, but it did not hamper or distort his development of a more sophisticated theory of human psychology.

The exact nature of this thesis is unclear. Bentham often treated it as a fundamental *empirical* thesis: the ultimate causes ("springs of action") of voluntary human actions are pleasure and pain. However, if we are to understand this thesis as an empirical psychological thesis, to be of use explaining voluntary human behavior, we should expect some empirical demonstration of it. Bentham never offered any; he simply took it as obvious. Or rather, he took it as an "innovation," a "new idea ... derived from logic," (*ibid.*) that is, from his theory of real and fictitious entities. But the idea of explaining behavior in terms of pleasure and pain was not new with Bentham; it was no "innovation." It was, rather, a staple of eighteenth-century empiricist philosophy. Perhaps, then, it should not be treated as an empirical thesis after all, but as the linguistic axiom: treat all language referring to affections, interests, motives, and the like as, or ultimately referring to—or rather anchored to—the language of pleasure and pain. Neither proposal fits Bentham's practice precisely. Let us look more closely at this practice.

Pleasure and Pain

Pleasure was a basic psychological concept in the British philosophical lexicon of Bentham's day. It is not surprising that he would have associated subjective experience, enjoyment and suffering, with the familiar concepts of pleasure and pain. Moreover, pleasure and pain were thought of as simple, immediately accessible "sensations." "We all know but too well what pain is, he wrote early in his career. "It is a simple idea. It is felt. It is not to be defined," and he thought the same is true of pleasure (UC 69.94). Also, like Hume, he thought that the immediate experience of pleasure and pain provided a unique point of sympathetic contact between sensitive beings. We cannot help but recognize the sufferings and joys of others and, by nature, we respond sympathetically to them. Further, he thought, recognizing the value of such experiences for ourselves, we immediately recognize their value for others. We will explore the role of the concepts of pleasure and pain in Bentham's theory of value in Chapter 4; here we will focus on their role in his theory of human psychology.

Bentham often seems to assume a simple model of pleasure and pain.[3] To begin, we need to notice an ambiguity in the common use of the word "pleasure." We often speak of this or that pleasure, or pleasurable experience—eating butter pecan ice cream, drinking a peaty single malt whisky, watching the sun set behind the mountains from one's cabin door, participating in a performance of Bach's *St Matthew Passion*, engaging in conversation with a friend, watching one's child score a goal, sharing a friend's joy over the birth of her child, and the like. Each of these "pleasures" is an instance of pleasure, although they differ greatly in their complex

[3] Further dimensions of this simple model will be explored in Chapter 4.

natures. Bentham was well aware of the vast variety of such pleasures. Sometimes, however, we might think, further, that all these "pleasures" have something in common, that accompanying, or intrinsic to, them is some simple, discrete, homogeneous felt quality—a positive hedonic *quale* we call *pleasure*. Likewise, common to the vast variety of painful experiences is a simple, discrete, homogeneous negative hedonic *quale*: pain. Moreover, Bentham was inclined to think that it is this hedonic something that is the active ingredient in human motivation, that this hedonic *quale* is the "spring of action." Bentham's language often suggests that he has this simple model in mind; however, there are several reasons to think that he had a more nuanced understanding of pleasure.

First, he recognized an important asymmetry between pleasure and pain. In his *Influence of Natural Religion on the Temporal Happiness of Mankind* (1822), Bentham wrote,

> Pain is a far stronger more pungent, and more distinct sensation than pleasure; . . . pain alone, or want or uneasiness, which is a species of pain, are the standing provisions of nature. . . . What is called *pleasure* is a secondary formation, something superadded to the satisfaction of our wants by a farther reach of artifice; and only enjoyable when that satisfaction is perfect for the present, as well as prompt and certain for the future. Want and pain, therefore, are natural; satisfaction and pleasure, artificial and invented (*Influence* 34, 35).

What Bentham has in mind in this passage is not clear and we must not make too much of it. However, we can safely infer that he regarded pain and pleasure to be significantly different in subjective quality. Pains—or most of them[4]—are immediate, discrete sensations of a decidedly unwelcome kind. So, too, is the experience of *want* (as opposed to wanting or desiring). These are immediate experiences usually with discrete physiological locations. Pleasure, Bentham suggests, is different. We use the language of pleasure to talk about the satisfaction of wants. While pains are natural and primordial, pleasures are derivative or "artificial." They are artificial, perhaps, because they are experiences we come to take pleasure in or take an interest in, and that interest taking is often influenced by our social circumstances. Also, pleasure is a more complex sensation than pain. Unlike the immediate experience of pain, pleasure builds into the experience some view of appropriateness or fullness in the present or belief in its future prospect. Taken as universal claims about pains and pleasures, Bentham's characterization appears to be inconsistent with much of what he says elsewhere. But if we take them as broad generalizations, highlighting an important asymmetry between pain and pleasure, they shed light on, rather than contradict, other things Bentham was inclined to say.

[4] Bentham left out of consideration here his notion of "the pain of disappointment," which was very important in his political and especially legal theory. See Chapter 7 and BCLT 5.3, 12.2.

This passage recalls other passages in which Bentham stepped back from the simple model of pleasure as a discrete, homogeneous subjective *quale*. John Dinwiddy called to our attention the fact that Bentham embraced what we might call an "attitude" notion of pleasure. Bentham wrote, "I call pleasure every sensation that a man had rather feel at that instant than feel *none*. I call pain every sensation that a man had rather feel none than feel."[5] What is common to all pleasurable experiences is not some discrete felt quality, but the fact that one would like to have it, and continue to have it; and pains are experiences one avoids if one can. Pleasure picks out an *attitude* of persons *toward* certain experiences they have or might have—their wanting the experience and wanting it to continue—rather than a discrete *quality of* that experience. The attitude is positive, and it may also have some motivational potential, but there may be no hedonic *quale* accompanying this attitude; thus, the motivation is not to reproduce or continue this feeling. The positive attitude has for its intentional object the pleasurable experience, not the feeling of pleasure. Thus, on this understanding, what Bentham had in mind when he spoke of pleasure was that which someone *takes pleasure in*, that is, that which someone cares about, or is emotionally or motivationally invested in. On this view, it will often lead to confusion to look further for the pleasure returned to the person who takes pleasure in some person or state of affairs. To take *pleasure in* something, we might say, is not to take *pleasure from* it, let alone to seek it for the pleasure one can take from it.

However, Bentham frequently encouraged confusion of these two different concepts. One such confusion concerns experiences lying in the future. He frequently moves back and forth between the *idea* of pleasure one might experience in the future (the idea of future pleasure—or pleasures) and the *pleasure* one might take *in* the idea of some future state of affairs. In the former case, the idea has for its intentional object some pleasurable experience; in the latter, one entertains favorably some idea the object of which is not specified, something one cares about, in which one is invested. The latter, of course, is and can only be *one's own*. If James takes pleasure in the idea of X, it is James's caring, James's engaged idea—it is in James that the idea, the caring, is psychologically located. Of course, the same idea (the idea with the same content) or a similar caring might be located in Joan, as it were, but then there would be two such carings, James's caring and Joan's. In neither case does the fact that the engaged idea is located in these individuals license the inference that they are caring about *their own* pleasure. There is a fundamental difference between my idea of the pleasure X and the idea of my pleasure X. Bentham is often insensitive to this difference. He was often inclined to say that if some pleasure is located in me and it motivates me, then it is my pleasure that I am seeking to promote. Yet, he had the conceptual resources to mark and maintain this distinction. Already early in his career, Bentham clearly distinguished between

[5] UC 96.128; Dinwiddy, *Bentham*, 27.

motives *in esse* and motives *in prospect* (IPML X.6). If something is a motive *in prospect*, then that state of affairs is the intentional object of one's voluntary action; one acts so as to bring about that state of affairs. One's future pleasure, or financial advancement, or health, or general welfare might be the object of one's action, one's motive *in prospect*. One could also take the future pleasure, financial advancement, health, or well-being of some other person or persons as the object of one's striving, one's motive in prospect. It may be true, at the same time, that the idea of the well-being of the other person, or of one's doing something significant to promote that well-being, causes one pleasure. In that case, one's "pleasure" would be the motive *in esse*—the prompting cause—of the action, although not its aim or end (motive in prospect).

Once we make these distinctions explicit, it is not too difficult in most cases to keep them in mind, but Bentham often failed do so, and this led him to make implausible observations. For example, in *Deontology*, he imagined a certain man, Liberalis ("generous man") who observes another, Egenus ("poor man"), in distress. "By the force of sympathy," Bentham wrote, "the pain felt by Egenus becomes, by means of the manifestations made of it, productive of correspondent pain in the bosom of Liberalis. To relieve himself from this pain and to obtain, at the same time, by means of the same act, a portion of the opposite and correspondent pleasure, he applies relief to this distress" (*Deont.* 194). Of such cases, and many like it, Bentham maintains that Liberalis acts from "self-regarding interest" (*Deont.* 195). But, as Bishop Butler argued many years before Bentham wrote this piece,[6] this apparent argument for the basically egoistic motivations of all human beings rests on a very implausible analysis of Liberalis's motivation. If Liberalis truly sought to relieve himself of the pain of Egenus's distress, the most efficient and least costly course of action would have been to turn his attention elsewhere. It may be plausible to say that Liberalis's pain motivated (caused) his benevolent act, but his motive—the object of his action—was to relieve the distress of Egenus, someone whose well-being he cared about. As we shall see presently, Bentham decisively rejected psychological egoism as a universal thesis regarding human motivation, but throughout his life he insisted on using egoistic language even when it was misleading and threatened to sow confusion, the threat of which he clearly anticipated.

Motives, Interests, and Sanctions

Pleasure and pain are, in Bentham's spare ontology, "real entities," because they are mental events, as we learned in Chapter 1. But he understood that the work of "practicable" psychology could not be done in the language of pleasure and

[6] Joseph Butler, "Sermon XI," in Butler, *Fifteen Sermons* (1729) (New York: Robert Carter & Brothers, 1860; reprinted 1993).

pain. For that work, he needed the language of *affections*, *motives*, *interests*, and *sanctions*—all of them names of indispensable "fictitious entities." "Affections" was, in Bentham's usage, the most general of these terms, encompassing all motivationally active human sentiments. To the other three terms Bentham assigned specific tasks in his theory. Because his use of these terms was somewhat idiosyncratic—and not entirely consistent—it is important to pause briefly to fix their meaning in Bentham's theory.

Motives

The core notion, in Bentham's psychology, was *motive*; he defined *interest* and *sanction* in relation to the notion of *motive*. Motive, Bentham held, is a necessary condition of voluntary action; motives move agents to action (this he calls the "impelling motive") or restrain their actions ("restraining motive") (IPML X.43; XI.29–30). It is the *cause* of action or omission (motive *in esse*). But he often also used "motive" to refer to the idea of the prospect of some future state of affairs, for example, of some future pleasure or pain (motive *in prospect*). The idea of motive, he wrote in an early manuscript, is "the idea of some pleasure or pain, the pleasure conceived as about to exist, or the pain as about not to exist, as a consequence of an action" (UC 69.70). Although he clearly distinguished the two, he often allowed himself to run them together. Typically, he thought of the motive of an action as its end or aim, the causally efficacious idea of some future state of affairs to be brought about by the action in view. Bentham also thought that motives (and interests) have a necessary self-referential dimension. As we noticed above, his slipping from motive *in esse* to motive *in prospect*—from motive as that which moves the agent to motive as the end or aim of the agent—often makes it unclear where he thought this self-referential dimension is located. We will seek to clarify Bentham's view on this matter presently.

The motive in prospect, on Bentham's view, necessarily includes the idea of some future pleasure or pain consequent upon performing the action, plus a judgment that the action is likely to bring about that state of affairs, both of which are products of memory and imagination (*Deont.* 90; FPP 214). Because a judgment of the efficacy of action (Bentham sometimes called it its "power") is essential for an end or aim to take on motivating force, Bentham realized that it is possible to influence motives of people by influencing their judgments of efficacy of their actions. The force of a motive can be reduced or even eliminated, he thought, if the agent can be convinced that it will be difficult to bring about the desired state of affairs. This insight proved central to his thinking about the design of social and especially governmental institutions.

The psychic force of a motive, their capacity to bring about action (or restrain it), is a function of its strength relative to that of other motives. This psychic force is, under ideal conditions, a matter of the rationally assessed value of the end sought. However, it is more directly a function of three other features of the agent. First, it depends on the general sensibility of the agent. The same state of affairs conceived of as an end of a person's action might have more force for one agent than another due to differences of their respective sensibilities. Because sensibility is not entirely determined by the rationally considered value to the agent of the end in view, the force of a motive is not a direct product of a rational judgment of the value of the end. Second, the force of a motive depends on whether it is present to the mind of the agent. It is possible for an agent to have a motive of which she is to some degree unaware (UC 69.88); however, to be causally efficacious, to move an agent to action, the motive must be present to the mind of the agent prior to her acting (IPML X.37; TSA 98; *Deont.* 195–6). Moreover, motives that are present to mind tend to capture the attention of the agent, focusing her attention on certain features of the present circumstances and future consequences, potentially obscuring or concealing others. Third, the force of a motive also depends on the light in which the end in view is considered by the agent at the time of action. Bentham believed that it is possible to alter the force of a motive (increasing or decreasing it) by changing the light in which its object or end is viewed by the agent.

Although the force of an agent's motives (and interests) may deviate from that agent's rational assessment of his aims and interests, it is also possible for that force to be altered by adjusting the degree to which motives are present to mind, by altering the light in which ends are viewed by the agent, and by introducing competing motives or alerting the agent to competing motives. Bentham's interest in "practicable" psychology was always the interest of an engineer of human conduct, whether this be the "deontologist" working at the micro-level of interpersonal advising or the constitution writer working at the macro-level designing "securities against misrule."

Interests

The concept of interests lies at the foundations of Bentham's theoretical structure. It is anchored to pleasure and pain (*Deont.* 336), but it incorporates pleasure, pain, and motive into a wider conceptual frame that enabled Bentham to move easily between explanation and evaluation. It plays an especially important role in his theory of institutional design. For that purpose, the idea of universal or public interest was critical. We will explore this in detail later in Chapter 6. But we must start, as Bentham did, with an understanding of interests of individual human beings.

We can view an individual's interests from perspectives marked by two different verbal formulations: (a) *J has an interest in X*, and (b) *J is interested in X* or *J takes an interest in X*. The conceptually prior notion is expressed in the language of (b). It not only looks at matters from J's point of view, but it looks to J *herself* for insight into that interest. It considers what she cares about, what is the focus of her attention, and so, Bentham thought, what she takes pleasure in (although not necessarily what she gets pleasure from). For J to take an interest in X or for J to be interested in X is for X to be mindfully engaged in seeking X. Possible objects of J's interest include her future condition, happiness, or well-being. They might also include the well-being of others. Bentham clearly recognized that a person may, from sympathy, "experience an interest" in the well-being of another person (B iii. 291). J may even take an interest in states of affairs not directly involving anyone's well-being. In contrast, Bentham held that J *has* an interest in X insofar as X is considered likely to be a source of pleasure or exemption from pain for J (TSA 91); or, more broadly, insofar as X is considered something in which J is likely to take pleasure. To judge that J *has* an interest is to take an external observer's view on J's carings. It may be true that J *has* an interest in X even though J does not at the moment *take* an interest in X. This external perspective is as important for Bentham's theoretical purposes as the internal perspective suggested by talk of what J takes an interest in.

Bentham frequently asserted what we might call "the best judge principle." For example, he wrote, "it may be delivered in the character of a general proposition [that] every man is a better judge of what is conducive to his own well-being than any other man can be" (*Deont.* 131). But in several of the passages in which he states this general principle he also qualified it. Bentham was always very clear that, with respect to J's immediate pleasures and pains and present and near-term future well-being, J is the best judge. The quality of his own sensibility is known to every person "by the most impressive and infallible of all direct evidence, the evidence of a man's own senses," Bentham wrote (*Deont.* 130). The individual himself is "the only proper judge" of what is to him pleasure or pain (*Deont.*150; see *Deont.* 195 and 250). Thus, for me to judge that something is unpleasant and to conclude from this that it is not or should not be pleasant for you is "folly" and "tyranny" (*Deont.* 151). Indeed, Bentham insisted, if we ignore for the time being the agent's consideration of future circumstances, the fact that an agent freely chooses to act in a certain way is "of itself conclusive proof" that the act produces "pure or preponderant good," that is, pleasure, for him (*Deont.* 151).

However, when it comes to judgments regarding his future interests or pleasures, Bentham conceded that the agent may not be the best, or even an adequate, judge. Bentham mentioned three reasons for this qualification of the "best judge" principle. First, to judge what has been and hence will be most conducive to his well-being requires that one be "accustomed to correct and complete reflection" and "inference to the most probable means," and he must be "permitted by his passions to employ it" (*Deont.* 250 n 2). It is clear that not all individuals are adequately disciplined in these respects. Second, human agents are prone to a kind of temporal myopia. "To the eye of the mind, as well as to that of the body, [temporally] more remote objects are apt to be eclipsed by less remote and, more especially, by present ones" (*Deont.* 151 n. 1). Bentham does not have in mind here the circumstance determining the value of a lot of pleasure that he calls "propinquity or remoteness" (*IPML* IV; see also *Deont.* 187). Bentham regarded the temporal discount rate as a determinant of the practically rational value of some pleasure or pain. Rather, here he has in view the non-rational phenomenon that present pleasures or advantages can "undervalue," obscure, or even remove from an agent's practical perspective other countervailing considerations, while "to the eyes of other persons they are sufficiently present" (*Deont.* 151–2 n. 1). Third, and most interesting, Bentham observed that, with respect to a one's future interests, pleasures or pains, one *can only* take an observer's perspective. "Like a third person his future contingent individual pleasure and pain can not be judged of by him otherwise than from the species it belongs to" (*Deont.* 195 n. 1). One judges one's future good, advantage, or interests not by consulting private and incorrigible experience, but rather by consulting the common experience of others of similar states of affairs ("species").

As we have seen, interests like motives are, in Bentham's theory, anchored to pleasure and pain, but we must be careful about how we think understand this connection. If, following Bentham, we understand pleasure as taking pleasure in something (rather than getting pleasure out of it), and see that pleasure as a matter of what one is personally (emotionally or practically) engaged with, then the link between pleasure and interests is easy to see. That which one cares about or takes pleasure in is that in which one takes an interest. What one takes an interest in is not the pleasure to be derived from it, but rather the "source" of it. Suppose J takes a ("self-regarding") interest in, say, power or wealth. Although Bentham's regimentation of language requires that ultimately this talk of interest must be anchored to pleasures or pains, it would be a mistake—in general, and as an interpretation of Bentham's view—to conclude that J is "really" or ultimately only interested in pleasure, viz., the pleasure J gets from possessing or exercising power or acquiring wealth. The proper object of J's interest may just be power or wealth.

Bentham is often inclined to link "interest" very closely to "motive," to the point of treating them as synonyms (TSA 99–100; FPP 192–3). Interests can have motive force, but Bentham regularly spoke of interests abstracted from their immediate motivational force. Sometimes, he also was inclined to speak of motives that are not present to the agent's mind. If his usage had been consistent, he would have used "motive" for the directly action-guiding affection and "interest" for the concern or aim an agent has, even if she is not at the moment moved to act in a way that would serve that interest (or may not even be entirely aware of it). In *Deontology*, Bentham maintained that an important part of the task of the personal moral advisor is to bring to mind interests understood in this way (*Deont.* 174f, 195).

Again, Bentham believed that there is an inescapable self-referential element in the concept of interest. We will explore presently exactly what Bentham had in mind, but the question we might ask at this point is whether this self-referential element is present to the mind of the agent when an interest motivates her action. In at least one place, Bentham clearly said yes. He wrote, "By his own interest, and even by his own self-regarding interest, that is, by that which *in that character presents itself to his view*, will, on every occasion, the conduct of every man be determined" (*Deont.* 195, emphasis added). However, elsewhere, in work written at the same time (1814), he concedes that when, out of sympathy with them, a person pursues the interests of others, he still pursues "his own [interest] at the same time, even though it be *without thought about his own*" (TSA 36, emphasis added). Later he wrote that there is a significant difference between self-regarding and sympathetic affection—between the case where the pleasure or pain by the consideration of which a man's conduct is determined is his own purely and immediately, and the case where it is his own no otherwise than in consequence of a correspondent pleasure or pain being regarded as experienced or about to be experienced by another person—between the case where the pleasure or the pain is his own purely and directly, and the case in which it comes to him no otherwise than as it were by reflection, and through the medium of a portion of pleasure or pain of a different nature, regarded as having place in another breast (iii. 291).

Actions taken out of sympathy with another person's suffering or enjoyment are self-regarding only indirectly, without that self-regarding element figuring in the direct motivation of the act. [7] It appears that Bentham recognized that it is possible for people who seriously take an interest in the well-being of others to act from that interest without a thought to its being *their* interest, or act for the pleasure they may nevertheless experience indirectly as a result.

We must note one further idiosyncratic feature of Bentham's use of the term "interest." He distinguished between J's *interests* (plural) and J's *interest* (singular). The former refers to the various states of affairs in which J takes an interest. These interests can be many, diverse, and potentially conflicting. J's *interest*, in contrast, refers to the ordered aggregate of J's diverse interests—or as Bentham sometimes put it, J's interests maximized (*Col.* 31, 239–40). Extended to whole communities, this use enabled Bentham to talk about the potentially opposed interests of various members of a community and about *the* universal or public interest, that is, the aggregate or ordered interests of the various members of the community. We will have much more to say about Bentham's idea of the universal interest in Chapter 6.

Sanctions

Perhaps the most curious and potentially misleading term in Bentham's psychological lexicon is "sanction" (see IPML III; *Deont.* 176–7; B iii. 290–3). Sometimes, like "interest," he treated "sanction" as a synonym of "motive." But when he was trying to use his technical terminology precisely, he reserved "sanction" for the "sources" of motives of certain specific kinds (B iii. 290, 292). What distinguishes sanctions from other motives is that they are apt tools or instruments for encouraging or discouraging human conduct. They are potential "inducements" to action or potential restraints on other motives (*Deont.* 175). Bentham called the

[7] However, in his memoir book, Bentham wrote late in his life, "if it be through the happiness of another, or others, in whatsoever number, that a man pursues his own happiness, still the direct and immediate and nearest object is no less than his own happiness" (B x. 532).

latter "tutelary motives" (IPML XI.29–30). The party deploying these instruments may be a party other than the agent whose conduct is in view, perhaps a legislator, legal official, moral advisor, the public (what Bentham later called "the Public Opinion Tribunal") or God, although, in some cases, it may also be the agent herself, seeking to modify her behavior.

Initially (in the 1780s), Bentham singled out four kinds of motives as sanctions: physical, legal–political, moral–popular, and religious. In the 1820s, he added two more: the sympathetic sanction (TSA and *Deont.* 175–6) and the retributive (*Deont.*175, 182, 262).[8] Bentham had already recognized sympathy as a (source of) motives in the 1780s (*IPML* X.25 and *Limits* 6), but he was not inclined at that time to think of sympathy as a sanction. Bentham regarded the (prospect or experience of) the immediate, uncalculated retaliation for evil done to another as the "retributive" sanction. It played a minor role in Bentham's scheme. Sympathy, on the other hand, was central not only to his account of human motivation, but also to his hopes for inclining human beings to act in accord with the principle of utility. Sympathy was the sanction by which Bentham hoped benevolence of the most extended sort might be taught and encouraged.

Bentham also regarded another class of motives as a kind of sanction, but he never incorporated it into his canonical five (or six). This is class of motives of "amity." These are motives that seek the well-being of others, in the hopes of securing the good-will and good offices of others. We might think of these as motives of (anticipated) reciprocity.

Bentham thought that the five canonical kinds of sanctions fell naturally into two groups: (i) the (purely) natural and (ii) the volitional (*Deont.*176). The latter include religious, legal–political, and the moral–political sanction. In the case of volitional sanctions, some agent other than the person whose action is directed by the sanction imposes the sanction or the threat of it on her. The ultimate "source" of the religious sanction, in Bentham's view, is God, but it operates through human agents' fear or apprehension of divine punishment. This fear is encouraged and aided by the religious establishment, which is the immediate source of the sanction. Legal sanctions are administered by authorized legal officials, according to formally determined procedures. Courts and those governmental organs that enforce their judgments are the primary agents of the legal sanction. The moral–popular sanction, as Bentham sometimes portrayed it, is the informal analogue of formal legal sanctions. He even used quasi-legal language to describe its primary *modus operandi*. In his late work on the constitution, "the Public Opinion Tribunal" (POT) imposes the moral sanction. The POT operates as a "quasi-jury" holding officials and individuals alike accountable to informal social norms.[9] The

[8] See Philip Schofield, *Utility and Democracy: The Political Thought of Jeremy Bentham* (Oxford: Oxford University Press, 2006), 36–7. Schofield traces Bentham's notion of the retributive sanction to Grote Papers, BL Add MSS 29,809.67 (17 Feb 1819).

[9] For a discussion of the Public Opinion Tribunal and its role in Bentham's political and legal theory, see Chapter 13.

moral sanction is the upshot of the judgments of the public at large, extending or withholding its good-offices. Although he did not include "amity" among the official sanctions, he did from time to time refer to it as "the popular or moral sanction in miniature" (*Deont.* 195, 222). It is "in miniature," because it involves interpersonal relations and the extending or withholding of good-offices by determinate individuals, rather than by "unassignable" individuals or the public at large, as in the case of the moral sanction as he usually understood it.

Volitional sanctions are what we are inclined to think of as proper sanctions, that is, they are incentives *added to* any reasons the agent already has to act in a way directed by the party imposing the sanction. Natural motives, in contrast, have their source in the "pre-established nature of things and not in any human agency" (B iii. 290). They comprise reasons agents have to act in certain ways, independent of any human intervention, although they may not be sufficiently aware of them. The class of natural sanctions includes various natural consequences of one's actions—for example, emphysema from smoking, a hang-over from drinking too much alcohol, and the like—but it also includes the immediate angry retaliation of injured persons against those who have done harm to them. The latter can operate as a natural sanction in the same way that the likely response of an angry dog might give one reason to let it sleep.

On this understanding, the retributive sanction is a kind of natural motive. Bentham also thought sympathy was a natural sanction (B iii. 291). This may strike us as a bit more puzzling. His thought is that one's sympathetic identification with the suffering of another itself can generate a motive for one, "without the intervention of any exterior will" (*ibid.*). Responding to suffering sympathetically, of course, typically involves one's will, but it is one's own will, not the will of someone who seeks to impose the sanction on one. The natural motives comprising the sanction are thought of as reasons that can be brought to the attention of agents, reasons that might then incline them to act or not act in certain ways, or not to act from some other motives against which the sanction-motives are deployed.

Bentham also distinguished sanctions in terms of the extent to which the motives involved are "self-regarding" or "other-regarding." In Bentham's view, the sympathetic sanction stands out as focused exclusively on the interests or well-being of others (B iii. 292–2; *Deont.* 201). As Bentham treated them, the physical and legal–political sanctions are purely self-regarding. The incentives or disincentives they provide concern the well-being or interests narrowly construed of those to whom they are addressed. This seems straightforward. Similarly, he typically treated the religious sanction as strictly self-regarding. But sometimes he included love of God, pious devotion, and religious ardor among the motives of the religious sanction (TSA 83). The latter are not strictly or predominantly self-regarding, if they are self-regarding at all.

More complex, however, is the moral–popular sanction. It comprises what Bentham calls the motives and pleasures (and pains) of reputation (TSA 83; UC

15.8) or esteem. But these pleasures and pains are very different in source and content from legal or natural sanctions. Unlike loss of property or liberty, damage to reputation involves judgments of one's standing in the community and appeals to common standards of evaluation, standards to which an individual's self-esteem is attached (*Deont.* 234–5). "It is from the opinion expected to be on each occasion inwardly entertained by them, that the good is looked for" (B ix. 42). A person punished by the moral sanction suffers loss of the esteem; the "characteristic evil of the moral sanction" involves a "sense of disgrace" (B i. 453). The "natural punishment" experienced by the sovereign—not being liable to formal, legal sanction—is "dishonour" (UC 33.79).

This kind of motive is never entirely selfless, as the sympathetic motives might be, for with loss of esteem comes loss of the good-will and, hence, the good offices of others in the community (B i. 453). But the motives are *social* and require that the person consider the interests and well-being of others, in conjunction, of course, with her own (*Deont.*195). Moreover, it depends on cultivation of moral judgment in those imposing the sanction and those subject to it. The "culture of the moral sanction" involves moral education, education of the virtue, Bentham maintained in *Indirect Legislation* XV (UC 87. 18, 19). The moral sanction inclines individuals to take as a primary concern the well-being of the whole community ("the most extensive benevolence") and in consequence directs them to compliance with the dictates of the principle of utility (*Deont.* 236, 237). Of course, this sanction can be distorted or corrupted; the most common corrupter, in Bentham's view, was religion (*Influence* 112–13).

The sympathetic sanction, as we have seen, contrasts with all the others in that its motives have for their aim and object the well-being of others. Viewed as a *sanction*, sympathy can be mobilized to motivate actions benefiting people other than the agent (beneficent actions) from the reason that those actions benefit them (benevolent motive). Sympathy as source of motives is central to Bentham's understanding of human motivation and an important instrument for encouraging beneficent action in compliance with the principle of utility. However, this conclusion runs counter to much of the language one finds in Bentham's moral, legal, and political writing. So, we must look more closely at his view of the relationship between motives, interests and the self.

Interests and the Self

"Were it not for the operation of this [sympathetic] sanction, no small portion of the good, physical and moral, which has place in human affairs, would be an effect without a cause" (B iii. 292). Although it is sometimes weak when it competes with other motives, sympathy cannot be left out of our repertoire of tools to encourage human conduct, Bentham held (*ibid.*). However, this clear statement appears to stand in sharp contrast with frequent statements we find throughout his corpus. One who serves the interest of others out of sympathy, Bentham insisted, at the same time serves his own (TSA 36). "On every occasion, the conduct of every human being will be determined by his own interest" (FPP 68; see also B ix. 43, 46; TSA 69; *Deont.* 195; UC 18.173). Against those who point to countless examples of disinterested actions, Bentham replied, "properly speaking … no human act ever has been or every can be *disinterested*" (TSA 99, author's emphasis; see also TSA 12; *Deont.* 128).[10] Yet, very often these strongly worded apparent denials of other-regarding motivations are set adjacent to passages in which Bentham called attention to clear examples of the operation of sympathy. For example, after writing, "the intrinsic and ultimate object of pursuit to every man at all times" is his own pleasure and his own pain, he wrote, "to deny the existence of this social affection [sympathy] would be to talk in the teeth of all experience. Scarce in the most brutal savage would they be found altogether wanting" (*Deont.* 148; see also *Deont.* 128, 129, 201). Setting them side-by-side, Bentham suggests that he thought these claims are not contradictory. This is a puzzle.

The solution to this puzzle lies in Bentham's broad use of the term "disinterested," and his inclination to speak of interests *of* oneself in ways we would normally speak of interests *in* oneself.[11] In *Deontology*, he distinguished "interest" and "disinterested" used in "the most extended … and strictly only proper sense of the word" from their "more confined" use (*Deont.* 99–100). In its "extended" sense, "interest" applies to all those matters in which a person takes interest, regardless of nature of these matters. These are interests *of* oneself. In this sense, no action is *disinterested* because interests are motives to action. Of course, Bentham conceded, many actions are disinterested, if we use "disinterested" in its "confined" sense meaning: "not motivated by narrowly self-regarding interests" (*Deont.* 100; B iv. 430)—that is, interests *in* oneself. He states his view clearly in his constitutional writings:

> Of action the sole efficient cause is interest, if interest be taken in its most enlarged sense: *i.e.* according to each man's perception of what, at the moment in question, is his most forcibly influencing interest: the interest determined by social sympathy and antipathy, as well as that which is of a purely self-regarding complexion, included (CC (B) 46).

Even more strongly he wrote, early in his career, that it is either "trite" or "indubitably false" to maintain that human beings are governed only by their interest.

[10] See also TSA 12; *Deont.* 128. Elsewhere Bentham puts the same point in terms of pleasure and pain. For example, he says the "intrinsic and ultimate object of pursuit to every man at all times" is his own pleasure and his own pain (*Deont.* 147–8).

[11] I follow here Rawls's distinction; see John Rawls, *A Theory of Justice*, revised edn. (Cambridge, MA: Belknap Press, 1999), 110.

> This observation in a large and extensive sense of the word interest (as comprehending all sorts of motives) is indubitably true [but trite]: but as indubitably false in any of those confined senses in which, upon such an occasion, the word *interest* is wont to be made use of (*Limits* 93 n. a).

Yes, Bentham insisted, everyone is moved ultimately by pleasure; pleasure is the efficient cause, the motive *in esse*. Hence, one is moved by one's pleasure, one's motives, one's interest. How could it be otherwise? This is as true of other-regarding interests and "pleasures" as of self-regarding ones. "The pleasure I feel at the prospect of bestowing pleasure on my friend, whose pleasure is it but mine? The pain which I feel at the sight or under the apprehension of seeing my friend oppressed with pain, whose pain is it but mine?" (*Deont.* 148; see TSA 69).[12] If we think of interests as motives, then, necessarily, one is moved by one's interests, and not those of another. That is a trite observation, a tautology. However, it is false to conclude that all actions are motivated by self-regarding interests, interests in the self.

Bentham could be entirely clear on this matter, when he wanted to be clear. It is unfortunate, then, that he was often willing to fudge the difference between interests of a self and selfish interests. Bentham's reason for doing so were twofold, I think. First, he drew on a language and conceptual frame familiar to him and his intended audience, although he recognized that it was likely to cause confusion. His repeated attempts to fend off critics who resisted his broad generalizations about the inevitably interested nature of human action are testimony to his awareness of this problem. Second, he needed something like this language for his larger theoretical purposes. We must keep in mind that he was not interested in developing a general theory of human nature—"speculative" psychology as he called it (TSA 71)—but only in developing a working theory for his project of designing legal, political, and social institutions (and, later, providing resources for the moral advising activities of the "deontologist"). For these purposes, Bentham thought it was important to stress repeatedly that to encourage and direct human conduct it was necessary to address human beings directly, personally. To move human beings, one must look to their actual interests, to that in which they are personally and emotionally invested. Abstract or impersonal reasons that do not connect with actual and potentially effective motivations are useless for this purpose. In this respect, his view is more focused and strategic than meta-ethical internalism,[13] which it otherwise resembles. For this purpose, he found the available egoistic language useful, albeit potentially misleading to readers (and to himself). So, as we noticed above,

[12] Earlier in the same work, Bentham argued that, from the fact that one pursues the interest or well-being of another person, it does not follow the one does not pursue one's own, for "his own is the breast in which the pain and pleasure of sympathy are seated" (TSA 36). In these passage, he makes clear that one can pursue an interest "without thought about [its being] his own" (*ibid.*)

[13] See Bernard Williams, "Internal and External Reasons", in Williams, *Moral Luck* (Cambridge: Cambridge University Press, 1981); Michael Smith, *The Moral Problem* (Oxford: Basil Blackwell, 1994).

sometimes Bentham claimed not only that one is always motivated by one's own interests, but that one always does so with its (trite or tautological) self-regarding dimension clearly in mind (*Deont.* 195); for example, that one serves the interests of others for the reason that one takes an interest in their interests. This is an unwarranted, unnecessary, and for Bentham's purposes, unwanted inference, an inference that his choice of language misleadingly encouraged. Nevertheless, while we may regret his use of this language, it we must acquit him of the charge of unqualified psychological egoism.

The Range of Human Affections

All human action is motivated by interest, "but by what branch of his own interest?" Bentham asked (*Deont.* 195). He distinguished the branches of interest with respect to the relation of their objects to the agents who possessed them. He distinguished strictly or purely self-regarding interests from purely extra-regarding interests, but he also identified several mixed cases (*Deont.* 126). In the former category fall the agent's particular interests. Actions serving these interests benefit only the agent, considered as if she were a socially unconnected individual (*Deont.* 126, 306). We might say they are interests a solipsist might pursue, except that successful pursuit of them might require interaction with other agents and take into account their opinions and attitudes. But they do not require that the agent consult the well-being, interests, or happiness of other persons. In contrast, agents motivated by extra-regarding interests must consult the interests of others not only for strategic reasons, as it were, but also because the interests of others are the primary focus of the agent. They are social (or interpersonal) interests: interests "of a member of society" who is socially connected and takes an interest in the interests of others, their cares and concerns, as their own (*Deont.* 126; *Limits* 6). Bentham distinguished two subclasses of extra-regarding interests (IPML X.34; TSA 84–5): *social* interests proper stemming from the activity of sympathy (*Limits* 6), and *dissocial* interests, stemming from antipathy (IPML X.26, 42).

In the purely self-regarding group, Bentham included, bodily interests like desires (for oneself) for food, drink, and sex, sensual pleasures and leisure, as well as aversions to pain and death; more general desires for (one's) preservation, security, and safety (TSA 79–80, 85–6). Also included were "the external instruments of felicity," especially interests in power and authority, wealth, and "factitious dignity" (*Col.* 289; SM 183; FPP 154; TSA 81).[14] Extra-regarding interests, in contrast, manifest "social regard, sympathetic regard, the desire to see others happy" (FPP 14). Social interests have their source in the operation of sympathy, the faculty by

[14] "Now the motives, whereof the influence is at once most powerful, most constant, and most extensive, are the motives of physical desire, the love of wealth, the love of ease, the love of life, and the fear of pain: all of them self-regarding motives" (IPML XII.33).

which we can experience, "as it were, by contagion," the suffering or joy of another person (*Deont.* 203; see *Deont.* 129, 194, 201). This faculty is embedded in human nature. There is a "primeval and constant source" of sympathy in human nature (IPML VI.27). "The general and standing bias of every man's nature is ... towards that side to which the force of the social motives would determine him to adhere" (IPML XI.42, p. 141). "In no state of society," Bentham insisted, "can social affection be wholly without place" (*Deont.* 201). Sympathy is so natural for human beings to experience that, to lack sympathy is akin to lacking the sense of smell (FPP 14). This affection has motivational force; it moves people to actions that benefit those with whom they sympathize (B iii. 291–2; *Deont.* 201).

The scope of social interests can vary widely in two dimensions: (i) they can focus on any or all of the interests of others with whom they have some sympathetic connection; and (ii) they can range over the interests of any number of individuals: interest of a single individual, of a group of individuals, of members of one's own community or one's nation, even interests of all human beings (*Deont.* 203). Bentham pays special attention to the latter variable scope (TSA 84; IPML X.36). He was inclined to think that the scope of our interests in the well-being and interests of others can expand as our awareness of others and the scope of our "field of action" expands (*Deont.* 333). Bentham thought of benevolence as the disposition to act from social or sympathetic motives and he regarded the dictates of the principle of utility as "dictates of the most extensive and enlightened (that is *well-advised*) benevolence" (IPML X.36, author's emphasis).

Although the utilitarian principle dictates "universal benevolence" (*Deont.*129), an agent's benevolent attention can focus on smaller groups of individuals and can motivate actions that sacrifice the good of others. "By sympathy, if exercised for the few against the many, as much mischief may be done as by antipathy" or "selfishness" (TSA 17, 108; UC 15.68). Bentham, in his political writings, developed the notion of "sinister interests." Defined broadly, sinister interests are interests focused on benefits to a smaller group at the expense of benefits to a larger one (TSA 18). One's own interests are "sinister" if they are pursued at the expense of the interests of others (FPP 27; SM 183). Sinister interests may be purely self-regarding, but also they may be the social interests of a group smaller than some relevant larger ("universal") group. Although his definition of the term is broad, Bentham limited his use of it largely to contrast the public or universal interest in a community with the restricted, particular interests of subgroups in that community, especially groups to which officials belong (the ruling elite—"the ruling few"—or the legal elite—"Judge and Co").

Bentham recognized a range of mixed cases between pure self-regarding and pure extra-regarding interests; some of them are of considerable interest. He characterizes this middle group in different ways, sometimes as "semi-social"—these are social motives with a self-regarding element (IPML X.35; *Limits* 6)—other times as self-regarding motives with a significant extra-regarding element. He wrote, "Into the composition of a man's self-regarding interest enters, on every occasion, a quantity of extra-regarding interest, and that in a variety of shapes" (*Deont.* 193). Bentham also recognized what he calls "compound" interests or pleasures, for example interpersonal love, love of liberty, love of justice (*Deont.* 96–7). These are not discrete interests, but combinations of a number of interests, some self-regarding, some extra-regarding, some mixed. In contrast, the mixed or impure interests have self-regarding and extra-regarding features intertwined; he called them a "conjunct kind of interest" (*Deont.* 193). In these cases, not only are one's own self-regarding interests affected by the actions of others (TSA 69; *Deont.* 126), but one must also consider the interests of those others with whom one interacts and on whom one depends.

Two such classes of mixed interests or motives are assigned important roles in Bentham's "practicable psychology": love of amity and love of reputation. Amity involves acting in ways that (manifestly) benefit others in hopes of securing their good-will and good offices for oneself. The circumstances must be ripe for reciprocity. Interactions over time give rise to expectations of it. Bentham thought motivations of amity combined extra-regarding and self-regarding elements. The interest one takes in the interests of certain specific other persons is genuine, but not entirely selfless. "By every act of virtuous beneficence which a man exercises, he contributes to a sort of fund—a sort of Savings Bank—of general Good-will, out of which services of all sorts may be looked for as about to flow on occasion out of other hands into his" (*Deont.* 184). The "service" sought is not that expected from a specific beneficiary (as a *quid pro quo*), but rather some eventual return from a kind of common stock. For the transactions to succeed over time, the interest one takes in the interests of others must be genuine. Yet, it could not arise, nor could it be sustained without some hope of eventual reciprocation. Amity is not altruistic; self-regard is involved in more than the trivial sense in which, according to Bentham, it is always and necessarily involved (every action being in this trivial sense "interested").

Likewise, as we saw earlier, love of reputation involves a mix of other-regarding and self-regarding elements, in Bentham's view. One is moved to act, perhaps to an extent against one's personal interests, for the good of others or to conform to social or legal norms, but serving the interests of others or complying with social norms implicates one's self-esteem, because one's actions are judged in the court of public opinion. This, clearly, is a self-regarding concern, but it cannot be an exclusively or purely self-regarding concern, in Bentham's view, because it is tied to something like shared norms and a publicly recognized need to serve the interests of the group of which one is a part.

In view of this, one may be inclined to see these two classes of motives in a crudely Hobbesian light, as lightly papered-over self-interest, and Bentham's typical language would seem to encourage this interpretation. However, another reading is possible, one that echoes Grotius rather than Hobbes. Bentham's account of the genesis and nurturing of motives of amity and sympathy (*Deont.* 202–3) suggests the emergence of a kind of cautious solidarity, rather than calculating knavery.[15] Recognition of interdependence and the possibility of reciprocity brings individuals together to explore opportunities for cooperation. Also, it often happens that pure social affection inclines some to pursue the well-being of certain other persons and that good-will is reciprocated. These interactions are then seen as contributing in a way to the common stock, not just to the private goods of the individuals; they lay the ground work for people working together. Individuals observe the operation of these extra-regarding motives and the natural responses to them and are, by the mechanism of sympathy, "excited and brought into action, as it were by contagion," moved to do the same. "From the example of the services thus rendered by his next neighbor to his next neighbor but one, a man, by a process more prompt than that of reflection, contracts and catches, as it were, a propensity to requite upon occasion the author of those benefits with similar benefits" (*Deont.* 203). This is further reinforced by the good opinion of others thus earned and the popular or moral affection thus engaged. This picture borrows little from a crude Hobbesian perspective on human nature and suggests, rather, the emergence of a more robust solidarity—not entirely altruistic, for it depends on a manifest cycle of reciprocity and a keen sense that the parties each have a stake in the common stock of well-being thereby generated, but also not reducible without distortion to the operation of opportunistic and clever ulterior motives. A "community of interest," Bentham argued, engenders a "community of sympathy" (FPP 71). As Bhiku Parekh put it, this "is not the selfishness of a barbarian, but of a civilized man, not of a man in a Hobbesian state of nature, but living in a settled society,"[16] a society populated by people who, under favorable circumstances, are inclined to act from sympathetic regard for others.

PSYCHOLOGICAL DYNAMICS

According to Bentham, interests of any kind, if present to the agent's mind, are capable of motivating action. Some kinds of interest tend in general to be strong, others relative weak. Self-regarding interests are, in general, the strongest; social motives tend to be weaker, but every interest has the potential to motivate (B iii. 292). This is especially true when they face little or no competition from countervailing interests. "Social motives . . . wherever the self-regarding ones stand neuter, regulate and determine the general tenor of [one's] life" (IPML XI.42, p. 141; *Deont.* 334–5). Sometimes, even when there is competition, social motives can overpower other motives (B iii. 292).

[15] See Bikhu Parekh, *Ten Critical Essays* (London: Frank Cass, 1974), xiv–xv.

[16] Parekh, *Ten Critical Essays*, xii. A similar conception seems to be at work in Bentham's understanding of the international order. See Chapter 11, 260.

Bentham distinguished usefully between *standing* and *occasional* motives (IPML XI.30). Standing motives are regular, steady, and constant, almost always available. Purely self-regarding and sympathetic motives are standing motives (IPML VI.27, XI.42; *Limits* 6), although sympathetic ones may be somewhat less so (SM 183). Dissocial motives are only occasional (IPML XI.42). Semi-social motives depend on various social and circumstances, but they too can be relatively constant, once their conditions are in place and stable.

Interests and motives interact in various ways in the mind of the person considering action, according to Bentham. They can compete or conflict, of course. Between strictly self-regarding and extra-regarding interests there is "almost continual" competition (*Deont.* 193); but interests of any kind can conflict—as is true, for example, between social motives that differ in extent. As we have seen, self-regarding interests, in general, are stronger than extra-regarding interests, but it is possible for the latter to overpower the former (B iii. 292–3; *Deont.* 193). "Each of [the sanctions] is according to the circumstances susceptible of such a degree of force as may prove sufficient, perhaps even the weakest of them, to enable it to overpower any one or more of the rest—i.e. to give determination to human conduct even while all those others are operating in opposition to it" (BL Add MS 33.550.034; see B iii. 293).

"Vulgar prejudice ... assigns the heart for the seat of all moral diseases," Bentham observed in the 1780s, but, he insisted, "the principal and more frequent seat is really the head: it is from ignorance and weakness that men deviate from the path of rectitude, more frequently than from selfishness and malevolence." This is fortunate, he argued, because ignorance and weakness is susceptible to "the power of information and reason (B ii. 553). As his thinking about institutional design progressed, he became increasingly aware of the possibility of enlisting competing motives to supplement efforts of providing information and reason. Bentham believed that motives not only compete, side by side as it were with other motives, but they also can affect and even modify each other. They can work together, in an "alliance" (*Deont.* 195, 201), and some can generate new motives, as we noticed earlier with the operation of sympathy (*Deont.* 203–4), or expand the extent of some extra-regarding motives (*Deont.* 333; CC (CW) vol. 1, 119). Some motives can "counter" or "check" others. "Tutelary motives," Bentham suggested, weaken or diminish the force of other motives (IPML XI.29–34). In some cases, they "extinguish" other motives (IPML XI.42, p. 141; *Deont.* 155–6). This may be what he has in mind in the opening essays of his *Constitutional Code* dealing with constitutional design. In the political domain, he argued, "sinister interest" is pervasive; those in power will dependably sacrifice the universal interest to their particular (class or group) interest.

What can be done to prevent this "sinister sacrifice"? "The nature of the case admits but on one method," he replied,

> which is, the destroying the influence and effect of whatever sinister interest the situation of the individual may expose him to the action of; this being

> accomplished, he will be virtually divested of all such sinister interest; [what] remains, as the only interest whereby his conduct can be determined, [is] his right and proper interest, that interest which consists in the share he has in the universal interest, which is the same thing as to say that interest, which is in accordance with the universal interest, taken in the aggregate (CC (B) 6–7).

Bentham did not explain how exactly this this is accomplished, but we can get some idea about what he had in mind by drawing on some features of his psychology that we have already noticed. We know, for example, that interests operate as motives only when they are present to the mind of an agent and that the force of a motive depends on the agent's attention, steadiness of mind, intelligence and sensibility (*Limits* 6; *Deont.* 194 n 4, 201). If a non-self-regarding interest is made strongly salient, it may have enough strength not only to outweigh, but even to diminish, competing self-regarding motives. They can do so by setting the latter in a different or even "dimmer" light. For example, if someone vividly represents to the agent the cost to another person of her pursuing her personal interest, the latter may lose its luster. (This is how the agent's immediate present interest might be extinguished by vivid portrayal of her future interest (*Deont.* 155).) Similarly, when the prospect of public disapprobation of the action serving the self-regarding interest (and sacrificing the interest of others) is brought to the agent's mind, she may just weigh the cost of that disapprobation against the other benefits to herself of the disapproved act; but, to the degree that she shares the judgment on which the disapprobation is based, she may some to see the act in a different light, and it thereby may lose some of its practical appeal.

Similarly, Bentham argued that when opportunities to advance one's private interest at the expense of larger interest are seen to be limited, considerations of respect and reputation, amity, and even sympathy have room to operate. One comes to recognize more vividly the stake one has in the larger interest, or the strength of one's desire for the good of another (FPP 14). Compared to Hume's much richer moral psychology, Bentham's resources are meagre, but they are rich enough to fund something like this explanation.

SELF-PREFERENCE AND INSTITUTIONAL DESIGN

Strategic Egoism

It is evident from the preceding discussion that Bentham recognized that the range of human motivation is large, spanning purely self-regarding motives to purely extra-regarding ones and complex mixtures of these pure types in between. However, Bentham never wavered from the view that "in the general tenor of life, in every human breast, self-regarding interest is predominant over all other interests put together" (CC (B) 5). He calls this "the self-preference principle," but I will refer to it as the *predominance thesis*. According to this thesis, there is a

> propensity in human nature, by which, on the occasion of every act he exercises, every human being is led to pursue that line of conduct which according to his view of the case, taken by him in the moment, will be in the highest degree contributory to his own greatest happiness, whatever be the effect of it, in relation to the happiness of other similar beings, any or all of them taken together (*ibid.*)

To this, Bentham frequently added that the very survival of the species depends on this predominant propensity (CC (B) 6, 61; *Col.* 288; SM 183; FPP 27, 58). It is remarkable that one finds this thesis throughout Bentham's writings, especially in his political works, and in almost the same words.[17] This was not only one thesis or principle among many in Bentham's repertoire, it was his mantra. It was no slip of his pen. How are we to square this very strong thesis with what we have already learned about Bentham's understanding of human psychology?

To understand the thesis, we must see it in light of Bentham's general project of social and political institutional design. First, we must not over-estimate the strength of the predominance thesis. It identifies a general "propensity," a generally observable tendency, not a universal law of human psychology. Second, while it purports to identify a major constituent of human nature, we know from other passages, most of them in the same works in which the predominance thesis is articulated, that Bentham thought the sympathy-derived social motives were also deeply rooted in human nature. For example, in his *Constitutional Code*, as he set out his rationale for various institutional devices to manage the predominance of self-preference, he stated clearly, "in all human minds, in howsoever widely different proportions—self-regard, and sympathy for others or say extra-regard, have place" (CC (CW) vol. 1, 119). Self-preference sets the general tenor of human life—the ordinary tenor of life for ordinary people (CC ((B) 61)—but it does not do so for all of life; indeed, social motives also have a role to play in determining the tenor of life (IPML XI.42). Moreover, as we have seen, human motivation is not fixed; it can be changed, cultivated, and managed. Human beings are inclined to sacrifice public to personal interest, "unless, by some means or other, intentional or otherwise, prevented from doing it" (CC (CW) vol. 1, 119). Self-preference is the default, before we set our minds to the task of managing it.

It should not be surprising, then, that the strongest statements of the predominance thesis are found in his writings on the design of political institutions, in particular, his project of constitutional design. Indeed, the predominance

[17] See, for example, FPP 27, 58, 233, 264–5; CC (CW) vol.1, 119; CC (B) 61, 192; SM 183; *Col.* 288; TSA 35; *Deont.* 132.

principle provides one of the three pillars of Benthamite institutional design.[18] Considering private life, Bentham still recognized the strength of self-regarding motives, but his view is more moderate. In his early discussion of private ethics, Bentham acknowledges that self-regarding interests will always provide adequate motives for action, but, he added, no person lacks some motive for consulting the interests of others (*Limits* 6; see also FPP 14–15). Moreover, Bentham thought that the propensity to prefer personal to public interest, and thus to motivate the "sinister sacrifice," was notably stronger among those in positions of power, especially political power. Hume gives us a clue to Bentham's understanding and use of the predominance thesis.

> Political writers have established it as a maxim, that, in contriving any system of government, and fixing the several checks and countrouls of the constitution, every man ought to be supposed a *knave*, and to have no other end, in all his actions, than private interest.... Without this, say they, we shall in vain boast of the advantages of any constitution, and shall find, in the end, that we have no security for our liberties or possessions, except the good-will of our rulers; that is we shall have no security at all.[19]

Hume suggests in this passage that the predominance thesis is a widely held *political maxim*, that is, a heuristic adopted for the purposes of institutional design. Still, Hume acknowledged that it is "somewhat strange, that a maxim should be true in *politics*, which is false in *fact*."

> Men are generally more honest in their private than their public capacity, and will go greater lengths to serve a party, than when their own private interest is alone concerned. Honour is a great check upon mankind: But where a considerable body of men act together, this check is, in a great measure, removed.[20]

Like Hume, Bentham regarded the predominance thesis, not as a universal law of human psychology, but as a practical maxim, a heuristic. It articulates a doctrine of psychological egoism as a strategic doctrine. Although it is not universally true, it a safe assumption to adopt for purposes of institutional design. To the rule there may be exceptions, "still, with a view to practice," Bentham wrote, "there may as well be none" (CC (CW) vol. 1, 119), because institutions must be based on generalizations, not on exceptions (CC (B) 6, 61; *Col.* 289). For this purpose, "no man can reasonably be expected" to sacrifice personal (or group) interests to the universal

[18] See CC (B) 5–7; FPP 232–7 and John Stuart Mill, *A System of Logic*, 9th edn. (London: Longmans, Greene, 1875), Bk VI, Ch. VIII, §3.

[19] David Hume, "Of the Independency of Parliament," in Hume, *Essays Moral, Political and Literary* (1758), Eugene F. Miller, ed. (Indianapolis: LibertyClassics, 1985), 42. A posthumous edition of the *Essays* was published in 1777. They were surely familiar to Bentham.

[20] Hume, "Of the Independency of Parliament," 43.

interest (CC (B) 6). "It is on what is common to the many, not only what is peculiar to the few, if to any, that all calculations and expectations on the subject of political conduct ought to be grounded" (*Col.* 288). Not surprisingly, those who oppose the predominance thesis, tend to be rulers, or those who speak for them, who try to convince "the subject many" of their honor, good-will and purity of motives. This, Bentham warned, is "the language of ruler craft." In contrast, he insisted on speaking "the language of simple truth" (albeit not the whole truth) (SM 186; (CC (B) 60–1). Naïve praise of the good-will and self-sacrifice of those holding ruling power serves only to enable "oppression and depredation" (CC (B) 61).[21]

Thus, Bentham clearly embraced a version of psychological egoism, but it is a limited, strategic version of the predominance principle, designed to serve the needs of his project of institutional design.

Cultivation of Human Affections

We have seen that, in Bentham's view, human affections are not static; they often change in response to changes in circumstances that affect individuals' experiences and expand their fields of action (*Deont.* 333). This fact was important for Bentham's strategy of institutional design. When it comes to political life, human beings, especially those exercising ruling power, tend to prefer promoting their personal interests at the expense of the universal interest. The constitution designer must not lament this fact, but must address it directly. The third pillar of Bentham's theory of institutional design is what he called "the duty-and-interest-junction principle" (CC (B) 5–7). "Duty" in this context is determined by the first pillar of that theory: the principle of utility, the principle of universal benevolence. The constitution designer's task is so to arrange political institutions that the interests of those exercising political power coincide with the dictates of the principle of utility, which require actions and policies that serve the universal interest. Commentators on Bentham's political theory typically assume that the duty-and-interest-junction principle requires that institutions be constructed such that strictly self-regarding interests track the dictates of utility. On this reading, the "junction" is to be achieved exclusively by giving political officials self-regarding incentives or disincentives sufficiently strong to overpower any other self-regarding interests that counsel actions contrary to utility. It is true that Bentham did countenance this incentive-giving strategy, modeled after his deployment of legal sanctions, but the strategy he adopted was more nuanced and resourceful. The fundamental aim of

[21] Bentham, at least in one early work, recognized that there might be costs associated with following this general maxim. The diffidence regarding the place of England in international affairs, which he thought was endemic to the English character, was due to "the jealousy and slight opinion we entertain of our ministers and public men." "Jealousy," he complained, "is the vice of narrow minds. Confidence the virtue of enlarged ones" (B ii, 553). This attitude, however, is rarely evident in his later constitutional writings.

constitutional design was to prevent the sinister sacrifice and to give increase and scope and efficacy to what he called "the moral aptitude." Bentham understood that this moral aptitude responded to the promptings mainly of both the moral sanction and the sympathetic sanction—to the semi-social interest in reputation and self-esteem and to the purely social motives rooted in sympathy. "To give increase to the influence of sympathy at the expense of that of self-regard, and of sympathy for the greater number at the expense of sympathy for the lesser number—is the constant and arduous task, as of every moralist, so of every legislator who deserves so to be" (CC (CW) vol. 1, 119). This involves, critically, the *cultivation* of social and semi-social motives (*Deont.* 334).

Cultivation is both an individual and a cultural process. As an individual increases in experience, strength of mind, and command over her faculties, her affections and interests also mature (*Deont.* 201–2). Education not only increases knowledge and understanding, it also alters the bent of one's inclinations and sensibility (IPML VI.38), engaging and expanding human affections and enhancing their relative motive force (UC 87. 18, 19; *Deont.* 202–3). This process is not strictly individual; it typically depends on social contact, observation, and interaction. "As experience encreases and mental culture advances, the field of operation of [sympathy] enlarges itself more and more" (*Deont.* 203; *Deont.* 194 n. 4). The cultivation of the sympathetic and the semi-social motives depends on interaction and reciprocity. Appreciating that they cannot adequately supply their needs by their efforts alone, individuals recognize that they can do better through working together. But, Bentham suggested, working effectively together requires that each attend to the interests of others and the emerging common interests. Moreover, they come to realize that usually they each do well by taking up and manifesting a spirit of solidarity and mutual caring. Like Hume, Bentham understood that the psychological mechanism facilitating this development is not rational calculation, but sympathy, a kind of social "contagion" of sentiments and associated ways of perceiving interests and advantage (*Deont.* 202–3). Moreover, "as in the individual, so in society, as age and experience advance, [the sympathetic] affection and its force and efficiency receive encrease" (*Deont.* 202). A similar process of cultivation happens at the social level and beyond.

The shape, direction, and force of human affections are, on Bentham view, sensitive to circumstances, natural environmental circumstances, and especially social circumstances—as a ship's motion is determined by gravity, wind, and the resistance of the water (IPML VI.5n b). The sensibilities of human beings, and hence that in which they take pleasure and the intensity of their pleasures are shaped by cultural norms and social practices. While physical harms are universal, other harms, especially those tied to "condition in life" or reputation ("mental injuries") can be much influenced by circumstances.[22]

[22] Bentham, *Place and Time*, edited by Philip Schofield and Stephen G. Engelmann, in *Selected Writings: Jeremy Bentham*, Stephen G. Engelmann, ed. (New Haven: Yale University Press, 2011), 159–60.

But, just as in some circumstances human affections may enlarge, in others they may shrink or turn malevolent. Antipathy, unlike sympathy, is not a constant or natural constituent of human nature, Bentham maintained; it arises "only in particular circumstances, and on particular occasions" (IPML XI.42). Perhaps the most fertile soil for growth of the dissocial motives is religious fanaticism and social or economic rivalry. In his *Influence of Natural Religion*, Bentham writes,

> The boundless range of human desires, and the very limited number of objects adapted to satisfy them, unavoidably leads a man to consider those with whom he is obliged to share such objects, as inconvenient rivals who narrow his own extent of enjoyment. Besides, human beings are the most powerful instruments of production and therefore every one becomes anxious to employ the services of his fellows in multiplying his own comforts. Hence the intense and universal thirst for power; the equally prevalent hatred of subjection. Each man therefore meets with an obstinate resistance to his own will, and is obliged to make an equally constant opposition to that of others, and this naturally engenders antipathy towards the beings who thus baffle and contravene his wishes (*Influence* 104).

"Religion," he adds on the next page, "becomes a powerful coadjutor to these predisposing causes. Almost all her influence ... is derived from the system of rivalry and mutual compulsion which she introduces among mankind." Differences of power and capability underlie and exacerbate these tensions (*Deont.* 234–40; *Influence* 47–52). This picture, painted in far more starkly Hobbesian tones, balances the more optimistic picture we have seen elsewhere in Bentham's work. It seems to be limited to this highly polemical attack on religion, which does not share the more programmatic intentions of his work on political institutions. But we might see it in light of that project as providing instruction, such as it is, about the nature of the work of building social and especially economic institutions that work to mitigate the conditions, reduce the scope and violence of rivalry, and moderate the inequalities that pit individual against individual. In addition to altering the circumstances of antipathy, Bentham thought the forces of antipathy can best be countered by building up the forces of sympathy, which were capable of countering and even extinguishing dissocial motives (IPML XI.42).

Self-Regard and Class

Bentham's mode of analysis was always individualist. In his view, communities must always be seen as aggregates of individuals. Nevertheless, after the turn of the nineteenth century, his analysis of political realities increasingly relied on group psychology. "Sinister interest," defined largely in terms of economic class, became one of his most important analytical concepts. Bentham came to see that individuals often act not to promote their strictly personal interests, but the interests of the groups with which they most closely identify, which, of course, in turn greatly influences their perception of their own personal interests. Although he gave the notion of sinister interest a wide definition, he conceived of sinister interest in narrower terms when he thought about the political domain. It comprised mainly the self-regarding interests in wealth and power of social groups or classes. He saw these narrow interests of the ruling elite—the "ruling few"—as fundamentally and directly opposed to the "universal" interest of the "subject many." The root cause of this group identity or convergence of interest was, in Bentham's view, economic.

The relative importance of purely self-regarding interests compared to other, especially social, motives was, in Bentham's view, a function of social and economic conditions in which people live.[23] The cultivation of the affections we observed above had cultural features—increase in "intellectuality," for example—but a key element was development of social and economic conditions—increase in "intercourse" (*Deont.* 194 n. 4; *Deont.* 202–3). In undeveloped societies, human wants are few and narrowly defined, and the life of individuals is solitary; human beings face manifest threats to survival and little opportunity to work with others to withstand them. "His time is divided between pursuit of food, enjoyment of means, and reckless apathy."[24] Narrow self-regarding interests dominate human motivation. Sympathetic response to the needs of others is possible, but conditions conspire to limit opportunities to encourage and develop these affections.

However, as material conditions improve and opportunities for interaction and intercourse increase, human wants and awareness of interdependence increase as well. Semi-social and eventually sympathetic interests emerge and begin to develop motivational force. Individuals begin to see that their own interests are intimately linked with the interests of others, but they recognize that they can enlist the aid of others only with respect to those interests that overlap with the interests of those others (CC (B) 63). As they pursue these "common" or mutual interests, they come to incorporate the interests of their group or community into their own (*Deont.* 203). Under favorable conditions, this process of expansion of the scope of interest in the well-being of others, seeing one's own interest as a component of the interests of the group, proceeds from smaller to ever larger groups. The expansion is not inevitable; under some circumstances, the process may be arrested and a clannish or tribal mentality can develop.

Bentham's main examples of this process are economic. The circumstances of life and the work of the "productive class"—the solid middle-class and

[23] I follow here my discussion of this issue in BCLT, 11.3. See also Parekh, *Ten Critical Essays*, xiii–xv.

[24] Parekh (at p. xv) quotes Bentham, but does not give a precise reference.

working-class—enable them to take an expansive view of their interests. They became the "uniformly beneficent class."

> In the laboring—the productive class, life in its general tenor is a life of beneficence: whatever maleficence has place forms the exception, and in comparison with the beneficence, those exceptions are extremely rare. By the produce of his labour, he procures his own subsistence, and contributes to that of the family to which he belongs ... At the same time to an indefinite amount according to the nature of his employment, he contributes to the gratification of others in abundance (CC (B) 62).

Producing for himself, the member of the productive class, produces for others, and they in turn for him. They pursue mutually beneficial activities, serving overlapping interests.

Bentham casts in sharp contrast with the interests of the productive class the interests and activities the "ultra-opulent class," the "consuming class that produces nothing" (B viii. 569). Members of this class are dependent on the services of the productive class, but they do not need to invite or encourage those services; they *command* them (*Influence* 49). Lacking any need to reciprocate the beneficial acts of others, members of this class do not develop any sense of the interests or needs of those outside their own class. Not being dependent on the good-will of others, their esteem is not engaged by the judgments of those outside their class (*Deont.* 238). The semi-social motives of amity and love of reputation (the source of the power of the moral sanction) look only to members of their own limited class. And lacking meaningful intercourse with people outside their class, they are unable to sympathize with their plight. "Proportioned to the correctness, clearness, and completeness of the conception a man has of [the] enjoyments and sufferings" of people of lower station "is the strength of the sympathy of affection with relation to those same objects of his sympathy" (CC (B) 110). With few checks on their power, members of this "aristocratical" class tend to exercise it extravagantly and without heed to its effects on the lives and well-being of others outside of their own limited circle.

The "ultra-indigent," also, are incapable of developing social and semi-social motives. Being powerless and lacking opportunity to work productively with others, they cannot produce enough for themselves, let alone contribute significantly to the good of others. Rivalry for the very basics of human survival encourages in them dissocial motives and an especially narrow sense of their own interests. They are likely to focus solely on their short-terms personal interests to the expense of all other' interests. A life of malevolence and crime is their destiny, depredation their primary means of support. But, compared to the activities of the "ultra-opulent," the depredations and oppression of the "ultra-indigent" operate on a small scale, and are usually within the competence of the criminal law to control. The depredations of the rich, however, operate on a grand scale, and, because they also hold the reins of power, they are often beyond the reach of the law (B viii. 569).

Bentham deployed this analysis primarily in his political, especially constitutional, writings. His social psychology was not deterministic. This class analysis is a special case of his predominance thesis and we learned above that Bentham meant that thesis to capture the political realities that any constructor of political institutions must take fully into account. These conditions enabling and encouraging sinister sacrifice will prevail unless resisted; self-preference (or class preference) will predominate *unless prevented*. The task of the designer of political institutions is to find instruments with which to prevent the sinister sacrifice among government officials and nurture the development of their "moral aptitude," which depends on the semi-social motivation of reputation and the social motive of extended sympathy. In this way, the interests of officials can be engineered to track utility-determined duty and ultimately to take the universal interest to heart.

CONCLUSION

It is evident that, although Bentham's "practicable" psychology has strongly egoistic elements, human nature is not egoistic, in his view. Human beings always act from what they take their most dominant interests at the time to be, but these may be entirely disinterested concerns for the well-being of others, even those of mankind in general. It is a trivial and misleading claim to insist that human beings are motivated only by their interests. But this claim, recast into something more meaningful, can be understood to call to the attention of moral advisors and designers of political institutions alike to the fact that to motivate voluntary human action, one must start with the interests and motives that the individuals in question have at the time. Affections can be created and nurtured, and competing motives can be weakened, but voluntary human action issues from the subjectively recognized interests of human agents. While self-regarding interests are always powerful, it is possible to construct institutions that encourage socially oriented motives, even extensive benevolence, to counter powerful self-regarding interests. Human affections are rooted in the constitution of human nature, but they are plastic, responding to education and enlightenment. Bentham's psychology was not egoistic, but neither was it naïve about the potential for spontaneous, other-regarding virtuous human action. It combined realism about the potential goodness of human motivation and its limits with a typical Enlightenment optimism about the capacities of culture and education to improve human conduct and direct it to fundamentally utilitarian objectives.

3

Normative Theory

The Principle of Utility

In the previous two chapters, we have explored two of pillars of Bentham's moral, political, and legal philosophy—his theories of meaning and the technology of thought and his theory of human psychological.* It remains for us to explore the third pillar, the ultimate ground of his normative theory: the principle of utility.

THE PRINCIPLE OF UTILITY

The principle of utility—or, as Bentham often preferred to call it, the "Greatest Happiness Principle" (IPML I.1 n. a)—was the fundamental normative axiom of his moral and political philosophy, its "*principium generalissimum*" (UC 96.75). Utility reigns as the "sole and sovereign arbitress of all disputes" (UC 69.232), the "all-directing principle," (Article 295), Bentham insisted. As "ruler and decider of all things" (UC 96.73), it sits in judgment on any individual, official, or governmental act, any law or measure of government, any form or system of government (LW 256); it is "the only just standard for trying all sorts of moral questions" (RRR 188). As such, Bentham meant it to function as an evaluative principle and as a decision principle. As an *evaluative principle*, it set out the ultimate grounds of the rightness of action and offered the ultimate standard by which all acts, laws, and institutions were to be judged, and thus the ultimate court of appeal for moral and political disputes. As a *decision principle*, it was meant to guide the deliberations and decisions of all moral agents, officials, and functionaries of government, as well as ordinary lay individuals. In addition, he saw it as the fundamental principle of *institutional design* (CC (B) 5–7; FPP 232–7). Throughout his career, Bentham focused his attention primarily on matters of public and institutional, rather than interpersonal, morality. He sought to articulate a public philosophy, addressed primarily to legislators and constitution designers. This orientation greatly shaped his understanding of the principle of utility. Bentham did find a place in his scheme of thought for interpersonal morality—"private ethics" he called it (*Limits* §1)—and he devoted an entire work to the topic late in his life. He entitled it, *Deontology*—a

* Adapted from G.J. Postema, "Bentham's Utilitarianism" in *The Blackwell Guide to Mill's Utilitarianism*, H. West, ed. (Malden, MA: Blackwell Publishers, 2006). Copyright © 2008, John Wiley & Sons.

term he, the reputed father of utilitarianism, invented. But even this work was addressed to the "deontologist," an individual moral advisor whose aim was to encourage those in his charge to do the right thing as determined by the principle of utility.[1]

Utility

Utility, according to Bentham, is the sole ultimate measure of moral right and wrong (IPML, 12–13). Bentham's use of 'utility' differs in important ways from its use current in economic theory, and in moral and political philosophy influenced by it.[2] Economic theory identifies utility with a person's good as measured by her preferences revealed in her choices or behavior. Bentham never regarded utility as a possession of a person, or quality of her experience; rather, he saw it as a property of actions, laws, practices, or institutions, namely, their *tendency to produce* good or benefit (UC 69.71, 124; IPML I.3). Community happiness, or universal interest, is the end, the good sought; utility is the ability of something to produce it (FG, 415). It is important to keep this point in mind, but we must add that Bentham meant the terms to specify the end as well. Bentham criticized Hume for treating 'utility' and 'usefulness' as synonyms, both meaning, simply, conduciveness to some end, regardless of what that end might be (Article 296, 322–3). Bentham insisted on specifying the end in terms of happiness of the community, and that, in turn, in terms of pleasure and the absence of pain (FG 446 n; Article 289–90, 296–7).

The Structure of the Principle of Utility

Bentham's understanding of morality was borne of three fundamental intuitions or insights. The first he borrowed from Hume and never thought to question: that promoting the overall good of the community is the basic aim of morality. We might call this *universal consequentialism*, since the rightness of actions is said to be strictly a function of the consequences of actions for all who may be affected.

His second insight was more complex. It was that, first, the fundamental moral concern is the good or well-being of individual human beings (even extended to all sentient beings—*Limits* 4 n a). All other concerns, when viewed from the perspective of morality, take their force and importance from, and must ultimately be rooted in, this concern. "Directly or indirectly, *well-being*, in some shape or other, or in several shapes, or in all shapes taken together, is the subject of every thought,

[1] John Dinwiddy, "Bentham on Private Ethics and the Principle of Utility," in *Bentham: Selected Writings of John Dinwiddy*, William Twining, ed. (Stanford: Stanford University Press, 2004), 134–54. For further discussion of Bentham's "engineering" model of ethics, see Chapter 11.

[2] John Broome, "Utility," *Economics and Philosophy*, 7 (1991), 1–12.

and object of every action, on the part of every known ... sensitive and thinking Being" (Stark iii, 82). Second, individual well-being must be understood in terms of how well or badly a person's life is going; well-being is a matter of *that individual's good*. Third, an individual's good must be assessed from the inside, as it were; that is, how well or badly an individual's life is going must be assessed subjectively, by the extent to which she or he experiences that life as satisfying or disappointing.[3] The concept Bentham found ready to hand to capture this intuition was "happiness." "Any thing that has no influence on happiness, on what ground can it be said to have any claim to man's regard," especially his *moral* regard? Bentham asked (LW 250). "In a proper system of morality, every proposition must be a source of happiness either to the man himself or to [some] other or others."

However, the concept of happiness was not sufficiently refined for Bentham's purposes. The word "happiness," he complained, ignores pain and focuses only on pleasure; it fails to capture the more complex idea of *net* positive or *net* negative consequences of an action. For this, he suggested, "well-being" (for net positive) and "ill-being" (for net negative) do a better job (*Deont.* 130). But more fundamentally, he proposed to capture this basic moral insight with the names of the "real" entities: "pleasure and pain" (LW 251). Reference to happiness, and more specifically to pleasure and pain, "gave determinateness" to the notion of utility (BL Add MS 33.550.007). "In morals, as in legislation," he wrote, "the *principle of utility* is that which holds up to view, as the only sources and tests of right and wrong, human suffering and enjoyment—pain and pleasure" (RJE vi. 238, original emphasis). "Utility is the property of an action to increase happiness. Happiness is no otherwise increased than by averting pains and increasing pleasures" (UC 69.124; UC 69.232). Pleasure and pain alone are good or bad in themselves (IPML 88–89, 100). "*Good*," Bentham wrote, just is "pleasure or exemption from pain: or a cause or instrument of either"; and *evil* "is pain or loss of pleasure; or a cause or instrument of either" (LW 256). Bentham embraced *ethical hedonism* because it expressed his fundamental moral insight in terms that could be anchored ultimately to "real" entities.

Bentham's third insight was that morality insists that the good or evil, pleasures and pains, of individual human beings be regarded *impartially*. "On what grounds, in the eyes of a common guardian, can any one man's happiness be shown to have any stronger or less strong claim to regard than any others?" (LW 250). *Moral good* is a matter of pleasure and pain *impartially considered*, insofar as they tend to be produced by *voluntary human action* (FPP 235 and TSA 89). Joining this *impartial hedonism* with *universal consequentialism* yields the view that what moral agents *ought* to do, or what is *right* for them to do, is that which promotes the overall

[3] I follow Sumner's suggestion here. See L.W. Sumner, "Welfare, Happiness, and Pleasure," *Utilitas*, 4 (1992), 199–200. Similarly, Bikhu Parekh writes, in Bentham's view, "we must start with what human beings *themselves* find good and bad, and build a moral theory on that basis." Parekh, *Bentham: Critical Assessments*, vol. 1 (New York: Routledge, 1993), xxxii.

happiness of people impartially considered. To this Bentham added that only when words like 'good', 'evil', 'right' and 'wrong' are understood in this way do they "have a meaning," otherwise "they have none" (IPML I.10; TSA 89). That is, as we learned in Chapter 1, although they are names of "fictitious entities," their legitimate and indispensable role in moral discourse is anchored in this way to mind-independent and language-independent reality.

Linking his individualist ethical hedonist understanding of value with his universal or communal consequentialist understanding of moral right or duty was an implicit, but rarely articulated, assumption I shall call his *compositional* assumption. The good or welfare of any group or community is strictly a composite of the well-being or happiness of its individual members. The end of government fixed by the principle of utility, Bentham maintained, is "the maximum happiness with reference to the several members of the community taken together" (Stark iii, 307). "The community is a fictitious *body*, composed of the individual persons who are considered as constituting as it were its *members*. The interest of the community then is . . . the sum of the interests of the several members who compose it. It is vain to talk of the interest of the community, without understanding what is the interest of the individual" (IPML I.4–5).

The Meta-ethics of Value

Bentham did not address himself systematically to meta-ethical questions, but we can identify with some confidence his views on some of the most important ones. Bentham proposed that we think of moral *ought*, *right*, and *wrong* in terms of *utility* and *good*, and those, in turn, in terms of *pleasure* and *pain*. Commentators have long taken these suggestions as textbook examples of his naïve attempt to derive an *ought* from an *is*, or to simply *define* evaluative concepts in purely descriptive terms. This, critics have charged, is to confuse *fact* with *value* and *is* with *ought*, a confusion that Hume clearly identified forty years before Bentham began his career.[4] Bentham's hedonistic theory of value, and hence his entire utilitarian moral theory, critics have argued, rests on a fundamental mistake.

More recent commentators have successfully acquitted Bentham of this charge.[5] They point out, first, that Bentham frequently expressed his commitment to the Humean distinction between *is* and *ought*; indeed, he celebrated the distinction (UC 10.129; *Chrest.* 275 n. a). It was, he said, a "most important discovery in moral philosophy" (UC 100.5(a)). Moreover, the charge that Bentham was committed to definist naturalism fails to understand Bentham's theory of fictitious entities and his method of conceptual analysis and explication, which we explored in

[4] See G.E. Moore, *Principia Ethica*, rev'd edn. (Cambridge: Cambridge University Press, 1993), 69–72.
[5] Ross Harrison, *Bentham* (London: Routledge & Kegan Paul, 1984), 100–3, 109–10.

Chapter 1. He did not intend to reduce "good" to "pleasure," or "ought" to "utility," but rather he sought to explicate these terms in a way that locates the content of moral or evaluative judgments in publicly accessible and verifiable facts. Bentham's "analysis gives the verification of the expression to be analyzed. That is, it gives in more directly perceivable terms . . . what has to be true if the [evaluative or normative] expression being analyzed is to be true."[6]

More importantly, Harrison pointed out that Bentham, like Hume, embraced an early form of meta-ethical expressivism.[7] Moral judgments are "expressive of a judgment or sentiment of approbation or disapprobation, as intended by the author of the discourse to be attached to the ideas of several voluntary actions" (B viii. 93; FPP 223, 244; UC 100.114). If I say James ought to help his neighbor, I express my approval of his doing so and disapproval of his failing to do so (*Deont.* 149, 209). Bentham sometimes suggested that such statements are merely disguised statements about the contents of one's mind (*Deont.* 149, 229–30). It seems that Bentham found it difficult to hold fast to the distinction between *saying that* one approves or disapproves of something and one's *expressing* these sentiments. But his weakness in this regard is evident in his discussions of any kind of attitude, beliefs as well as sentiments of approval; it was not a view he reserved for moral judgments.[8]

Moral judgments, then, are expressions of approbation or disapprobation regarding actions, dispositions, laws or institutions (*Deont.* 209). However, they are not *mere* expressions of sentiment—"mere averment[s] of unfounded sentiments" (IPML I.14) or "mere opinion[s] of men self-constituted into Legislators" (UC 69.190). At this point, Bentham borrowed an insight from Hume and used it to inform his understanding of moral judgments, deliberation, and discourse. "Determinations of the understanding," Hume wrote, "have a reference to something beyond themselves, to wit, real matter of fact; and are not always conformable to that standard."[9] This thought inspired Bentham's fourth key insight into morality: that moral judgments are necessarily public.

We can distinguish two key components of this insight. First, our moral approvings and disapprovings, like judgments of the understanding, are subject to rational assessment.[10] The expression of opinion regarding what ought or ought not to be done "leads naturally to the inquiry after a reason" (RRR 188). If one blames or approves of some mode of conduct, one should expect to be asked for one's reason for the judgment (UC 69.72), "something that points out some external consideration, as a means of warranting and guiding the internal sentiments of approbation

[6] Harrison, *Bentham*, 29.
[7] Harrison, *Bentham*, 192.
[8] See Chapter 1, 8, and Chapter 9, 211-13.
[9] David Hume, "Of the Standard of Taste," in *Essay Moral, Political, and Literary*, Eugene F. Miller, ed. (Indianapolis: LibertyClassics, 1985), 230.
[10] See Chapter 1, 8, 9 regarding judgments in general and Chapter 9, 213–6, for judgments of probability.

and disapprobation" (IPML II.12), "a foundation for [the] judgment . . . distinct from that judgment itself" (*Com.* 199). Proper moral judgments purport to direct attention to something beyond the sentiment of the appraiser. They purport to be guided by or grounded in reasons independent of the sentiment that is communicated to others. Moreover, the appraiser is answerable to such grounds. One may always ask for the reason or ground of another person's moral judgments (*Deont.* 209). Moral judgments claim authority for themselves rooted in the reasons that can be given for them, which are considerations independent of the appraiser's *ipse dixit* ("[because] I said so"). Without this potential backing by reasons, moral judgments would be mere expressions taste—"sounds instead of sense . . . caprice instead of reason" (IPML I.1). More colorfully put, the expressions of approbation or disapprobation offered up "without any specific grounds produced or referred to . . . may be compared to the careless housemaid who, without regard to the heads upon which it might chance to fall, should cast the contents of her receiving pail into a crowded street out of an upper window" (*Deont.* 153).[11] Bentham called those who issued such groundless judgments partisans of "*ipsedixitism*," who offer nothing more than their "I said so" to fund their judgments (*Deont.* 304–5).

Moral judgments, then, must appeal beyond the sentiments of the appraiser, to something in the world, "a quality or property of the act or object" being appraised (LW 256), and hence to "a general matter of fact; the truth of which rests upon experience" (UC 69.72; FG IV.41; *Com.* 199). This appeal to the world beyond the appraiser is important, precisely because it is to that publicly accessible world in which others participate to which the appraiser addresses her moral judgment. The matters of public fact are potentially matters of common knowledge, because they are presumed to be matters of common experience. This is the second component of Bentham's insight. His concern is not that evaluative language be tied to bare physical reality, but rather that otherwise private sentiments be given a public expression and public foundation. "The catechism of reasons is worthless if it cannot be a catechism of the people," Bentham insisted (B i. 163). Moral judgments must be public, appealing to considerations that are "fixed and certain, and that all men are agreed about" (*Com.* 159). A moral judgment expresses a sentiment that purports to be "a standard of right and wrong, with respect to every other man" (IPML II.14). But, as such, it must be neither "despotical" (imposing one's idiosyncratic sentiments on everyone else, without permitting them the same privilege), nor "anarchical" (allowing "as many different standards of right and wrong as there are men") (IPML II.14, p. 16). Moral justification, as Bentham saw it, has an essential *public* dimension: it is justification "by a person addressing himself to the community" (IPML II.14 n. d, p. 28). Thus, reasons in support of moral judgments must be capable of being communicated to and appreciated by others.

[11] The editors of *Deontology* note that this passage was bracketed for possible omission, suggesting that the prose may have been too colorful even for Bentham.

Those who practice *ipsedixitism* commit two major errors regarding their understanding of moral discourse. First, they purport to offer judgments that rest on appraiser-independent considerations as their grounds, but the judgments disguise mere averment of sentiment. The expressions of sentiment fail as moral judgments. Second, those who practice *ipsedixitism* engage in a morally objectionable exercise of power: they set themselves up as law-givers in the moral domain, hence as moral despots (*Deont.* 253, 337). They seek to secure agreement with their sentiments by sheer exercise of will and rhetoric, not by persuasion that proceeds by calling attention to the reasons or grounds underwriting their judgments (*Deont.* 209).

Thus, Bentham argues, "morality, as well as policy [politics], is a matter of account" (B vi. 238; UC 106.170) in two respects. First, it is a matter of accounting, as it were, that is, a matter of deliberation and reasoning. Second, this reasoning is public and discursive in the sense that it involves giving and receiving, tracing and evaluating, assessing, and challenging reasons and arguments that are offered in a public domain. Properly functioning moral discourse rests every dispute on matters of fact. "Now the question is put as every political and moral question ought to be, upon the issue of fact; and mankind are directed to the only true track of investigation which can afford instruction or hope of rational agreement..." (RRR 189). Yet, the hope of agreement is no a guarantee. "Agreement to be sure is not even thus made certain: for certainty belongs not to human affairs. But [this method]... bids fairest for leading to agreement" (*ibid.*), or at any rate, those who are disputing "see clearly and explicitly, the point on which the *dis*agreement turned." Thus, "the door to reconcilement would be much more open, when they saw that it might be not a mere affair of passion, but a difference of judgment, and that, for any thing they could know to the contrary, a sincere one, that was the ground of the quarrel" (FG IV.39; original emphasis; see also UC 106.170–171).

Morality is brought to account in a second regard, morality provides a language and a framework of deliberation and discourse by which moral agents—and by extension, citizens in a polity—can hold each other accountable. Responsibility is understood to involve answerability for one's actions and for one's judgments. Morality settled on a firm public footing, provides the resources for this practice of accountability holding. This is important in interpersonal relationships, of course, but in Bentham's view, it becomes utterly vital for politics in a well-ordered polity. In his *Fragment on Government*, Bentham equated the "responsibility of governors" with "the right which each subject has of having the reasons publicly assigned and canvassed of every act of power that is exerted over him" (FG 485).[12]

This general analysis of the necessary features of moral judgments and discourse provided Bentham with the resources he needed for an argument in support of his ultimate normative principle.

[12] See Chapter 13.

AN INDIRECT ARGUMENT FOR THE PRINCIPLE OF UTILITY

Bentham acknowledged that because the principle of utility was the sole ultimate principle of rational practice, it is not possible to derive it from some yet more basic normative principle (IPML I.11). Nevertheless, in an essay introducing his *Constitutional Code*, Bentham offered some words in support of his "greatest happiness principle" (CC (B) 4). When I say that the greatest happiness of the whole community alone ought to be the end of law and government, he wrote, I give expression to "my wish, my desire, to see it taken for such, by those who, in the community in question, are actually in possession of the powers of government." In so doing, Bentham asserted, I make a statement about a matter of fact, a fact about something in my mind. Readers may then consider whether they entertain the same sentiment. If some do, they may find some profit in reading on; if some do not, they have little reason to read on.

However, if this bit of writing was meant to give support to the Bentham's sovereign principle, it is a manifest failure, even on Bentham's own terms. While it brings to view a matter of fact, the fact expressed (Bentham mistakenly says "stated") by his judgment, it is a fact about Bentham's state of mind. It cannot, on Bentham's principles, be offered as a reason for the judgment, since it fails to point beyond the appraiser and the appraiser's judgment to something in the world that might be thought to support the judgment. It is nothing more than "a mere averment" of sentiment. That leaves Bentham's enterprise on a most unstable footing, and subject to the same dismissive gesture that he used at the opening of *Introduction to the Principles of Morals and Legislation* to wave away all competitor principles to his principle of utility.

Yet, Bentham had a more plausible argument—or at least a start of an argument—available to him. The argument begins with the meta-ethical observations we surveyed in the previous section. Moral judgments, and hence the foundational principle or principles on which they rest, must appeal to appraiser-transcendent reasons that are accessible to and assessable by all those to whom the judgments are addressed. These reasons must be rooted in facts of common experience, facts that all can acknowledge and assess. Bentham's meta-ethical principle set the test. The question is what species of facts, if any, passes the test. Bentham's candidate is facts concerning human well-being, the satisfaction and disappointment of human aims, the realization of human interests, in short, human suffering and enjoyment, ultimately rooted in experiences of pleasure and pain. These facts are known, intimately, to each and all of us. They are "matters of experience" for all of us, and hence they can be "rendered familiar to all the world" (*Deont.* 169; B i. 163). Moreover, they only such facts can do the job, in Bentham's view. "Pleasures and pains ... are the only clear sources of ideas in morals," he argued (B i. 163). They alone meet the publicity test. On this basis (and only on this basis), moral right and wrong can be made known and demonstrated ... [and made a] matter of account" (RJE vi. 238; FG IV.39–41). Bentham concluded that the principle of utility, although it expresses a sentiment of approbation, refers beyond itself to a publicly observable property of actions, namely their utility, and ultimately to the pleasure and pain they produce. This property provides a measure by which the sentiment expressed by moral judgments can be assessed as reasonable or not.

Bentham's argument is incomplete in several respects. First, Bentham asserts, but does not plausibly argue, that utility alone meets the publicity test. Most of his attempts to do so beg the question. They rest on the premise that in each case the supposed competitor principle is not properly tethered to the only relevant "real" entities, pleasures and pains, but that only shows that they are not at bottom hedonist. It does not show that they cannot do the job of focusing public deliberations and disputes. Bentham's argument ultimately fails for this reason. But we shall put this (not inconsiderable) problem to one side to consider two other points at which the argument is incomplete.

Second, to establish the principle of utility as the ultimate moral principle it is not enough to show that pleasures and pains are matters of common experience (we shall see later that Bentham himself backs off this claim), and even less that they are "real entities." At the very least, Bentham must show that pleasures and pain are morally *relevant*; indeed, for this purpose, they need to be morally *fundamental*. That is, Bentham's argument depends on the other insights or intuitions on which Bentham built his moral theory. In particular, it depends on the assumption that we all recognize that the suffering and well-being of individual human beings is of fundamental moral importance and that well-being must be regarded, as it were, from inside of the experience of each person. This is something that is, also, a matter of common experience. "We all know but too well what pain is" (UC 69.94). Anything that does not affect human happiness has no claim to our moral regard (LW 250). The *value* of enjoyment and *disvalue* of suffering, Bentham thought, are matters no one would deny and all would recognize that all others recognize. Furthermore, not only do we seek pleasure, but we regard it as good. Anticipating the much-discussed argument in Chapter 2 of Mill's *Utilitarianism*, he linked the two, writing "After experience had of it by the person in question, the very fact that his pursuing [is] conclusive proof of its goodness" (*Deont.* 150). The fact that an agent freely chooses to act in a certain way is "of itself conclusive proof" that the act produces "pure or preponderant good" for him (*Deont.* 151).

But, and this the third point regarding which the above argument is incomplete, this might explain why we ought to pay attention in our evaluative judgments to suffering and enjoyment, but it does not yet show why *I* ought to pay attention to *your* suffering and enjoyment. Yet, the principle of utility calls for *impartial hedonism*. How do Bentham's considerations support this important move? Perhaps, at this point we can deploy the publicity condition to explain and underwrite the requirement of impartiality that lies at the heart of Bentham's utilitarian principle. Suppose one accepts that considerations of one's own happiness provide one with compelling reasons to act. Could a principle that gives singular weight to considerations of my happiness pass the publicity test? Surely not, Bentham insisted, for moral judgments are put forward as binding on all moral agents, and no principle that privileges my point of view could hope to secure the agreement of other moral agents. "The principle of self-preference," Bentham wrote in his *Constitutional Code*, "has for its regulator in the breast of each, the consciousness of the existence and power of the same principle in the breasts of all the rest" (CC (B) 63). Public argument in support of moral judgments is possible only if equal importance is given to the point of view of each agent. Because the moral point of view is *public*, it must be *impartial*. Viewed impartially, the happiness of one person is no more or less important than the happiness of any other person, Bentham insisted; so, the fundamental moral principle must give the same weight to the happiness or interests of any one person as to any other. Only one version of a utility principle fulfills this requirement, Bentham argued, the greatest happiness principle.

> In the eyes of every impartial arbiter, writing in the character of legislator, and having exactly the same regard for the happiness of every member of the community in question as for that of every other, the greatest happiness of the greatest number of the members of that same community can not but be recognized in the character of the right and proper, and sole right and proper, end of government (FPP 235).

In *Constitutional Code*, this argument gives a distinctive but somewhat different shape to the principle of utility. Bentham writes,

> In so far as his aim is, to sacrifice all interests to his own ... no man finds any effective number of hands disposed to join with his: in so far as his aim is, to serve such of his interest alone, as are theirs as well as his, he finds all hands disposed to join with his: and these common interests correspond to the immediately subordinate right and proper ends of government, maximization of subsistence, abundance, security, and equality (CC (B) 63).

PESTILENTIAL NONSENSE: RIGHTS, JUSTICE, AND UTILITY

In 1792, Bentham was made an honorary citizen of France by its new revolutionary government. However, this honor did not prevent him from excoriating the historic *Declaration of the Rights of Man and of the Citizen*.[13] He dismissed the idea of

[13] *Nonsense upon Stilts* in RRR 317–401; see also *Supply without Burden*, section V, in Stark I, 332–7. Useful discussions of Bentham's and others' critiques of natural rights can be found in Jeremy Waldron, ed., *Nonsense Upon Stilts* (London: Methuen, 1987), 151–206; Philip Schofield, *Utility and Democracy: The Political Thought of Jeremy Bentham* (Oxford: Oxford University Press, 2006), Chapter 3;

natural rights, which lay at the center of the revolutionary *Declaration*, as "pestilential nonsense" and the idea of natural and *imprescriptible* rights as "nonsense upon stilts." His famous attack fits a pattern of Benthamic hostility to appeals to justice, natural law, natural rights, and related notions in legal and political discourse. Justice, he quipped, "is an imaginary personage feigned for the convenience of discourse" (IPML 120n). To the proud authors of the *Déclaration des droits de l'homme* he responded curtly, "instead of rights talk of expectations" (UC 29.6). All such appeals suffered from "*ipsedixitism*," he charged. We should not be surprised, then, to find that his critique of natural rights drew directly on the argument for the publicity of moral judgments that we just considered.

Bentham's critique of the French *Declaration* in the 1790s was specifically aimed at the use of natural rights ideology in political constitutions. He addressed what he saw as largely a jurisprudential problem. His arguments presupposed his earlier critique of natural-law thinking, which not only targeted its jurisprudential use, but its pervasive use in contemporary moral and political discourse. His root criticism was meta-ethical, drawing on his analysis of the necessary features of moral judgments. In this chapter we will consider Bentham's meta-ethical critique. In Chapter 10, we will consider his deployment of that critique in his jurisprudential and especially constitutional thought.

Natural Law

Bentham observed that when moral judgments of people conflict and when they disagree about matters of public policy, many are inclined to try to convince their opponents by claiming that their opinion is grounded in natural law, or supported by "reason"; and when that fails, they appeal to God's will. Those who rhetorically appeal to natural law imagine that law that exists apart from positive law and stands in judgment of it. Bentham regarded such appeals as either empty or fallacious. He was not opposed to appeals to what is "natural"; indeed, he deployed the rhetoric of "the natural" for his own purposes. But he thought he could tie all such appeals to matters of common experience, experience rooted in publicly accessible facts about human nature, human happiness, pleasures and pains. Such legitimate appeals did not invoke *law*; the dictates of utility are not themselves laws, but rather reasons or grounds for laws.

However, natural law, he believed, was alleged to be law that is at the same time not law—that is, not anything properly called law. And so, appeals to natural law are, he argued, contradictory. This argument, of course, begs the central question of jurisprudence, namely, whether law is to be identified only with *positive law*, law

Schofield, "Jeremy Bentham's 'Nonsense upon Stilts,'" *Utilitas* 15 (2003), 1–26; and Schofield, "A Defense of Jeremy Bentham's Critique of Natural Rights," in *Bentham's Theory of Law and Public Opinion*, Xiaobo Zhai and Michael Quinn, eds. (Cambridge: Cambridge University Press, 2014), 208–30.

of the state and of the law-giver who makes it. But, perhaps this is not an entirely question-begging argument, for what positive law possesses is a kind of public standing, providing "common standard[s] which all men acknowledge and all men are ready to resort to" (UC 69.188). Natural law, Bentham insisted, manifestly lacks this public standing. Moral judgments appealing to natural law purport to appeal to something beyond the judgments themselves, and the appraiser's sentiments that they express, but the alleged standard is imaginary, or rather it is a standard of and for each person, and nothing more (*Com.* 197–8; UC 69.124). If they had appealed to utility, rather than "reason" or "natural law," Bentham insisted, "they would have said something." They would have offered a foundation for their judgment, "to something distinct from the judgment itself" (*Com.* 199). Some moralists do appeal to something beyond their judgments; they appeal to God. But such appeals, he argued, are intended not to persuade but only to silence or simply to frighten. "Unable to convince, his aim has been to silence; unable to reason them into assent, he has tried to frighten them into submission" (UC 69.132).

The core themes of Bentham's meta-ethical analysis of moral judgments are clear in this critique of natural-law language. Moral judgments necessarily point beyond themselves to matters that can be accessed and assessed by others. This is required by the fact that moral judgments are not meant to be exercises of power, but contributions to deliberations about how one ought to act and what laws and institutions ought to govern us, deliberations which must be public, engaging ordinary people. Appeals to utility, according to Bentham, fill this moral discourse bill, but appeals to natural law fail; indeed they fail spectacularly. His critique of natural rights follows this pattern.

Natural Rights and Justice

Natural rights are said to be moral rights that exist apart from law and are rooted in the nature of human beings; moreover, they are said to trump the claims of law and of general welfare. This notion of natural rights, Bentham argued, is either contradictory or empty. His demonstration presupposes his analysis of the concept of a right. To claim a right, according to Bentham, is to demand that someone do something for one's benefit or refrain from interfering with one's liberty in some respect. If this claim is to amount to anything more than the expression of an idle wish, that is, if it is to be taken seriously as a *moral* claim, it must assert the existence of an *obligation* of the other party to provide that service or to refrain from liberty-interfering actions. This moral judgment is credible, according to Bentham, only if it is underwritten by a public standard that imposes the obligation on the other party and supports it with a credible sanction. Positive law provides such standards, but natural law cannot, precisely because it cuts itself off from the only possible sources of such public standards. Rights are real when the obligations they imply are sanctioned by positive law, but in the absence of positive law, rights are empty, self-contradictory fictions.

> Lay out of the case the idea of a *law*, and all you get by the use of the word *right* is a sound to dispute about. I say I have a right: I say you have no such right. Men may keep talking on at that rate till they [are] exhausted with vociferation and rage, and when they have done be no nearer to the coming to a mutual conception and agreement than they were before (SM 23).

Law alone offers a credible promise of providing "determinate and intelligible meaning" (B ii. 218). A right is "the child of law," Bentham insisted, but "a natural right is a son that never had a father . . . a species of cold heat, a sort of dry moisture, a kind of resplendent darkness" (Stark i, 334, 335).

Bentham thought that the rhetoric of rights is especially problematic if we seek to try to incorporate it in the fundamental constitutional law of the land as a means of restraining the arbitrary exercise of power by those in positions of authority, as the French Revolutionaries (and their American counterparts) proposed to do. One major problem, Bentham argued, is that the language of natural rights is indeterminate (UC 69.6–7, 102). Another is that claims made based on natural rights trades on a confusion. It is said legislators "cannot" make laws which threaten this or that alleged natural right. But, strictly speaking, the claim is false; they certainly *can*. What is meant, Bentham argued, is that legislators *ought not* to make such laws. But, if they say that, they must appeal to some reason or fact beyond the mere expression of opposition (RRR 187–9; NS 327–8). It is tempting to read this bit of argument as a typical legal positivist rejection of the incorporation of substantive moral standards into the conditions of validity of law.[14] However, this does not capture accurately Bentham's concern. He did object to the typical natural-law claim (e.g., Blackstone's) that a law in violation of natural law is not morally binding, but he did not reject the idea that a law may properly be judged morally objectionable and worthy of resistance. Rather, he objected to the idea that conformity to *natural law* could be a ground of one's obligation to obey positive law. Indeed, he insisted that utility is the only proper test of law's morally binding force.

In this argument, Bentham seems to quibble about *cannot* vs *ought not*, but the "cannot" here refers to limits on legal powers, and he clearly recognizes that there can be (must be) such limits. So his objection is not conceptual. His objection against incorporating natural rights language in constitutional law was substantive, not conceptual. In *Securities against Misrule*, he argued that putting principled limits on the exercise of legislative power is not the best or most effective way to curtail the arbitrary exercise of legislative power. Rather than announcing vague

[14] See Philip Schofield, "Bentham's 'Nonsense upon Stilts,'" *Utilitas* 15 (2003), 23–6.

and toothless *rights*, all exercises of power should be subjected to ruthless public scrutiny (see Chapter 12).

Bentham charged that the language of natural rights was dangerous—"anarchical" was his term. However, the danger does not arise from people taking a critical attitude toward all exercises of governing power; indeed, after the turn of the nineteenth century, he thought a decent and liberal society should take major steps to encourage and empower active criticism. The problem, rather, was that the language of natural rights was vacuous. It could not ground rationally focused criticism or opposition; it could only encourage each person to launch opposition from his own private stock of ill-formed and ungrounded sentiments. Opposition appealing to vacuous natural rights and natural law was "anarchical," because it opposition without a rational, principled basis. The proper source for and discipline of such criticism and opposition was, in Bentham's view, his principle of utility. This principle alone focused the attention of everyone in the community, officials, and members of the public alike, on matters of universal interest.

Bentham was especially critical of the idea of *imprescriptible* rights; he thought it practically incoherent and unworkable—"nonsense upon stilts" he called it. To recognize Jean's right is to recognize John's correlative obligation, but that obligation restricts John's freedom and frustrates his interests. Inevitably, some interests will have to be compromised. Doing so may be justified, but only if the competing interests of all the parties are clearly kept in view. Imprescriptible rights, however, focus our attention exclusively on the interests of the lucky person claiming the right, and blind us to the interests of all others.

Bentham's critique of natural rights, like his criticism of justice more generally, was at bottom a critique of the *rhetoric* of rights and justice. In his view, the problem with these important moral notions is that, in moral and political discourse, they are cut off from the one context in which they could be given rational content, namely, consideration of the community's universal interest or well-being. In less polemical moods, Bentham tended to think of justice as a *species* of overall utility. Early in his career he wrote "Utility [is] two-fold: 1. original, 2. derived from expectation. The term justice … [is a] substitute for (or dependent on) the term utility in the latter sense" (UC 96.74). Similarly, he wrote, "Justice (that is utility in so far as it consists in observation of Justice) depends upon expectation" (UC 70a.21). Later he tended to think of justice as utility concerned with certain especially important resources that are necessary for the protection and promotion of community welfare, for example, security of action and of the means of subsistence and well-being.

Late in his life Bentham jotted down an intriguing idea in his commonplace book. "Justice is beneficence," he wrote,

> in cases in which the non-performance of it is considered as punished, or punishable by the force of one or other of the several sanctions: principally the political, including the legal, and the moral or popular (B x. 511).

The idea seems to be that justice and moral rights are among the most important concerns of morality, so important to social welfare in fact that the substantial costs of enforcing them by law can be justified on utilitarian grounds. This is the kernel of the analysis of justice and moral rights that Mill later developed in Chapter V of *Utilitarianism*. Mill may have gotten his idea from Bentham, but it was never more than temporarily entertained by the senior utilitarian. Rather, he consistently maintained that justice is nothing more than a *species* of utility, and rights are real just insofar as they are actually enforced by law, not merely that certain goods or opportunities ought to be enforced. In *Nonsense Upon Stilts*, he wrote, "reasons wishing there were such things as rights, are not rights: a reason for wishing that a certain right were established, is not that right: wants are not means: hunger is not bread" (NS 330).

However, Bentham's way of making his peace with the rhetoric of rights and justice by treating them as species of utility, leaves his public philosophy vulnerable to a very common criticism. It has often been argued that utilitarianism fails to take rights, or individual persons, seriously.[15] The principle of utility, it is argued, requires that we sacrifice the happiness of individual human beings whenever a net increase of community welfare can be achieved through or despite violation of the right. This sacrifice of the individual to the good of the larger community is not prevented by insuring that the good or happiness of all members of the community is considered impartially, it is argued, because good that can be done for the community, even if the good is only marginal, can utterly dwarf the sacrifice of the few.

In the twentieth century, philosophers sympathetic to utilitarianism have sought to answer this criticism, by removing the principle of utility from its role as the sovereign decision principle to which Bentham assigned it. They argued that the principle plays an indirect, background role, providing the normative bases for ordinary rules of morality, including rules of justice, rights, and the like. Bentham, I believe, had resources to mount a plausible if not ultimately conclusive answer to these criticisms, but they do not rely on this strategy of indirection. His resources lie not in the structure of his grounding principle, but rather in the theory of value incorporated into it. The familiar criticism of Bentham is fair if (1) Bentham understood the welfare of a community at any point in time to be the simple sum of the pleasures enjoyed by its individual members minus the pains they experience, and (2) the greatest happiness principle requires that we maximize the happiness of the community understood in this way. However, there is evidence (significant, but perhaps not conclusive) that he had a quite different, more complex and subtle, understanding of the principle of utility, especially the theory of value at its core. I will explore in the immediately following two chapters this more subtle understanding of the principle of utility.

[15] John Rawls, *A Theory of Justice*, 2nd edn. (Cambridge, MA: Belknap Press, 1999), 24, 163.

Also, Bentham's argument for his principle of utility from the requirement of publicity, suggests another direction from which he might try to answer to this challenge. Recall, Bentham argued that publicity forces each of us to seek a principle by which to live in our social world that we could hope others can embrace as well. This, he argued, forces each to embrace a principle that does not permit self-preference to blind us to the well-being of others, but that also does not force altruistic self-sacrifice. It drives us to embrace an understanding of the principle that focuses on serving *common interests*, "such of his interest alone, as are theirs as well as his." These common interests, he proposed "correspond to the immediately subordinate right and proper ends of government, maximization of subsistence, abundance, security, and equality" (CC (B) 63). In Chapter 6, we will explore Bentham's attempt to recast his principle of utility in terms of the *public interest*.

4
Publicity and the Development of Bentham's Theory of Value

At the opening of his inquiry into the principles of morals, Bentham crowned pleasure and pain sovereign masters of the moral life (IPML I.1).* Although he immediately repented of the rhetorical fanfare of this coronation, he never repented of the hedonist theory of value it announced. A consequentialist theory of moral right and duty is incomplete without a theory of value to tell us which consequences are good and which evil. Bentham's utilitarian consequentialist theory needed a compelling theory of value. From the outset of his career he was inclined to cast that theory of value in terms of pleasure and pain. Why was he tempted to concede royal authority to these otherwise common and humble concepts?

In the preceding chapter, we answered this question by looking at an intuitive idea that decisively shaped Bentham's moral outlook. Promoting the good of the community as a whole (universal consequentialism) is the central aim of morality, but the fundamental moral concern, as Bentham saw it, is the well-being or welfare of *individuals*. The most general end of morality is "giving encrease in some shape or other to man's well-being," the well-being of each individual being separately considered (*Deont.* 125). Morality is focused not on the good of some abstract entity ("the community"), but rather on the good of individual human beings—in particular, on how well or badly their lives are going—and, in Bentham's view, we assess this from the point of view of the individuals living those lives. The morally relevant good of a person is good *in that person's eyes*, something she cares about, something in which she takes an active interest. Thus, whether a person's life is going well or badly must be measured by the extent to which she *experiences* it as satisfying or disappointing.[1] "Happiness" is an empty word, he often said, unless it is understood in terms of human feelings, the subjective experience of individuals. "The principle of utility . . . holds up to view, as the only sources and tests of right and wrong, human suffering and enjoyment" (RJE vi. 238).

As we saw in Chapter 2, pleasure had long been a basic term in the British philosophical lexicon, so it was natural for Bentham to associate subjective

* Adapted from G.J. Postema, "Bentham's Utilitarianism" in *The Blackwell Guide to Mill's Utilitarianism*, H. West, ed. (Malden, MA: Blackwell Publishers, 2006). Copyright © 2008, John Wiley & Sons.

[1] L.W. Sumner, "Welfare, Happiness, and Pleasure', *Utilitas*, vol. 4 (1992), 103.

Utility, Publicity, and Law: Essays on Bentham's Moral and Legal Philosophy. Gerald J. Postema.

experience—suffering and enjoyment—with the simple and familiar concepts of pleasure and pain. To care about something just is to take pleasure in it. Moreover, like Hume, he thought that the immediate experience of pleasure and pain provided a unique point of sympathetic contact between sensitive beings. By nature, we respond sympathetically to the suffering and joys of others, so, he thought, we can hope to move people to recognize the moral value of the sufferings and joys of others by reflecting on the moral significance of their own experience. "Who is there, that is not susceptible of discomfort and comfort—of pain and pleasure?" he asked, and assumed that we naturally join him in drawing the conclusion that the "happiness and unhappiness of any one member of the community ... [is no] greater or less [a] part ... of the universal happiness and unhappiness, than that of any other" and for that reason is due full respect (B iii. 459). Also, most importantly, Bentham was inclined to think that pleasures and pains have a kind of empirical solidity and public accessibility that makes them especially appropriate as bases for public moral discourse.

THE CALCULUS OF PLEASURE

With pleasures and pains as the basic units of value, and the welfare of the community as a whole as the ultimate end prescribed by the principle of utility, it was tempting for Bentham, who hated abstractions, to think of the welfare of the community as a grand composite of the pleasures and pains of individuals. But this thought raises a number of questions: how are these essentially subjective values to be measured, related, and weighed with respect to each individual and combined to yield a meaningful assessment for each proposed act, law, or institution?

The Model

Bentham suggested that it is possible to construct a powerful ethical deliberating machine capable of churning out precise, determinate, and publicly verifiable judgments and prescriptions for all moral occasions, both private and public. On this view, once we make a precise and determinate assessment of the quantities of pleasure and pain of each of the persons affected by some range of actions or policies open to us, we can calculate the hedonic sums for each individual and from them determine a composite hedonic sum for the community as a whole. The principle of utility, then, requires that we choose the action or policy that comes out on top. In his relatively late *Codification Proposal*, Bentham wrote, "To exhibit reasons" of utility "is to draw up the account ... apply arithmetical calculations to the elements of happiness" (LW 250–1) and in the succeeding pages (LW 251–6) he described how such a calculus of pleasure would work. One finds a description of a similar model in his manuscripts written in the 1770s and 1780s,[2] and it received its canonical and most familiar formulation in Chapter IV of his *Introduction to the Principles*.

According to this simple model, the "value" of each pleasurable or painful experience likely to be consequent upon a given act is a number determined by the net quantum of pleasure or pain experienced by each individual, measured in terms of intensity, duration, probability, and remoteness (i.e., temporal distance), combined with a similar assessment of other consequences of the act for that individual; the results of this assessment is then aggregated to determine the happiness quotient for the community as a whole (or of all those affected by the action in view). The welfare of the community is modeled as a function of the welfare, thus calculated, of each individual member of it. This arithmetic function is usually thought of as simple summation (UC 69.198; LW 256); however, in one manuscript account, Bentham took the function to be multiplication. Since, the community is nothing more than a multitude of individuals, the good or happiness of the whole community consequent upon some act is the value of it for an individual multiplied by the number of individuals in the community (presumably, counting only those actually affected by the action). The "total value of the stock of pleasure belonging to the whole community is to be obtained by multiplying the number expressing the value of it as respecting any one person by the number expressing the multitude of such individuals" (UC 27.34 (Baumgardt 556)). This formulation requires that when one uses Bentham's model to calculate the happiness total for the community, one must regiment the assessment of each individual's total pleasures and pains to some index or perhaps some representative person. If we take this formulation seriously, it is clear that we have abstracted from the idiosyncrasies of each individual's experiences of pleasure and pain and adopted a perspective that is in some sense common to, and representative of, all of them. Bentham did not specify how this representative position is to be constructed.

It is not clear how we should regard this alternative formulation of the compositional function, but it does focus attention on fact that the ordinary formulation of the simple model rests on assumptions which may prove difficult for Bentham to sustain, especially in light of the requirement of publicity that he insisted constrains all modes of moral and political reasoning. His simple model of a calculus

[2] UC 69.198 (PPI—1770s) and UC 27.33–5 (1782). The latter was published as "Appendix IV" in David Baumgardt, *Bentham and the Ethics of Today* (Princeton: Princeton University Press, 1952), see 555–62. For an extended discussion of this model in Bentham's works, Michael Quinn, "Bentham on Mensuration: Calculation and Moral Reasoning," *Utilitas* 26 (2014), 61–104. Although I depart at points from Quinn's interpretation of Bentham's appeal to this model, his essay is invaluable because it brings together and insightfully discusses all the relevant texts in which Bentham described, commented upon, or used the model. For a very different interpretation, see Tom Warke, "Multi-dimensional Utility and the Index Number Problem," *Utilitas* 12 (2000), 176–203 and Tom Warke, "Classical Utilitarianism and the Methodology of Determinate Choice, in Economics and Ethics," *Journal of Economic Methodology* 22 (2000), 1–27, esp1–12.

of pleasure assumes (1) that pleasure is a simple, discrete, and homogeneous felt quality that accompanies every enjoyable experience (and that pain is the corresponding quality of experiences of suffering, frustration, and disappointment), (2) that they come in publicly measurable quantities (psychic packets, or *quale*, as it were), and (3) that the *quale* experienced by one person can be compared, at least with respect to their morally relevant quantities, with those experienced by all others affected by the acts under consideration such that the quantities can be meaningfully added together. Also, (4) if the combinatorial function is multiplication, as Bentham suggested, the model assumes that the experiences of each individual can be expressed adequately for purposes of moral deliberation as the experience of some representative person.

A little reflection, however, reveals that these assumptions are very implausible. Moreover, Bentham himself recognized the limitations of this model, often in the very same passages in which he suggested the main outlines of the simple model (e.g., LW 251–6). Indeed, scattered throughout Bentham's writings are sophisticated critiques of these assumptions and the model they underwrite. One wonders, then, just how seriously we should take Bentham's characterization of moral reasoning as a kind of mathematical calculation. There is no doubt that he was fond of the image for this purpose,[3] but how deep did his commitment to the model go? Should we treat it as rhetorical flourish—"metaphor and declamation"—as he explicitly treated his "two sovereign masters" language (IPML I.1)? Or should we, following Lord Robbins, treat Bentham's talk of a "felicific calculus" as "all shop window."[4] In at least one place, Bentham suggested that he used "calculation" rather loosely to mean "reasons applied to the subject in the manner best adapted to the subject" (TSA 43),[5] but on the same page he offers a characterization more in line with the simple model. "To calculate," he wrote, "is to take an account of quantities (under the principle of utility) of such pleasures and pains as seem likely to be the result" of actions under consideration (*ibid.*).

We should not try to settle whether Bentham took seriously his talk of "calculation" on a mathematical model just by looking at passages in which he used the *term*; rather, we must consider whether used the *method* in his own moral and political reasoning, and even more critically, we should consider how he managed to square his searching critique of the simple model with his apparent reluctance to repudiate it.

[3] Quinn quotes the following from Bentham's pseudonymous work, "Not Paul, but Jesus": "No calculation! exclaims the shallow and empty-headed sentimentalist, … as if the distinction of right and wrong—as if the determination of an act in respect of conduciveness or destructiveness to human happiness—depended on any thing else than calculation" (UC 161.322). Quinn, "Bentham on Mensuration," 67.

[4] Lionel Robbins, *The Theory of Economic Policy in English Classical Political Economy*, 2nd edn (London: Palgrave, 1978), 181, quoted in Quinn, 67.

[5] Quinn argues that we must not take this suggestion seriously; see Quinn, "Bentham on Mensuration," 66.

Bentham's Critique of the Model: Epistemic Distance from Experience

Moral judgments, Bentham repeatedly stressed, point beyond themselves to *facts* in the world, and the only relevant facts, he insisted, are facts about the pleasures and pains of individual human beings. These are the facts to which moral reasoning is anchored and which alone make moral reasoning possible. Not only are they are among the ultimate constituents of psychical reality—"real entities"—but they are also matters of direct experience, immediately accessible to introspection. "In respect of the actual state of my sensations, meaning the sensations themselves, I am scarcely liable to be deceived or in error" (B viii. 330). This seems to put moral reasoning on a secure, unchallengeable footing. However, Bentham was aware that these sensations—secured by unassailable first-person authority—make up only the smallest portion of the materials used in moral reasoning, even reasoning of the most elementary sort. This is due to the fact that first-person authority extends only to the matter of the *existence* of a *present* sensation. However, just to get moral reasoning going, one must assess the "value" of any given pleasure, whether immediately present or likely to occur in future. The value of a given sensation, in both senses of "value"—its evaluative status and its quantum—is not something immediately given in experience; it is the product of an exercise of intellect. The "value" of a given pleasure, the building block of the calculus of pleasure, is not a primary psychical fact, but rather the product of an "inference" or construction of the intellect.[6] It is, in Bentham's language, a "fictitious entity." That is not to say that there is anything dubious or even, in a proper sense, "unreal" about such values, as we learned in Chapter 1. These "fictitious entities" stand on the same ground as all other "inferential entities," like tables and chairs, dispositions and motives, rights and duties. Reasons denominated in these values may be entirely legitimate objects of our thought—indeed, they are absolutely essential to thought—but they are not "real entities," and they exist by virtue of our mastery of the technology of thought. Thus, although moral reasoning of even the most elementary sort may be *ultimately* rooted in pleasures and pains, but moral reasons are more proximately, and thus usably, matters at some greater or lesser epistemic distance from these foundations.

Moreover, on Bentham's understanding, the reasoning of a moral agent focuses not on his or her sensations, but rather on their causes and their likely recurrence. It depends on associating subjective experiences with events in the world, human actions and all the other factors that conspire to bring about those experiences. At its most elementary level, moral reasoning must connect events in the external world, and their causes, with subjective experiences.[7] Judgments about these

[6] Bentham acknowledged that "the elements of [moral] calculation being in so large a proportion of the psychical class—such as intentions, affections and motives—are in a proportional degree situated out of the reach of direct observation" (UC 102.71 (DO 146)).

[7] Quinn, "Bentham on Mensuration," 93–5.

matters are not judgments about primary facts, but inferences, or the products of inferences. In addition, the deliberating agent must think in action *types* (and event types), which she must construct by analogy and inference from past (i.e., remembered) and shared experience (UC 70.23). Bentham put this point in a striking way in his *Table of the Springs of Action*. "It is no otherwise than through the medium of the *imagination*," he wrote, "that any pleasure, or pain, is capable of operating in the character of a *motive*," and hence as a reason (TSA 90).

It should be evident that the epistemic distance between the primary facts of pleasure and pain and ordinary moral reasoning is large. This is not in itself a problem or challenge to Bentham's understanding of moral reasoning. We should not think that this distance opens the door to "uncertainty" threatening the viability or rationality of moral discourse, any more than the distance from immediate perceptions and the empirical world of ordinary objects and events motivate any worry about our grasp of that world.[8] We learned in Chapter 1 that despite his spare ontology, and the absolutely necessary role of human reason in the construction of the world of our ordinary experience, Bentham was no epistemic skeptic. He read Hume with some care and admiration, but he was never tempted by Hume's skepticism.

Canvassing these facts of epistemic distance are not meant to cast doubt on Bentham's understanding of moral reasoning, but rather to bring to mind that the way he is often inclined to characterize the process of moral reasoning may not neatly fit together with deeper views of the nature of experience and human reasoning on which his model must depend. Whatever "calculations" are done, they are not done with or upon the "real entities," pleasures and pains; indeed, any credible and creditable reasoning will take place at epistemic levels so distant from these entities that it would be pointless and enormous waste of effort to follow the tether from any given constituent of moral reasoning to some one or more of these real entities.

We must take note of another dimension of epistemic distance between the usual reference of reasons of utility and well-being in Bentham's account and the primary facts of the individual sensations of pleasure and pain. As we observed in Chapter 3, Bentham often insisted that each person is the best judge—indeed, "the only proper judge"—of his or her own pleasure (*Deont.* 150). But in his *Deontology*, he qualified this general claim: Each of us is the best judge of our *present* pleasure or pain, but not of our *future* ones. "*Like a third person* his future contingent individual pleasure and pain can not be judged of by him otherwise than from the *species it belongs to*" (*Deont.* 195 n. 1, emphasis added). Bentham here astutely observed that we are not especially good at what recent social psychologists call "affective forecasting."[9] We systematically overestimate the emotional satisfaction or

[8] *Pace* Quinn, "Bentham on Mensuration," 94.

[9] B. Pelham, "Affective Forecasting: The Perils of Predicting Future Feelings," *APA On-line*, 18: No. 4, 2004 [http://www.apa.org/science/ about/psa/2004/04/pelham]; T.D. Wilson and D.T. Gilbert, "Affective Forecasting," in *Advances in Experimental Social Psychology* (San Diego: Academic Press,

distress we will get from experiences we anticipate as great pleasures or horrible pains (e.g., owning a BMW or one's team losing the championship). We are better able to anticipate the value of these future experiences by looking at them from the outside, Bentham maintained. The resources we have for the purpose of predicting our future well-being are the resources available in much the same way to observers. Such predictions depend on our "general" sensibility to pleasures, not our *particular* sensibilities. The "quality" of an experience, in Bentham's terminology (*Deont.* 130–1), is a matter of the *immediately felt* property of a pleasurable experience. This is *strictly present*, immediate to the experiencer's mind, but once it is gone, or when it is considered in prospect or in the abstract, one's own access to it is no different from the access of any other person.

This leads to a further problem, for Bentham acknowledged that the *quality—quale*—of an experience is not publicly available. "To no man, can the quality of sensibility in the breast of any other man be made know by anything like equally probative and unfallacious evidence" (*Deont.* 131). At best, we can make inferences from "countenance, gesture, deportment, contemporary conduct at the time, subsequent conduct at other subsequent times," and the like (*ibid.*). Beyond the present moment, even our access to our own experience is only indirect, inferential. Thus, Bentham's understanding of the resources on which moral reasoning must draw is more nuanced than the simple model can recognize. It is perhaps not surprising, then, that when Bentham came to consider "subordinate ends" of law and government—subordinate to the single, overriding end of the universal interest—he focused on broadly shared interests that function like public goods, viz., security, subsistence, abundance and equality (*Civ. Code* 302).

The epistemic distance between Bentham's own moral reasoning practice and the simple model of that reasoning is evident also in his understanding of the utilitarian significance of expectations.[10] The notion of expectations, and utility associated with expectations and their disappointment ("expectation utilities") is a, if not the, central notion of Bentham's utilitarian theory of law and legislation. In his assessments of and arguments for formal and substantive aspects of law, expectation as a species of utility plays a dominant role. In the utilitarian calculus, expectation-utilities routinely outweigh all competitors. The reason for this dominance is, Bentham's view, that the capacities and sentiments involved in shaping and realizing expectations are fundamental to human life (*Civ. Code* 308). Security of expectations, he argued, is the precondition for achieving anything meaningfully satisfying in human life beyond momentary pleasure. He even suggested

2003), 35, 345–411; J. Gertner, "The Futile Pursuit of Happiness," *New York Times Magazine*, September 7, 2003 (available at http://www.wjh.harvard.edu/~dtg/Futile_Pursuit.htm).

---

[10] For further discussion of the role of expectations and "expectation utilities" in Bentham's political and especially legal thought, see Chapter 7 and BCLT, Chapter 5.

that it is necessary for recognizably *human* life. He wrote in his *Principles of the Civil Code*,

> In order to form a clear idea of the whole extent which ought to be given to the principle of security, it is necessary to consider, that man is not like the brutes, limited to the present time, either in enjoyment or suffering, but that he is susceptible of pleasure and pain by anticipation, and that it is not enough to guard him against an actual loss but also to guarantee to him, as much as possible his possessions against future losses. The idea of his security must be prolonged to him throughout the whole vista that his imagination can measure (*Civ. Code* 308).

The disposition to look forward generates *expectation*. Powers of imagination and foresight, and the sensibility of anticipation, enable human beings to live meaningfully across time. It is distinctive of human good that it consists not merely in pleasures of the moment and the actual security of future good, but also in the security of expectations regarding the future.

> It is by means of [expectations] that we are enabled to form a general plan of conduct; it is by means of this that the successive moments which compose the duration of life are not like insulated and independent points, but become parts of a continuous whole. Expectation is a chain which unites our present and our future existence, and passes beyond ourselves to the generations which follow us. The sensibility of the individual is prolonged through all the links of this chain (*Civ. Code* 308).

Expectation plays a key role in well-being considered from the inside, that is, *in the individual's eyes*. And it threads all or very many of the other elements of an individual's good together into a meaningful human life. For this reason, on Bentham's view, it has singular importance in any assessment of a person's well-being for purposes of utilitarian moral and political reasoning. It is true that Bentham was inclined to speak of "the pains of disappointment" and "the pleasures of anticipation," but he had to admit that, beyond the very simplest cases, such talk is metaphorical. Such pleasures look and feel radically different from the pleasure of eating a butter pecan ice cream cone. They are far more complex, not only temporally, but also conceptually. It is unlikely that anything like such pleasures could be intelligibly combined in a calculus on the simple model. Yet, these are the pleasures and pains that figure most prominently in Bentham's own political reasoning, when he has left behind his favorite simple model and is doing actual utilitarian deliberation. It also seems to be true that, unlike the discrete and homogeneous real entities favored by the simple model, these conceptually structured and articulated utilities can contribute to an enterprise of *public* deliberation and justification.

Questioning *Qualia*

Bentham recognized challenges to the simple model that go deeper than the epistemic considerations we have just considered. They represent conceptual, rather than merely epistemic challenges. Several such challenges can be found in Bentham's writing, often within a few paragraphs of descriptions of his calculus of pleasures and pains. One challenge is directed against the assumption that pleasures and pains are discrete, homogeneous properties (*qualia*) that accompany all pleasant and painful experiences (see Chapter 2, 28–30). It is sometimes argued that Bentham rejected this assumption, on the ground that he recognized the vast heterogeneity of pleasures and pains that human beings are capable of experiencing (IPML V–VI). "Pleasure and pain in general," he wrote, are "apt to flow from so many distinguishable sources" (RJE vii. 569). However, heterogeneity of the things in which human beings find pleasure is no challenge in itself to the simple model, as long as there is a discrete and homogeneous property that accompanies the all the heterogeneous pleasurable experiences. It is this latter thesis that Bentham's core doctrines challenge.

In at least one place, Bentham explicit asserted, albeit in passing, that "words . . . like pain and pleasure [are] names of homogeneous real entities" (IPML VI.6 n c (p. 53)). But, while this may be true regarding those real entities that ultimately anchor all practical thought, it may not be true of the deliberation-level fictitious entities on which moral reasoning primarily depends. Bentham's understanding of the referent of "pleasure" poses a challenge to this *qualia* doctrine. We observed in Chapter 2 that Bentham endorsed what I called an attitude conception of pleasure. In an unpublished manuscript, he wrote, "I call pleasure every sensation that a man had rather feel at that instant than feel *none*. I call pain every sensation that a man had rather feel none than feel" (UC 96.128). Bentham suggests here that what is common to all pleasurable experiences is not some discrete, felt quality, but the fact that people like to have them and that pains are experiences people would like to avoid.[11] Pleasure, on this view, picks out an attitude of persons towards certain experiences they have—their wanting the experience, and wanting it to continue—rather than any particular discrete quality of the experience. I suggested in Chapter 2 that we might express this attitude in terms of what a person takes pleasure in. This attitude might accompany each pleasurable experience, but it is not a property, let alone a discrete and homogeneous *quale*, of that experience.

The shift to the third person perspective that is required, in Bentham's view, by consideration of one's future well-being, marks a shift from the *quale* conception to

[11] Quoted by John Dinwiddy in *Selected Writings of John Dinwiddy*, William Twining, ed. (Stanford: Stanford University Press, 2004), 27. This way of reading Bentham's notion of pleasure was not lost on earlier commentators on Bentham's psychology. For example, John Hill Burton, in his introduction to Bowring's edition of Bentham's *Works*, suggested something along these lines as well (B i, 22) and the suggestion was endorsed by C.K. Ogden in his introduction to Bentham's *Theory of Legislation*, C.K. Ogden, ed. (London: Kegan Paul, 1931), xv.

the attitude conception of pleasure. For when we shift to the third person, we are dependent on others to help us grasp the impact of contingent features of our world on the availability of pleasures, and we are also forced to look to sensibilities that we tend to share with others. Experiences we know by participating with others in daily life are the kind that I and many others would like to have again. For these purposes, these pleasures are not adequately portrayed in terms of some single, homogeneous *quale* accompanying them. The relevant conception of pleasure, for these purposes, is the attitude conception.

Interpersonal Comparisons of Utility

Bentham was inclined at times to express an even more radical skepticism regarding the suitability of the simple model of the calculus of pleasure. Already in the 1770s, he wrote, "There is no marking out by any description a determinate lot to serve as a common measure of pain or pleasure: nor were such an aliquot marked out is there any way of knowing whether it subsists or not in a given subject" (UC 69.41).[12] "Money is divisible into parts capable of being numbered: pleasure or pain itself is not" (UC 143.39).[13] We find the same thought expressed in the 1820s in his *Codification Proposal*: "Pleasure itself [is not] ponderable or measurable ... Weight, extent, heat, light—for qualities of all these articles, we have perceptible and expressible measures: unhappily or happily, for quantities of pleasure or pain we have no such measures" (LW 251, 253). The problem of comparing pleasures or pains arises for an individual agent seeking to take her own hedonic temperature; the problem is magnified many times, if she seeks to take into account the well-being of others. Pleasure and pain, while facts of experience and real entities the existence of which is a matter of immediate, first-person perception, are not interpersonally measurable (*Deont.* 131). Bentham was no radical skeptic of other minds. He never doubted that we can correctly judge that another person takes pleasure in some activity, object, person, or state of affairs. But he realized that the kind of access even we have to our own present pleasures and pains, and our ability to compare and evaluate them, is not available to us regarding the pleasures and pains of others. We can gain some insight into the working of another person's sensibility through imaginative projection or empathy (UC 69.238-9), but the usefulness of this exercise for purposes of interpersonal comparison of the experiences is limited. And, more importantly, we have no common standard by which to measure and compare experiences of present pleasure or pain.

The problem is at its most serious level, Bentham acknowledged, when it comes to assessing the *intensity* of an experience of pleasure or pain. Bentham

[12] Quoted in Philip Schofield, *Utility and Democracy: The Political Thought of Jeremy Bentham* (Oxford: Oxford University Press, 2006), 43 n 52.

[13] Quoted in Quinn, "Bentham on Mensuration," 70 n. 30.

distinguished seven determiners of "the value of a lot of pleasure or pain" (IPML IV; see Chapter 5, 96–8). Four such determiners—intensity, duration, probability ("certainty"), and remoteness—are non-relational properties of the pleasures or pain in the sense that they are thought to be properties of the pleasurable experience itself. To these Bentham added fecundity, purity, and extent. These three are not properties of the experience, but rather properties of that which gives rise to it. *Fecundity* is its ability to produce other or more such experiences; *purity*, the extent to which it also gives rise to experiences of the opposite valence (e.g., pains associated with pleasurable experiences); and extent, number of other people who may also have like experiences from the same cause.

Of the four non-relational determiners of the "value" of pleasure and pain, duration is easiest to measure; probability less easily, perhaps, but not in principle problematic, although neither of these is a *felt* quality of the experience. Remoteness is the property of a future pleasure considered in the present. It measures the effect of the temporal distance between the present and the time at which one expects to experience the pleasure on one's estimate of its "value" for one's current deliberation. It is not a felt quality of the experience either. It may be measurable, perhaps, by measuring preference revealed in behavior. Of the four determinants, it appears that only intensity is intrinsic to the experience itself. It is the primary or core dimension, which other dimensions qualify or amplify. However, of these dimensions, intensity "is the least capable" of being measured, Bentham conceded, "for this there is no common standard" for it (UC 69.19). He echoes this assessment made at the outset of his career in his late *Codification Proposal*. Intensity "is not susceptible of precise expression: it *not* being susceptible of measurement" (LW 254). The problem, of course, is acute if we are trying to compare the intensity of pleasure that Peter takes in working in his garden on a sunny April day with the intensity of the pleasure James takes in watching him work. It is also a problem if Peter wants to compare the pleasure he is about to experience working in his garden with the pleasure of a long walk in the woods that he must forgo to work in the garden; and even more problematic when he must do so in deliberations concerning his plans for a month hence.

Bentham acknowledged early on that interpersonal comparisons are problematic (IPML VI.2–3), and that this problem poses a serious challenge to the simple model for computing aggregate community welfare. The depth of the problem becomes apparent once we recognize that it arises even for individuals. If there is no common measure, then there is no way of assigning a unit value to the intensities of pleasures and hence no way of comparing one experience of pleasure with another with an eye to determining their aggregate "value" (i.e., quantity). This problem is intensified if one wishes to compare a present experience of pleasure with one in some middle-distance future, or two future pleasures. For, as we observed earlier, Bentham was keenly aware that, with respect to one's experiences lying beyond a perhaps generous horizon of the specious present, one is in a position not unlike that of a person trying to assess the experience of another person. This determination of intensity must be done, according to the canonical understanding, before the qualification of the remoteness dimension can be factored into the calculus of pleasure. But if this is true, then we face a radical incommensurability at the point of departure of moral reasoning as modeled by the calculus of pleasure. It arises even before we get to the point of aggregating the results across members to yield an initial assessment of community welfare.

Bentham seems to have been aware of the problem. He does not say merely that intensity does not admit of *precise* expression, but that it is *not susceptible of measurement* (LW 254). Bentham acknowledges that the problem is not a problem of vagueness or imprecision—as when one paces off a lot to determine its dimensions rather than using a precisely calibrated measuring tool—but rather a problem of incommensurability *in principle*, with respect to the dimension to which all other dimensions refer and on which they depend. This is not to say, and surely Bentham did not ever say, that we do not and cannot with some confidence make comparisons of the importance or significance of various experiences within our own lives or in the lives of others (see *Deont.* 130–1). But it does imply that, however we make these comparisons, we cannot make them based on the privately felt quality of these experiences, as the simple model requires.

This *in principle* limitation of the simple model creates serious problems for its use as a model for public moral and political reasoning. The problem is not that individual minds are inscrutable; Bentham willingly acknowledges that it is possible sympathetically to enter into the experience of another and thereby grasp with some confidence the quality of it. The problem comes, rather, when one attempts to articulate and communicate this grasp in terms that can be appreciated and assessed by others. To lack a common measure is to lack a language in which publicly to communicate one's qualitative assessment of some matter and a quantitative measure of it. "The use of a common measure is to enable the person who speaks to communicate to any one he is speaking to the same idea of the quantity of any thing he is speaking of as he himself conceives. A common measure must therefore be some instrument the name of which suggests upon being mentioned to both parties an idea of the same quantity" (UC 27.36 (Baumgardt 560)).

One problem created by the lack of a common measure is illustrated in Bentham's early discussion of judicial decision-making. Bentham argued that, in deciding disputes over property, judges ultimately must determine where the balance of expectation-utilities lies, considering the expectations of both parties and the public at large (BCLT 208–10). He suggested that the judge might consider trying to enter sympathetically the minds of each of the parties to determine the subjective intensities of these expectations, because "the stronger a man's expectation is of having a thing the stronger is his disappointment … if he fail to have it … [and hence] the greater is the pain of disappointment" (UC 70 (a).20). However, the judge will have to take into account that the intensity of expectation and disappointment is likely to vary with temperament. The judge may determine this to his own satisfaction, Bentham conceded, but the reasons that lead the judge to his conclusions are themselves "uncommunicable" leaving the judge with "no means of satisfying the public of the existence of them" (UC 69.238–9). This problem is especially acute for public officials, but the problem infects all moral and political reasoning, which, as we have seen in Chapter 3, always involves justification addressed to the community (IPML 28).

Proxies

Occasionally, Bentham suggested that it might be possible to use money as a proxy measure of well-being.[14] The suggestion is clear in his *Codification Proposal.* Since pleasure itself is not ponderable or measurable, we might use "the general source, and thence representative, of pleasure, viz., money" to estimate pleasures and pains (LW 251, 252). But here Bentham proposed to use money only to estimate the impact of remoteness on the intensity of a pleasure or pain. From time to time, he suggested in passing that we might be able to assess the impact of certain legal measures or punishments on behavior by looking to money as a surrogate for the strength of motives.[15] But in an early text on "Value" (UC 27.32–6 (Baumgardt 555–62)), he gives the idea of money as a proxy for pleasure a more extended discussion.

To speak of quantities of pleasure and pain we need a common measure, he wrote, but "the only common measure that the nature of things affords is money" (UC 27.36 (Baumgardt 561)). Perhaps, then, we might hope that our appreciation of the value of money tracks the intensities of our pleasurable and painful experiences reliably enough for us to use the cardinal measure that money provides in place of direct calculation of pleasures and pains. Bentham did not claim that all the interests of which human beings are capable might be "reducible to the pecuniary interest."[16] Rather, his more modest claim is that money might provide a rough approximation of the relative intensities of pleasures and pains, such that we can rely on its convenient cardinal measure to compare, weigh, and eventually combine pleasures and pains with respect to each individual with whom one's moral reasoning is concerned and within the community of which they are members. To establish this approximation, Bentham suggested, we can ask Jane, "how much money would you give to purchase [some given] pleasure?"[17] For example,

[14] See Quinn "Bentham on Mensuration," 77–93.

[15] *Limits* 203–4; B vii. 398. See Quinn, "Bentham on Mensuration," 79–81.

[16] Quinn, "Bentham on Mensuration," 83.

[17] This may be the earliest use in economic literature of the "willingness to pay" measure of utility. On this measure, see, for example, Richard Posner, *Economic Analysis of Law*, 1st edn. (Boston: Little, Brown, 1973); Posner, "Wealth Maximization and Tory Law: A Philosophical Inquiry," in *Philosophical Foundations of Tort Law*, David Owen, ed. (Oxford: Oxford University Press, 1995), 99; Gerald J. Postema, *Legal Philosophy in the Twentieth Century: The Common Law World* (Dordrecht: Springer, 2011), 190–3.

if she is willing to pay £5 for pleasure X and the same for pleasure Y, then we can say that, as far as she is concerned, the pleasures are of equal intensity (UC 27.36 (Baumgardt 561)). We can extend this analysis to other pleasures that are not available for purchase. If Jane is indifferent between pleasures X and Y, and pleasure X is produced by £5, then we can infer that pleasure Y can be adequately quantified at £5 as well. That is, X = Y = £5 (UC 27.25 (Baumgardt 559)).

The philosophical problems facing this method of approximation are very well-known in the literature of the philosophy of economics, and Bentham, himself, was aware of some of them. Perhaps, the most important objection is that an individual's willingness to pay for something is a function not only of how much he wants or takes pleasure in it, but also of his current stock of money. On the principle of the diminishing marginal utility of money, the marginal utility "cost" to a person of the loss of £1 decreases in some proportion to the increase in one's wealth. Bentham was aware of this principle and deployed it in a crucial argument for equality of income (other things being equal) in his *Principles of the Civil Code*. Moreover, he explicitly recognized a more general version of this principle in the text under consideration, observing that "there are it is true some men to whom the same sum would give more pleasure than to others; to the same man likewise the same sum would give more pleasure at one time than at another" (UC 27.35 (Baumgardt 559)). And in *Principles of the Civil Code*, he counseled that, when "speaking of the effect of a portion of wealth upon happiness" of a number of persons, "abstraction is always to be made of the particular sensibilities of individuals" (*Civ. Code* 305). So, Bentham himself had convincing reasons to treat skeptically the proposal of money as a proxy for the measurement of the intensity of pleasures and pains. Nevertheless, one might argue that we should take his explicit appeal to this idea at least twice and at widely varying times in his career as strong evidence that he took the idea seriously. However, this inference is mistaken. We can identify the mistake if we take a closer look at the passages in which Bentham suggested the idea.

In the passage in his *Codification Proposal*, Bentham introduced the idea of a monetary measure, not as a proxy for a measurement of the intensity of pleasures and pains, but rather as a device to illustrate how we might conceive of the effect of remoteness on a given quantity of pleasure. "The magnitude of a pleasure, supposing it present, *being given*," he wrote, we need to measure the extent to which it is "diminished" by its being remote rather than present (LW 251, emphasis added). Thus, the core determiner of the "value" of a lot of pleasure is not to be measured, even roughly or approximately, by money, but rather that value is, for purposes of illustration of the operation of remoteness on that value, assumed to have been determined—a task that Bentham had already conceded is not possible in principle.

Furthermore, Bentham's discussion in his essay, "Value," was very carefully qualified. First, the context of his discussion was limited to an exploration of the instruments available to a legislator who seeks to motivate conduct to enhance community welfare, not as a means of estimating that welfare (UC 27.35 (Baumgardt 557–8)). Second, he proposed money as a measure of the capacity of certain "instruments" to produce pleasure, not as a measure of the quantity of the pleasures themselves (UC 27.35 (Baumgardt 558–9)). Third, Bentham admits that his indifference or willingness-to-pay test is reliable only *ceteris paribus*, and only where the quantities are small and ordinarily occurring (UC 27.35 (Baumgardt 559)). Elsewhere, Bentham is also clear that it only makes sense to use money as proxy for measuring the intensity of a small range of interests, primarily the pecuniary interest (RJE vii. 397). These texts, we must conclude, do not provide evidence of Bentham's hope, let alone aspiration, to use money as a proxy for measurement of pleasures and pains in general. No such common measure, he conceded, is possible.

UTILITARIAN CALCULATION AND PUBLIC REASONING

At this point in our reconstruction of Bentham's theory of value we face a problem of interpretation. There is no question that when Bentham talked about the process of utilitarian moral reasoning he liked to talk in terms of "arithmetic calculus" of utilities or pleasures and pains. And yet, Bentham was keenly aware that moral and political reasoning cannot, except in the narrowest range of cases, conform to this model. The assumptions on which the model rests are simply false, for reasons Bentham fully appreciated. But, then, the model is not merely fictitious; it can only be taken to be a straightforward *fiction*. And, if it is just a fiction, it would seem he would have to conclude that reasoning on the utilitarian model is no better able to meet the conditions of public reason than appeals to natural law, moral sense, or the principles of sympathy and antipathy. Bentham's challenges to the simple model seem to throw his entire project into doubt. Of course, it is possible that Bentham embraced *both* his simple model and the assumptions on which it rests *and* the views that undermined them without making any effort to reconcile them. If this is the case, one must conclude that his theory of value, and the theoretical enterprise of which it is a part, is inconsistent at its foundations. The question for us is whether there is a plausible interpretation of the various claims Bentham made that can allow him to escape this threat to his theory at its foundations.

Imperfect Rationality

Various attempts have been made to solve this interpretive problem. One approach has been to regard Bentham's talk of a "felicific calculus" on a mathematical model as window dressing, not meant to be anything more than an attractive metaphor.

This is the approach Lord Robbins took, and others have argued for a similar reading.[18] Philip Schofield and Michael Quinn have challenged this strategy.[19] They have maintained that Bentham embraced the simple model of the calculus of pleasure, and the assumptions on which it rests, as his understanding of practical rationality. Not only did he embrace a hedonist theory of value, but he took pleasures and pains—the only relevant "real entities"—as the fundamental common denominators of value, capable of quantitative measurement and intrapersonal and interpersonal comparisons, and thus capable of being added together to determine the community welfare value of the consequences of any act, law, or institution. The principle of utility, relying on this method of calculation, took as its ultimate end the maximization of welfare thus determined. Thus, in their view, Bentham was the first "classical utilitarian" as canonically defined by Sidgwick and later Rawls.[20]

To be sure, they argue, Bentham was aware of, and in several cases was the first to point out, the limitations of this model. He held that reasoning on this model inevitably was imperfect, imprecise, fuzzy, and indeterminate. It cannot meet the high standard of determinateness—"fine-grained analysis"—that model sets as an aspiration. Actual moral reasoning, when it is done correctly, must conform to this model, but it can do so only imperfectly. Nevertheless, although it is imperfect, it is better than any alternative on offer, for example, appeals to natural law, moral sense and the like.[21] Moreover, they argue, Bentham must embrace this model, for if he were to accept that the pleasures and pains that figure in utilitarian reasoning are not homogeneous, discrete entities, not intrapersonally or interpersonally comparable, and not publicly accessible, his entire theory would collapse; he would have to abandon rationality.[22]

There is some textual evidence that Bentham thought that ordinary moral reasoning did, and perhaps could, only approximate the precision and determinacy he had hoped for. "Of evil, in none of these shapes," Bentham conceded, "can any exact measure be taken: on this as on so many other subjects, instead of the strong and steady lights to which all wishes ought to point, we must content ourselves with such glimmerings as an be collected."[23] Yes, he wrote in an early manuscript, doing the utility calculation work is difficult and the results uncertain, but "bad as the chance may be which this method gives us of judging right no other method is there that affords so good an one" (UC 69.69). This point is expressed most fully in

[18] Robbins, *The Theory of Economic Policy in English Classical Political Economy*, 181; Fred Rosen, "Individual Sacrifice and the Greatest Happiness: Bentham on Utility as Rights," *Utilitas* 10 (1998), 129–43; Tom Warke, "Classical Utilitarianism" and "Multi-dimensional Utility."

[19] Quinn, "Bentham on Mensuration"; Schofield, *Utility and Democracy*, 42–4; Schofield, *Bentham: A Guide for the Perplexed* (London: Continuum Books, 2009), 58–60.

[20] John Rawls, *A Theory of Justice*, 2nd edn. (Cambridge, MA: Harvard University Press, 1999), 19–30, 160–8.

[21] Quinn, "Bentham on Mensuration," 102–3; Schofield, *Utility and Democracy*, 43–4.

[22] Quinn, "Bentham on Mensuration," 76–7.

[23] Jeremy Bentham, *Of Sexual Irregularities and Other Writings on Sexual Morality*, Philip Schofield, Catherine Pease-Watkin, and Michael Quinn, eds. (Oxford: Clarendon Press, 2014), 29.

his *Codification Proposal*, not two pages from the passage in which Bentham conceded that for pleasures and pains there is no common measure. He wrote,

> To return to the application thus made of arithmetic to questions of utility. How far short soever this degree of precision may be, of the conceivable point of perfection—of that which is actually attained in some branches of art and science,—how far short so ever of *absolute* perfection,—at any rate in every rational and candid eye unspeakable will be the advantage it will have over every form of argumentation in which every idea is afloat no degree of precision being ever attained because none is ever so much as aimed at (LW 255, author's emphasis).

Bentham, then, did acknowledge that engaging in utilitarian "calculation" was difficult, that ordinary people (and perhaps even experts) will and can engage in it only imperfectly, and that the results are inevitably if regrettably imprecise.

However, this reply, and the interpretation of Bentham's theory that depends on it, is unconvincing. It fails to appreciate the nature and depth of the problems facing the simple model of the calculus of pleasure, problems that Bentham himself identified. In the passage quoted in the preceding paragraph, he represents the problems as merely epistemic, due to imprecision of our instruments of measurement and limited intellectual capacities, limitations that make the model less than ideal, but perhaps still better than alternatives for achieving at least some creditable results. However, the problems Bentham uncovered are not merely epistemic; they challenge the *intelligibility* of the model. The problems Bentham uncovered are of two basic kinds.

First, the problems are conceptual, making the intelligible operation of the calculus of pleasure impossible *in principle*. He showed that pleasures and pains are not the kind of things the calculus of pleasure assumes as inputs. They are not discrete and homogeneous entities, properties of every pleasurable or painful experience. Thus, they are not the kind of thing that *can* be compared intrapersonally or interpersonally. There is no common measure to make this comparison possible. An imprecise measure is a measure that fails to achieve some desired degree of precision, but Bentham's argument and his explicit text maintains that there is no common measure, not that the common measure is imprecise. Moreover, attempts to devise proxies that might promise to estimate the relevant reality indirectly fail because, strictly speaking, there is no such (discrete, homogeneous, comparable) reality. The fact that we are able to make assessments of our own future well-being and the well-being of others (still considering this as a matter of how a person's life goes in the eyes of that person) is not due to the fact that we are able, albeit imperfectly, to detect the kind of inputs the calculus of pleasure assumes, but rather are due to the fact that we track, assess, and make inferences from other morally relevant things.

Second, the problems Bentham uncovered cannot be dismissed as matters of imprecision, because they threaten the standing of the calculus of pleasure as a model for moral and political reasoning. As we saw in Chapter 3, moral and political reasoning, by its nature, *must* be public, Bentham insisted. The currency in which it deals is the currency of reasons that are accessible and assessable by people in the community: "The catechism of reasons is worthless if it cannot be a catechism of the people" (B i. 163). But the imperfections of the simple model undermine the claim to publicity of reasoning undertaken under its auspices. The absence of any common measure of pleasures and pains undermines the claim made for the simple model that the "reasons" it generates can meet the demands of publicity. Again, this is not to say that utilitarian reasoning, reasoning Bentham himself sought to use in his substantive political institution-building work, cannot meet that standard, but rather that whatever that mode of reasoning is, it is not that which is alleged to be modeled by the simple understanding of the calculus of pleasure. If that calculus is the only possible rational method, then, indeed, rational moral deliberation is not possible. Pointing out this consequence does not restore rationality to the method; it only convicts Bentham of basing his moral and political theory on a failed and incoherent foundation.

So much the worse for Bentham's theory, we might say—unless an alternative account of moral and political reasoning, one that abandons the simple calculus model, or gets it up and running on quite different, less problematic assumptions.

Calculation with Expectations and Interests

Bentham's use of the model of "calculation" may not have been merely rhetorical or cynically manipulative. Bentham never gave up on the idea that moral and political reasoning involves "calculation" of some sort. But he was forced to treat circumspectly the simple model of such calculation, and this involved more than owning up to the inevitable epistemic imperfections of the model.

When seeking an interpretation of the details of his theory of value, it is important to keep in mind three key three key determinants of that theory: (i) Bentham's theory of meaning, (ii) his view of the structure of the principle of utility, and (iii) his pivotal meta-ethical principle of publicity. From his theory of meaning we get what we might call "moral-meaning hedonism," the view that for purposes of understanding the moral life, the foundational "real entities" are present sensations of pleasure and pain. His meta-ethical principle requires that moral reasoning is a form of public discourse, offering and assessing reasons that are intelligible to and assessable by others in the general public. The general structure of the ground principle of Bentham's understanding of morality, to which the theory of value contributes an essential component, is defined by universal consequentialism, individual welfarism, and a principle of composition according to which the universal good is a composite of the welfare of individuals. In addition, individual welfarism is understood in light of the requirement that the well-being of each individual is to be understood as the good of each individual as seen through his or her own eyes.

We know from Chapter 1 that, according to Bentham's theory of meaning, the basic constituents of the world are physical and psychical events. Bentham's view of the general structure of the principle of utility singles out pleasures and pains among the basic mental events, that is, present pleasurable or painful sensings, as uniquely relevant for moral life and thought. This locates Bentham's individual welfarism in the natural world and commits him to "moral-meaning hedonism." We also know from our study of Bentham's theory of meaning that the world of ordinary experience, especially the interpersonal, social world, is not limited to this base world of natural and mental events. The quotidian social world is rich and complex, intersubjective, and in a sense constructed (together) by active minds governed by principles of rationality that discipline discourse in and about that world. Among these principles are certain foundational principles of moral reasoning, the cardinal one being the requirement of publicity and the related requirement of impartiality. Many of the concepts we find indispensable in our quotidian social world, while tethered to basic physical and mental reality, travel well beyond it. It is possible to live our lives and understand the world of our ordinary experience only by means of these concepts which in Bentham's idiolect are names of "fictitious entities." (Recall, "fictitious" does not mean "false.") Thus, the demands of quotidian moral and political life drive us to construct concepts essential to moral discourse and reasoning. The central concepts of value, then, will likely be names of fictitious entities that operate at some constructive distance from present pleasurable sensings. It is possible to see the development of the vocabulary of Bentham's theory of value as the story of his effort to articulate a language of value adequate for the purposes of moral discourse as he came to understand them.

The story begins with the foundations of moral reasoning laid in sensations. "Sensation is the highest evidence," Bentham held (UC 70.23). The core moral notion of individual well-being, as viewed from the inside, must be anchored in pleasure or pain sensations. But the quotidian life of moral experience cannot be restricted to these sensations. For one thing, because the moral life concerns the well-being of others as well as oneself, the relevant sensations include sensations of others, and they are not matters of immediate experience or direct observation (*ibid.*). As Fred Rosen observed, Bentham "fully acknowledged that there was no possible way that individual perceptions of pleasure and pain, however successfully they might be measured by the individual, could be added up to form the public interest."[24] And, for that matter, one's own pleasure or happiness are also not immediately accessible. To consider one's future happiness, one must shift to a third-person perspective. Moreover, morality's fundamental demand of publicness of reasons entails that all moral considerations must be communicable, capable of being articulated in a language referring to matters of experience to which others have access as well. The *quale* conception of pleasure and pain cannot fund

[24] Fred Rosen, "Individual Sacrifice and the Greatest Happiness," 143.

quotidian moral reasoning. However, the attitude conception allows access of a kind, because the attitudes involved are manifest in behavior; one chooses to continue that in which one takes pleasure.

Also, the shift to the third person perspective brings assessments of one's own good into potential conversation with that of others. We depend on others to help us grasp the impact of contingent features of our world on the availability of pleasures. We are also inclined to look to sensibilities we tend to share with others. Experiences we know by participating with others in daily life are the kind that I and many others would like to have again. Pleasure understood in this way is more likely to be publicly available. At the same time, the publicly available facts are no longer a matter of immediate experience; they are "inferential" rather than ontologically of the first order, as Bentham thought of these things. This shift is clear even in a very early manuscript where he wrote that the morally relevant pleasure "is not of him who announces the proposition concerning it," but of others, "formed upon recollection, observation and analogy—recollection of one's own sensations upon past occasions—observation of the conduct of others—analogy according to which our conduct or discourse is presumed to originate from like sensation as those which give birth to the same conduct in ourselves" (UC 70.23).

Thus, pleasure on the *quale* conception ultimately anchors pleasure on the attitude conception in immediate experience. Pleasure on the attitude conception, by the same token, is more closely tied to public features of the states of affairs, objects, or persons in which people take pleasure. Indeed, it is not the pleasure *qua quale*, but the *taking pleasure in*, that seems to be important for the ordinary business of moral and political reasoning, reasoning that takes place in public or at least with members of the public as regularly expected addressees. That is the kind of thing we can track across time and across people, the kind of thing we can gather into kinds ("species") and attribute to people in the community generally with a degree of confidence based on our experience. The things we talk about together as "pleasures" are the kind of things about which over time our judgments may even to some degree tend to converge.

It is perhaps this third person perspective that yields the "representative person" that figures in Bentham's alternative (multiplication) formulation of the compositional function by which community well-being was said to be constructed (UC 27.34 (Baumgardt 556)). The demands of publicness force us to look to matters of general sensibility, to abstract from individual idiosyncrasies, and focus on commonalities (*Civ. Code* 305). Equal intensity, equal valuation of that in which various persons take pleasure, must be assumed, equality must be taken as the measure of quantity, unless the differences can be articulated publicly (UC 69.238–9).

These demands of quotidian moral reasoning inclined Bentham to put at the center of his understanding of such reasoning the concept of expectation early on and the concept of interests later in his career (see Chapter 6). Expectations, as we have seen, come to hold a dominant place in Bentham's theory of value, not because of their unique or especially impressive felt quality, but rather because giving shape to expectations and pursuing them enable human beings to give meaningful continuity to their lives over time. It is their functional role in everyone's grasp of their well-being viewed from the inside that explains their importance in Bentham's theory of value. In a similar way, the concept of interests gives shape and focus to the idea of individual well-being as publicly accessible and communicable facts about members of the community.

In his work on matters of constitutional design, Bentham typically formulated the principle of utility itself in terms of the "universal interest," rather than happiness or pleasure. We observed in Chapter 2 that Bentham always thought of the concepts of pleasure and interest as close kin. He referred to pleasure and pain as "interesting perceptions" (IPML V.1), that is, as sensations that attract and hold our attention. An interest, for Bentham, is never merely a legally protected benefit, abstractly conceived; rather, it is something that we *care about*, something in which we take an active interest. Moreover, he believed (implausibly, I think) that interests always have motivational force. "It is by his own particular interest," he wrote, "that on every occasion, be it what it may, a man's conduct will be governed" (*Deont.* 192).

We shall see Chapter 6 that Bentham held that the concept of interest can do much of the work in his theory of value that he wanted the public concept of pleasure to do. It has the advantage of allowing one to abstract from immediate felt experience and to focus on the object of one's interest. Unlike present sensations, interests are intelligibles rather than mere sensibles, taking the shape of publicly accessible concepts, rather than immediately felt sensations. They can be articulated in an accessible, public language. This makes it possible to think about how interests might fit together with others into more or less coherent packages. The ways in which they intersect with, and reinforce or conflict with, other interests can be articulated and submitted for public discourse. While rooted in the subjective experiences of persons and their stake in how their lives are going, interests have a public dimension that allows us to think about shared or common interests and to assess the compatibility of some interests with others. Moreover, interests are tied to resources, opportunities, security, and capabilities, and these are the kinds of things that utilitarian legislators and policy-makers (the primary intended audience of his philosophy) can focus on. From the very beginning of his career, Bentham conceived of his utilitarian creed as a public philosophy—a rational guide for managing public affairs—and for this purpose the notion of interest proved especially useful. While he always insisted that pleasure and pain must ultimately anchor all talk of interests, insuring that when we talk of interests we talk about something real and do not merely express an idle wish, nevertheless, he also insisted that the language of the ordinary business of utilitarian moral deliberation, policy-making and law-making must fully public, and for this the language of interests was best suited.

We can conclude that despite his criticisms of the *quale* conception of pleasure, Bentham did not abandon rationality or the principle of utility. He did uncover compelling reasons to treat the simple model of utilitarian calculation (the "felicific calculus") with circumspection. Proper utilitarian reasoning still, in Bentham's view, involved "calculation"—that is, tracing out the consequences of all the options for action, laws, or institutions, consequences assessed in terms of their impact on the welfare of all the members of the community in view. But these calculations need not fit the simple model, in fact, they must not, since the simple model cannot meet the demands of moral reasoning, in particular the demands of publicity. Bentham's universal consequentialism took for its core theory of value concerns about expectations and interests, rather than immediate sensings of pleasure or pain.

Bentham sought to articulate a principle of utility sensitive to the demands of his commitment to universal consequentialism, individual welfarism, and publicity. These concerns led him to several attempts to incorporate equality into his foundational principle. Equality, too, we shall see in the chapter to follow, found its way into his theory of value.

5
Bentham's Equality-Sensitive Theory of Value

In the previous chapters, we have seen that Bentham's general understanding of morality and his keen grasp of the limits of the simple hedonist model of value gave him strong reason to adopt a theory of value understood in terms of the interests of individuals.* The ground of moral judgments, he argued, must not be mere expressions of wish or whim; they must be public reasons accessible to all observers who view the matter impartially. In Chapter 4, we saw that the demands of publicity at the foundations of morality forced him to cast utilitarian value in terms of that which is representative or common. Similarly, in Chapter 3 we saw that Bentham took the fundamental requirement of publicity pragmatically to entail an impartial understanding of individual welfare. Subject to the demands of publicity, he argued, no one could hope to convince others to adopt a formulation of the principle of utility biased in one's own favor.

Sometimes Bentham cast the conclusion of this kind of argument in terms of equality. For example, in his "Essay on Representation" of the 1790s, he wrote, "Any unequal plan whatever, whatever were its good points otherwise, would always have this disadvantage over the equal: in order to show its utility, it requires demonstrations less capable of being presented to everybody in a successful fashion" (Representation, 452). For Hobbes, the constraint that forces rational agents to accept a principle of equality is the alleged empirical fact of rough equality of power among the parties (*Lev* 107), but for Bentham the constraint is provided by the fundamental moral demand of publicity. Equality, it appears, lies deep in Bentham's moral, political, and legal theory.

Equality of resources is one of the four immediately "subordinate ends" of government and law, subordinate only to the demand of the principle of utility itself. Equality of goods, especially wealth, is required by the principle of utility, other things equal, Bentham argued, due to the pervasive fact of the diminishing marginal utility of wealth and many other such goods (PF 228–30). Similarly, arguing for near universal suffrage in his *Plan of Parliamentary Reform* (1817), he wrote:

> If, in the instance of any one individual, it *be right* that he should possess a *share*, of a certain *magnitude*, in the choice of a person, to form one in the aggregated

* Adapted from G.J. Postema, "Bentham's Equality-sensitive Utilitarianism," *Utilitas* 10(2) (1998), 144–58. Cambridge University Press, 1998, reproduced with permission.

Utility, Publicity, and Law: Essays on Bentham's Moral and Legal Philosophy. Gerald J. Postema.

> body of the representatives of the people—how can it be right that, in the instance of any other individual, the share should be either *less* or *greater*? (B iii. 452)

Important as this theme was in Bentham's jurisprudence and political theory,[1] the notion of equality plays a much more fundamental role in his practical philosophy. Equality lies at the foundations of his theory. His commitment to equality of the means of happiness—especially wealth, but also legal rights—is carefully calibrated, qualified by a *ceteris paribus* clause (*Civ. Code* 311); however, in its foundational role equality is unqualified. "Everybody to count for one no one for more than one"—this is the way John Stuart Mill formulated Bentham's deep equality principle (*Utilitarianism* 257). And, as we shall see, there is convincing evidence for Mill's attribution.

The thesis of this chapter is that a proper understanding of the foundational role of equality in Bentham's moral and political theory will give us further insight into his distinctive theory of value. I shall argue that equality was not merely an *ad hoc* addition to his principle of utility, undermining the coherence of the entire theory, as A.J. Ayer once charged.[2] Rather, Bentham thought of equality as internal to the principle of utility itself. As Mill put it, equality is "involved in the very meaning" of the principle (*ibid.*). Moreover, I shall argue, this equality-sensitive principle of utility has its roots in a conception of value that contrasts sharply with the one standardly attributed to classical utilitarians.[3]

EQUALITY AT THE FOUNDATIONS OF UTILITY

In his early essays on international law, Bentham formulated a principle of utility for use by sovereigns in their interactions with other sovereign nations. The object or end of a "universal international code," he wrote, is "the greatest common utility of all nations taken together," that is, "the [greatest] common and equal utility of all nations" (PIL 538, 537). Designed for this particular context, the principle of utility builds equality directly into its ultimate goal. The "utility" to be promoted or sought in all international interactions, Bentham insisted, is the greatest *common* well-being of nations, provided it is available equally to all nations. I will discuss at greater length in Chapter 11 how to understand this principle, but I think it is safe to say that this is not a principle *derived* from the foundational principle of utility, as was the principle of equal distribution of wealth (other things equal). Rather, it is a *formulation* of the fundamental principle for this particular context.

[1] We will consider at the end of this chapter just how important this derivative equality is in Bentham's political theory.

[2] A.J. Ayer, *Philosophical Essays* (London: St. Martin's Press, 1954), 257.

[3] As, for example, by John Rawls, *A Theory of Justice*, 2nd edn. (Cambridge, MA: Harvard University Press, 1999), 19–30, 160–8; and H.L.A. Hart, "Bentham's Principle of Utility and Theory of Penal Law," in IPML, *Collected Works* (1996), xci.

Bentham's argument for the formulation parallels the argument for impartiality we considered in Chapter 3. This represents one way that Bentham sought to incorporate equality into his utilitarian theory at its foundations; I will consider another way in this chapter.

Extent as a Dimension of Value

Fred Rosen called attention to a dimension of Bentham's assessment of what he called "the value of a lot of pleasure" that is rarely considered: the dimension of extent. By "value," Bentham meant the *quantity* or *magnitude* of a lot of pleasure. This seems to involve a relatively simple matter of counting, but in Bentham's hands, the notion is neither simple nor merely a matter of counting. On Rosen's reading, it implicitly includes one or more normative dimensions; equality is among them. Rosen maintained that, by including *extent* as a dimension of the value or amount of pleasure, Bentham incorporated equality into the very notion of utility. "To extend happiness (i.e, its maximization)," Rosen wrote, "is to distribute it equally."[4] This intriguing suggestion invites a closer looks at Bentham's notion of the value or magnitude of pleasure and the role of extent in its determination.

Bentham identified seven dimensions of the magnitude of pleasure: intensity, duration, probability, remoteness, fecundity, purity, and extent (IPML IV; see Chapter 4, 82). At the outset, two features of this list stand out. First, it is diverse and the dimensions are related to the pleasure, or the causes or occasions of pleasure, in different ways. Second, these dimensions are identified as important specifically for the purposes of moral (or moral–political) assessment of actions, laws, institutions, and the like. Thus, value qua magnitude has an *evaluative* and, thereby (in Bentham's theoretical framework) *normative* valence. Implicit, in this assessment is the root idea that more is better. Moreover, at least one dimension (and, if Rosen is correct, two dimensions) clearly involve a kind of rational assessment.

The dimensions fall into three groups: (a) intensity and duration; (b) probability and remoteness; and (c) fecundity, purity, and extent. Intensity and duration are immediate properties of the pleasurable experience itself. The pleasurable experience is, necessarily, the experience *in the present*. Future pleasures are notional, imagined, or projected. Actual pleasure one might take in some future pleasure is the pleasure one presently experiences while entertaining the prospect of the future pleasure. (In this way, Bentham is often inclined to say, one can also experience someone else's pleasure—i.e., one takes pleasure in the idea of another's pleasurable experience, as we observed in Chapter 2.) If we could conceive of present pleasure coming in uniform chunks, or better like money in recognizable denominations,

[4] Fred Rosen, "Individual Sacrifice and the Greatest Happiness: Bentham on Utility and Rights," *Utilitas* X (1998), 140.

then intensity and duration would determine this size of the pile; the greater the intensity or duration of a pleasurable experience, the more dollars, pounds or yen in the pile.

Probability and remoteness are rather different from intensity and duration. Strictly speaking, they do not affect the experience, because they concern notional or imagined pleasures. The pleasure units are not themselves diminished by being to a degree uncertain or in the future. They mark relations between the pleasurable experiences and the person contemplating the experience of them. They affect not the size of the pile, but rather how the person contemplating the experience of them feels about them; we may say they affect "the value" of that pile to the person, if Bentham had not already commandeered that term for a broader use. It appears that *remoteness* should be distinguished from another property of contemplated pleasures that Bentham considered. In *Deontology*, he observed that untutored people are subject to a kind of myopia. The subjective attraction of immediate or near immediate pleasurable experiences causes them to misrepresent to themselves the relative intensity of the near pleasures to the temporally more distant possible pleasures (*Deont.* 151 n. 1). Advice and counsel can correct this myopia by bringing more vividly into view the temporally more distant experiences, thereby allowing a more accurate subjective assessment of the relative value of the various pleasures. This implies, however, that remoteness, as a dimension of the value of a lot of pleasure, is not strictly a matter of the felt quality of subjective experience, but involves a rational assessment of that subjective experience, an assessment made ultimately by each individual, but sometimes with the assistance of an outside party. Thus, both probability and remoteness are relations between the subject and the notional pleasurable experience with a normative aspect.

Fecundity, purity and extent differ from the other dimensions in that they are not properties of the experience, immediate or contemplated, but rather of the causes or occasions of the pleasures. The pleasurable experience is just one thing, so it is pure and, as it were, self-contained, not causally linked to other experiences. Fecundity and purity are not properties of pleasurable experiences. The same is true of extent. Extent concerns the number of sentient beings who are likely to be caused to experience pleasure of a similar kind. Extent seems to operate on the "pile" of units of pleasure initially fixed by the measure of intensity and duration in a way similar to the way probability and remoteness do. Probability and remoteness do not change the size of the pile, but they change the value of that pile to the subject of the contemplated experiences—in particular, they diminish it by some regular discount rate. Extent also affects the "value" by increasing it. To whom does it increase the value of the pleasure? Not, surely, to any given subject. Like fecundity and purity, extent increases the "value" to an agent viewing the pleasure from a moral point of view. No *subject's* attitude to the pleasurable experience or its cause is implicated. The value qua magnitude of a lot of pleasure is not an empirical quantity; rather, it necessarily has an evaluative, moral dimension.

How are we to understand this moral dimension? The general property of value in this context, we observed, involves the idea that more is better. This implies that the wider the extent of the pleasurable experience, that is the more who are likely to enjoy it, the better. At a minimum, this suggests that the extent dimension implies that all who are affected by some potential cause of pleasure must be taken into account and, when comparing actions (or laws or institutions) and their pleasurable experience-causing properties, those that promise wider extent are to be preferred. The wider the extent, the more there are who are likely to enjoy that pleasurable experience. We must ask who are included in the "more," what is the scope of extent? The idea of extent itself does not supply the answer to this question, but without an answer it is an empty measure. Thus, it appears that the idea of extent presupposes some determination of the range of the principle of utility that this account of the value of a lot of pleasure is meant to serve. And it requires, as a determinant of the rationally and morally relevant magnitude of a given pleasurable experience, that subjects who fall into that range must be taken into account and, comparing one such pleasure-consequence of an option (action, etc.) with others, the widest extent is to be preferred.

Read in one way, this seems to embed a distributive dimension into the heart of Bentham's notion of utility. Rosen pushed this reading a step further, maintaining that not only must the wider spread (greater number) be preferred, but also that an equal distribution is to be preferred to an unequal one over this range. However, to my eye, this is expands than the notion of extent, as it figures in Bentham's account, beyond what it can bear. The notion of extent presupposes a notion of the relevant range and some view of how each individual in that range is to be considered, but the idea of extent alone does not entail a distributive component within this range. However, another key element of Bentham's theory of value might do the job, namely the maxim that Mill attributed to him: "everybody is to count for one and no one for more than one." We must look carefully into the meaning and provenance of Bentham's dictum. We have learned from our exploration of Bentham's account of the dimensions of the value of a lot of pleasure that this dictum is embedded in Bentham's understanding of *utility*, the value-notion at the heart of his fundamental moral–political principle.

Every Individual Tells for One

J.S. Mill, taking his lead from his father[5] and ultimately from Bentham, argued that the idea of equality plays a foundational role in utilitarian theory. Recall Mill's well-known comments toward the end of Chapter V of *Utilitarianism* about impartiality and equality. He argued there that the principle of utility requires not only that

[5] See Terrence Ball, introduction to *James Mill: Political Writings* (Cambridge: Cambridge University Press, 1992), xxii.

judges apply laws impartially, but also that the principle itself embodies the ideal of equality. He explicitly refers to Bentham's dictum, "everybody to count for one, no one for more than one." The commitment to equality evident in this maxim, he insisted, is not something *added to* the utilitarian's fundamental principle, but rather, it is "involved in the very meaning of ... the greatest happiness principle." It "might be written under the principle of utility as an explanatory commentary" (*Utilitarianism* V, n. 4). This dictum was part of the folklore of the Philosophic Radicals. Doubtless, it captures a maxim Bentham expressed.

In his *Rationale of Judicial Evidence*, which Mill edited early in his life, Bentham wrote, "the system of arithmetic, which, as long as I remember, I have been in the habit of employing on all political occasions [is]: every individual in the country tells for one; no individual for more than one" (RJE vii. 334). James Crimmins objected that this cannot be the source of Bentham's dictum, since it is found in a work on the law of evidence, not one devoted to foundational work on the principle of utility. In Crimmins' view, "the implication is that each individual ought to be treated equally by law and by those who apply the law."[6] However, there is reason to believe that Bentham took this principle to have a more fundamental role in his moral and political theory. No doubt, Bentham used the thought behind this dictum when discussing applications of his principle of utility to legal and political matters, for all of his work was devoted to such matters. In his *Principles of the Civil Code*, he wrote, "I have placed equality among the objects of the law. In any arrangement intended to give to every man the greatest possible happiness, no reason can be assigned why the law should give one man more than another. There are, however, good reasons why it should not do it" (*Civ. Code* 302).

Moreover, it is reasonably clear that Bentham did not intend his dictum merely as a version of equality before the law. He thought of it as more fundamental. In his *Rationale of Reward*, he wrote that when determining who should bear the burdens of service to the common good, "one man's interest weigh[es] neither more nor less than another's," and thus, wherever practicable, they should be distributed equally (B ii. 207). In a similar vein, recall, he wrote, "The happiness or unhappiness of any one member of the community—high or low, rich or poor—what greater or less part is it of the universal happiness and unhappiness, than that of any other?" (B iii. 459; see also CC (B) 107–8). And, as we saw in Chapter 3, impartiality requires that "exactly the same regard [be had] for the happiness of every member of the community in question as for that of every other," and upon this equal regard rests the demand of the greatest happiness principle (FPP 235). The entire passage reads as follows: "In the eyes of every impartial arbiter, writing in the character of a legislator, and having exactly the same regard for the happiness of every member of the community in question as for that of every other, the greatest happiness of the greatest number of the members of that same community cannot but

[6] James E. Crimmins, *Utilitarian Philosophy and Politics* (London: Continuum, 2011), 102.

be recognized in the character of the ... sole right and proper end of government" (FPP 235). In his "Essay on Representation," Bentham wrote that "the happiness of any [one person] has no more value in his eyes than the equal happiness of any other" (Representation 449).[7]

In view of the legacy of the principle of the greatest happiness principle, Bentham had reason to write this dictum under his principle of utility as an explanatory commentary, as Mill suggested. Bentham inherited his characterization of his principle of utility from Hutcheson (via Beccaria), who may have been the first to articulate the principle in English. Hutcheson said, "that action is best, which procures the greatest happiness for the greatest numbers." He intended this as a summary of his view that "in equal degrees of happiness, expected to proceed from the action, the virtue is in proportion to the number of persons to whom the happiness shall extend." But, to this he attached the crucial rider: "and here the dignity, or moral importance of persons, may compensate numbers".[8] Whatever its role in Hutcheson's moral theory, Bentham would surely have been anxious to make clear to readers that "dignity" does not qualify the utilitarian significance of pleasure or happiness.[9] What better way to do so than to write under the principle of utility, "every individual in the country tells for one; no individual for more than one"?

These considerations put to rest the criticism that Bentham introduced incoherence into his utilitarian moral theory by adding to his principle of utility a second, independent principle of equality. The principle of utility, in Bentham's hands, as in Mill's, was meant to give expression to an ideal of equality that lies at the very foundations of morality. But how is this commitment to be understood? How must the principle of utility be formulated to honor this commitment? We can start down the road toward answers to these questions by considering a criticism of utilitarian doctrine that some believe is not silenced by the "every individual tells for one" slogan.

[7] For a discussion of this essay, see Marco E.L. Guidi, "Everybody to Count for One, Nobody for More than One: The Principle of Equal Consideration of Interests from Bentham to Pigou," *Revue d'etudes Benthamienne* 4 (2008), available online at http://journals.openedition.org/etudes-benthamiennes/182.

[8] Francis Hutcheson, *Inquiry into the Original of our Ideas of Beauty and Virtue* (1725), in *British Moralists: 1650–1800*, vol. I, ed. D. D. Raphael, (Oxford, 1969), 284, 283 (author's italics suppressed). Joachim Hruschka pointed out that Hutcheson probably followed Gershom Carmichael's commentary on Pufendorf. (J. Hruschka, "The Greatest Happiness Principle and Other Early German Anticipations of Utilitarian Theory," *Utilitas* iii (1991), 171). But Carmichael gave "dignity" a clearly utilitarian gloss: "dignity, being a person's utility for many other people" (*Supplementa et Observationibus ad C. V. Sam. Pufendorfi libros duos De Officio Hominis et Civis*, Glasgow, 1718, 75). It is not clear what to make of Hutcheson's silence regarding Carmichael's gloss, but without the gloss, Hutcheson's phrase is open to anti-utilitarian interpretations. This alone would have given Bentham strong reason to attach the "each for one" gloss to his principle of utility.

[9] At the turn of the twentieth century, Hastings Rashdall built his ideal utilitarian moral theory on a similar rejection of equality at the foundations of utility. See Rashdall, *The Theory of Good and Evil: A Treatise on Moral Philosophy*, 2nd edn. (Oxford: Oxford University Press, 1924), 234–42, discussed by Jeremy Waldron in *One Another's Equal: The Basis of Human Equality* (Cambridge, MA: Belknap Press, 2017), 20–9.

As we just noticed, Bentham seems to have thought that his "each tells for one" maxim entails that when determining what is to be done on utilitarian grounds, the happiness of "the most helpless pauper" should not be regarded any differently from that of "the most powerful, the most opulent member of the community"; neither may the "happiness and interest of a person of the female sex" be regarded any differently from that of "a person of the male sex" (CC (B) 107, 108). This seems to rule out certain standard forms of discrimination, requiring the utilitarian moral agent to ignore certain distinguishing features of those who are likely to be affected by her actions. We might call this the *anti-discrimination* or *anonymity* principle.

However, Bentham's twentieth-century critics argue that this is an empty, merely formal principle. It demands: don't consider properties of the people affected that are not relevant from a utilitarian perspective. Because the only thing relevant from a utilitarian perspective, they argue, are pleasure and pain—or more broadly happiness or welfare—the principle requires that we *not* consider social status, wealth, gender, virtue, or dignity, or other familiar bases for discrimination. Utilitarians are no respecters of persons, we might say. Prince or pauper, male or female, rich or poor, English, Irish, or Indian, blue-blooded aristocrat or black former slave, nothing about persons, except the pleasure and pains they may experience, have any utilitarian moral significance. But far from a substantial demand of equality, Herbert Hart objected, Bentham's dictum is "only a weighting principle, to be used in calculating what will maximize aggregate happiness; it treats persons as equals by securing that in the determination of what measures are required by the general welfare equal weight must be given to the equal happiness of all persons."[10] Moreover, equality understood in this way has no direct distributive implications. At most, the principle of utility is indifferent to distribution and it provides no protection against sacrifice of the interests of individual to the aggregate general welfare. "It treats individuals as mere receptacles with no intrinsic value for the experiences of pleasure and pain."[11] Rawls argued that classical utilitarians approach calculation of the general welfare of the community as if the community were a single, undifferentiated being whose welfare is the simple composite of the welfare—the happiness and unhappiness or pleasures and pains—of its members. Utilitarianism, he charged, fails to take the separateness of persons seriously—it fails to recognize that welfare, happiness, and pleasures and pains are possessed by individuals who are each morally entitled to separate consideration.[12]

This reading of Bentham's equality concern rests on a familiar understanding of Bentham's conception of happiness or utilitarian value, but it is not Bentham's conception; his understanding of the principle of utility, incorporating this alternative

[10] H.L.A. Hart, *Essays on Bentham*, 99. Mill says explicitly that the equality involved is merely "the truths of arithmetic... applicable to the valuation of happiness..." (*Utilitarianism* V, n 4).

[11] H.L.A. Hart, "Bentham's Principle of Utility and Theory of Penal Law," in IPML, *Collected Works* (1996), xci.

[12] Rawls, *Theory of Justice*, 21–30, 160–8.

conception, is, I think, subtler and more complex than twentieth-century defenders and critics of utilitarianism recognized.

Two Conceptions of Happiness

Critics have regularly attributed a particular conception of happiness to Bentham and classical utilitarians. I will call it the "Abstract Happiness" conception. On this conception, happiness is abstracted from the persons who enjoy it: happiness and happiness alone has intrinsic value; and it has value irrespective of who experiences it. According to Mill, "equal amounts of happiness are equally desirable [that is, valuable], whether felt by the same person or different persons" (*Utilitarianism* V, n. 4), and whether enjoyed by *one* person or *many* persons. It is a natural fact, of course, that pleasure is always someone's pleasure, but this fact has no moral significance on this conception of utilitarian value. With respect to its moral significance, happiness is abstracted from those who experience it; like *wealth* as viewed by the partisans of law and economics, it is a good to be maximized without regard to who holds it. More precisely, not only must moral agents ignore *who* experiences it, but they must also ignore the fact that *someone,* some morally considerable *person*, experiences it. All that matters is the net amount of the happiness that is produced.

This conception of happiness as an abstract good implies the anti-discrimination principle I mentioned earlier. Each person, on this conception, counts no more than any other; and in particular, neither race, gender, nor social status, neither wealth, honor, nor any other person-distinguishing feature may count in utilitarian calculations. But this is not because each person counts equally in the calculation, but rather because *no* person, qua person, counts for *anything* at the most fundamental level of moral consideration. Understood in this way the principle of utility is literally no respecter *of persons*. Pleasures and pains, and they alone, count in utilitarian calculations. Bentham insisted that each person counts for one; but on this reading, "each is to count for one" is not to be read as "each person" ("everybody" or "every individual") is to count for one, but rather each *unit of pleasure* counts for one. Derivatively, we may say, "each person is to count the same" because no one is to count for *anything*: pleasures and pains, they alone count morally. Because happiness for moral purposes is abstracted in this way from those who experience it, utilitarian deliberators need not pay attention to the way in which this intrinsic good is distributed amongst potential recipients. The principle of utility, on the Abstract Happiness conception of value, is indifferent to distribution (except, of course, derivatively).

I believe there is a different, more complex and interesting, conception of utilitarian value at work in (much of) Bentham's writings on the foundations of political morality. On this conception, which I will call his Individualist, or Person-Respecting, conception, the fact that happiness is the happiness *of someone* is of fundamental moral importance. Happiness is morally relevant because it is the happiness *of individual persons* who experience it and integrate it into their lives. Happiness is not abstracted from the persons who experience it. The fundamental moral fact for the person-respecting utilitarian is not that *suffering happens*, but that this, that, or another *individual person* suffers or flourishes, they take delight in or are distressed by the events of their lives, and these experiences cannot meaningfully be abstracted from the significance the experiences give to the lives of those who have them.[13] What gives pursuit of well-being its moral point, on this view, is that we ought to care about *the people* who experience it.[14] Thus, the legislator must consider the effects of laws and policies on each member of the community taking them one by one.

This conception of the value underlying utilitarian morality builds a concern for its distribution among human beings into the very content of the principle of utility. Regard for the suffering and well-being of individual human beings cannot be expressed in a concern for maximization of happiness in the abstract without considering how individual human beings participate in this stock of happiness. Moreover, this concern for distribution is not *derivative* of a commitment to produce the greatest net aggregate happiness. It is not concerned with the distribution of the means of happiness, but with the spread of happiness itself. At the same time, equality is not an *independent* moral concern. It is not a *supplementary* principle, brought in to break ties in utilitarian calculation, or to add an egalitarian dimension to the utilitarian concern. Rather, it is an immediate expression of the fundamental utilitarian theory of value itself. Thus, this utilitarian notion of intrinsic value builds into it equal concern for each person, recognizes the equal moral claim each person's well-being has on our moral attention, and yields a structuring principle requiring that equal weight be given to the happiness of each. Thus, "each for one" has a *dual* function: (1) it undermines all claims to status (as does the anti-discrimination reading), *and* (2) it expresses the complexity of the underlying Individualist value of happiness.

I must hasten to add that this does not entail that there is never any moral justification for sacrificing the well-being of one person for that of another.[15] In a world

[13] Is this inconsistent with Bentham's famous argument for extending moral consideration to animals: "[T]he question is not, Can they *reason*? nor, Can they *talk*? but, Can they *suffer*?" (*Limits* 5n)? I do not think so. He argues in this passage that sentient beings must be given moral consideration, not that the moral significance of their suffering is the same as that of human beings. Note also that it is capacity for suffering, not merely capacity for pain, *that* qualifies such beings for moral consideration. "Suffering" is a wider term incorporating more than merely pain, and it locates the experience, whether painful or not, in the context of the lives of the creatures in question and the ways in which those lives can go well or badly. When speaking of non-human animals, it may be a stretch to talk in terms of "integrating the experience meaningfully into their lives," but it does make sense to talk about the role of that pain in the going-well or -badly of their lives as they experience them. That, it would seem, is enough to retain the focus of moral consideration for Bentham's purposes even in the case of non-human animals.

[14] I here paraphrase Elizabeth Anderson, *Value in Ethics and Economics* (Cambridge, MA: Harvard University Press, 1993), 27.

[15] In the passage from his *Rationale of Reward* that we noticed earlier, Bentham wrote "one man's interest weigh[es] neither more nor less than another's." These words appear in a discussion of who

in which human lives are intertwined, it is often not possible to promote the well-being of one person without affecting that of another as well, sometimes to its detriment. Not to sacrifice Cain to Able, under these circumstances, is to sacrifice Able to Cain. This underlying concern to count each for one requires that when such sacrifices are inevitable, we impose them always guided by the overriding aim of giving equal consideration to the interests of all who are affected by our actions.

BENTHAM'S INDIVIDUALIST CONCEPTION OF HAPPINESS

I believe that Bentham often had something like this individualist conception of happiness in mind.[16] In an otherwise puzzling argument, Bentham signals his commitment to the individualist conception. "If it be proper to sacrifice the fortune of one individual, in order to augment the fortune of the others," he argued, "it would be still better to sacrifice a second, a third," and so on to any greater number, "without it being possible to assign any limits; for, whatever may be the number of those you have sacrificed, you always have the same reason for adding one more. In a word, the interest of the first is *sacred*, or the interest of no one can be so" (B i. 321, emphasis added).

Further evidence of its influence can be found in his view of the relationship between happiness and expectations, in various expressions of his dictum, and in his various formulations of the principle of utility. Let us consider some of this evidence.

Equal Consideration and its Distributive Implications

First, we observed in Chapter 3 that Bentham was skeptical about the possibilities of meaningful interpersonal comparisons of pleasure or pain. In one manuscript

should bear the burden of service to the general welfare, for "the interest of any one man ought to give way to the interest of all" (B ii. 207). And, more pointedly Bentham asked in his *Codification Proposal*, "On what ground, in the eyes of a common guardian, can any one man's happiness be shown to have any stronger or less strong claim to regard than any others? If, on the ground of delinquency, in the name of punishment, it be right that any man be rendered unhappy, it is not that his happiness has less claim to regard than another man's, but that it is necessary to the greatest happiness of the greatest number that a portion of the happiness of that one be sacrificed" (B iv. 540).

[16] Not always, however. The Abstract Happiness conception may be at work in IPML chapter IV (concerning how to measure "the value of a lot of pleasure"). Still, in a related manuscript, Bentham admitted that his use of "value" here is misleading, because it normally implies an assessment of quality rather than mere quantity, represented mathematically, which is his meaning here ("Value of a Pleasure or Pain" (1778) in *Bentham's Political Thought*, Bikhu Parekh, ed. (London: Croom Helm, 1973), 113, note c). Also, later in his *Table of the Springs of Action*, Bentham wrote, "Consequences apart, magnitude the same, one pleasure is as good as another" (TSA 66). But he wrote this in a context in which he argued more generally, in a latitudinarian vein, that pleasures are not to be judged as worthy or unworthy (TSA 16, 105). I believe that at this point in TSA he is not entertaining or rejecting the abstract conception of happiness.

he wrote, "'Tis in vain to talk of adding quantities which after the addition will continue distinct as they were before, one man's happiness will never be another man's happiness: a gain to one man is no gain to another: you might as well pretend to add 20 apples and 20 pears."[17] Our current concerns shed new light on this passage. The problem of interpersonal comparisons that Bentham considers here is not a problem of inadequate epistemic access of one person to another person's interior life; rather, the distinctness of each man's happiness is a moral (or perhaps a metaphysical) fact. The happiness of one person *will never be another person's* happiness; no gain to one can be regarded as a gain to another. On the Abstract Happiness conception, this comment makes little sense. Whether it is one person's happiness or another's is morally irrelevant—that one person does not gain (directly) from another's gain is of no moral significance—because *whose* happiness it is, *who* stands to gain or lose, is of no moral significance. On the Individual Happiness reading, however, this passage it makes plain sense. The problem of aggregating happiness across persons faces a critical moral obstacle. On the Abstract Happiness conception, it is of no *moral* significance that one person's happiness will never be another's, whatever importance it might have from that person's private point of view. According to this conception, morality abstracts happiness from this personal location. However, on the Individual Happiness conception, aggregating the happiness of two incomparable sources of experience cannot do justice to the moral significance of the happiness in view.

Similarly, second, on several occasions Bentham expressed the view that the happiness of each member of the community is an equal part of the happiness of the whole. "As a faggot is comprised of sticks, so is the public of individuals: that one individual is as large a part of the public as another individual: and the happiness of the one as much a portion of the happiness of the public as the happiness of the other" (UC 100. 179; see also B iii. 459). And in his *Constitutional Code*, Bentham wrote, "the happiness of the most helpless pauper constitutes as large a portion of the universal happiness, as does that of the most powerful, the most opulent member of the community. *Therefore*, the happiness of the most helpless and indigent has *as much title to regard* at the hands of the legislator, as that of the most powerful and opulent" (CC (B) 107, emphasis added). This suggests that the universal interest or social happiness, as Bentham saw it, is not the net aggregate of abstract happiness. To read this passage in the tone of the Abstract Happiness conception would make Bentham's claim nonsensical on its face. Surely, the happiness of each is not equal. He means rather that each individual is to be considered an equal part of that happiness; each person's happiness is to be considered individually. The "universal happiness" is the inclusive combination of the happiness of each individual member. "Each to count for one" is not to be understood to say, as Bentham's critics insist, that each *pleasure* is to count for one; but rather, that every

[17] UC 14.3, quoted in John Dinwiddy, *Bentham* (Oxford: Oxford University Press, 1989), 50.

individual, *each person*, in the community is to be so regarded, that *each person's* happiness is to be considered alongside every other person's happiness, taking them one by one.

Moreover, third, both Bentham and Mill thought that viewing the principle of utility as they proposed had immediate implications regarding how happiness or well-being is to be distributed. "Each is to count for one," Mill argued, entails that each person has an equal claim to happiness, from which he infers further that, other things equal, each has an equal claim to the means of happiness (*Utilitarianism* V, para. 36). Even more strongly, Bentham insisted that "each man has an equal right to all the happiness that he is capable of" (Representation, 449). It is not entirely clear what to make of this alleged inference, but what is clear is that they believed that "each counts for one" has morally significant implications for how happiness was to be distributed. This is underscored by the fact that they thought that this foundational principle had direct implications for the distribution of what they called "the means of happiness"—the resources, offices, rights, and opportunities at the legislator's disposal. For example, Bentham argued that *since* "[n]o reason can be assigned, why a person of the one sex, should as such, have less happiness than a person of the other sex", there is no reason "why a female should have a less portion of... [the] means [of happiness]." Moreover, if "the possession of a share in the constitutive power, be a means of securing such equal share of the external means of happiness, the reason in favour of it, is, therefore, at least as strong in the case of the female sex, as in the case of the male" (CC (B) 108).

Again, as we have seen, Bentham argued that if we have "exactly the same regard for the happiness of every member of the community in question as for that of every other" we will be led to the conclusion that "the greatest happiness of the greatest number of members of that same community cannot but be recognized in the character of the ... sole right and proper end of government" (FPP 235). The spread or extent, i.e., the scope of the distribution, of happiness in a community is central to its moral appeal and moral demand. Bentham later came to regret his formulation of the principle in terms of "the greatest number," not because of its distributive dimension, but rather because it gives a misleading suggestion about how that dimension should be conceived (OAM 352).[18] He worried that one might think that the principle of utility would sanction ignoring the welfare or happiness of a minority in the community as long as the welfare or happiness of a majority of its members was made as great as it could be. This worry would not have occurred to Bentham had he the Abstract Happiness conception in mind.

This concern with distribution is echoed elsewhere in Bentham's work. In his discussion of international law and international relations, he formulated the fundamental principle of the domain in terms of "the greatest common utility of all nations taken together," that is, "the [greatest] common and equal utility of all nations"

[18] See Fred Rosen, *Jeremy Bentham and Representative Democracy* (Oxford: Clarendon Press, 1983), 201–2; John Dinwiddy, *Bentham*, 25–6.

(PIL 538, 537). Similarly, we see it at work in his understanding of the subordinate ends of legislation, especially those to which Bentham assigns priority, namely, subsistence and security. As we have already seen, security, according to Bentham, is maximized by being made universal and thereby in a certain respect equal. The same is true for subsistence. The legislator's aim is to "maximize" each of the four ends, "in so far as is compatible with the maximization of the rest" (B ii. 269). Maximization of subsistence, Bentham claims, entails *universality*—"securing the existence of and sufficiency of the matter of adequate subsistence of all members of the community"[19]—and *equality*—"in regard to subsistence . . . equality is . . . included in the very conception of it."[20] My claim is not that, in Bentham's view, the universal happiness *just is* the maximization of these equality-sensitive aims. My point is, rather, that the subordinate ends mirror in their structure the shape of Bentham's Individualist conception of happiness, and thereby the moral concern at the foundations of his theory.

Equality, as Bentham understood it, is not formal, not merely a matter of pleasures being the sole focus of the legislator's concern. Bentham thought each person has a legitimate claim on happiness and hence on the means of happiness. Equal consideration has direct distributive implications. On the Abstract Happiness conception this would be a logical howler, but it is plausible if we see, as now we must, that Bentham is working with an Individual Happiness conception of utilitarian value.

Expectations, Persons, and Human Happiness

Bentham's understanding of the moral importance of the location of pleasures and pains in the lives of persons lived over time is also apparent in his view of the role of expectations in distinctively human lives.[21]

In his earliest reflections on justice, utility, and the moral foundations of law in the 1770s, Bentham carefully distinguished two species of utilities: "original utility" and "utility derived from expectation."[22] He argued that the moral importance of expectation utilities far outstrips that of original utilities.[23] Original utilities include all pleasures or pains, many also experienced by sentient beings other than human beings, which do not depend directly or indirectly on expectations. Expectation utilities include, of course, satisfactions attendant upon fulfillment

19 BL Add. MSS 33,550.52.

20 UC clx, 160; quoted in Paul Kelly, *Utilitarianism and Distributive Justice* (Oxford: Clarendon Press, 1990), 123. Bentham adds: "for as consistently involved with the supposition no man can in this case have more of the means of subsistence than another, so consistently with his existence no man can have less" (*ibid.*).

21 In Chapter 4, 91-2, I discuss a different dimension of Bentham's view on the nature and moral significance of expectations.

22 See Chapter 7, 150-1.

23 UC 70(a). 20; UC 96. 74; UC 72. 1; *Com.* 231; see BCLT 155-8.

of expectations and pains experienced upon their disappointment,[24] but they also include most of the other pleasures, satisfactions, and enjoyments, and their contraries, to which human beings are susceptible, because, in Bentham's view, they depend fundamentally on certain capacities and sensibilities at the core of human life. He writes in his *Principles of the Civil Code*, "man is not like the brutes, limited to the present time, either in enjoyment or suffering, ... [rather] he is susceptible of pleasure and pain by anticipation ... The idea of his security must be prolonged to him throughout the whole vista that his imagination can measure" (*Civ. Code* 308). Imagination and foresight enable human beings to live beyond the discrete present and to project their lives and the goals that give them significance onto the stream of time. By means of this distinctively human capacity, he wrote,

> we are enabled to form a general plan of conduct; it is by means of this, that the successive moments which compose the duration of life are not like insulated and independent points, but become parts of a continuous whole. Expectation is a chain which unites our present and our future existence, and passes beyond ourselves to the generations which follow us. The sensibility of the individual is prolonged through all the links of this chain (*ibid.*).

Thus, for Bentham, well-being in its most important and most *human* form consists in the realization of integrated "plans" for our lives, coherent structures of aims extending over time and knitting our existence into "a continuous whole." This explains the greater, perhaps singular, moral significance of expectation utilities for Bentham. It gives *human* happiness a distinctively individualist cast. The view that human beings are mere "receptacles" for pleasure and suffering is clearly inconsistent with it.[25] The locus of Bentham's concern for human well-being and suffering in the individual person is evident.

This is consistent with and reflects the general orientation of Bentham's psychology and theory of value that we noticed in Chapter 3. There we argued that his apparent (psychological and evaluative) egoism is better seen as a form of "internalism." On his view, our grasp of the experiences of others and of value starts "from the inside." We grasp the experience of others by reflecting on our experiences and noting an analogy between our situations and behavior and those of others. This basis of rapport enables individuals to grasp the nature and quality of their experiences in the future, which are available to them only from a third-person perspective. Similarly, we grasp what is of value by reflecting on what we take pleasure in and what we wish to repeat. This grasp is extended by a kind of universalization, driven by the demand

[24] UC 69. 239; UC 70(a). 20; BCLT 206.

[25] Bentham did speak of persons as "receptacles" of happiness and unhappiness in a passage in his late "Article on Utilitarianism," 310. However, his tone is clearly ironic and implicitly critical. He says that people, who, through an egregious misunderstanding of his greatest happiness of the greatest number principle, ignore the claims of each person to consideration are also inclined to regard people as mere receptacles of happiness and unhappiness.

of publicity that is intrinsic to morality. There are two key features of this psychological and evaluative dynamic: the ground or starting point is *experience*, enjoyed and valued, which is *indexed*: it starts with *my experience* and extends to *her experience*. The root of value at the heart of the utility principle is *located* empirically and evaluatively in indexed human experience. Moral demands depend on an extension from this indexed experience, not by way of abstraction, but rather by way of universalization. What one recognizes, when one takes up the morally required public point of view is not some abstract good, but rather the parallel location of such experience and its value in the lives of others. When we add to this simple basic picture Bentham's appreciation of the fact that, for human beings, valued experience is not one off, but rather a matter of meaningful linkage over time like notes in a melody, it becomes clear that Bentham could not have consistently entertained the Abstract Happiness conception of value. His conception was distinctively Individualist. Thus, again we can see that the locus of Bentham's concern for human well-being and suffering was in the individual person.

This feature of his conception of happiness is reflected in the high priority Bentham gives to security; it is the first among the four ends of legislation immediately subordinate to the end of maximizing happiness. Security has this priority, in Bentham's view, because it provides the necessary infrastructure for personal continuity over time and so for individual human happiness. Moreover, security mirrors in its own structure, the individuated nature of the ultimate end of happiness which it serves.

When Bentham spoke of "maximization," Fred Rosen observed, he did not use it in the now common sense of producing the greatest aggregate quantity of some good, but rather in the sense of giving that good the broadest possible distribution.[26] The distributive sense of "maximization" is at work, Rosen argued, in Bentham's late constitutional writings where Bentham argues that the fundamental aim of constitutional design is to "maximize official aptitude" and "minimize expense." I confess that I find Rosen's evidence for this reading inconclusive,[27] and I think we cannot accept that Bentham used the term "maximize" exclusively in the distributive sense. Nevertheless, I believe that Rosen has pointed out an important feature of Bentham's frequent use of this term. We find "maximization" in the distributive sense especially in contexts directly or indirectly implicating his principle of utility. His discussion of security is one of them.[28] Security, in Bentham's understanding of it, has an important distributive dimension. He understood security

[26] Rosen, "Individual Sacrifice and the Greatest Happiness," 138–9.

[27] I find Rosen's distributive reading of "minimize official expense" strained and I think that the phrase "maximize official aptitude" can be taken in either aggregative or distributive senses. Does it make sense to permit trade-offs of official aptitude? Perhaps. Might it not make sense to economize on demands for impartiality, say, or practical judgment, and use our resources, and define official responsibilities, such that our needs for impartiality and practical judgment are optimally met. Isn't this a kind of aggregative rather than distributive use of "maximize"?

[28] Both distributive and aggregative senses are at work in Bentham's characterization of the four subordinate ends of legislation in the following passage: "Maximizing universal security – securing the existence of and sufficiency of the matter of adequate subsistence of all the members of the community,

to be a kind of public good in which, in so far as it is available to some, it is available in roughly like measure to all. To maximize security is to insure its "universality" over the whole community.

Perhaps, then, Bentham's injunction to seek the greatest happiness in the community should be understood in the same distributive sense. This is suggested in a passage from his *Plan of Parliamentary Reform* (1817). The ultimate end of government, elsewhere stated as "the greatest happiness of all" or "the greatest happiness of the greatest number," is put in terms of "advancement of the universal interest" which means, he says, "*comprehension* of all distinguishable *particular interests.*" All interests must be included or incorporated, and "with exceptions to as *small* an extent as possible, interests *all* to be *advanced:* without *any* exceptions, all to be *considered*" (B iii. 452, author's emphasis).[29]

FORMULATIONS OF THE PRINCIPLE OF UTILITY

Throughout his long career, Bentham typically referred to his fundamental principle as "the greatest happiness principle" or the principle requiring "the greatest happiness of the greatest number." Yet, when he turned his attention directly to the formulation of his principle he was curiously unsatisfied. He often tinkered with it. He tried not only to make it precise, but also to make it useful for his public, practical purposes. Equality in one dimension or another always played some role in his formulations of the principle, and he made that role most explicit in a late formulation of the principle. A brief tour of his efforts to formulate his principle will, I believe, further support the individualist reading of Bentham's utilitarian theory of value set out in this chapter.

We can begin with his discussion of the principle in his early work *A Fragment on Government.* The "fundamental axiom" of this work, Bentham declared, is that "it is the greatest happiness of the greatest number that is the measure of right and wrong" (FG 393). He used this formulation throughout his life, but he grew increasingly uncomfortable with it and altered it several times in the last decade of his life. It is tempting to think that he *abandoned* the greatest number formulation and embraced the straightforward, greatest happiness principle, thereby confirming his commitment to utility maximization in the aggregative sense and the Abstract Happiness conception of value on which it rests. However, Rosen has shown that the story actually took a very different shape.[30]

maximizing the quantity of the matter of abundance in all its shapes, securing the nearest approximating to absolute equality in the distribution of the matter of abundance and the other modifications of the matter of property" (BL Add. MS 33,550.52). Kelly quotes this passage in *Utilitarianism and Distributive Justice*, 106.

[29] The distributive aspect of Bentham's notion of universal interests is explored in Chapter 6.

[30] See Rosen, *Jeremy Bentham and Representative Democracy*, Chapter XI.

In his "Article on Utilitarianism" (309f), Bentham did worry about the greatest number formulation. As we have seen, what worried him was the likely misunderstanding and distortion of the utilitarian doctrine that this formulation might encourage. To an unsympathetic reader it might appear committed to policies that would deprive a minority of happiness, and possibly even impose on them enormous burdens, whenever a majority (the greater number) of the members of the community stood to benefit. This reading, Bentham argued, ignored the claims to happiness of each of the members of the disadvantaged minority. He thought that the greatest happiness principle—"the sole proper end of government is the greatest happiness of all in the community"—expressed better the fundamental utilitarian aspiration (PF 211; CC (B) 5). Yet, he did not abandon the greatest number principle; rather, he subordinated it to the more general principle. Thus, Bentham gave the principle of utility a more complex structure.

Bentham made the distributive dimension of his principle of utility clear later in his career. The basic principle was the greatest happiness principle, he insisted, but behind it was the "happiness enumeration principle." It was designed to handle situations in which it was not possible to advance the interests of all. In *Deontology*, he articulated a general choice strategy which he deployed in all such cases: first, determine "in what cases, by what means, and in what quantity happiness may be obtained gratis, [i.e.] without sacrifice"; and "when these means are exhausted," inquire "how the greatest quantity of happiness may be obtained with the least quantity of sacrifice" (*Deont.* 122). Bentham's suggestion is not entirely clear here. One way to read it is to see it as a recommendation to maximize the aggregate benefit offered by the options available to the decision maker. But this would not explain the two-step process, nor would it explain the first step recommendation to seek that option which involves no sacrifice, for a simple maximization strategy would recommend choosing the greatest net benefit and that might involve trade-offs even when there is an option that involves no sacrifice.

A different reading is possible, especially if we keep in mind Bentham's "enumeration" concern. He recommended something like the following. First, take the Pareto optimal option, if one is available, where at least one potentially affected party is benefited and no party is made worse off. Second, when all options involve trade-offs, some gaining and others losing, choose that option which promises the greatest benefit for the least amount of sacrifice. Note, the choice strategy does not recommend seeking the greatest net benefit (aggregative maximization). Rather, it requires, first, that all parties benefit, or at least that one benefits and no one else bears a loss to secure this benefit; and then that agents choose that the option which secures the greatest benefit—benefit to the greatest number—subject to the condition that the number of those who must bear the costs is minimized. This seems to be the way Bentham thought of his fundamental utility principle. As we noticed earlier, he often articulated that principle in terms of "advancement of the universal interest." This calls for "comprehension of all distinguishable particular interests."

Without exception, all interests must be included or incorporated, *and* all interests to be advanced, "with exceptions to *as small an extent as possible*" (B iii. 452, emphasis added).

Bentham developed this thought in his constitutional work. In situations in which it is not possible to promote the greatest happiness of each, he argued that we must prefer that option which advances the happiness of the greatest number. In his *Constitutional Code*, he wrote:

> I recognize, as the *all-comprehensive*, and only right and proper end of Government, the greatest happiness of the greatest number of the members of the community: of all without exception, in so far as possible: of the greatest number, on every occasion on which the nature of the case renders it impossible by rendering it matter of necessity, to make sacrifice of a portion of the happiness of a few, to the greater happiness of the rest.[31]

Very late in his career he made the equality-sensitivity of his greatest happiness principle even more explicit.

> I recognize, as the *all-comprehensive*, and only right and proper end of Government, the greatest happiness of the members of the community in question: the greatest happiness—of all of them, without exception, in so far as possible: the greatest happiness of the greatest number of them, on every occasion on which the nature of the case renders the provision of *an equal quantity of happiness for every one* of them impossible: it being rendered so, by its being matter of necessity, to make sacrifice of a portion of the happiness of a few, to the greater happiness of the rest.[32]

In this passage, Bentham makes clear that his *basic principle*, which defines the target of utilitarian aspiration, is committed not to aggregate net happiness in the community, but rather to the *greatest equal* happiness.[33] This echoes the principle he articulated in the 1790s that "each man has an equal right to all the happiness that he is capable of" (Representation, 449). Only when this goal cannot be achieved and some sacrifice is inevitable does the backup principle come into play: in cases where the benefits cannot be distributed universally distribute them as widely as possible.

Bentham was keenly aware that a viable and realistic moral principle had to tell us how to decide in situations in which we can improve the lot of some only at the

[31] CC (CW) vol. 1, 136. See also FPP 3, 234f; PF 211.

[32] *Parliamentary Candidate's proposed Declaration of Principles: or say, A Test proposed for Parliamentary Candidates* (London, 1831), 7 (second emphasis added); quoted in Rosen, *Jeremy Bentham and Representative Democracy*, 212.

[33] Compare here Bentham's formulation of the principle of utility for the domain of international relations: "the [greatest] common and equal utility of all nations" (PIL 537).

expense of others. His conception of welfare did not force him to hold that there is never any moral justification for sacrificing the welfare of one person for that of another. In a world in which human lives are intertwined, it is often not possible to promote the welfare of one person without affecting that of others as well, sometimes to their detriment. Bentham's underlying concern to count each person for one required, in his view, that when sacrifices are inevitable, we impose them always guided by the overriding aim of giving equal consideration to the interests of all those who are affected by our actions. So, he proposed a "compromise" principle to handle cases in which it may be necessary to sacrifice some for the good of others. Greatest Happiness of Each Person Principle requires,

Treating the greatest equal happiness as a baseline:

a. choose that alternative which most improves the welfare of each member of the community;
b. when it is not possible to improve the welfare of each, choose that alternative which spreads the improvement most widely over the community.[34]

This may not be a very satisfying principle. It is hard to see, for example, how to prevent the exceptions from entirely overwhelming the baseline rule of equality. But it does make manifest that Bentham sought to give expression to a utilitarian creed that is sensitive to equality and to the moral claims of individual persons. He built equality as a baseline requirement directly into the principle. On the Abstract Happiness conception of welfare, this would either be a logical mistake, or an illegitimate smuggling of a distinct, and conflicting, moral principle into utilitarian theory.

Bentham, I suggest, had a different conception in mind. On this Individual Happiness conception, the fact that happiness, or welfare, is the happiness *of someone* is of fundamental moral importance. Happiness is not abstracted from persons. Happiness is morally relevant because it is the happiness of the persons who experience it, and integrate it into their lives. To care about happiness for moral purposes is to care about the people who experience it. But this is just to say, in slightly different words, that the fundamental moral fact to which we must attend, on Bentham's version of the utilitarian creed, is individual welfare, how a person's life goes as that person experiences it. Maximization of happiness in the abstract without regard to how individual human beings participate in this stock of happiness is inconsistent with this creed. An attempt is made to "recognize the separateness of persons" and incorporate that recognition into the structure of the principle of utility itself. If the above reading of Bentham's intentions is correct,

[34] Bentham was not always consistent in his commitment to this theme. In *Legislator of the World*, he wrote, "But on every occasion, without detriment to the greatest happiness of the greatest number, a burthen may in any shape be imposed upon any individual or individuals in any number for the benefit of an individual or individuals in any number, so that this condition be fulfilled: viz. that the sum of the benefits conferred be greater in value than the sum of the burthens imposed" (LW 206).

Bentham's theory of value—his understanding of the fundamental moral significance of suffering and happiness—is the root of his attempt to incorporate equality into his fundamental moral–political principle. His utilitarian notion of intrinsic value builds into it equal concern for each person, recognizes the equal claim that each person's well-being has on our moral attention, and yields a structuring principle requiring that equal weight be given to the happiness of each.

Bentham's struggles over the formulation of the principle of utility, I believe, were struggles to give expression to the individualist insight, captured by the "each for one" byword, on which he built his moral and political theory. He was never satisfied with the results, and he was right to remain unsatisfied. He never specified what circumstances would make pursuit of the more fundamental, equality-sensitive goal "impossible." Unless they are carefully spelled out, however, such circumstances threaten to swallow the basic principle. Yet, if we keep in mind Bentham's four subordinate ends and their distribution-sensitive deployment in his political theory, that theory retains some plausibility. At least, his struggles are instructive. They indicate a direction utilitarian theory might have gone, had not Bentham's followers developed a clearer, simpler, more consistent, and far less morally sensitive rendering of Bentham's underlying utilitarian motivation.

EQUALITY: BASIC vs DERIVATIVE

It is important to distinguish theoretical levels at which a commitment to equality might be articulated. Much contemporary debate among egalitarians, and challenges to them, focus on what we might call "derivative" equality, equality concerning distribution of resources, capabilities, freedoms, rights, opportunities, powers, and more generally the benefits and burdens of cooperative social life. These goods, benefits, and burdens may be socially and personally of great significance, but they are derivative from a general theoretical point of view. Many egalitarians argue that equality in one or more of these derivative dimensions find their ground in a deeper egalitarian principle, for example, a principle of equal concern and respect.[35] Of course, commitment to deep or basic equality is consistent with people being treated differently in a wide variety of ways. Deep equality does not entail universal uniformity of treatment. Indeed, commitment to deep equality may even require differential or unequal treatment in certain important respects. A good example of this is Rawls's "difference principle," which justifies unequal distribution of some primary goods (when a more equal distribution would not improve the position of the least well-off) on the ground that it best serves the principle requiring respect for all as free and equal moral persons.[36]

[35] Ronald Dworkin, *Sovereign Virtue* (Cambridge, MA: Harvard University Press, 2000), esp. Chapters 1 –2; Rawls, *Theory of Justice*, 441–9; Waldron, *One Another's Equals*.

[36] Rawls, *Theory of Justice*, 86–92; Rawls, *Justice as Fairness: A Restatement* (Cambridge, MA: Belknap Press, 2001), 130–2.

I have argued that Bentham incorporated equality into the formulation of his single, most fundamental moral–political principle, the principle of utility. He was committed, I have argued, to deep or basic equality, equal consideration of the interests and happiness of each member of a community—every individual in the country is to count for one, no one for more than one. We have also noticed that he believed that this commitment to basic equality of consideration had strong distributive implications. Equal consideration, he thought, commits us to regarding each person as having an equal claim on happiness, even an equal claim to the means of happiness. And the equal claim to the means to happiness implies derivatively a claim to equal access to these means of happiness, subject to constraints that deep equality, equal consideration of the interests of all, imposes on the production and allocation of these means of happiness. Like other deep-equality egalitarians, Bentham recognized and defended social and political arrangements that countenanced significant forms of differential treatment. Considering only his views on such derivative matters, one might be inclined to doubt the conclusions I have sought to establish regarding Bentham's commitment to deep equality. We would do well to conclude this discussion of Bentham's equality-sensitive theory of value with a brief discussion of his views of such matters of the distribution of the goods, benefits and burdens of social and political life.

Bentham's commitment to deep equality finds expression in his political and legal theory in several different ways. To illustrate his approach, consider two such contexts, his constitutional theory and his theory of civil law. In his constitutional theory, the effect of his commitment to deep equality is evident in his theory of political structure. The fundamental principle of institutional design in this domain is to organize all institutions and offices, and the incentives and constraints that make them work, to serve the universal interest. This, in Bentham's view, comprises two main tasks: (1) to prevent "the sinister sacrifice" and support and motivate optimal exercise of official aptitudes, especially the moral and intellectual aptitudes; and (2) to focus the work of government, through both legislation and policy, on matters of the public interest. The latter is a relatively direct expression of Bentham's equality-sensitive utility principle. For, as we will see in Chapter 6, matters of public interest are matters in which for the most part each individual has some material stake, and none are completely excluded. The former is served in at least two ways in Bentham's constitutional theory. (a) Government institutions are set up such in a way as to maximize the transparency and openness of official activities.[37] No imprescriptible natural rights may be embedded in fundamental law, but rather government and non-governmental civic institutions are designed to provide a series of interrelated "securities against misrule." "Inequality in the scale of power is a source of evil: but inequality in this scale is necessary to the existence of society: still the less there is of it, consistently with the well-being of society in

[37] This dimension of Bentham's commitment to publicity in government is discussed further in Chapter 12.

other respects, the better" (FPP 320). The aim is to protect each individual against the arbitrary imposition of the will of one party, or of a powerful elite. Such rule is "arbitrary" in the dual sense that it serves the sinister interests of the ruling individual or group, and that the power is exercised without accountability to the public. Equal consideration at the foundations of his political theory led Bentham to find ways to direct the inevitable inequalities of power and authority to the universal interest (FPP 158), subject to control of the public in which each individual can play a role. (b) While power and authority must be vested only in some members of the political community, all of the people, on Bentham's democratic design, must play an active role in what he called "the Supreme Constitutive"—the body entitled to vest ruling power in some persons and remove it for cause. For this purpose, the people acts as a whole; participation is made possible through universal suffrage. His argument for universal suffrage started from the premise of equality that we encountered earlier. The happiness or interests of any one person is no more or less important than that of any other, that of the poorest or least regard-worthy any less than that of the most eminent, that of women no less than that of men. Since "possession of a share in the constitutive power [is] ... a means of securing such an equal share in the external means of happiness," the case for extending the franchise to women and the poor is at least as strong as the case for providing it to powerful men (CC (B) 107–8). As we have seen, Bentham wrote in his *Plan of Parliamentary Reform*, "If, in the instance of any one individual, it *be right* that he should possess a *share*, of a certain degree of *magnitude*, in the choice of a person, to form one in the aggregate body of representatives of the people—how can it be right that, in the instance of any other individual, the share should be either *less* or *greater*" (B iii. 452, original emphasis). Deep equality sets a strong presumption in favor of equality of distribution of constitutional powers. That presumption can be defeated by persuasive, publicly articulated reasons, but the underlying equality must be evident even in the resulting inequalities.

Similarly, deep equality also has implications for the arrangements of civil law—that is, for economic and social institutions defined or governed by law. The fundamental principle of utility determines for this domain four immediate "subordinate ends": security, subsistence, equality and abundance (FPP 153). These also are arranged in a rough order of priority, security being the most fundamental, and each taking precedence over any other policy that might be considered desirable in this domain. All subordinate ends, in their way, serve the more fundamental object of equality, in Bentham's view, each being components of public or common good in which each member of society has a stake. Security does so in the most obvious way. As we have seen, to secure a population against external and internal threats is a public good in which all participate to a significant degree. Its "maximization" calls for extending protections universally. Security of possession—protection for property rights—not only serves the interests of property owners, but the whole polity by encouraging industry and productivity. Of course, legal and governmental efforts aimed at providing security do not benefit everyone to the same degree, but, Bentham believed, all benefit to some degree and in a way that, in this domain, respects equally the interests of each member of the polity.[38]

Moreover, Bentham explicitly argued for a (qualified) policy of movement toward equalization of wealth in a way that anticipated arguments made familiar a century later. He began with the psychological fact that certain goods, money and wealth most prominently, conform to the "axiom" of diminishing marginal utility (PF 228–30; *Civ. Code* 304ff). According to this axiom, the size of the utility benefit produced by the addition of one unit of wealth varies in inverse proportion to the amount of money or wealth the recipient already holds. Thus, with a given stock of money, the utility benefit is greater if we give it to a relatively poor person rather than to a better off person. This argues for policies that have the effect of approximating equal distribution of income and wealth, *other things equal*—that is, taking into account only the direct or first-order benefits and costs of allocations of wealth. Furthermore, Bentham argues that if we were to start from a status quo of rough equality, movements to greater inequality would lack utilitarian justification, because of the further psychological fact that a person's utility is diminished more by the loss of a given sum than another party would gain by acquiring that same sum (*Civ. Code* 307). In addition, the loser would experience the second-order pain of disappointment by losing the sum, a disutility that would not be compensated by any equivalent gain by the one who benefits. So, there is good utilitarian reason not to disturb an existing roughly equal distribution.

However, Bentham recognized that things are not equal. All law and governmental policy works *in medias res*, and, in the status quo, resources—wealth and property—are already possessed. This brings into play second-order and third-order costs which militate against efforts to promote greater equality of wealth. Primary among these higher-order costs, in Bentham's view, are potential disappointments of expectations and fear of loss, as well as potential depression of industry and productivity. Security, especially security of possession, Bentham insisted, takes priority over equality of resources, and considerations of security outweigh any utility gains that could be reaped by greater equal distribution of wealth (*Civ. Code* 311). Thus, despite his egalitarian commitments, Bentham seems to counsel acceptance of potentially vast inequalities of wealth, and to advise lawmakers to do all they can to maintain the existing distribution of wealth. Michael Quinn concludes a survey of Bentham's arguments in this area with the observation that "ultimately ... it appears that the room explicitly left by Bentham for policies which directly pursue the goal of distributional equality was vanishingly

[38] The argument sketched here moves at a very high level of abstraction and without attention to much necessary detail. Were we to dig more deeply into the argument we would likely find reason to challenge Bentham's conclusions. However, the point of the discussion here is not to determine the success of his arguments, but rather to see to what extent proposals that are apparently inegalitarian at the derivative level might be consistent with, and even plausible be seen to express, his commitment to deep equality.

small."[39] This conclusion might still stand after we recognize that Bentham justified some policies to mitigate inequalities of wealth on utilitarian grounds. For example, some of the worry about defeat of expectations can be obviated, Bentham argued, by policies of post-mortem redistribution—because expectations of the dead cannot be defeated, and the living can adjust their expectations in advance of possessing what they might otherwise inherit—and carefully planned efforts at taxation that avoid sudden governmental invasion of property rights.[40]

Yet, although it is possible credibly to challenge the arguments Bentham offered to justify resistance to redistribution, one might still recognize the shadow of his commitment to deep equality even in these arguments. First, Bentham insisted that "all inequality is a source of evil—the inferior loses more in the account of happiness than the superior is gained" (FPP 319, see also 316). Equal consideration of the interests of each requires that this psychological fact be given full weight in utility-determined policy. Second, equality in the distribution of the "means of felicity" takes a back seat only to substantial considerations of security. "The greatest felicity of the greatest number of the people requires that the external instruments of felicity, whatsoever they may be, be shared by the whole number in proportion as near to equality as is consistent with universal security, and with that abundance at each moment of time which is itself necessary in the character of a security for the permanency of universal subsistence" (FPP 16, see also 142). Security, itself, in Bentham's view, is the first demand of his equality-sensitive principle of utility. Taking security of the community and security of possession within was, in his view, the best way to provide the basis for expectations of each citizen and hence for their planning and execution of a meaningful life over time.

It is reasonable to conclude, I believe, that Bentham's inegalitarian social policies do not challenge the plausibility of attributing to him a commitment to deep equality, even if arguments for them remain unpersuasive. To settle the matter, I suppose, a careful analysis of a wide range and variety of his arguments on political, social and economic policy issues would be necessary. Such a survey may force us to abandon this interpretation, for, with Bentham, the details of his argument are always relevant to interpreting and assessing his general and abstractly articulated commitments. The arguments developed in this chapter, however, set a high bar for defeat of this interpretation.

I cannot conclude this discussion of Bentham's alleged deep egalitarianism, and the Individualist conception of happiness on which its rests, without acknowledging that Bentham sometimes says some shockingly inegalitarian things. Michael Quinn has brought some of these to our attention.[41] Bentham's troubling

[39] Michael Quinn, "A Failure to Reconcile the Irreconcilable? Security, Subsistence and Equality in Bentham's Writings on the Civil Code and on the Poor Laws," *History of Political Thought* 29 (2008), 343.

[40] See Quinn, "Failure to Reconcile," 331–2.

[41] Quinn, "Failure to Reconcile," 336–40.

remarks have their roots in his social psychology, which we explored briefly in Chapter 2. Bentham believed that human sensibilities are shaped by their circumstances, experiences, and modes of life. Needs and hardships are experienced quite differently depending on the histories and circumstances of different individuals. Circumstances shape attitudes and even capacities to deal with the vicissitudes of life. One who is poor after having been affluent cannot deal as well with deprivation as a person who has always known it, Bentham argued (LW 205). Likewise, Bentham held that only some members of the society will truly benefit from education. One who has just read the various passages in which Bentham utters, in one form or another, his "dictum"—"every individual in the country is to count for one . . ." will be drawn up short by the following passage that Quinn quotes from Bentham's papers on poor laws.

> Setting man against man, numbers out of the question, the superiority of importance [of providing education] is on the other side. Why?—because it is only from the class of gentlemen that it is usual for the members of the governing body in all its branches . . . to be taken. In point of fact, a gentleman tells for more in the general account, than a common man: his conduct has more weight, more influence in society, than that of a common man: in point of reason and utility, it is right that he should tell for more—Why? because more is apt to depend upon his conduct than is apt to depend upon the conduct of the common man. Man for man, it is to the gentleman that the superiority is due: class for class, it is the class of non-gentlemen that stands foremost in the order of importance. In the account of happiness that of one man is equal to another. In the eye of the philosopher and in the eye of the philanthropist, all men are equal: and it is for this very reason, that in the eye of the same person, the gentleman, compared with the common man, man for man, will be he whose education will appear to be of superior importance.[42]

Without a doubt, this sounds more like Hutcheson (and Rashdall) than the Bentham I presented throughout this chapter. Yet, a shadow of his commitment to deep equality is evident even here. *Because* every man is equal to every other at the level of deep principle ("in the eye of the philosopher and . . . philanthropist"), Bentham argues, it is possible and important to determine who is constitutionally able to benefit from education and who is not, and who is more likely to benefit society from education. Bentham's argument, shocking and objectionable as it is, is of a form that is consistent with his deep egalitarian principle. It recognizes that society inevitably allocates its benefits and burdens differentially. Such inequalities may be justified, if they can be shown to serve the universal interest in which the individual interests of all are properly included. Bentham's argument here is, to my

[42] UC 153.87, quoted in Quinn, "Failure to Reconcile," 340.

eye, utterly unconvincing, but it is of a form that fits roughly with the account of the equality-sensitive principle of utility developed in this chapter. The problem with his argument lies not in the egalitarian foundations of Bentham's moral philosophy, but rather in his failure to follow through on his fundamental egalitarian commitments.

6

Interests, Universal and Particular

> In the whole moral sphere ... there is nothing more glorious nor of wider range than the solidarity of mankind, that species of alliance and partnership of interests [*societas et communicatio utilitatum*] and that actual affection which exists between man and man ... [which] is termed Justice.*

Bentham learned from Hume that "the foundations of all *virtue* are laid in *utility*" (FG 440, author's emphasis).[1] Perhaps it was the following passage from Hume's *Enquiry* that made the scales fall from Bentham's eyes.

> In all determinations of morality, this circumstance of public utility is ever principally in view; and wherever disputes arise, either in philosophy or common life, concerning the bounds of duty, the question cannot, by any means, be decided with greater certainty, than by ascertaining, on any side, the true interests of mankind.[2]

Surely some such passage did the trick, for the basic concept of Bentham's moral and political philosophy was not simply utility, but rather *public utility*. All moral judgments, Bentham insisted, are ultimately grounded in "the cause of the people" (FG 440).

Moreover, following Hume's lead, Bentham linked this concept directly with the concept of interests. For classically trained philosophers, the link between utility and interest was manifest in the Latin root *utilitas*. This is evident in the passage from *De Finibus* quoted above. Of course, it was Hume, not Bentham, who drew inspiration from Cicero and readily coupled justice with utility. Yet Bentham heartily embraced the singular "species of alliance and partnership of interests" that attracted Cicero's praise, and he placed it at the core of his utilitarian theory of value. Or so, at least, I shall argue in this chapter.

Of course, for Bentham, pleasure is our "sovereign master" and the anchor of all practical judgments (IPML I.1), but, in Bentham's argumentative practice, this sovereign rarely appears in public, and is seldom recognized when it does. It is known

* Adapted from G.J. Postema, "Interests, Universal and Particular: Bentham's Utilitarian Theory of Value," *Utilitas* 18(2) (2006), 109–33 Cambridge University Press 2006, reproduced with permission.

[1] Cicero, *De Finibus*, H. Rackham, tr. (Cambridge, MA: Harvard University Press, 1914), V. 65.
[2] David Hume, *Enquiry Concerning the Principles of Morals*, L.A. Selby-Bigge, ed., 3rd edn., revised by P.H. Nidditch (Oxford: Clarendon Press, 1975), 2.17.

Utility, Publicity, and Law: Essays on Bentham's Moral and Legal Philosophy. Gerald J. Postema.

primarily by its effects, wearing the mantle of the universal interest, which comprises in Bentham's mature public philosophy a distinctive partnership of the interests of all members of the community. The ultimate end of government, Bentham insisted, is "the advancement of the universal interest" (B iii. 452). Indeed, this is the aim of all of morality: "To the art and science of *morals* belongs the indication of the sorts of acts, by which, in the various situations of life, the universal interest is served or disserved" (LW 142, original emphasis). In this chapter, I undertake to articulate the structure of Bentham's notion of universal interest and locate its place in his theory of value. I continue here the project of rethinking the philosophical core of Bentham's utilitarianism begun in the preceding chapter, which explored the place of equality in his theory of value. There I argued that Bentham's life-long concern with the distribution of happiness did not issue from his commitment to a principle of equality distinct from his principle of utility, but rather from his understanding of the moral concern that lies at the heart of his theory of value. The most fundamental morally significant fact, in Bentham's view, is that individuals suffer and flourish, and his many formulations of the principle of utility represent attempts to give clear and effective expression to his commitment to individual happiness. This commitment is most aptly expressed, I shall argue, in the concept of the universal interest, which took shape in his work late in his career.[3]

HAPPINESS, EQUALITY, AND THE PRINCIPLE OF COMPOSITION

"Public welfare," Bentham wrote in *Chrestomathia*, is "the great and universal end" to which all action and institutions (indeed, to which "all art, all science, all language") ought to be directed (*Chrest.* 120). Recall our discussion in Chapter 3 of the structure of the fundamental principle of Bentham's theory of political morality, the principle of utility. The principle consists of four components. The first, *universal consequentialism*, set the unquestioned horizon of Bentham's thinking about morality and politics. Morality is, at bottom, the business of promoting the overall good of the community.[4] Bentham took this lesson from Hume. All virtue is founded on utility, he learned, and he understood utility, at a first approximation, in terms of social welfare. Thus, according to this second component, *social welfarism*, the good of the community is to be understood in terms of its welfare or well-being. Third, as we saw in the preceding chapter, Bentham believed that the

[3] The basic themes discussed in this chapter are evident throughout his writings, but they come strongly to the foreground in the 1820s. My project here is to offer a reconstruction of Bentham's theory of value and its philosophical motivations. There is an important story to tell about how this theory developed over the course of his career, but I will not attempt to tell that story here.

[4] We will see in Chapter 11 that Bentham devised a version of his principle of utility for agents who act in the global domain. His principle was meant to apply only to actions of sovereign rulers and focused directly on the welfare of nations. It was meant to be only indirectly concerned with the welfare of individuals of those nations.

fundamental moral concern is the well-being or welfare of individuals. *Individual welfarism* insists that all other concerns, when viewed from the perspective of morality, must be rooted in the welfare of individuals. Thus, somehow the fundamental concern with individual welfare must be modulated in some way to yield a measure of social welfare. The fourth component, *compositionalism*, unites the two parts of his welfarist understanding of universal consequentialism: the welfare of the community is a composite of the welfare of its individual members.

The key to understanding Bentham's fundamental utilitarian principle lies in understanding the *principle of composition*—the nature of the function that composes the welfare of the community, public utility, out of the welfare of its individual members. On the received view of classical utilitarianism, evident, for example, in Rawls's familiar treatment of it in his *Theory of Justice*,[5] the welfare of a community is the net sum of the welfare of its individual members measured in hedonic units of positive and negative valence—pleasure and pain—viewed impartially and so given strictly equal weight. Promotion of social welfare, on the received view, requires that actions be chosen and institutions constructed so as to maximize this net sum of aggregated pleasures and pains. The principle of composition requires the simple summation of the pleasures and pains of all those affected by proposed actions, policies, or laws. The principle of choice, given this composition of the social welfare, is maximization: the principle of utility instructs us to choose that alternative which promises to produce the largest net sum of pleasure. I argued in Chapters 4 and 5 that this was not Bentham's view, because this view is fundamentally at odds with the theory of value at the center of his utilitarianism. Bentham's principle of composition reflects his understanding of moral value. It is not entirely clear whether Bentham was committed to maximization as the canonical principle of choice regarding public utility, but even if he was committed to it, it should become clear as we proceed that his very different principle of composition of social welfare gives a rather different meaning to the idea of maximization than is familiar to students of utilitarianism in this century and most of the last one. A brief reminder of what we have already learned about Bentham's understanding of moral value will put us in search of his alternative principle of composition.

Pleasure and its Problems

Bentham frankly acknowledged that measurement of pleasures and pains was greatly limited. "Pleasure itself [is] not ... ponderable or measurable," he wrote. "Weight, extent, heat, light—for quantities of all these articles, we have perceptible and expressible measures: unhappily or happily, for quantities of pleasure or pain,

[5] John Rawls, *A Theory of Justice*, 2nd edn. (Cambridge, MA: Harvard University Press, 1999), 19–30, 160–8.

we have no such measures" (LW 251, 253). Meaningful comparisons of pleasurable experiences across persons are not possible.

> To every man, by competent attention and observation the quality of his own sensibility may be made known: it may be known by the most impressive and infallible of all direct evidence, the evidence of a man's own senses. To no man, can the quality of sensibility in the breast of any other man be made known by any thing like equally probative and unfallacious evidence (*Deont.* 130–1).

The problem is especially acute regarding the fundamental quality of a pleasurable experience, its *intensity.* Intensity, Bentham conceded, "is the least capable" of being measured; "for this there is no common standard" (UC 69.19; see also LW 254).

Second, Bentham doubted whether there is any property common to pleasurable experiences such that that property could be identified, measured and then used in interpersonal comparisons. Rather, Bentham adopted an "attitudinal" conception of pleasure. What is common to all pleasurable experiences is not some discrete felt quality, but the fact that people like to have them and pains are experiences people would like to avoid. "Pleasure," on this view, picks out an attitude of persons towards certain experiences they have—their wanting the experience, and wanting it to continue—rather than any discrete quality of the experience.

Third, while Bentham maintained that, with respect to present pleasures and pains, the individual experiencing them is the best judge, this authority does not extend to *future* ones. "*Like a third person* his future contingent individual pleasure and pain can not be judged of by him otherwise than from the *species it belongs to*" (*Deont.* 195 n. 1, emphasis added). We systematically overestimate the emotional satisfaction or distress we will get from experiences we anticipate as great pleasures or horrible pains. Bentham believed that we are better able to anticipate the value of these future experiences by looking at them from the outside. The resources we have for predicting our future well-being are the same resources available to others assessing our well-being. Such predictions depend on our "general" sensibility to pleasures, not our *person-specific* sensibilities.

When we shift to the third person, we are not only dependent on others to help us grasp the impact of contingent features of our world on the availability of pleasures, but we are also forced to look to sensibilities we tend to share with others. Experiences I know by participating with others in daily life are the kind that I and many others would like to have again. For these purposes, such pleasures are not adequately portrayed in terms of some single, homogeneous *quale* associated with or caused by them. The relevant conception of pleasure, for these purposes, is the attitude conception. Pleasure understood in this way is more likely to be publicly available. At the same time, it is no longer a matter of immediate experience. It is "inferential," rather than ontologically of the first order, as Bentham thought of these things. Pleasure, on the attitude conception, is closely tied to public features of the states of affairs, objects, or persons in which people take pleasure. Indeed, it is not the subjective quality of the pleasurable experience, but the subject's *taking pleasure in* something that seems to be far more important for the ordinary business of moral and political deliberation. That is the kind of thing that we can track across time and across people, and that we can gather into kinds ("species") and on the basis of experience attribute with some confidence to people in the community generally. The things we talk about together as "pleasures" are the kind of things about which over time our judgments may even converge to some degree, despite differences of sensibility. Later in his career, Bentham was inclined to appeal to the notion of interests to do the work he had once assigned to pleasure and pain, thus understood.

Equality and Value

John Stuart Mill, Bentham's godson, memorialized Bentham's dictum—"every individual in the country tells for one; no individual for more than one" (B vii. 334)—in the last chapter of *Utilitarianism*. One way to understand the maxim, we saw in Chapter 5, is to take "each to tell for one" to mean *each unit of pleasure* (or pain) is to tell for one—that is, pleasure and pain *alone* are to count in fundamental utilitarian deliberation. This entails a principle proscribing certain widely practiced forms of discrimination. It prohibits any weighting of the pleasures or pains in the initial calculus according to features of those who experience them; thus, it seems to endorse a kind of equality. No ascribed status must affect the weight to be given to the pleasures and pains of different people in the utilitarian calculus. The principle of utility is no respecter of persons. Since pleasure alone is its concern, it matters not whether the units of pleasure are experienced by one person or many. This understanding of 'each tells for one' fits the received interpretation of classical utilitarianism and rests on a conception of happiness that regards the moral significance of happiness as entirely independent of its connection to the individuals experiencing it. I called this the Abstract Happiness conception.

I argued that Bentham did not understand the moral significance of happiness in this way. Rather, on his Individual Happiness conception, the fact that happiness is the happiness *of some particular person* is of fundamental moral importance. Happiness is not a moral good considered apart from the persons who experience it. Happiness is morally relevant just because people experience it and can integrate it meaningfully into their lives. The fundamental moral fact for the individualist utilitarian is the suffering experienced by concrete individual people. It is people who suffer and flourish, people who take delight in or are distressed by the events of their lives. If these experiences are abstracted from the meaning that they have within the lives of individual human beings, they lose their moral significance.

"One man's happiness," Bentham wrote, "will never be another man's happiness: a gain to one man is no gain to another: you might as well pretend to add 20 apples to 20 pears" (UC 14.3). Each person's happiness remains distinct, not just epistemically, but morally.

On this conception of value, "each is to tell for one" requires that, exceptions kept to a minimum, the interests of *all* must be advanced (B iii. 452). Late in his career, he wrote that the only proper end of government is the greatest happiness of all members of the community, "an equal quantity of happiness for every one of them"—in so far as that is possible. When this proves impossible, and the happiness of some must be sacrificed for the happiness of others, government must seek the greatest happiness of the greatest number of them. Bentham's basic principle, which defines the target of utilitarian aspiration, is committed to the greatest equal happiness, not to maximizing total net (abstract) happiness. Only when this goal cannot be achieved and some sacrifice is inevitable does a fallback principle come into play. However, this principle does not require that happiness considered in the abstract be maximized, but that the greatest and widest possible distribution of happiness be achieved.

Thus, I argued in the preceding chapter that Bentham did not accept the view, often attributed to him, that the good or welfare of individuals could be entirely subordinated to the welfare of the community. However, he also clearly recognized that the utilitarian principle applied in a world in which conflicts of interest are pervasive and where sacrifices of the happiness of some for the happiness of others are unavoidable and sometimes are morally justified. There is an evident tension in these views and Bentham struggled with it over much of his lengthy career. Yet, he seemed to think that, for the domain of politics and public policy at least, this tension could be substantially relieved even if not eliminated. The key to his solution, and to a principle of composition consistent with his individualist conception of happiness, I shall argue, lies in his understanding of the notion of the universal interest.

UNIVERSAL INTEREST

In the last two decades of his life, the concept of interest became a central organizing notion of Bentham's political sociology and his theory of political morality. Ultimately, perhaps, pleasure and pain remained for him the two sovereign masters of our lives—dictating what we will do and what we ought to do—but interest was their first minister and chief operating officer.

The Interest of Interests

According to Bentham, the word "interest" has no superior genus and so cannot be defined in the traditional way, *per genus et differentiam* (IPML 12n). Thus, he argued, we must analyze it as the name of a fictitious entity, in the same manner as he proposed to analyze "obligation," "law," "rights," and the like. All these fictions are necessary to our thought and practice. They remain harmless, or at least are not seriously misleading, if they can be tethered ultimately to real entities. "Interest" is rooted ultimately in the psychic entities, pleasure and pain (TSA 5–7, 74–9, 98–100). This way of thinking about the relationship between interests and pleasure or pain allowed Bentham to articulate his principle of utility in the language of the universal interest, while contenting himself that, if necessary, he could cash any specific discussion of utility into ultimate (but practically unwieldy and epistemically problematic) hedonic terms. For all practical purposes, on the analysis we explored in Chapter 1, the language of interests can be taken as fundamental.

It was, indeed, for specific practical purposes that Bentham devised his principle of utility. His aim from the outset was to articulate a public philosophy, addressed primarily to legislators, constitution makers, and engineers of social reform, who could be enlisted in the enterprise of designing and constructing social, economic, and political institutions. For this purpose, the language of interests is especially well suited. Robert Goodin captured Bentham's theoretical outlook when he observed,

> People's pleasures are varied, their preferences idiosyncratic. People's basic interests, in contrast, are (at least at some suitable level of generality) pretty standard across all individuals (at least all individuals in any given society at any given moment). Policy makers are of necessity making choices that must affect a wide range of people at one and the same time. They might well be overwhelmed by the diversity of pleasures and preferences ... Their task is rendered far more manageable by the relative commonality of people's basic welfare interests.[6]

This picture fits Bentham's outlook well (see *Civ. Code* 304–5). The language of interests enabled him to articulate a subtle theory of individual and group motivation with which he structured his analysis of the fundamental problems of constitutional design. It also provided the resources for a carefully nuanced articulation of the fundamental aim of all government and of the principle of utility which made that aim imperative. Bentham's tendency to use a core concept for both normative and analytical-positive purposes led him to obscure the important, if sometimes subtle, features of the concept in its different modes of deployment. I am interested here in Bentham's normative theory. I seek here to understand Bentham's theory of value and the principle of composition on which his principle of utility relies. The notion of the universal interest will be the focus of the inquiry, but it

[6] Robert Goodin, *Utilitarianism as a Public Philosophy* (Cambridge: Cambridge University Press, 1995), 14.

will be necessary to keep in mind Bentham's tendency to use this concept for both purposes.

Consider briefly the notion of interest as Bentham typically used it.[7] In legal usage, an interest is a legally protected benefit. Bentham's use is different. For Bentham, (1) interests are matters that one *takes an interest in*. Thus, it is the focus of an agent's attention or caring, and it has an object. (2) As we have seen, officially (i. e., when he is on duty as a hedonist), Bentham connected the notion of interest with pleasure. "A man is said *to have an interest in any subject* in so far as that *subject* is considered as more or less likely to be to him a source of pleasure or exemption [from pain]" (TSA 91, original emphasis). (3) Interests can and often do have motivational force. Sometimes, Bentham put this point in very strong terms: "On every occasion, the conduct of every human being will be determined by his own interest" (B ix. 43); but interests are not always motives. Motives, as Bentham understood them, are necessarily *present* to the mind at the time of action, and are momentary (*Deont.* 210). In contrast, an individual may have temporally persistent interests of which she is not immediately aware. Interests are matters one takes an interest in, but they need not be occurrent. Moreover, interests can be considered and deliberated with when the agent is motivationally off-line, as it were. So, it is more accurate to say that Bentham understood interests to have a motivational dimension. (4) We noticed in Chapter 2 that Bentham believed that, unlike pleasures, interests have an implicit, if not explicit, self-referential character. (5) Also unlike pleasures, interests have a conceptual structure. We not only think about them, but we can also deliberate with them; and deliberating with them is not a matter of counting and adding, but rather a matter of connecting, assessing, combining into coherent, practically meaningful and feasible packages. (6) While interests are always the interests *of* some subject or group of subjects, they are not purely subjective. They are can be grasped by people other than those who have those interests. People can help us think about our interests; they can help us appreciate better their practical importance or salience, enable us to put them in a proper perspective, illuminate the relations among several of our interests, and help us achieve greater coherence among them.[8] (7) Interests of different people can fit together into coherent packages, combinations that can make sense from the practical perspectives of the individuals involved.

Thus, the language of interests enabled Bentham to articulate a conception of individual well-being that is tied to the good of individuals viewed from the inside and that is accessible from the outside and can be combined into an intelligible measure of social well-being. It was, ultimately, for public practical purposes that Bentham sought to define his principle of utility in terms of the universal interest.

[7] Here I build on the discussion in Chapter 2, 33-6, 42-5.

[8] That is a major task of the private moralist ("deontologist") (see *Deont.* I.1, I.2, and *passim.*).

Composition and the Universal Interest

The principle of utility, Bentham repeatedly tells us, requires that we seek the greatest happiness, and that in turn requires that we take seriously the distribution of happiness among all members of the community—as he often put it: the greatest happiness of the greatest number. It is common for Bentham to capture this aim with the concept of the universal interest (or sometimes the public interest). In a typical passage, he wrote that we should "Take for the description of the *ultimate* end [of government the] *advancement of the universal interest*" (B iii. 452, original emphasis). He often used interchangeably the phrases "universal interest" and "greatest happiness" or "greatest happiness of the greatest number" (FG 514–15; LW 140n, 142; SM 69, 252–3).

Bentham established the connection between utility (and happiness) and "the interest of the community" already in the opening paragraphs of his *Introduction to the Principles*. There he told us that the interest of the community is the composite (he says "sum") of the interests of the individuals that compose it (IPML 12). The question, of course, is what is the nature of this composition? In 1820, he characterized the relationship between interests and happiness (and pleasure) as follows: An individual's interest "is either the interest of the moment, or the interest of the sum of life." The former is accounted for in terms of the individual's immediate pleasures; the latter "is what is most commonly meant by the phrase his interest" (*Col.* 239–40). Not only is it summed over the individual's whole life, but it also embraces all that the individual may take an interest in, including the well-being of others (TSA 99; FPP 68n). An individual's interest (in the singular, i.e. comprehensively considered) is that his happiness and interests (plural), summed over his whole life, "be as great as possible" (*Col.* 31; IPML 12). The interest of the community, in turn, is just "the interest of all the individuals taken together," that is, "that the happiness of all those same individuals taken together be as great as possible" (*Col.* 31). The thought expressed here seems to be that, as the interest of an individual is to maximize the net sum of the satisfaction of all her interests (of all that she takes an interest in) over her life time, so the interest of the community—the universal interest—should be conceived as the maximization of the net sum of the satisfaction of the interests of individuals so conceived. This suggests the simple aggregative or summative notion of utility that is standardly associated with classical utilitarianism. Indeed, Bentham often characterized the universal interest as the aggregate of individual interests. He wrote in his *Constitutional Code* that the universal interest is "the good of the community taken in the aggregate" (CC (CW), vol. 1, 43), and in his essay, "Identification of Interests," he wrote that "the universal interest is nothing else but the aggregate of all individual interests" (FPP 133, also 192).

But we must proceed with some care at this point. For, by "aggregate," Bentham typically meant only a collection, not a sum which carries with it the idea of a common measure. Moreover, when Bentham spoke of "the interest of all the individuals taken together" he had just been speaking of interests that are in fact common to them (*Col.* 31); and when he identified the universal interest with the aggregate of all individual interests, he focused on those that survive "the additions of the changes effected by birth and immigration and the subtractions made by death and emigration" (FPP 133). These are only a subset of the interests of the persons in question, not the sum of all their individual interests. Also, clearly in the background, shaping his understanding of the aggregate of individual interests is his assumption of equality (FPP 133, also 97). No individual's interest may be excluded from the universal interest. "As a faggot is comprised of sticks, so is the public of individuals: that one individual is as large a part of the public as another: and the happiness of the one as much a portion of the happiness of the public as the happiness of the other" (UC 100.179). Considering what we have already learned about the role of the notion of equality in Bentham's theory and its impact on his understanding of value, it would appear that the universal interest, in his usage, should be understood not, as the net sum of individual interests, but rather as the composite of the interests of individuals. Thus, we do not yet have a clear view of Bentham's principle of composition. All we know is that the universal interest relates to that which is common to a group of individuals and respects in some way their equal status.

The universal interest, as Bentham understood it, cannot be the net sum of all individual interests because it is both *composed of* individual interests and *opposed to* them—it is composed of certain of the interests of the individuals of the community as a whole, and opposed to others. In fact, the concept of the universal interest is given shape by its contrast with its opposing term "particular interests." The universal interest is not opposed to individual self-interest, but rather to the *particular* interests of individuals. Bentham delimited the universal interest by analyzing the composition of an individual's overall interest. "In every political community," he wrote, "every member has a share in the aggregate interest composed of that of all the members of the community taken together—in a word in the universal interest. [But also] every member has a particular interest in which the rest of the members have no share" (FPP 192; see CC (B) 127). He elaborated this analysis in his *Book of Fallacies*, using the terms 'public' and 'private' to mark the key distinction.[9]

> The mind of every public man is subject at all times to the operation of two distinct interests—a public and a private one. His public interest is that which is constituted of the share he has in the happiness and well-being of the whole

[9] The terminology is interchangeable. He made the same point in his *Constitutional Code* using the contrast between "universal" and "particular" interests: "Be the community what it may, to every member of it belongs two opposite and continually conflicting interests: 1. His share in the universal interest . . . which is common to himself and every other member of the community: 2. That interest which is particular and peculiar to himself, with or without some comparatively small number of associates" (CC (B) 127).

> community, or of the major part of it: his private interest is constituted of, or by, the share he has in the well-being of some portion of the community less than the major part; of which private interest, the smallest possible portion is that which is composed of his own individual—his own personal—interest (B ii. 475).

Within the set of all the interests of a given individual, Bentham distinguished several subsets, each with its own center of gravity in the life of the individual. These centers of gravity are determined by the groups or communities to which the individual belongs, and the interests he shares with members of those groups. With respect to any group, it is possible to distinguish its members' "aggregate interests," those interests they share with other members of the group, from their "several particular and distinct interests," which can diverge from and conflict with their aggregate interests (SM 56). It is possible to distinguish for any given individual his public interest from his particular interests. *His* public interest is his share in the common interest of the community as a whole—that is, of the most comprehensive community presently in view (*Col.* 290). *The* public interest—or universal interest—is that set of interests held in common by all members of the community in the realization of which each member has a distinct and positive share. The universal interest in a community excludes the particular interests of its members. These are the interests which individual members do not hold in common with all members of the community at large, but which are held in common with members of a sub-community of it, or are entirely "personal," and which in every case are defined without regard, and possibly in strict opposition, to the common interests of the community at large. They are interests "in which the rest of the members have no share" (FPP 192). Bentham further decomposed an individual's particular interests into his "personal interests" and his "private interests." The latter can be shared jointly with others in a subgroup of the community at large; indeed, in so far as an individual may belong to several such subgroups, he may have distinct centers of private interest as well. With respect to any one of them, it is likely that a part of a person's "particular" interest will overlap with like interests of other members of the group, and a part may stand in opposition to them as well.[10]

We may conclude that it is possible to identify three defining features of Bentham's notion of the universal interest: (1) it excludes all particular interests; (2) it includes interests of members of the community taken together, where these are understood as interests common to all members of that community; and (3) each member has a share in this universal interest, which is in turn "constituted of" the aggregate shares of each. To clarify further Bentham's notion, let us take a closer look at each of these features.

[10] See Bentham's letter to Diego Colón, 6 December 1820 (*Corr.* 10, 223–4).

UNIVERSAL vs PARTICULAR

By definition, the universal interest does not encompass the particular interests of members of the community at large; correspondingly, particular interests are those interests of members of that community that are not shared by all (or by the greatest number) in the community. Thus, in a first approximation (I will qualify this claim presently), we can say that, for any individual, the universal interest is composed of those interests she has along with all (or almost all) other members of the community—their convergent interests—or at least those which they could (under relatively relaxed conditions) come to share in this way. Her particular interests, in contrast, are those interests that converge with some subgroup of the community (private interests) or are entirely idiosyncratic (personal interests). Because particular interests are not universally shared, pursuit of them in some circumstances can conflict with more widely shared interests.

Hence, particular interests (whether private or personal) can motivate "the sinister sacrifice" (FG 514, also 212f), that is, sacrifice of the morally imperative universal interest to special interests of the few. "By sinister interest understand every particular interest by which, it being opposite to the interest of, that is detrimental to the greatest happiness of, the greatest number, a man is prompted to sacrifice to it that all-comprehensive interest" (FPP 151). Thus, while components of the universal interest are also constituents of each member's overall interest, it is possible that some of one's particular interests will loom larger in one's overall scheme of interests than one's share in the universal interest. If this leads one to pursue one's particular interests rather than support the universal interest, and circumstances are such that pursuit of one's particular interests works against the universal interest, then these particular interests are also sinister. However, we should note that, for Bentham, these interests are not particular because they are sinister, but rather they are (likely to be) sinister because they are particular (CC (CW) vol. 1, 105), and because the payoff to individuals of serving their particular interests is likely, especially in the short run, to appear greatly to outpace the benefit they can expect from realization of the universal interest (FPP 276).

Thus, for the most part (and it is in Bentham's view a very large part), the universal interest and rival particular interests stand in a relationship of "implacable hostility" (OAM 43; SM 252–3). Of course, when there is no particular interest to challenge it, one's "fractional share" of the universal interest will be sufficient to motivate action (FPP 276). And, Bentham admitted, there are times when "the value of his share in the universal interest may in the breast of each man outweigh the value of any particular and sinister interest by which he may be solicited to seek to gratify it at the expence of the universal interest" (SM 241; also *Col.* 51–2). But, he added, these times are rare and fleeting (CC (B) 127; SM 241)—as "frequently exemplified as insanity" (CC (B) 61). Even though the universal interest is the "exclusively rightly directed" end (CC (CW) vol. 1,105), Bentham counseled us not to expect willing and spontaneous sacrifice of personal or particular interest to the universal interest (CC (B) 61).

What is somewhat more likely is that the implacable hostility between the universal and particular interests can be diminished to some degree, not by changing the weight or "value" that an individual assigns to his respective interests, but by reducing the occasions for their coming into conflict. This may simply be the result of the happy, if temporary, coincidence of some particular interests with the demands of universal interest (FPP 151; *Col.* 50). Sometimes, also, an individual's personal interest, when added to his share in the universal interest, can appear to him greater than some other, sinister particular interest and thus move him to prevent the sinister sacrifice (*Col.* 40–1). Moreover, Bentham seemed to think that many desires will simply atrophy in the absence of any hope of satisfaction. Thus, an individual deprived of the means of securing his sinister interests is likely to abandon them, or at least such interests will be drained of their saliency for him (FPP 135, 213). Shrewd political actors (with the universal interest in view) will exploit such happy circumstances when they arise (FPP 56; *Col.* 51–2). Legislators and constitution-makers, guided by Bentham's utilitarian blueprint, will engineer such a junction of private or personal interest with duty directed to the universal interest. A strictly natural harmony of (particular) interest and (utilitarian) duty is not inconceivable or even without example, in Bentham's view, but he thought it was rare. Most of his work on legal, economic, and social institutions was devoted to the artificial identification of duty and interest (FG 513–15; FPP 13–17, 125–47; B ii. 475).

The inevitable conflict between the universal interest and particular interests of all sorts tells us something important about Bentham's principle of utility. Consider again Bentham's claim that spontaneous, willing sacrifice of personal interests to the universal interest is rare. With wry wit he wrote,

> It is the interest of the highwayman that all passengers, of the housebreaker that all householders, be as rich as possible, and that they be as secure as possible against all depredation but that which he practices for his own benefit: but this community of interest does not prevent the highwayman, does not prevent the housebreaker, from being what he is.... [For his] share in the universal interest is never of sufficient value in his eyes to prevent him from making the sacrifice which he is constantly making of it to his own peculiar interest (*Col.* 290).

The echo of Rousseau here is striking, if unintended. Rousseau wrote in the Geneva Manuscript of his *Social Contract*:

> Each person, detaching his interest from the common interest, sees perfectly well that he cannot completely separate himself from it; but his share of the public

> misfortune seems like nothing to him compared to the exclusive good that he claims he is getting.[11]

If the principle of utility is to be understood in terms of the universal interest and if this is how the universal interest is to be understood—that is, if this is the conception of social welfare at the core of the principle—then the principle instructs us to promote some interests of members and not to promote others. This is exactly what Bentham said in his *First Principles Preparatory to Constitutional Code*, where he wrote:

> In this way, in the instance of each individual such part of the whole mass of his happiness as is not adverse to the happiness of any other individual will be, in so far as depends upon the agency of the government, secured to him: the correspondent part of his interest will be provided for: the correspondent part of his desires, of his wishes, will receive its gratification: while all such portions of happiness as he could not be made to enjoy without depriving others of happiness to greater amount will not be given to him: the correspondent part of his interest will be left unpromoted: the correspondent part of his desires, of his wishes, left ungratified (FPP 135–6).

Thus, Bentham's principle of utility looks very different from the principle Rawls attributed to the classical utilitarians. When it is applied to matters of public (especially political) morality, it is not simply a version of individual utility-maximizing applied to the interests of the community as a whole regarded as a kind of super-person. Bentham's principle focuses on only some of the interests of individuals, and leaves aside other interests.

Universal Interest: Inclusive or Oppositional?

Before we proceed to consider the other key features of Bentham's notion of the universal interest, we need to pause for a moment to acknowledge the confusion that a certain inconstancy of Bentham's language can generate. To capture the key idea mentioned in the previous paragraph, Bentham sometimes relied on the phrase "the universal interest" and sometimes on the phrase "the general happiness" or "the greatest happiness of the greatest number." What is more, Bentham often equated "the universal interest" with the aggregate interest of the greatest number in the community, rather than with the interest of all. His strong tendency to portray the universal interest and particular interests as yoked in relations of

[11] Jean-Jacques Rousseau, *The Social Contract and Geneva Manuscript*, R.D. Masters, ed., J.R. Masters, trans. (New York: St. Martin's, 1978), 109.

"implacable hostility" combined with the dominant theme of his late constitutional and institutional writings—the bitter battle between "the ruling few" and "the subject many"—may explain in this imprecision (FPP 69). Let us briefly take a closer look.

When he deployed the notion of the universal interest, Bentham frequently identified it with those interests or concerns that are common to all members of the community in view, those in which each member of the community has a share (CC (CW) vol. 1, 43; FPP 76, 192). I will call this the *inclusive* use of the term. However, other times he associated "the universal interest" with the interests common to the greatest number, or the subject many (the "democratical class"), in the community, clearly implying opposition to the interests of "the smaller number," the ruling (or "aristocratical") class (FPP 68–9, 193, 205; FG 514–15). I will call this the *oppositional* use of the term. Bentham was clearly aware of this duality,[12] admitting that "the phrase universal interest may be employed as corresponding indifferently to the interest of the greatest number as to the interest of all" (FPP 234). This, of course, will not do, since they have very different implications. Used in the oppositional sense, there is a whole class of members of the community whose interests are systematically excluded from the universal interest (although in some cases, their particular interests may temporarily coincide with the universal), while the distinctive point of the inclusive use is to stress that *every* member has a stake in the universal interest. The interests of members of this class may be excluded just to the extent that they are particular. In his constitutional writings on Spain and Spanish America, he acknowledged that it is appropriate to think of the interests that are common exclusively to the subject many, or majority, as particular interests opposed to the particular interests of the few, and he distinguished both from the universal interest. Interests "common to those of the most numerous class" are broader but no less particular, he conceded (*Col.* 31). Later in the same work he tries a different tack: still linking "universal interest" to the aggregate interests of the greater number, he invented a new term, "the all-comprehensive interest" (and later yet: "the great universal interest"), to refer to that which is composed of the interests of all, including members of both the subject many and the ruling few (*Col.* 286, 335).

I am inclined to think that nothing of substance rests on Bentham's shifting usage. It is due, rather, to the fact we noticed in Chapter 2 that he wanted the term "universal interest" to do work in both his positive political-sociological theory and his normative political theory. His willingness to identify the universal interest with the interest of the greatest number comes mainly in those passages in which

[12] In a curious passage in his *First Principles Preparatory to Constitutional Code*, Bentham wrote: "be the community what it may, the aggregate interest of all the members of it [the community as a whole] is never so opposite to the interest of the smaller number [the few] as the aggregate interest of the smaller number may be and generally is to the aggregate interest of the greater number [the majority or subject many]" (FPP 76).

he attempted to analyze political forces in terms of his embryonic class theory. He portrays the aristocratical class (including not only politicians and landed aristocracy, but also clerical and legal elites) as largely idle and predatory, while productive work in society is done by the democratical class, which is vastly larger and largely powerless (FPP 68–76). After the turn of the nineteenth century, he was increasingly inclined to argue that the latter is better able to exercise political power—at least "constitutive power," establishing and overseeing government institutions—and thereby can more reliably serve the universal interest. It is not surprising that, in this context, he was inclined to slip (perhaps not entirely unintentionally) from the inclusive to the oppositional uses of the term, and back again. I see no good reason to place the oppositional use of the term at the center of his theory of value. When it was important for him to articulate carefully the fundamental aim at the core of his utilitarian public philosophy, he relied mainly on the inclusive use of the term.

SACRIFICE AND THE SHARE OF EACH MEMBER IN THE UNIVERSAL INTEREST

Consider now the third defining feature of the universal interest. In his critique of Spanish colonialism, Bentham wrote, "In every political community ... every man has not only an interest which is peculiar to himself, but an interest which is common to him with every other member, and which constitutes his share in the universal interest" (*Col.* 290). Moreover, he insisted that typically one's recognition of this commonality produces a sense of solidarity: "by this community of interest is produced a community of sympathy" (FPP 71; B ii. 476; see Chapter 2, 45). So, in Bentham's view, it is possible for us to identify to some degree with the interest of the community. We might say, following Rousseau, that when each person detaches his interest from the common interest, their respective shares in that common interest begin to lose in comparison with their private or particular interests.[13] Bentham argued that social sentiment, especially this kind of social sentiment, rooted in a sense of common interest, can motivate self-sacrificing actions, but he thought it was more likely to happen among the young than among those more advanced in age.

> The less advanced the age, the greater the probability of an adequately strong propensity to an occasional sacrifice of a man's personal interest to the universal interest: the stronger in a word the force of sympathetic affection operating on the national and other enlarged scales: the more advanced, the more constant the

[13] Rousseau, *Social Contract*, 109.

> preponderance of personal, domestic and other comparatively narrow interests over the universal interest (SM 219n. 4; see also FPP 103–4).

With age, we may not get any wiser, Bentham seems to think; we just wise up. Youthful idealism and the absence of weighty responsibilities of career and family, perhaps, might explain this difference, but Bentham did not pursue this question. It is important, however, not to confuse this kind of sacrifice with a more exacting sort that Bentham also acknowledged, namely, sacrifice motivated by purely extra-regarding interests, which we might call pure altruism. In exceptional circumstances, especially in times of extraordinary danger, Bentham observed, some people may be moved to extraordinary efforts of self-sacrifice, yielding all "the instruments of felicity" and even life itself (SM 185; CC (B) 127). But he sharply distinguished this "all-comprehensive" or heroic sacrifice from the sacrifices we are all regularly called upon to make "at the expence of [our] own particular interest to the universal" (SM 185).

This, too, tells us something important about Bentham's notion of the universal interest, and thereby about the focus of his fundamental utilitarian principle. Bentham's principle of utility, as we have seen, readily countenances sacrifices of individual interests—namely, personal and private interests—but it does not call for or justify imposing more heroic sacrifices. Focused on securing those interests of the community in which each member has a share—and, in some sense, an equal share—it countenances sacrifices only when the individual called upon to sacrifice also receives a significant benefit. Bentham's thought here is not as precise as we might like, but what is clear is that although the principle of utility may countenance and call for sacrifice of (some of) an individual's interests, it never sanctions complete sacrifice of individuals. This point is brought home dramatically, albeit problematically, in two different discussions of the idea that individual interests must give way to the public interest.

The first such discussion appears in his *Principles of the Civil Code*. In this discussion, Bentham professed not to understand the thought that the interest of an individual must be sacrificed to the public interest. (In his *Constitutional Code*, he called such talk "the language of sentimentalism" (CC (CW) vol. 1, 451).) What could this mean? he asked, repeating his frequently uttered challenge: "Is not one individual as much a part of the public as any other?" (see also B iii. 459; B iv. 540; CC (B) 107; UC 100.179). After all, what is properly called the public interest "represents only the mass of the interests of individuals." These individual interests must all be taken into account, instead of considering a part as the whole, and the rest as nothing. The interests of individuals are "sacred"; they are "the only real interests," he insisted. "Take care of individuals; never injure them, or suffer them to be injured, and you will have done enough for the public [interest]" (*Civ. Code* 321). This passage commits Bentham to the Individualist conception of utility, as opposed to the Abstract Happiness conception. However we work out the details of this position—and there are many details to work out—we will need to honor Bentham's deep commitment to the well-being of each individual member of the community. It is that commitment that his notion of the universal interest is meant to articulate.

This commitment is further underlined by his discussion of the problem of the inevitable sacrifice of the interests of some for the good of the community at large in *Official Aptitude Maximized*. In this work, he suggested that even when private interests are sacrificed to the public interest, efforts should be made to compensate those losses "out of [the public's] profit from the arrangement," beyond what is equivalent to their losses (OAM 387). This passage is remarkable for three reasons. First, Bentham here calls for actual compensation, not merely hypothetical compensation (as the familiar Kaldor-Hicks formula counsels). Second, it calls for compensation of losses to private interests, not merely losses to members of the public who do not share equally in the promotion of public interest. This goes beyond that which concern for the universal interest requires. Third, he goes even further, suggesting that the compensation exceed the strict equivalent of the losses incurred. I think we should not rest very much on the details of this suggestion, for I do not know of other places in Bentham's work where this generous scheme is endorsed, let alone elaborated. However, we can confidently conclude that it would be a mistake to attribute to Bentham a view of the welfare of the community that simply submerges the interests and well-being of individuals into an undifferentiated sum of interests of the whole. However we understand it, the universal interest must be seen as an articulated, individually differentiated composite of core interests of individual members of the community.

Interests in Common with Every Other Member

The universal interest, according to Bentham, is "that interest [of a person] common to himself and every other member of the community" (CC (B) 127). How are we to understand this key part of Bentham's notion of universal interest? At this point, Rousseau offers a useful foil. He wrote,

> If the general society did exist somewhere ... the public good or ill would not be merely the sum of private goods and ills as in a simple aggregation, but would lie in the liaison uniting them. It would be greater than this sum, and public felicity, far from being based on the happiness of private individuals, would itself be the source of this happiness.[14]

Bentham could agree with Rousseau that the universal interest is not merely the simple aggregation of private goods and ills, but rather lies in a "liaison uniting

[14] Rousseau, *Social Contract*, 159–60

them." Yet, he could never accept that this liaison consists in some public felicity existing over and above the interests of individuals. He resolutely rejected Rousseau's thesis that "general society [is] ... a moral being with qualities separate and distinct from those of the particular beings constituting it" (*ibid.*). More specifically, whatever Bentham means by "interests common to himself and every other member of the community," he did not mean to include what we might call communal goods—that is, goods which members of a community regard as theirs collectively—as they would say, "not mine or yours, or mine and yours, but ours."[15] As we have seen, Bentham did believe that there is some connection between a community of interest and a community of sympathy (FPP 71; B i. 476), but he thought this kind of solidarity was the product of identification of the common interests, not its precondition.

On the other hand, the liaison Bentham had in mind is not merely a matter of the simple congruence of interests, each member focusing attention on goods or states of affairs of the same kind, for these may be in sharp opposition. You and I may both pursue wealth or fame, but our interests in wealth or fame may not be common. (I seek wealth or fame for me, you seek them for you. In one respect, the objects of our pursuits are the same, but in a more important respect they are opposed.) Moreover, Bentham recognized that the kind of common interests he had in mind can often be realized only through cooperation and collective action. He was keenly aware of what we now call collective action problems. Particular interests are relatively easy to achieve, he argued, because "the individuals who compose the particular interest always are, or at least may be ... a compact, harmonizing body," while "the individuals making the universal interest are on every such occasion an unorganized, uncombined body" (*Col.* 373). A group in pursuit of particular and hence sinister interests is "a chain of iron," but the community at large is often nothing more than "a rope of sand" (*ibid.*). The source of the problem of mobilizing action on behalf of the universal interest lies in the fact that the expected payoff from realization of the universal interest (the share of each in that realization) is outweighed by the cost to each of efforts to achieve it. "Of the partakers in the universal interest, the proportion of interest centered in one individual is too small to afford sufficient inducement to apply his exertions to the support of his trifling share in the common interest" (*Col.* 373). Bentham's point, I think, is not that it never pays to participate in efforts aimed at achieving some element of the universal interest, but that coordinated efforts of large numbers of members are needed and cannot reasonably be expected to happen spontaneously.

It appears that the "common interests" Bentham had in mind resemble what we now call public goods.[16] They are, in fact, convergent interests, interests of all members of the community in certain conditions, or states of affairs, the achievement of

[15] I discuss such collective goods in G. Postema, "Collective Evils, Harms, and the Law," *Ethics* 97 (1987), 425.

[16] So argued Michael James in his "Public Interest and Majority Rule in Bentham's Democratic Theory," *Political Theory* 9 (1981), 51–4.

which benefits each of them. If they had the power, Bentham admitted, individuals would pursue their own personal interests without regard to the interests of others, and willingly sacrifice those interests to their own. Since this is not possible for most of them, they must enlist the aid of others to achieve their interests, and this forces them to focus their attention on only a certain range of their interests. Thus, Bentham wrote,

> In so far as his aim is, to sacrifice all interests to his own—the interests of others, to that which is peculiar to himself, no man finds any effective number of hands disposed to join with his: in so far as his aim is, to serve such of his interests alone, as are theirs as well as his, he finds all hands disposed to join with his (CC (B) 63; see also FPP 135).

He expanded on this in *Securities against Misrule*:

> The way in which, by expression and effect given to the several individual wills, contribution is made to the universal happiness is this. If the result depended upon himself each individual would give expression and effect to such will as in his judgement would in the highest degree be conducive to his own greatest happiness, whatsoever became of the happiness of others, and consequently on most if not all occasions at the expence of the happiness of all others.... But, in so far as the effect of it is by others seen or thought to be detrimental to their own happiness, the will of each individual finds an opponent and bar in the will of every other, and in the will of all together a bar absolutely insuperable. On the other hand, in so far as the effect of each one's will is by every other individual seen or thought to be conducive to his own greatest happiness, the will of each one finds a support and coadjutor in the will of every other: in a word each separate and sinister interest finds a bar, and that an insuperable one, in every other separate and sinister interest: but each man's share in the universal interest finds an ally and coadjutor in every other man's share in the universal interest (SM 265–6).

The common interests in a community can be represented as the product of a kind of virtual negotiation, projects in which one can, or can hope to, enlist others in the community to pursue with them. One's purely personal interests are not intrinsically hostile to the interests of others, but with regard to them one is indifferent to their impact on others—they are, as it were, interests of a solipsist. For the satisfaction of such interests, Bentham delighted in pointing out, one has no reason to hope that one could enlist others in their satisfaction. But there is a range of one's interests in pursuit of which one would could reasonably hope to engage others' efforts. Each party, under the constraint of similar lack of power to achieve his or her own private interests, is forced to seek cooperation of others, and thereby, they are forced to find those interests they share, or can come to share. These are interests in the achievement of which all benefit, because they involve the kind of goods which, if provided to some, will thereby be provided for all.

Bentham offered several examples of such virtually negotiated common interests. In *First Principles*, he wrote:

> In his endeavours to secure himself against depredation and oppression, each man finds all others in general disposed to become co-operators and supporters: for against depredation and oppression at his own expense, no one of them can find any means of security but such as can not but afford the like security to other individuals in general (FPP 213).

Security—public defense against a common enemy and protection of property against common predators—is the most frequent of Bentham's examples of common interests (B ii. 477; *Col.* 290). "It is the interest of every member of the community to possess in the compleatest degree security against evil from all these several sources: against misdeeds by individuals at large and against misdeeds of [government] functionaries" (FPP 153). We might also include public health, economic prosperity, community infrastructure and services like roads, bridges, and the like. They all share the characteristics of public goods. They require co-operative, collective action to provide them, and if they are provided for some they will be provided for all. Thus, each has a share in the realization of components of the universal interest.

Of course, these are the kinds of goods concerning which one would do even better if one did not have to pay the price of one's own contribution to their provision; recall Bentham's wry description of the highwayman and housebreaker. Each has an interest in the abundance and security of everyone, including themselves, but this does not prevent them from being highwaymen and thieves: the "share [for each] in the universal interest is never of sufficient value in his eyes to prevent him from making the sacrifice which he is constantly making of it to his own peculiar interest" (*Col.* 290). Note, the contrast here is not between the cost to the thief of his contribution to security (refraining from housebreaking) and the cost to him of no security, but rather the cost of his contribution and the loss he is likely to realize if he does not contribute (assuming most others will). This is a clear case of a free-rider's calculation.

With this in mind, we can dispel what might look like a problem for Bentham's reliance on the notion of universal interest to articulate his principle of utility. According to his view, it is conceivable that for each member of the community it is the case that their private or personal interests add up to more than their share of the universal interest. It would seem then that promoting the universal interest in some cases will not be in the best overall interest of any of them. This might at first sound paradoxical, but it makes sense if we look more closely at Bentham's idea. Consider such a case. It is true for every member of the community that there is some alternative to the pursuit of the universal interest that would better serve her overall interest, one that she would prefer, looking to her interests alone. But, by hypothesis, there is no single alternative that improves the lot of all, for if there were, presumably, that would better serve the universal interest. But that is just to say, as Bentham stressed all along, that serving particular interests is not the sort of enterprise that one can get all the others in the community to join. It is precisely because particular interests may point in very different directions, that the universal interest is normative for the community taken together; any alternative will serve only some insufficiently extended sub-group, at the expense of others.

Are there any interests of individuals on which all members of the community might converge? It is conceivable that there are very few, but Bentham's public philosophy is not interested in what is conceivable. It is focused on what is likely, given basic features of human nature and the technologies available in society at large to meet the needs of its members. Like Mill, Bentham thought that human beings are sufficiently similar, when it comes to matters of public philosophy, that there will be a substantial core of converging interests, sufficient to constitute a robust universal interest. "The feelings of men are sufficiently regular to become the object of a science or an art" (*Civ. Code* 304). He was sensitive to the vast range of what human beings might take an interest in, but he also was convinced that these idiosyncrasies operate on the margins of social experience. At the core—that is, amongst most members of the community, and at the center of what is important to them—are a largely predictable range of needs, goods, and interests on which they converge.

Bentham gathered these goods together primarily under four closely related heads. These "common interests," he wrote, "correspond to the immediately subordinate right and proper ends of government, maximization of subsistence, abundance, security, and equality" (CC (B) 63).

> The universal interest requires that, in regard to subsistence, abundance, security, and equality, the aggregate mass in the community in question, be maximized: and that in particular the shares, which are the result of the three first, be as near to equality as consistently with security in all other shapes they can be (CC (B)127; see also FPP 153).

These four ends are the focus of Bentham's utilitarian theory of the foundations of civil law (*Civ. Code* 311–26; CC (B) 11–22). These immediate ends, and the goods they provide, are not regarded as means to maximizing the sum of happiness regarded in the abstract, but rather as constituents of the universal interest. They are "immediately subordinate," not in the sense that they are *derivative*, but rather in the sense that they are *constituents*. They are first in line as constituents because they are fundamental to all other potential constituents. They are not the most important interests of individual members of the community in the sense that they form the center of most people's meaningful and happy lives, but rather in the sense that without them any happy and fulfilled lives would not be possible. They are the universal goods that each member needs whatever her (other) interests are. The focal aim of government is not to maximize the aggregate happiness in the community, nor the equal happiness of all, but rather to maximize those common resources that are necessary for all members of the community to pursue their own interests, so long as doing so does not conflict with the equal chances of others to do so as well, promoting "the interest of each in those points in which it is not opposed by any other interests" (FPP 135).

CONCLUSION

As Bentham understood it, the universal interest limits the pursuit of personal interest. Social institutions designed to serve the universal interest are likely to call for the sacrifice of personal interests. But, he made clear, the universal interest also makes pursuit of such personal interests possible, and it always includes each in the benefits resulting from the realization of the universal interest. In both respects, Bentham's view entails that while the (personal or private) interests of individual members may be sacrificed, individuals are not. Each is accorded a substantial share in the interest of all.

The universal interest understood in this way provides the compositional principle presupposed by Bentham's principle of utility, the principle that defines how the welfare of the community is composed out of the welfare of its members. "The more perfect the enjoyment of [goods secured by the four immediately subordinate ends of government], the greater the sum of social happiness" (*Civ. Code* 302). Social happiness is a composite of the welfare of individual members, namely, where the interests of all members of the community focus on the public goods and common interests, primarily those organized under the heads of security, subsistence, abundance, and equality. This principle is not added to his principle of utility, but is a direct expression of his understanding of the value—individual human well-being or happiness—that he placed at the center of his utilitarian theory. Pleasures and pains, abstracted from individuals who experience them, make no moral claim. So, the fact alone that some interests are not given weight at the moral level is not itself an objection to this construal of the compositional principle. It is an objection only if this way of treating individual interests does not respect the fundamental moral value of the well-being of each individual as lived from the inside.

The argument for understanding Bentham's compositional principle in terms of the universal interest rests on the claim that the way to respect this fundamental value, understood as equal for every person, is to focus moral attention primarily on those interests broadly compatible with the interests of others in the community, and especially those interests all members share or can come to share. When choices must be made among alternatives which may benefit some more or differently than others, everyone must be included in the benefits. No one may be completely excluded—not only may they not be excluded from formal consideration in the calculation leading to decisions on the alternatives, but they also may not be excluded from reaping the actual benefits. No one may be sacrificed entirely for the good of any other person or group of persons, even the whole community. Everyone must be able to recognize that, while losers in certain respects, they are gainers in others. The foundations of morality, in Bentham's utilitarian vision, lies in public utility, in that "alliance and partnership of interests" that Cicero liked to call "justice." Bentham called it "the universal interest."

PART II
JURISPRUDENCE

7

Utility, Public Rules, and Common-Law Adjudication

A central theme running through all of Bentham's jurisprudential writings is the conflict between the demands for stability and certainty of law on the one hand, and the need for flexibility in adjudication on the other. Keenly aware of the utility, indeed necessity, of relatively fixed general rules for social conduct, Bentham nevertheless regarded the principle of utility as the sole and sovereign rational decision principle.* Thus, he sought ways to constrain the decision-making of judges while leaving them room to respond to the constantly varying demands of utility in particular cases. The complex history of the development of Bentham's theories of law and adjudication is the history of a series of increasingly sophisticated attempts to solve this central problem of utilitarian political and legal theory.

This history begins to unfold in, and is largely shaped by, Bentham's early reflections on justice, utility, and common-law adjudication. In these early writings, Bentham defined the basic terms of the conflict, surveyed with remarkable insight the issues at stake, and proposed a unique utilitarian solution for his native common-law system. He soon became dissatisfied with this solution and this dissatisfaction set him on a course of increasingly deeper reflections on the nature of law and adjudication that eventuated in a complex and sophisticated jurisprudential theory only a small part of which is presented in his classic jurisprudential work, *Limits of the Penal Branch of Jurisprudence*. However, abandoning his initial solution signaled not the abandonment of the principles underlying his early argument, but rather an increasingly firm conviction that no common-law system, even a substantially revised and reformed one, could adequately satisfy those principles. Only a systematic arrangement of comprehensive codes—the "pannomion"—could hope to answer the demands of publicity on the law. Thus, his early reflections play a pivotal role in the development of his mature jurisprudential theory. In this chapter, I will sketch out his main arguments in these early writings. The rest of the story is told in detail in *Bentham and the Common Law Tradition*, Chapters 5–9. It is revisited and revised in the Afterward to that work.

* Adapted with permission from G.J. Postema, "Bentham's Early Reflections on Law, Justice and Adjudication," *Revue Internationale de Philosophie* No. 141 (1982), 219–41.

Utility, Publicity, and Law: Essays on Bentham's Moral and Legal Philosophy. Gerald J. Postema.

JUSTICE, UTILITY, AND EXPECTATIONS

John Stuart Mill once remarked that, when it came to jurisprudence, Bentham found the battering ram more useful than the builder's trowel.[1] This comment hardly does justice to the careful and sophisticated analysis of jurisprudential concepts one finds in *Limits*, for example, but it is an accurate description of Bentham's standard treatment of some central moral notions. No moral concept suffers more at Bentham's hand than that of justice. There is no sustained, mature analysis of this notion to match the quality of Mill's discussion in *Utilitarianism*. A germ of Mill's analysis can be found in a late (1818) entry in Bentham's commonplace book. "Justice is beneficence," he wrote, "in the cases in which the non-performance of it is considered as punished and punishable by the force of one or another of the several sanctions: principally the political, including the legal, and the moral or popular" (B x. 511). The link between justice and utility by way of the notion of reasons for sanctions is, of course, the cornerstone of Mill's utilitarian theory of justice (*Utilitarianism* V). However, Bentham seems never to have developed this thought. He was most inclined to respond to talk of justice in an entirely polemical fashion, dismissing it summarily as innocently vague, potentially obscurantist, or a mask for social antipathy and malevolence (IPML 10.40 n. b^2; CC (B) 123; UC 14.103–7).

It is remarkable, then, that we should find in his earliest discussion of law and legislation a sketch for an essay on justice.[2] Opening this sketch, he remarked that systematic reflection on law and legislation must begin with determination of the "import" of, and relations between, the two fundamental notions of political theory: justice and utility. "Perhaps there is not a topic in the whole field of political disquisition more universally nor frequently applicable than this nor on which it more behooves men to have their ideas settled" (UC 70(a).17). Our ideas, however, are often "fluctuating," and even when settled, they often betray an inadequate understanding of the idea. For example, it is commonly believed that justice and utility are in direct and constant conflict and that, despite the attractions of utility, justice is the popular favorite in this conflict.

"Why is justice more highly regarded than utility?" Bentham asked. Because, in popular opinion, the demands of justice are clear, determinate, easy to discover and to observe, and easy to determine whether others are observing them; thus, they promise uniformity and stability of judgment. Justice sets a fixed and inflexible standard, while the demands of utility, it is believed, are unpredictable, constantly changing with the changing circumstances. "Justice feigns a rule ready

[1] John Stuart Mill, "Austin on Jurisprudence," *Dissertations and Discussions*, vol. 4 (London, 1874), 159.

[2] In drafts of work written in 1807 and intended for, but not published in, *Scotch Reform* (B v. 1–53), a short essay on utility and justice echoes some of the themes of this early essay (UC 106.170–80, 194–7). For a discussion if this essay, see BCLT, Afterward, 486-7.

fixed and established. Utility recognizes the rule as yet to seek.... Utility is spoken of as something that will yield—Justice as an inflexible line—something that will break rather than bend. Utility as applicable to many measures at a time and these opposite—Justice ... as applicable to but one" (UC 70(a). 17, 18).

As Bentham characterized the conflict between justice and utility, the justice in question is not economic or political justice—a standard of justice against which laws can be measured. Rather, the justice Bentham had in view *presupposes* the existence of established rules (or, as we shall see shortly, of legitimate expectations). Like Hobbes and Hume before him, and Mill and Sidgwick after him, Bentham naturally associated justice with law or, more precisely, with the administration of law. The conflict between justice and utility is the conflict between adherence to established rules and the setting aside of a rule to secure a clear advantage in a particular case. But, of course, the conflict, set up in this way, admits of a relatively straightforward utilitarian solution. Bentham does not reject the general characterization of either justice or utility, but rather argues that what makes justice an attractive political ideal is the very utility of secure and determinate public rules.

> It was sufficiently understood that it was justice, that is the keeping of the chain of analogies ... unbroken, that kept the stock of happiness for the time being together: any decision or act therefore by which it should be manifest that [the] chain was intentionally/knowingly broken (viz: broken in the instance in question with such circumstances as indicated a disposition to break in an indefinite number ... [of] future instances) would have the effect of making it appear as if the whole stock was in danger.... A much greater, because indefinite, defalcation of happiness [is thereby] threatened than the utility of any particular measure assignable could make an addition. Justice ... being superior in utility to utility itself. (UC 70(a). 18).

A reasonably clear argument is discernible through the rough, tortured style of this passage. It is only when utility is mistakenly restricted to immediate expediency that a deep conflict between justice and utility can be seen to arise. Justice demands adherence to established rules in the face of arguments from immediate utility to the contrary; but a careful accounting of the relevant utilities yields the same conclusion, the argument insists. For intentionally setting aside an established rule (in circumstances indicating a disposition on the part of the official to do so in the future) is likely to cause greater insecurity and consequent loss of happiness, than can ever be gained by ignoring the unsatisfactory rule and deciding on the immediately available utilities. Narrowly restricting utility to immediate advantage yields the paradox that justice emerges superior in utility to utility itself. There is no deep conflict, Bentham concludes, between justice and utility, broadly and properly construed.[3]

[3] However, Bentham seemed aware even here that the conflict is not eliminated, for he restricted his argument to cases in which there is in the official action some indication of a general disposition to ignore the laws. It is not clear how important this restriction was for Bentham at this point.

There is no conflict between these two fundamental notions because, in the relevant contexts, the two principles yield the same prescriptions. What accounts for this harmony? Bentham's answer differs significantly from familiar attempts to reconcile justice and utility in Mill and Sidgwick. It also provides an important clue to the nature of the utilitarian foundations of Bentham's theory of law and adjudication. Justice, he insisted, insofar as it is an intelligible standard, simply focuses on a particular *species* of utilities, *and* because this species of utilities is, in the contexts in question, likely to be of overriding importance, the dictates of justice are also very likely to coincide with the dictates of the principle of utility.

Bentham distinguished "original utility" from "utility derived from expectations," which I will call for short "expectation utility" (UC 70(a).20; UC 96.74; *Com.* 235). The distinction is intended to define two exclusive and jointly exhaustive classes of utilities. Expectation utilities depend causally on some belief regarding likely future behavior of public officials or private persons. The class of original utilities includes all utilities which do not depend on such beliefs. However, the expectation utilities Bentham had in mind are those linked to the fulfillment or disappointment of expectations regarding only certain future events. Bentham's notion has little in common with the modern decision-theoretic notion of expected utility. His notion is concerned not with the proper utilitarian assessment of alternative future states of affairs in light of their relative probabilities, rather it focuses on certain *sources* of utility. Nor is he concerned with the pleasures of anticipation and pains of apprehension in general. Bentham does suggest (at UC 70(a).19) that "opinion of original utility" is to be counted among the sources of expectation utility. Yet in a related manuscript he dismisses the notion as a mistake; expectation determined by "expediency," he insisted, falls properly into the category of original utility (UC 96.74; *Com.* 231). Expectation utilities, then, derive primarily from two main sources: (a) habits, customs, or promises (and, more generally, the actions and patterns of behavior of other persons); and (b) law deriving from statute or from the custom of officials (the common law) which he calls the "opinion of praejudication" (*ibid.*). Thus, expectation utilities are those which have their origins in beliefs regarding the likely behavior of persons, private or official, in virtue of established practices, habits, customs, or the general rules (and in some cases the absence of them) which govern their behavior. Excluded from the class are expectations regarding utility-producing natural events.

With this distinction in mind, Bentham identified justice with expectation utilities. "Utility [is] two-fold: 1. original 2. derived from expectation. The term justice… [is a] substitute for (or dependent on) the term utility in the latter sense" (UC 96.74; UC 70(a).19–21). Thus justice, insofar as it is an intelligible political ideal, demands following established rules, practices, and patterns of behavior, which rest for their ultimate authority not on their intrinsic merit or utility, but on the expectations that they engender and protect. Thus, like Hume, Bentham associated justice with conventional arrangements of general rules which structure, underwrite, and seek to protect expectations essential to social interaction and individual planning and action. The model for Bentham, as for Hume, was the law of property. This link, quite clear already in the early manuscripts under consideration, is reiterated a decade or so later in Bentham's study of the principles of civil law. "Expectation is the basis of every proprietary right: it is this [which] affords whatever reason there can be for giving (or adjudging) a thing to one man rather than another" (UC 29.6). "The principle of expectation is the ground of civil rights—the only true principle of civil justice." However, these expectations, and thus justice that seeks to protect them, are given a distinctively utilitarian interpretation. The demands of justice are to be taken seriously just because they concern a species of utility which, in Bentham's view, is of overriding importance.

But why are expectation utilities given such prominence in Bentham's utilitarian scheme?[4] Bentham never explicitly defended the assumption, but we can find in his work suggestions of an explanation. First, Bentham seems to have regarded security of expectations not as desirable for its own sake, but as a necessary condition of achieving all but the most minimal level of individual happiness (the most important utilitarian "primary good," as it were). The passage from his *Principles of the Civil Code* (1780s), which we discussed in earlier (Chapter 4, 79; Chapter 5, 108), deserves our attention here as well. Bentham wrote,

> In order to form a clear idea of the whole extent which ought to be given to the principle of security, it is necessary to consider, that man is not like the brutes, limited to the present time, either in enjoyment or suffering, but that he is susceptible of pleasure and pain by anticipation, and that it is not enough to guard him against an actual loss, but also to guarantee to him, as much as possible, his possessions against future losses. The idea of his security must be prolonged to him throughout the whole vista that his imagination can measure (*Civ. Code* 308).

Bentham defined expectation as the "disposition to look forward, which has so marked an influence upon the condition of man" (*ibid.*). Through imagination and foresight human beings can live in into the future through plans, fears, and expectations. This marks a distinctive difference in the condition of human beings as compared to that of all other sentient beings. Human well-being consists not only in the good of the moment and the *actual* security of future good, but also in the security of expectations regarding the future. This, in Bentham's view, is not just one more source of pleasure and pain alongside all the others; rather, this disposition has a deeper significance for human beings that makes security of expectation a matter of primary utilitarian importance.

[4] For an extended discussion see BCLT Chapter 5.2.

> It is by means of [expectations] that we are enabled to form a general plan of conduct; it is by means of this, that the successive moments which compose the duration of life are not like insulated and independent points, but become parts of a continuous whole. Expectation is a chain which unites our present and our future existence, and passes beyond ourselves to the generations which follow us. The sensibility of the individual is prolonged through all the links of this chain (*ibid.*).

This is, of course, the barest sketch of an argument, but something like the following seems to be suggested. Due to the disposition of expectation, human beings are capable of living to some extent in the future, by planning, structuring, shaping that future, and even more deeply by projecting their present selves into that future. Without a secure, reasonably predictable future, such activities would be difficult, perhaps impossible, and often pointless. But these activities are of enormous value to us. The value lies, first of all, in the sheer delight of exercising these capacities and bringing to completion our own plans and projects. But their value and importance to us runs deeper, for only through such activities can we shape our own identity, and insure our personal continuity over time. Thus, without security of expectations, we experience both the frustration of curtailment of our liberty to plan and to carry out these plans, and the deeper pain of personal discontinuity, of alienation from one's past and future. And, Bentham suggested, a sense of personal continuity is essential to any individual's happiness beyond that restricted to the pleasures and sufferings of the immediate moment. Thus, it appears that security of expectations for Bentham, like the social bases of self-respect for Rawls,[5] is regarded as a necessary condition of any person's well-being, regardless of what the components of that well-being might be. On "stability" depends "every thing that is valuable to a man" (FG 409).

Given this understanding of the importance, as a matter of psychological fact, of security of expectations for individual human well-being, it is not surprising that Bentham should believe that expectation utilities bear great practical weight in utilitarian deliberation. Yet, they are not likely to have the same degree of prominence in all practical contexts. The extent to which human actions can influence expectations, either positively or negatively, will vary greatly with the circumstances and the positions of the agents in question. This suggests another reason for Bentham's assumption of the overriding importance of expectation utilities in the works under consideration. Law and legal officials, he thought, are in a nearly unique position dramatically to affect, shape, secure, or undermine expectations on a community-wide scale. It is not unreasonable, then, for Bentham, given his theoretical focus on law and adjudication, to regard expectation utilities to be of enormous practical importance. In Bentham's public philosophy, and especially the part of it devoted to jurisprudence, expectation utilities loom large.

[5] John Rawls, *A Theory of Justice* rev'd edn. (Cambridge, MA: Belknap Press, 1999), 386–91.

This goes some way towards explaining Bentham's special concern for expectation utilities in his jurisprudential writings, and the close association he sought to establish amongst justice, utility, and law. But despite this close association, it must also be clear that, according to his utilitarian theory of justice, justice is not simply to be *identified* with following established rules, nor is justice elevated, for utilitarian reasons, to the status of an independent decision principle which can, in particular cases, preclude consideration of the demands of utility (as the rule- or indirect-utilitarian understanding of justice would require). I will consider these two points in turn.

First, justice is essentially a matter of respecting expectation utilities, and only derivatively is it a matter of following rules. How far is it true, as Blackstone claimed, that justice is dependent upon law? Bentham asked. "Thus far," he replied: "Where Justice (that is utility insofar as it consists in the observation of Justice) depends upon Expectation and Expectation follows the finger of the law."[6] Justice consists in following the law where following it maximizes respect for expectation utilities. Although this may be true in most cases, it is not true in all. For once we recognize the connection between expectations and justice we can perceive "why certain exceptions [to established rules] may be made in some cases, without injuring or detracting from a rule of Natural Justice." And in some cases, considerations of original utility may provide, in part, the warrant for the exception, "because a manifest tho' less general utility in those particular cases may carry expectation with it" (UC 70(a).19). That is, where original utility seems to counsel setting aside or altering an established rule, expectations may not be seriously disappointed, indeed they may call for the decision, if the utility of the novel decision is sufficiently "manifest" (i.e., publicly recognized). It is not the amount of utility alone that is important here, but rather the assurance of common knowledge of that utility. (This, of course, is most likely to occur, for example, in cases in which great disutility would be caused by following the rule). Established rules have a justified claim on official attention because they provide a focus for public expectations.

Second, Bentham is not arguing for a principled restriction of official attention to consideration of expectation utilities, to the exclusion of all other potentially relevant utilities. His utilitarian theory of justice does not mark a departure from his fundamental view that the principle of utility is always the sovereign decision principle. Tied to expectations is a *species* of utilities which, in Bentham's view, are especially weighty in contexts of official decision-making, and this special weight explains why they tend to override relevant original utilities. Bentham never counseled officials to ignore other relevant utilities. Indeed, he had harsh words for the intellectual indolence of lawyers and judges caused by the doctrines of justice and precedent.

> When lawyers persist in giving to their maxims an authority original, without exception, and without appeal, the most salutary of them turn, upon many

[6] UC 70a.21, citing Blackstone (Bs Com. I, 55).

> occasions, poisonous. There is not one of them which should be established without a standing proviso tacked to it in favor of utility. There is not one of them of which some higher reason cannot be given, so far as it is reasonable, which higher reason ultimately is utility … [The lawyer's attitude] comes of getting certain maxims by rote and applying them undeviatingly as if they were *sui juris* without enquiring whether they may not be suspended by a utility superior to their utility (UC 70(a).31, 32; see also UC 106.172–4).

Where there are good utilitarian reasons for a rule or maxim, the judge must look past the rule to the reasons of utility and treat them as his ultimate reasons for decision and action; the judge will, thus, regard the rules as open to qualification by appeal to greater utility in particular cases. There is no inclination in Bentham, then, to counsel officials to ignore or overlook any relevant utilitarian considerations in their deliberations. Justice and utility are not in deep conflict, in Bentham's view, because justice properly understood is reducible to utility.

UTILITY AND COMMON-LAW ADJUDICATION

The necessary link between the concerns of the preceding section and Bentham's analysis of common-law adjudication is forged in a fragment entitled "Law: Common vs. Statute" which is contemporaneous with the essay on justice and utility discussed in the preceding section. It may have been intended for the same larger work. "Common Law Judges," this fragment argues, "cannot make any exception to a rule of Law, but what are deducible from some other—although it may happen that the rule beneficial upon the whole is so only *ex majori parte*, and not as to those exceptions" (UC 63.49). That is, the doctrine of *stare decisis*, according to Bentham, requires common-law judges scrupulously to adhere to rules established by past judicial decisions or to new rules drawn by analogy from them. This is so even when utility seems to call for an exception to the rule. The reason for this requirement is that:

> The course of expectation was fixed by the general rule which was formed without recourse to those exceptions: instance after instance has happened to confirm the rule before the case that (consistently with independent utility) called for the exception—people acquire a persuasion that any case that shall come within the aspect of the rule will be governed by it … [and] they act accordingly.… This is the expectation [which] was made up before the case calling for the exception was foreseen, it is now too late to alter it after the act has happened (*ibid.*).

Thus, in the name of securing the course of expectations in the community, common-law judges must strictly follow established rules of law, without regard to their individual merits.

From this fragment, it is not clear whether Bentham regards this statement as an accurate report of common-law practice (or theory) at the time, or as a proposal for the improvement of common-law adjudication as he knew it. However, it clearly departs significantly from both the theory and practice of common law in the rigidity of the requirement he attributes to it and in the proposed rationale for it. According to standard common-law doctrine, judges are bound to rules implicit in past judicial decisions, but these decisions themselves do not constitute the law.[7] Rather, as Blackstone put it, they are the best evidence of the law (Bs Com I. 71). The formulation of any common-law rule is always corrigible, even when the rule is formulated explicitly in the judicial opinion of the precedent case. "The *law*, and *the opinion of the* judge are not always convertible terms, or one and the same thing; since it sometimes may happen that the judge may *mistake* the law" (Bs Com I. 69–70). Furthermore, Blackstone and other common-law jurists allow that some precedents can be set aside when the precedent in question is "against reason," or there is very good reason for setting it aside (Bs Com I.71).[8] This relative flexibility is due in part to the fact that, according to common-law theory, established law rests on, and derives its authority from, a shared sense of the historical appropriateness and general reasonableness of the rules. An eighteenth-century judge, for example, wrote, "private justice, moral fitness, and public convenience, when applied to a new subject, make common law without precedent, much more when received and approved by usage."[9]

Bentham's view contrasts sharply with this approach. In his *Comment on the Commentaries*, responding to what he regarded to be Blackstone's garbled defense of *stare decisis*, he asks,

> Why should decisions be uniform? Why should succeeding ones be such as to appear the natural and expected consequences of those preceding them? Not because it *ought to have been* established but because it is established.... The deference that is due to the determination of former judgments is due not to their wisdom, but to their authority: not in compliment to dead men's vanity, but in

[7] See Gerald J. Postema, "Classical Common Law Jurisprudence, Part II" *Oxford University Commonwealth Law Journal* 3 (2003), 11–17.

[8] See generally Rupert Cross, *Precedent in English Law*, 3rd edn. (Oxford: Clarendon Press, 1977), 5, 8–11, 25, 28. This sentiment is echoed in the mid-nineteenth century by Lord St. Leonards: "You are not bound by any rule of law which you may lay down if upon a subsequent occasion you should find a reason to differ from that rule; that is, that this House, like every court of justice, possesses an inherent power to correct an error into which it may have fallen." *Bright* v. *Hutton* (1852), 3 H.L.C. 343 at 388 (quoted by Cross, *Precedent*, 23).

[9] J. Willis, in *Millar* v. *Taylor* (1769), 4 Burr. 2303 at 2312 (quoted in Cross, *Precedent*, 26). See also the following passage from Blackstone: "The authority of these maxims rests entirely upon general reception and usage; and the only method of proving that this or that maxim is a rule of common law, is by showing that it hath been always the custom to observe it. [I]n our law the goodness of a custom depends upon its having been used time out of mind, or, in the solemnity of our legal phrase, time whereof the memory of man runneth not to the contrary. This it is that gives it its weight and authority" (Bs Com I, 68, 67).

> concern for the welfare of the living. That men may be enabled to predict the legal consequences of an act before they do it: that public expectation may know what course it has to take (*Com.* 197, n. c, emphasis in the original).

The authority and practical binding force of past cases, on this view, rests solely on *the fact* that they are established, recognized, and taken to generate (or stand for) general rules, and that, consequently, public expectations come to be fixed to these rules. This authority is independent of the content—the wisdom, justice, or reasonableness—of the rules. Respect for legitimate expectations alone underwrites the binding force of precedent, and permits no deviation from the chain of analogies. Indeed, in Bentham's view, within the common-law system, no improvement of the law may be permitted to issue from the judiciary. He wrote, "I could wish to see it established by those magistrates as an inviolable maxim in the minutest article, to improve nothing: to relish, nay to thirst after improvement, but to fetch it ever and only from its proper source (UC 27.91). Here Bentham argues on utilitarian grounds for a doctrine of *stare decisis* which is more rigid than the contemporary common-law theory and practice itself.

An explanation of Bentham's doctrine might best begin with a passage from another early manuscript in which he articulates more fully his reasons for the "no improvement" maxim.

> Nothing can be of greater importance than that the provinces of the Judge and of the Legislator should be kept distinct. Better were it for the law [to] remain as it is at present, with all its numerous imperfections on its head than to receive amendment at their hands.
>
> Not that a man being a Judge is the less fit for a Legislator: on the contrary no man so likely to be fit as he. No man who has such good opportunities of being acquainted with the details of those imperfections of the law which want correcting. *Tis the provinces/functions that should be distinct and not the persons.* The same person who acting by establishing a rule in the character of a Legislator shall do eminent service, shall by establishing the same rule in the capacity of a Judge do infinite mischief (UC 159.264, emphasis added).

Improvement or reform of the law must not, in Bentham's view, originate from the bench, because judicial activity of that sort involves a deep confusion of function. He does not object to judges exercising legislative power, but to their doing so *in the course of attempting to decide particular cases.*

But we are entitled to ask of Bentham why we should strive to keep the functions of adjudication and legislation sharply differentiated. One possible, now common, argument appeals to democratic considerations. It is argued, for example, that since judges are not democratically elected, and the judicial process does not allow full public participation, judicial legislation is a violation of the democratic rights of citizens to participate meaningfully in the creation of laws that govern their activities and potentially limit their liberties. But this is clearly not Bentham's argument; nor is he ever—even in his later "democratic" period—much inclined to adopt this argument.

Rather, Bentham's argument, as always, depends on the great need to maintain the stability of the law and thus security of expectations. Improvement from the bench purchases "partial good" at the price of the "universal evil" of defeat of general expectations (*Com.* 223–4). The judge, sensitive to the evil or disutility worked by the established rule in the particular case before the bench, will be inclined to make an exception to the rule in a particular case without attending sufficiently to the insecurity he introduces, thus undermining the confidence of the public in the regularity and predictability of the law. The reason why "a new resolution made in the teeth of an old established rule" is mischievous, he argued in the Preface to the *Fragment on Government*, is that:

> it puts men's expectations universally to a fault and shakes whatever confidence they may have in the stability of any rules of Law, reasonable or not reasonable: that stability on which every thing that is valuable to a man depends. Beneficial be it ever so high a degree to the party in whose favor it is made, the benefit it is of to *him* can never be so great as to outweigh the mischief it is of to the community at large. Make the best of it, it is general evil for the sake of partial good. It is what Lord Bacon calls setting the whole house on fire, in order to roast one man's eggs (FG 409).

This argument is troubling in two respects. First, without justification it restricts the good or utility of setting aside, or improving, a rule to that enjoyed by the litigants. No doubt, good of even great magnitude to only one or a few will never outweigh disutility suffered by a multitude. But why ignore other relevant "original utilities"? Bentham gives no clear reason for this restriction, and it seems unnecessary, given the views and arguments regarding expectation utilities considered in the preceding section. Second, the argument from the *Fragment on Government* is framed in quite general terms and thus seems equally applicable against reform of established law issuing from any quarter, and not just against reform from, the bench. If the argument is to be restricted to judicial improvement, we are still due an argument to show that there is something peculiar about the position of judges (or at least judges in a common-law system) which makes doing only partial good at the expense of universal evil inevitable.

One such argument, which Bentham began to develop in the period under consideration, comes to play a central role in his later campaign for codification. He argued that only the legislator (more properly, the code writer) can take a sufficiently general view of the entire field of action and of law, and so alone can introduce reforms that are wide-ranging enough adequately to remedy the defects that exist in the law (*Limits* §21, and generally Gen. View 155–210). On this view, improvement from the bench can at best accomplish only "partial good." Furthermore, incremental adjustment from the bench is likely on the whole to be more disruptive than truly effectively reforming.

But in these early manuscripts we find a second, and in some ways more interesting, line of argument. In "Law: Common vs. Statute," Bentham noted that even in novel cases—cases to which no established rules or past decisions directly apply—common-law judges are bound to decide only by appeal to analogy to established rules and past decisions, and not by appeal, to utility or convenience. He defended this restriction on the ground that under it "those who are to act in any new case may be better able to conjecture beforehand what is likely to be the decision, and to order their conduct accordingly" (UC 63.49). Analogy is, he maintained, "more easily agreed upon" than utility:

> To judge whether such a rule—which is proposed as being like another rule, is so, a man has but to compare the rules themselves. To judge whether it be in itself right, he has a variety of other circumstances to consider, which presenting themselves in different numbers and differently upon different persons ... make this a task much more difficult than [the] former (UC 63.49).

Utilitarian calculation, he argued, is much more complex than argument from analogy, its complexity being a function of both the larger number and the unbounded variety of considerations that must be weighed as well as the fact that these considerations tend in some cases to appear different to different observers. Thus, people are more likely to come to agree on analogy than on utility. But why should that fact, if it is a fact, be important? Should not the relevant consideration for a utilitarian be whether the calculation of utilities is *correct*? Not, I think, in the sorts of situations Bentham had in mind. The utility of rule-governed social interaction often depends largely on the predictable pattern of behavior that the rules define. In such cases, the utility of one or another course of action depends largely on its being agreed upon. But in novel cases (i.e., situation not clearly falling under established public rules) citizens and (secondarily) officials face a special problem of coordination. One person's decision regarding future action may depend largely on the decisions and actions of many others, but their actions depend in turn on his. Sufficiently public rules might serve to focus expectations of all the affected parties and so coordinate their interaction, but in the absence of such rules the parties seem to be left to their own individual devices. In such circumstances, appeal to analogy, Bentham claimed, is much more likely to yield agreement on a desirable pattern of interaction (or rule), and thus succeed in coordinating that interaction, than is any direct appeal to utility. Therefore, established rules of law, and analogies naturally drawn from them, provide a focus for public expectations. From them citizens can, with some reliability, predict the decisions of judges and the behavior of their fellow citizens.

It is worth noting that this conclusion squares with an argument we considered at the end of the preceding section. There we saw Bentham maintain that sometimes it is precisely the superior utility of one course of action which carries expectations with it; so that appeal to original utility may require setting aside an established rule, but without defeating expectations. These two arguments are consistent because the argument for setting aside established rules rests not on the fact that the preferred alternative considered narrowly in fact *maximizes* utility, but on the fact that the utility in question is *manifest*. Where the utility is sufficiently clear and public, it, rather than analogy, may provide the best focus for the convergence of expectations. And since the concerns of justice, and of proper adjudication lie, according to Bentham, with coordinating judicial activity with public expectation (with what is "more easily agreed upon"), appeal to manifest utility under these circumstances, entirely satisfies these concerns.

Bentham goes on in the passage from "Law: Common vs. Statute" to consider an objection. If what is said is correct, then it seems to provide equally good reason for blocking the legislator's consideration of utilities as it does for blocking judges consideration of like utilities. To this objection Bentham mysteriously replies that it does not apply with the same force to legislators, because judges are more likely than the legislators to be "mistaken (i.e., disagreeing with the majority) in their notions of the utility of the alternatives" (UC 63.49). Why the judge is more liable to utilitarian error than the legislator? The key to the answer seems to lie in Bentham's equation of utilitarian error with "disagreeing with the majority." As we saw in Chapter 6, Bentham was inclined late in his career to equate dictates of the principle of utility with the public interest. It might be argued that a democratically elected legislature would be more likely accurately to gauge the majority's interest than judges insulated from the public, and thus be more likely to make correct utilitarian judgments. However, Bentham was never inclined to this sort of argument in his early career. Moreover, it ignores the importance Bentham in his constitutional writings put on transparency of judicial decision-making, and the accountability of judges to public opinion (see Chapter 12). Consequently, this potential reading must be rejected.

However, another and more plausible reading of his equation of utilitarian mistake with disagreement with the majority follows the line of argument already suggested. Implicit in the argument is a contrast between the conditions under which the legislator effectively makes law and those necessary for "judicial legislation." Roughly, on his view, coordination with the expectations of the public ("majority") is essential for successful judicial rule-making, but less important for effective legislative rule-making. The problem is not that the judge is more likely than the legislator to make mistakes with regard to the *actual* proper balance of utilities, but rather that, given the indeterminacy of utilitarian calculation, and the likelihood of different perceptions of the relevant utilities, the judge's determination of the right (i.e., correct by utilitarian standards) course of action may not square with that of the public; indeed, there may be no unanimity amongst the members of the community regarding the proper balance of utilities (UC 106.172–4). Thus, utility does not provide a sufficiently reliable focus of public expectations, whereas expectations naturally converge on "analogy"—that is, on settled rules of law and projections from them into novel or exceptional cases. Now this is of some concern for the legislator, since obedience to law depends (or ought to depend) on public perception of the overall utility of conforming to the law (FG, IV.22ff), but the validity of the products of legislation, their status as laws, does not depend on the convergence of expectations, according to Bentham (or at least not at this stage of his career). In contrast, the legislative effect of judicial activity does depend on just such convergence. Bentham's point seems to be that judicial activity—at least insofar as it has any legislative effect—must coordinate with public expectations in a way that the legislator's activities need not. Thus, if judges were to follow merely their best judgment as to the balance of utilities in a particular case, they would fail to take expectations into account, but in a way different from that which we have considered above. They may, in fact, be correct about the proper balance of utilities and yet, because they do not carry public expectations with them, their decisions defeat those expectations.

This interpretation is confirmed, and the argument is further developed, in another early manuscript. Bentham begins by supposing a case in which "the new anomalous rule . . . [is] in itself more conformable to utility than that which would have been the regular one. Still as things stand it is probable that all things considered the decision would be less conformable to utility" (UC 69.6). This is not because the judge has done his utilitarian sums wrong, but because merely doing utilitarian sums right will not guarantee that the rule so designated will become law. The anticipated utilitarian gains, however, depend on the optimal rules being regarded as law. There are two problems here; both of them are crucial. Such a decision will not conform to utility,

> because it cannot but be doubtful whether succeeding judges will be most swayed by the *insulated* (particular, simple, separate, independent) utility of the new rule or by the *concatenated* utility of the old which it supersedes. Consequently, it is doubtful whether the rule which it is designed to establish will in fact be established. If it be not, the particular mischief stands entirely uncompensated. Secondly, it is yet more doubtful which of the rules the *public* will *expect* the succeeding judges shall be swayed by (UC 69.6, original emphasis).

The key point is that judicial decisions, in particular those intended to have legislative effect, depend for their legal effect upon concurrence by both the body of active judges and the public. A new rule may be singularly attractive on utilitarian grounds, but unless there is concurrence by these two groups with the judge's opinion (even if it is correct on utilitarian grounds), the rule thus adopted by the judge will not be established. It will not be able to perform the essential legal task of providing in the future a focus for public expectations. Thus, effective adjudication under common law requires not so much that the judge get his utilitarian sums right, but that he coordinate his activities with the expectations of both his colleagues on the bench and the public generally. It is for this reason that in some cases *manifest* utility may provide a proper ground for judicial decisions, and in most other cases successful coordination will be achieved not by appeals to utility, but to precedent, or rules naturally projectable from the materials supplied by established rules.

Bentham's argument, then, seems to be the following. The primary and most important function of a system of laws is that of securing community expectations. Its greatest utility lies in defining a stable framework of publicly recognized rules that provide a focus for expectations regarding the behavior of both citizens and officials. In a common-law system, rules and standards of law must be extracted from the actions and decisions of judges and the validity and effectiveness of such rules depend on their being widely recognized or acknowledged by the public. Given such a system, the law can adequately perform its fundamental utilitarian task only if judges resist the temptation to introduce new rules or make exceptions to established rules (without guarantees that other judges and the public in general will come to the same view), even when original utility seems to demand it. Thus "it appears that it is not any degree of wisdom, or probity, however consummate, that can render [it] expedient for a judge to make a sacrifice of utility *concatenate* [expectation utility] to *insulate* [original utility]: in other words to depart from pre-established rules" (UC 69.6).

STARE DECISIS AND THE SOVEREIGNTY OF UTILITY

The originality and interest of Bentham's theory of common-law adjudication lies not in his linking of precedent to considerations of certainty and predictability of law (and thus to security of expectations). This, after all, was common fare already in eighteenth-century legal theory. Blackstone, for example, made a similar argument in his *Commentaries* (Bs Com I, 69). William Paley made a similar argument in his influential *Principles of Moral and Political Philosophy*:

> The general security of private rights, and of civil life, requires that such precedents, especially if they have been confirmed by repeated adjudications, should not be overthrown without a detection of manifest error, or some imputation of dishonesty upon the court whose judgment the question was first decided. And this deference to prior decisions is founded upon two reasons: first, that the

> discretion of judges may be bound down by positive rules; and secondly, that the subject upon every occasion, in which his legal interest is concerned, may know how to act and what to expect ... To remove therefore the ground of expectation, by rejecting the force and authority of precedents, is to entail upon the subject the worst property slavery—to have no assurance of his rights, or knowledge of his duty.[10]

The interest in Bentham's account lies, rather, in his insights into the interdependence of official and public expectations in common-law adjudication, and in his attempt to integrate the argument for *stare decisis*, and common-law adjudication in general, into his general utilitarian practical philosophy. What is distinctive of Bentham's theory is its attempt to weave the doctrine of precedent into the fabric of an essentially direct-utilitarian conception of proper practical decision-making. His is not an indirect-utilitarain or rule-utilitarian theory of adjudication. The principle of utility is, for Bentham, the sole ultimate decision principle. We have already seen evidence of this commitment to the sovereignty of the principle of utility in the first section. It is also clear in his early writings on common law.

As we have seen, Bentham insisted that (a) judges insure that their decisions conform to precedent and to analogies reasonably projectable from precedent, and that (b) these rules have practical force only in virtue of the expectations associated with them. Bentham insisted further that proper judicial deliberation should ultimately focus only on these expectations (or rather on the expectation utilities), and should be concerned with the rules and prior decisions only insofar as they in fact focus public expectations. Proper judicial decisions, in his view, must be made on the balance of expectation utilities:

> The business of the Judge is to keep the distribution of valuables and of rewards and punishments in the course of expectation: conformable to what the expectations of men concerning them is, or if apprized of the circumstances of each case, as he is, he supposed *would be*. To do that he is to put himself in their place (*Com.* 197 n. c; original emphasis).

In his "Preparatory Principles" manuscripts he illustrated his point with the example of a title dispute (UC 69.238–9). In deciding the right to some piece of property, he argued, judicial resolution of the dispute is determined by two sets of considerations (a) the balance of expectations of the litigants, and (b) the balance of expectations of the public at large. He gave the process of deliberation a distinctively utilitarian interpretation. The weight of the expectations, for example, is not

[10] William Paley, *Principles of Moral and Political Philosophy* (London: J. Davis, 1785), 508. Paley's work was written about a decade after Bentham penned the manuscripts under consideration here, although we have no reason to believe Paley was acquainted with these manuscripts.

to be assessed according to the strength of the legal-doctrinal *arguments* for title from existing rules of law, but rather by determining the subjective strength of the expectations according to the following method:

> What then has the judge to do? One thing and one thing only: ... to put himself in the place of both: of the parties and also of the public (to measure the strength of his own expectation). He supposes himself first in the situation of one of the parties then in that of the other. He observes in which of the situations his own expectations would be strongest, and that party in whose situation he finds his expectation to be the strongest is the party in whose favor he determines (UC 69.238).

But since in the present context expectation utilities are the overwhelmingly weighty utilities, this is equivalent to direct balancing of the relevant utilitarian considerations:

> The ratio of the number that represents the balance of pleasure accruing to the society in the case of its being given to Titius, to the number that represents the balance of pleasure accruing in the case of its being given to Sempronius, will represent the chance that the act of our legislator or judge has for being conformable to utility (UC 69.98).

Thus, proper judicial reasoning must look behind the existing rules to the utilitarian concerns underlying conformity to them. Powerful utilitarian arguments require judicial conformity to precedent, but the sole relevant decision principle is still the principle of utility itself. We might ask, however, does this not undermine the doctrine of *stare decisis*? Bentham considered this objection: "Hard, then, it will be said, and novel is the task you have set to Judges. Nice the test you have set up of a well-formed judgment. [But] where is the judge whose practice shall abide it?" To this he replied, "It will be proper to observe that in general the line of uniformity is the line of utility. That the road to utility lies in the beaten track of precedent; ... the more steadily they adhere to [precedent, the more] do they discharge the duties/business of their function" (UC 69.199).

There is no conflict, he insisted, between his requirement that the judge decide each case on its utilitarian merits and the doctrine of *stare decisis*, because both generate the same results. There is an extensional equivalence obtaining between the two doctrines. Not content to leave the matter here, however, he insisted further that his account is not only prescriptive—requiring judges to appeal to utility in each case—but also properly *descriptive* of the actual practice of (some model) judges.

> Many a grave Magistrate who judges causes as the Clubman before St. Dunstans sounded the horn and who like Mons. Jourdain in the play has been talking prose all his life time without knowing a syllable of the matter, may well be surprised, perhaps, at this account of what he has been doing, but let him reflect a while and then answer whether it is not a just one (*ibid.*).

The extensional equivalence between the dictates of *stare decisis* and the dictates of utility is no mere accident, since any judge, fully self-conscious of his decision-making activity, would have to admit that he in fact followed precisely the procedure Bentham outlined and recommended, although perhaps he would not readily admit that publicly. The doctrine of *stare decisis* then, does not describe actual judicial deliberation *(that* is determined only by utility), but it does issue a sort of public guarantee, and so (Bentham hoped) provides an adequate focus for public expectations to which, then, the utilitarian judge must direct his deliberation. The publicly recognized doctrine of *stare decisis* determines not so much what judges may or must do, but rather what they *can* do, what the available decision-relevant options are for them. The existing rules and projections by analogy from them to a large extent fix expectations and thereby expectation utilities, which, for Bentham, are the dominant utilitarian considerations judges must weigh.

Although he soon called for the complete abandonment of common law, we can see in this early account of common-law adjudication some of the central features of his mature theory of adjudication. We see here, as in his account of utilitarian adjudication under a code of laws, an attempt to unite his deep commitment to the sovereignty of the principle of utility with his recognition of the need for a device which can focus public expectations in a way that public knowledge of the practice of direct appeal to utility cannot. Within the common-law system, the doctrine of *stare decisis* was supposed, in Bentham's view, to do this job. Later, Bentham assigned the task to a comprehensive but ideally simple and publicly accessible system of codes of law (the "pannomion"). It is doubtful whether the strategy could succeed in either case. Bentham quickly came to see that even if, in the common-law system, it did meet with some success in securing expectations, it would do so at the price of substantial rigidity in adjudication. Bentham seems to have been acutely aware of this problem and he did not long remain happy with his solution. Indeed, his argument for *stare decisis* appears curiously half-hearted. He argued that common law, *if* it is to answer the purposes of law, must be governed by a strict and unbending doctrine of *stare decisis* (*Limits* 193). But the costs assessed in terms of its inflexibility and its inability, despite all efforts, to provide suitably determinate predictable legal standards were in Bentham's view so great that he came to the firm conviction that common law must be completely scuttled, to be replaced with a more suitable alternative form of law and adjudication. Common-law theory and practice soon became, for Bentham, the main target of a life-long critical attack.[11] Nevertheless, the early arguments designed to salvage what he regarded as the essentially unsystematic, unstructured, and largely unpredictable legal arrangements characteristic of common law remained the focus of his general theory of law and adjudication throughout his career.

BENTHAM'S CRITICUE OF COMMON LAW

When Bentham launched his withering attack on common law in the 1770s, he was entering an on-going debate with a familiar dialectic.[12] Like many critics of his day, Bentham decried the overwhelming technicality and impenetrability of common-law doctrine. The substantive doctrines of common law, having developed from a bundle of special writs defining simple causes of action, over the centuries were stretched and contracted by analogy, fiction, and liberal interpretation. As a result, they had become highly technical, complex, very specific, and resistant to any systematic general statement and even more resistant to reform. Bentham readily agreed with Coke that the "reason" of the common-law bench and bar was "artificial," but, to his mind, this in no way recommended it; on the contrary, it guaranteed that common law was "technical," "absurd," and ultimately "dishonest" (B iv. 498). Contrary to its orthodox doctrine, common law, according to Bentham, was quite literally *nothing*, if not judge-made.[13] Who made the so-called unwritten law? "If not judges, then, who ... [for] laws don't make themselves" (LW 124–6; see *Com.* 223).

Such a system of judge-made law is unavoidably retroactive ("dog law"), he charged,[14] and undermines responsible allegiance to the law. Judge-made law secures obedience and social order only by playing on the blind fear of citizens, not by addressing clear directives to them and articulating the reasons for these directives (B i. 161; UC 69.151, 163). As we saw above, fundamental problems with this system lay not in judges making new laws, nor in permitting a degree of judicial flexibility in the adjudication of specific cases. "Not that a man being a Judge is the less fit for a Legislator: on the contrary no man so likely to be fit as he." Rather, the problem lay in the confusion of the functions of law-making and law-applying in the common-law system (UC 159. 263). The potential utility of making new laws

[11] The arguments in the following section are discussed at greater length in BCLT, Chapter 8. See also David Lieberman, *The Province of Legislation Determined* (Cambridge, 1989), 219–40; Michael Lobban, *The Common Law and English Jurisprudence, 1760–1850* (Oxford: Clarendon Press, 1991), Chapters 6 and 7, and Michael Lobban, *A History of the Philosophy of Law in the Common Law World, 1600C–1900* Dordrecht: Springer, 2007), 162–7.

[12] Lieberman, *Province of Legislation Determined*, 219.

[13] See, B iii. 223–4; B iv. 483–5; B v. 546; RJE vii. 539 n. *; CC (B) 8.

[14] "When your dog does anything you want to break him of, you wait till he does it, and then beat him for it. This is the way you make laws for your dog: and this is the way the judges make law for you and me. They won't tell a man beforehand what it is he *should not do* ... they lie by till he has done something which they say he should not *have done*, and then they hang him for it" (B v. 235).

to meet changes in social conditions, or greater appreciation of the complexity of situations governed by law, and of responding flexibly to them, cannot be achieved without paying a prohibitively high cost in insecurity, uncertainty, and potential corruption.

Bentham's critique of common-law practice might appear inconsistent, charging common-law practice simultaneously with excessive rigidity and uncontrolled judicial flexibility, but his view was that the contradiction lay not in his critique, but in the institutional realities of the common-law system itself. Competing forces deeply embedded in the institutions, he argued, are constantly and disastrously at war with each other. The two forces, technical rigidity and arbitrary flexibility, are antagonistic but interdependent, arising from features deep in common-law practice itself. I have elsewhere called this "the paradox of inflexibility" (BCLT 273-9).

Bentham argued, first, that that common-law judges, finding that the flexible conception of precedent outlined in the previous section failed to provide the sufficient security and predictability, came to practice a more rigid doctrine of *stare decisis* as a "check to the Judges" and guarantee "that men may have a certain rule to guide them and know what they have to expect" (UC 50.124; see also UC 63. 49). Indeed, Bentham maintained, "It is only in as far as subsequent decisions are rendered comfortable to the rules that are fairly to be drawn from prior decisions that such prior decisions can answer, in any even the most imperfect degree, the purpose of a law" (*Limits* 193). However, the inevitable consequence of such a regime of *stare decisis* is rigidity of the judicial decision-making process. A certain "hardness of heart" became "predominant in the system."[15] This he attributed to the fact that a strict doctrine of binding precedent, for all its merits in underwriting citizen security and the predictability of the law, requires that judges and lawyers turn a blind eye to special circumstances and the harms done to particular parties by precedent-based rules (even when they are reasonable), in order not to lose the benefits of general perception in the community of adherence to predictable rules (*Com.* 195). Ironically, the allegedly vast experience of the common-law judges in "human affairs and conversation,"[16] which supposedly equipped them for the most sensitive and particularized grasp of practical problems, is deadened, even destroyed, under the necessary regime of *stare decisis*. This is inevitable, he thought, because the common law insists on combining the functions of judicial law-making and law-applying. For the judge must always keep uppermost in his mind the systemic effects of his decisions—in particular, its effects on the perception of security and predictability of the law in the general public.

But this rigidity has a paradoxical consequence. In reaction to the rigidity imposed by *stare decisis*, pressures develop both within the judiciary and outside

[15] OLG 194–5, n. i. This passage is not included in *Limits*.

[16] Matthew Hale, "Reflections upon Mr Hobbs His *Dialogue*," in Matthew Hale, *On the Law of Nature, Reason, and Common Law: Selected Jurisprudential Writings*, Gerald J. Postema, ed. (Oxford: Oxford University Press, 2017), 190.

of it to find some source of flexibility and reasonable sensitivity to the needs and circumstances of litigants that are ignored by the ordinary judicial standards and mode of decision-making. Thus, legal fictions, abstract and largely empty notions like "reasonableness," "policy," "natural law," and Latinized principles like "*contra bonos mores*" creep into law and the decision-making practices of common-law judges. Under these auspices, judges can assess the equities of particular cases while maintaining the appearance of merely applying the existing common law. However, they give no concrete guidance to the judge. In effect, they issue a blank check to the judge to decide on his best judgment. The door is opened again to unchecked and unaccountable judicial decision-making, and, thus, to arbitrariness, bias, and caprice. Thus, matters are even worse under this new regime, than they were under the original regime of judicial decision-making without *stare decisis*; for now, the common-law judge "to the great astonishment of the spectators, draws from the same fountain [of law/justice] bitter waters, or sweet" (B i. 326), as he wishes. He can never lose: if he conforms to precedent, he is praised for his principled stand, and if he sets precedent aside in view of the equities of the case, he is praised for his "liberality" (B vii. 308). This flexibility is available to judges in virtually every case because it is the product of features deep in the structure of common-law adjudication. Paradoxically, the increasing rigidity of *stare decisis* creates the opportunity for unconstrained flexibility of judicial decision-making.

This paradox enabled Bentham to focus with brilliant intensity his criticism of common-law practice, but the basic elements of this criticism were not unique to him. What sets Bentham's criticism apart is his insistence that the paradox of inflexibility signals incoherence of common law at a deeper level. If we take common law seriously on terms of its own theoretical self-understanding, he argued, we can only conclude, "As a System of general rules, Common Law is a thing merely imaginary" (*Com.* 119). Common-law theory is incoherent; whatever it is a theory of, it cannot be a theory of some kind of *law*. Common-law theory is committed to what we might call the "corrigibility thesis" according to which, although judges are empowered to settle particular cases, any formulations of rules justifying their decisions, even those of the deciding judges themselves, are corrigible, open to challenge and reformulation. (Recall that Blackstone wrote that the *law* and *the opinion of the judge* are different things, because it is possible for the judge to mistake the law.) Common law exists not in the case or judicial opinion, but rather in shared practice. This thesis, Bentham charged, is incoherent.

Bentham's argument takes the form of a dilemma arising from a single, uncontroversial premise. The premise is that in order for laws to guide the actions of those whom they address, they must be both authoritative and general: "To serve as ingredients in a system of Law we must have not ideas of individual items of conduct, but ideas of sorts of … conduct" (UC 69.151), and we must have some reason to take such general directives as *legal* and binding. From this, the dilemma for common-law theory arises immediately, according to Bentham. If a proposition of common law is authoritative, it can only be particular—the decision or command of a judge regarding just the resolution of the particular case before him—and hence is not law (because not general); and if it purports to be a statement of a general rule of law, it cannot, on common-law theory's own assumptions (the corrigibility thesis), be authoritative, and hence, again, is not law (*Com.* 153–4).

Bentham did not deny that it is possible for common-law lawyers to construct rules from cases—defeasibly but still reliably—by "induction" or "abstraction"; indeed, he thought these general propositions may "appear to be the just expression of the judicial practice in like cases."[17] Moreover, he allowed, judicial decisions can, "in virtue of the more extensive interpretations which the people are disposed to but upon them, have somewhat the effect of general laws" (*Limits* 161). However, he insisted that such rules are ultimately illusory, because they are merely "inferential entities," fictitious constructions. The problem is not merely that they are ontological fictions, but rather that these constructed propositions are nothing but conjectures (*Com.* 95), the expressions of nothing more than private opinion:

> From a set of *data* like these [namely, a set of judicial decisions] a law is to be extracted by every man who can fancy that he is able; by each man perhaps a different law: and these are the *monades* which meeting together constitute the rules ... of common or customary law (*Limits* 195).

Rules constructed in this way are nothing more than "the idea that *you* have formed of the act in question, the idea that *I* have formed of it, the idea that *Titus* has formed of it" (UC 69.151).

This creates two problems, according to Bentham. First, on common-law theory's own assumptions, no private conjecture or opinion has authoritative status. So, these cannot count as law. "To serve as ingredients in a system of Law, we must have not ideas of individual articles of conduct, but ideas of sorts of articles of conduct: general ideas taken off from these particular ones; ... But who shall take them off? Titus? Whose shall those words? Titus's? Then would Titus be a Legislator. But Legislator, by the supposition, there is none." (UC 69.151; see also *Limits* 185–6). More fundamental, in Bentham's view, was the problem that these private conjectures and personal inferences converge only by accident. "These ideas exist," he argues, "but are ... these ideas of one and the same description? Perhaps they are; perhaps not" (UC 69.151). And whether the rule that one party constructs happens to be the same as that of another, or either of them match that of a judge, are entirely matters of sheer chance. "Whether in any case [the rule] of the pleader shall happen to be the same with that of the Judge is a matter of cross and pile" (*Com.* 210).

[17] UC 100.98. In *Limits*, Bentham wrote, "to make a rule that can serve for cases yet to come ... a general rule must be created by abstraction out of this particular proceeding" (186).

In his *Dialogue between a Philosopher and a Student of the Common Law*, Hobbes complained that common law is not statute but "philosophy," a matter of conjecture and constant disputation (*Dialogue* 29). Likewise, Bentham charged that common law is nothing but a matter of "unauthoritative jurisprudence" (*Limits* 162). However, he insisted, law is—it must be—a matter of public standards, publicly declared, publicly authorized, publicly accessible. What we need from law are "common standard[s] which all men acknowledge, and all men are ready to resort to" (UC 69.188). Private conjectures, no matter how clever, or expert, or accurately capturing the import of a line of cases, cannot serve as law and cannot claim status as law. The corrigibility thesis of common-law theory, and the associated idea that law resides in the reasonable and disciplined practice of lawyers and judges, utterly undermines its coherence.

Thus, the uncertainty Bentham decried in the ordinary practice of common law was not merely an unfortunate failure to live up to its standards, a temporary flaw that might be remedied through devices like more systematic, accurate, and public reporting of cases. The source of the uncertainty and indeterminacy of common law lay at its root; it was a fault in the way in which law was conceived by common-law theory, a fault that had devastating effects on common-law practice. Can this fundamental problem be escaped by admitting, what common-law theory sought to deny and disguise, that judges actually make the rules they articulate in the course of adjudicating cases? This solution, however, just puts us face to face with the paradox of inflexibility again, Bentham argued. Forced to introduce some degree of stability into the system of judge-made law, it embraces a strict doctrine of *stare decisis*, only to find that it thereby increases rather than remedies the instability and unaccountable judicial arbitrariness endemic to the system.

It might appear that Bentham's critique of common-law theory and practice begs the most important question between positivist and common-law conceptions of law, viz., whether law should be conceived of on the model of discrete, publicly articulated rules *made* or *posited* by an authorized or authority-bearing law-maker. However, I think Bentham's commitment to this model is not presupposition, but consequence of a deeper assumption about law which he assumes he shares with common-law jurists: that law is necessarily a matter of common *public* standards. Common law fails, most fundamentally, not because it fails to fit the model of command, or because its makers cannot be manifestly identified, but rather because anything it puts forward as candidates for legal norms fails on this publicity test.

Bentham's dispute with common law concerns how to explain this feature of law, and the forms in which it is manifested. Bentham's quasi-positivist account of law can be seen as a product (in part) of his attempt to explain its essentially public character and the implications he drew from this explanation regarding the necessary formal characteristics of law. Frank Michelman captured Bentham's intuition well (no doubt without intending to do so) in the following passage:

> The very notion of law connotes both something that transcends individual deciders as well as individual decisions, and also something that binds deciders, as it binds decisions, together. The judge is to invoke as justification a standard that not only is generally and categorically framed, drawn not just from the instant case and applicable to all relevantly similar cases; but also is public, drawn from the same sources by the same methods, as other judges use.[18]

The notion of law's public character assumes, first, a realm of agency, of rational deliberation and action, and of justifications for actions taken. But it is not a realm of strictly individual or private action, but rather *common* or *public action*, as well as action *in public*. It is the realm in which agents, who are and will probably remain strangers, nevertheless interact, whose actions and decisions are interdependent in important ways, who thus exchange evaluations and criticism of those actions and decisions, and who often deliberate and act together. The intuition of the public character of law is that law is something which facilitates this activity, or a matrix within which it takes place. Law binds the deciders, their decisions, and those affected by the decisions together.

Bentham's position is clear in the familiar discussion in Chapter IV of his *Fragment on Government*. Bentham criticized natural-law theory for including standards for moral assessment of law among criteria *of validity* of laws, thereby treating the question of one's moral obligation to obey a particular law as *automatically* settled by settling the question of its validity. These, he insisted, are two different questions. The former is a question which one must decide on the basis of one's best judgment; the latter is essentially a matter of public criteria. While utility provides the only rational basis for obligation, it can at best only define for "each man in particular the juncture for resistance" (the limit of obligatory obedience), it cannot provide assurance that when resistance is justified for one person it is at the same time justified for everyone else (see BCLT 237-44). Bentham clearly distinguished between what is available to (or recognizable by) *each person individually*, and what is mutually recognizable and *publicly accessible*. While the deliverances of the principle of utility are, he believed, available to *each* of us, they cannot supply the relevant standard of the validity of law when they are not mutually available *to all*.

The problem with common-law theory, then, is that any convergence of interpretations of the law must be regarded as entirely accidental. "Whether in any case [the rule] of the pleader shall happen to be the same with that of the Judge is a matter of cross and pile"—that is, sheer luck (*Com.* 210). But convergence or

[18] Frank Michelman, "Justification (and Justifiability) of Law in a Contradictory World," *Nomos*, XXVII (1986), 73.

mutuality is an *essential* property of law. Thus, the absurdity lies in the suggestion at the heart of common-law theory that something could be a valid or true proposition of law while not publicly *recognized as such.*

Bentham's alternative was complex. Embracing the "thetic" conception of law, which we will discuss in Chapter 8, he insisted that law must be the product of authoritative law-making, identifiable by formal standards of authenticity; but also formally authenticated law must take the form of thoroughly systematic and manifestly reasonable code ("pannomion"). The reasons of each provision of the code must be articulated in the language of the general, public interest and must accompany the code.

ADJUDICATION IN THE SHADOW OF THE PANNOMION

Bentham's critique of common-law theory and practice revealed a theme that runs deeply through all his jurisprudential writings: law is an enterprise of public rules, procedures, and institutions, the primary task of which is to define and structure social relationships and thereby coordinate social interaction. The ultimate end, of course, is to promote the welfare of the community as defined by the principle of utility. Bentham came to see that the most fundamental problem that utilitarian universal jurisprudence had to address was the problem posed by the ever-present tension between the need for stability and certainty of the law, on the one hand, and its ability to respond flexibly and reasonably to constantly changing particular circumstances, on the other. Traditional common law bought flexibility at the price of radical uncertainty and vulnerability to corruption and abuse; and attempts to bring stability and predictability to the practice created rigidities and a mind-set of mechanical judicial decision-making that was blind to the substantive merits of particular cases and keen only to follow the rules even if absurd.

It is important to recall Bentham's diagnosis of the inevitable failure of common law. First, it fused the two very different functions of law-making and law-applying. Judges made law in the course of adjudication and, to maintain the integrity of the law-applying process had systematically to deny they were making law while all the time doing so. Second, the laws thus made were inaccessible to all but a professional elite and even then were at best only the product of conjecture. Common law lacked publicity. Third, judicial law-making had the benefit of close-to-the-ground experience, but no systematic view of the effects of decisions on the law or the community in general, hence the laws were likely to do local justice while causing larger scale and long-run disasters. Moreover, he argued that attempts to introduce stability and publicity through a principle of precedent and public recording and digesting of decisions ultimately made the problem worse because flexibility had to be sacrificed in order to achieve a reasonable degree of stability. Yet such flexibility was essential in his view. Rational (that is, proper utilitarian) decision-making,

Bentham argued, demands that the judge be empowered and equipped to respond to the unique circumstances and profile of needs and interests of particular cases. Because this was impossible in the common-law system, an entirely different form of law and adjudication had to be instituted.

Law, on this new model, was to take the form of a system of comprehensive, complete, and fully public codes with the reasons for all its components, drawn from the principle of utility, interwoven throughout. The defects of the common-law system were to be remedied, and the tension between certainty and flexibility resolved consistent with the demands of publicity and utility, through his scheme of codification.[19] The codes must be complete and comprehensive; in the codes all areas of life to which law might properly address itself were comprehended. "In a map of the law executed upon such a plan there are no *terrae incognitae*, no blank spaces: nothing is at least omitted, nothing unprovided for ... Such are the fruits of a method planned under the auspices of the principle of utility."[20] Bentham was convinced that a set of rational codes constructed on this model, naturally arranged according to universally recognized needs of public utility, and made fully public, would provide a reliable focus of expectations in the community and thereby guarantee security. Moreover, the functions of law-making (and law-amending) and law-applying were to be sharply separated. Expectations of citizens could be focused reliably on the activities and products of the recognized, authentic law-maker, and, at the same time, law-appliers could treat the legislation or code as the rules for them to apply. Since the codes attracted the expectations of citizens apart from the judge's activities, the judge would find that in most cases, the best decision on the merits all things considered was the decision required by the publicly promulgated and acknowledged law. Bentham built a firewall between adjudication of particular cases and procedures for recommending amendments to the code.

Yet, Bentham's solution, clear in its general outlines, becomes less clear when one digs deeper into its details. It is tempting to think that adjudication under the code, in Bentham's view, was to be strictly a matter of judicial application of the codified rules as they found them. On this reading, judges were to be nothing more than the handmaids of the code, except that they could suggest revisions of the code to a code revision committee. However, Bentham's early reflections on justice and adjudication make clear that he was keenly aware of the possibility of cases arising in which the law works an injustice (or fails adequately to serve the ends of utility) even though it may not be possible to construct a general exception that would not in the long run do more harm than good (UC 106.194–7). This might be so even when the very important "expectation utilities" are considered. Since Aristotle, such cases were thought to call for "equity" (or in

[19] See Philip Schofield, "Jeremy Bentham: Legislator of the World," in Michael D. A. Freeman, ed., *Current Legal Problems* 51 (1998), 115–47.

[20] OLG 246; this passage is not included in *Limits*.

Bentham's terminology, "reasonable flexibility"). A system that was unable to respond to these cases in a reasonable way would seem to share some of the defects of the common law and to violate Bentham's understanding of the role of his principle of utility in practical deliberation and decision-making. Based on evidence considered earlier in this chapter and the strong "anti-nomian" views manifest in his theory of evidence and throughout his procedural writings (see Chapter 9) I argue in BCLT that in fact Bentham's mature view of adjudication under the code provided for just such flexibility (BCLT, Chapters 10–12). Judges working under Bentham's system of codes were to decide particular cases according to their best judgment of the balance of utilities in the case, always mindful, of course, of the code and especially of the course of expectations that public knowledge of the code had established. The code, as viewed by judges, was not a set of fixed, peremptory rules, but a systematic and expertly drawn map of the relevant utilitarian considerations. It was a reliable guide to considerations that had to be weighed and to the best decisions balancing them in most cases. Yet, Bentham admitted, it anticipated all relevant utilitarian circumstances *in genus,* but not necessarily in every sub-species (B iv. 538). There is always a role for the dedicated, impartial, responsible judge to decide the particular case in front of him or her, he thought. He also insisted upon safeguards to protect this structure of adjudication against abuse. Most importantly, judicial decisions were denied all precedential effect. Only legislators, and judges acting in explicitly recognized and authorized law-making capacity, could alter or add to the law. The legal effect of judicial decisions was strictly limited to the parties to the litigation decided by them. In addition, judicial responsibility—"moral aptitude" as Bentham called it—was to be maximized, especially through publicity of all proceedings and decisions and other related institutional devices. Thus, Bentham sought systematically to resolve the tension between stability and flexibility in a way typically for Bentham: rather than qualify and restrict his fundamental principles, he built institutions which enabled them to flourish.

Several critics challenged this reading of Bentham's theory of adjudication.[21] Carefully surveying Bentham's late writings on codification, Dinwiddy argued that Bentham's code denied judges the power to decide cases against the code when they thought the balance of utilities required it. Bentham's anti-nomian strain is undeniable, Dinwiddy conceded, but argued that Bentham carefully limited it to the domains of evidence and procedure. He did not entertain it with respect to any areas of substantive law.[22] Flexibility was guaranteed, he argued further, not by allowing judges to decide on their best judgment of the relevant utilitarian

[21] John Dinwiddy, "Adjudication under Bentham's Pannomion," *Utilitas* 1 (1989), 283–9; Francesco Ferraro, "Direct and Indirect Utilitarianism in Bentham's Theory of Adjudication," *Journal of Bentham Studies* 12 (2010), 1–24; Francesco Ferraro, "Adjudication and Expectations: Bentham ion the Role of Judges," *Utilitas* 25 (2013), 140–60.

[22] Dinwiddy, "Adjudication under Bentham's Pannomion," 285–6.

considerations, but by the system of amendment in which judges were given a key role to play.[23]

Unfortunately, Bentham's several discussions of his proposed institutional arrangement for amending the law are complex and multi-layered. Resolution of this debate among interpreters of Bentham's theory of adjudication calls for a close reading of all these passages. I have attempted to do so in the Afterword to the second edition of BCLT. There I conclude that there may be no way to reconciling all parts of his jurisprudential theory into a single coherent account. The tensions he highlighted in common-law jurisprudence were, in his own view, tensions deep in law. He was convinced that English common law exacerbated them and his codification proposal, and constrained adjudication under the codes, went a long way toward resolving them, but could not ultimately eliminate them. If any resolution of this debate over the theory of adjudication Bentham developed in his late constitutional writings is possible, I argue in the Afterword, it must take into account a key distinction between Bentham's utilitarian account of practical reasoning, which lies at the foundation of his thinking about morals and law, and his utilitarian project of institutional design.

Bentham's institutional engineer is guided by the principle of utility, but he must build social, political, and legal institutions keeping in mind the prevailing modes of reasoning, and expected sources of motivation. They provide the materials and constraints of his project. The task is to design institutions to enable, structure, constrain, and manage the deliberations and decision-making of incumbents in the roles and positions of the institution in question in order best to serve its utility-determined ends.

The institutions of adjudication and law-amending that Bentham designed late in his career were meant to shape the decision-making of judges, by determining the inputs of their practical reasoning and defining the practical options available to them. They determine what judges can and cannot do, and what outcomes are possible or feasible to achieve through the exercise of their institutionally defined decision-making powers. The principle of utility directs judges to choose the course of action that promises best to promote the well-being of the community, but the institution determines the options and thus delimits the set of actions available to the decision-maker. Public knowledge of the substantive law and the constitutional structure will inevitably shape the expectations of ordinary law subjects—and hence, in Bentham's view, they shape the relevant "expectation-utilities"—thereby affecting materially the relevant inputs to proper judicial decision-making. Thus, what might be regarded in the abstract (i.e., abstracting from the limitations of options determined by the institution within which the decision-maker works) as an optimal outcome by utilitarian standards, may not be available to the judge.

[23] Dinwiddy, "Adjudication under Bentham's Pannomion," 286–9; see also Ferraro, "Adjudication and Expectations," 153–60.

Judicial decision-making, on this view, is still ultimately governed by the principle of utility understood as the sovereign decision principle, but what that principle dictates is determined by the institution-shaped alternatives available to the judge. Bentham's view about the institutional structures of judicial reasoning matured greatly over his career. But the basic outline of his view, and the main issues at stake, are clear already in his earliest reflections on justice, utility and law and on the dynamics and defects of common-law adjudication.

8

Utility and Command

Roots of Bentham's Universal Jurisprudence

Bentham located the foundations of his universal jurisprudence in two overlapping traditions.* From Horace's *Satires*, and the Epicurean tradition, he took his motto: "Utility is the mother of justice and equity."[1] From Hobbes, and a long tradition before him, Bentham took his model: laws "are not Philosophy as is the Common-Law, and other disputable arts, but are Commands or Prohibitions" (*Dialogue* 29).[2] These notions influenced thinking about law since classical times and inspired Bentham's thinking, but in his hands they were transformed. To gain perspective on Bentham's jurisprudence, and the uniqueness of his contribution to modern legal theory, I propose first to survey briefly these traditions and then take up Bentham's revisions of them.

BEGINNINGS

In his classic discussion of the question whether it is better to be ruled by a wise man or wise law, Plato articulated a common-sense understanding of key features of law.[3] Law, he assumed, is meant to provide rational agents with guidance to right or wise action, but it is addressed in public terms to a public consisting of individuals engaged in complex patterns of social interaction. So, it must give its guidance wholesale, i.e., for general circumstances and broad classes of people. He observed, however, that law's wisdom can sometimes appear to be folly; law and the right or rational can diverge. Nevertheless, he argued, we are well advised to opt for the rule of law rather than men, since the costs of permitting unregulated official discretion are high.

* This chapter is based on the following previously published texts. **a:** "Legal Positivism—Early Foundations," *The Routledge Companion to Philosophy of Law*, A. Marmor, ed. (NY: Routledge, 2012). Reproduced with permission of Routledge in the format Book via Copyright Clearance Center.
b: G.J. Postema, "Law as Command: The Model of Command in Modern Jurisprudence," *Philosophical Issues* (Supplement to Noûs), vol. 11 (2001), 470–501. Copyright © 2002, John Wiley & Sons. https://doi.org/10.1111/0029-4624.35.s1.18

[1] Bentham, Article 299, quoting Horace, *Satires*, 1.3.98.
[2] Hobbes's "philosopher" speaks of statues here, but later (at 31) generalizes the point to all laws.
[3] Plato, *Statesman*, Julia Annas, ed., Robin Waterfield, trans. (Cambridge: Cambridge University Press, 1995).

Plato spoke in terms of *nomos*, and, as Aristotle reminded us, *nomos* stood in contrast with *physis* (nature), in classical Greek. *Nomos*, Martin Ostwald explains, denoted "an order of living . . . of some kind, which differs from the order expressed in the early archaic age by *themis* in that it sees its sanction in its acceptance by those who live under it and who acknowledge it as valid and binding for themselves." And "even when it is attributed to a god or a lawgiver, the source of its validity always remains its general acceptance as a norm by those who constitute a given milieu."[4] In this sense, Aristotle spoke of *nomoi* when he had in mind a conventional, but not necessarily legislated, order.[5]

The Epicurean tradition (in the third to first century BCE) emphasized the adventitious features of law,[6] but invoked the watchword that "utility is the mother of justice" to answer the skeptics who charged that law was merely conventional and hence arbitrary. Epicureans argued that the ultimate good is a sense of well-being rooted in mental tranquility and absence of pain. Chief among disturbances of such tranquility is fear of harm suffered at the hands of others. Being free of the primary causes of the desire to harm (hatred, envy, low self-esteem), the sage is not inclined to harm others, because he knows that refraining from harming others sacrifices nothing of value. However, he also realizes that if he is known to be unwilling to respond to violence with violence, others who do not appreciate the pointlessness of violence will be emboldened to attack. Thus, Epicurus argued that justice, formally expressed in legal norms, "was never anything *per se*, but a contract regularly arising at some place or other in people's dealings with one another, over not harming or being harmed."[7] Justice and law are products of a mutual, consensual arrangement. Coercive sanctions are added to assure those who are independently motivated to comply with law that advantage will not be taken of them by those who are shortsighted and fail to recognize law's benefits.

Epicurean jurisprudence was one form of a more general view of law, common in late ancient and medieval theory, that understood law to be artificial or conventional, in the sense that it is temporally limited and changing, stemming in part from intelligent human activity, and rooted in potentially varying custom or practice, which manifests the "consent" or "consensus" of those subject to the law. Some laws might be made by the prince, on this view, but the bulk of law was planted deeply in the soil of custom, for, as Aristotle wrote, "*nomos* [law] has no compelling force beside that of *ethos* [custom]."[8]

[4] Martin Ostwald, "Ancient Greek Ideas of Law," in *Dictionary of the History of Ideas*, Philip P. Weiner, ed. (New York: Charles Scribner's Sons, 1968), 682.

[5] Aristotle, *Nicomachean Ethics*, Terence Irwin, trans. (Indianapolis: Hackett Publishing, 1985), 1094b15–16, 1134b18–5b6.

[6] Roderick T. Long, "Hellenistic Philosophers of Law, in *A History of the Philosophy of Law from the Ancient Greeks to the Scholastics*, Fred D. Miller and Carrie-Ann Biondi, eds. (Dordrecht: Springer, 2007), 122–7.

[7] Epicurus, *Key Doctrines 33, 32*, in *The Hellenistic Philosophers*, A. A. Long and D. N. Sedley, trs. (Cambridge: Cambridge University Press, 1987), 127.

[8] Aristotle, *Politics*, C. D. C. Reeve, trans. (Indianapolis: Hackett Publishing, 1998), II.8, 1269a20.

In the eighteenth century, Hume offered a sophisticated version of the convention-based understanding of law, grounding the formal elements of law in informal social conventions and practices (THN 307–45). Conventions, emerging over time from intelligent social interaction rather than contract, lie at the foundations of law, Hume argued; informal social practices, endorsed and extended by courts and law-makers, supply the rules of law. As social cooperation enables small groups to thrive and expand, natural relations based on trust and sympathy become strained and less personal, more formal devices are needed to refine, extend, and enforce the informal conventions that initially governed social relations. Formal legal institutions supplement rather than supplant informal conventions of justice, Hume argued, and the ground of both is public utility—mutual benefit arising from a stable scheme of social cooperation securing possession of resources necessary for survival and decent social life. The special utility of conventions of justice arises from their systematic interdependence, working together like stones in a gothic vault. Thus, although adherence to the rules sometimes appears to disserve public utility, the rules secure the systemic benefits they promise only if they are followed with few exceptions.

Late Medieval Jurisprudence

A conception of law more closely approximating the familiar positivist understanding is evident in the work of two important late medieval philosophers. Because the key term for law that was used was not *nomos*, but *thesmos*, I will refer to this as the "thetic" conception—taking the term from the Greek *tithenai*, meaning to put, as in *laid down* or *posited*—to highlight the fact that law, on this conception, is seen to be explicitly and intentionally made and imposed on law-subjects.[9] Two late medieval philosophers, Thomas Aquinas and Marsilius of Padua, integrated this notion into their respective understandings of law.

Aquinas, in the late thirteenth century, took *lex* rather than *ius* for the core concept in his discourse on law. The contrast he drew between these two concepts highlights the extent to which he embraced the thetic model of law. According to Aquinas, *ius* is the object of *iustum* (right or justice). It is a condition or state of affairs: the right ordering of the external actions or interactions of members of a community of equals.[10] *Ius* is established by nature (*ius naturale*), but it may also be instituted in part by agreement or mutual consent (*ius positiva*) (Aquinas, 161–3 (ST IIaIIae 57 a. 2), 201 (ST IIaIIae 60 a. 5)). *Lex* is the public expression of *ius*, that is, the rules or measures prescribing right order are publicly expressed and

[9] See Ostwald, "Ancient Greek Ideas of Law," 682.

[10] Aquinas, *Political Writings*, R.W. Dyson, ed. and tr. (Cambridge: Cambridge University Press, 2002), 158–60 (*ST* IIaIIae 57 a. 1).

typically reduced to writing (Aquinas, 160 (ST IIaIIae 57 a. 1, ad 2)). Moreover, *lex* does not merely declare or make public this order, it *makes* or institutes it through this expression, "giving it the force of authority" (Aquinas, 201 (ST IIaIIae 60 a. 5)).

According to Aquinas, *lex* differs from *ius* in nature, source, and force. First, *lex* is action-guiding; it consists of rules ("ordinances of reason") addressed to self-directing rational agents, prescribing actions to be performed. It guides action through the agency of another rational being: "Every law proceeds from the reason and will of a legislator" (Aquinas, 153 (ST IaIIae 97 a. 3)). *Lex* is a dictate of reason that exists first *in* that lawmaker who then "imprints" it on the minds of law-subjects (Aquinas, 110 (ST IaIIae 93 a. 5)), inducing or restraining ("obliging") their actions (Aquinas, 77 ((ST IaIIae 90 a. 1)). Thus, promulgation is essential to the nature and binding force of *lex* (Aquinas, 82–3 (ST IaIIae 91 a. 4)). Second, it is essential to *lex* that it originate in and is established by one who has the standing or authority to direct the actions of others. This must be a "public person" charged with care of the community (Aquinas, 81 (ST IaIIae 91 a. 3)). Third, since laws are not merely declared but are imposed on law-subjects (Aquinas, 110 (ST IaIIae 93 a. 5)), the relationship of lawmaker to law-subject is one of superior to inferior (Aquinas, 58 (ST IIaIIae 104 a. 10). The appropriate response of the law-subject is obedience, which involves taking the will of the legislator for one's own. "By obedience," Aquinas wrote, "we slay our own will" (Aquinas, 64–5 (ST IIaIIae 104 a. 3, ad 1)).

Aquinas's model of law is distinctively thetic, but it is not exclusively so, for a directive has the character of law, in his view, only if it is in accord with reason, and more specifically, only if it is properly directed to the common good (Aquinas, 78–80 (ST IaIIae 90 a. 2)). In the view of many, this addition is enough to consign his theory to positivism's rival camp, natural-law jurisprudence, but this should not obscure its contributions to the developing understanding of positive law. We should keep in mind that by "character of law" Aquinas did not have in mind the legal validity of norms, but rather the condition of having the full nature and force of law. So, he meant to say that when laws fail to be directed to the common good they fail in an important dimension to be and do what we reasonably expect laws to be and do.

Moreover, Aquinas's account of law is not merely a hybrid of positivist and naturalist elements, for the thetic elements of his account are internally linked to this substantive element. Juridical law (*lex*) is needed, in Aquinas's view, because the common good for a community is in large measure indeterminate both regarding the shape of the goal and detailed features of the means needed to achieve it. This makes coordinating our interactions with others especially difficult, for we often do not know what the common good requires of us, and even if we do, we lack adequate assurance that others share our understanding or are sufficiently motivated to comply with its requirements. In view of these conditions, we need publicly accessible, manifestly authoritative, and explicitly articulated directives to determine the indeterminate, or difficult to determine, common good, and to assure the community that a degree of general compliance with the resulting social order is likely enough to make any individual's compliance reasonable. This, on Aquinas's view, is precisely what law is designed to offer.

The thetic dimensions of law are even more marked in the work of Marsilius of Padua (ca. 1275–1343). Law, according to Marsilius, seeks to direct actions which are autonomous in nature and transitive in effect. Law elicits actions "as a result of [the agent's] empire," that is, it directs actions which fall within the control, liberty and agency of the agents addressed, and it concerns only actions that have the potential to affect others, especially to harm or injure them. Although we sometimes misleadingly use the term "law" to refer to principles of action to which we are habituated through "disciplines of work," law properly so-called lacks such habituation (*Defender*, 53, 215), and so "lacks a soul and moving principle" (*Defender*, 216). It needs a *maker* to issue the standard, a *judge* to assess acts relative to that standard and a coercive *incentive* to secure compliance. On Marsilius' view, laws are universal judgments of justice and public good which can be viewed in two ways: either as *indications* of what is just or advantageous, or as *imperatives* expressed in a "command ... which coerces by means of a penalty" (*Defender*, 53). Strictly speaking, a true judgment of what is just for a community is not yet a *law*, "unless a coercive command has been given in respect of its observation" (*Defender*, 54, 66). By the same token, although laws can fail as true indications of what is just, a coercive command that does not even pretend to offer an assessment of what is required by justice would have the form of law only but not its proper content, both of which are essential to law.

Marsilius required more of the form of law than that it express a coercive command. Laws, he argued, provide that "without which civil judgments cannot be made in a way that is simply speaking correct" (*Defender*, 56). That is, they are necessarily general and secure a kind of impartiality with respect to particular agents and circumstances. This makes possible a degree of equality or equity among parties governed by it, which is essential for the role law plays in social ordering (*Defender*, 56–7). Moreover, following Aristotle, Marsilius insisted that law is prince over all (*Defender*, 61). Law is the form of the prince's exercise of power (*Defender*, 51, 56–7, 61) in the dual sense (1) that it constitutes the office, standing, and power of the prince and (2) that it is the mode of ruling that the prince is bound to use. The source of law, however, lies not in the prince, according to Marsilius, but in the "human legislator" who holds supreme lawmaking authority and power. This power is located in community as a whole—the universal body of citizens, or its "prevailing part" (*Defender*, 66–72). It is supreme in a polity because it directs the actions of free individuals, and even more because it defines and constitutes the social order; it is located in the universal body of citizens because it most fundamentally touches their lives. According to Marsilius, law serves three important functions: (1) it defines and confines the exercise of lordship, and in particular warrants and vindicates the exercise of coercive force; (2) it constitutes and structures all fundamental social and political relations; and thereby (3) it secures the peace amongst people who, while by nature sociable, are nevertheless prone to passions that drive them into conflicts.

The Thetic Tradition in the Seventeenth Century

In the work of Aquinas and Marsilius we find most of the themes that figure in a tradition of thinking about the nature of law that extends from the thirteenth to the nineteenth century, a tradition in which the idea of command was the central organizing concept or metaphor. Considering only writers in the seventeenth century, we find it not only in the work of Hobbes (1588–1679), but also in Second Scholastic theorists like Francisco Suarez (1548–1617), Protestant theorists like Samuel Pufendorf (1632–1694), and even classical common-law theorists like Sir Matthew Hale (1609–1676).

Lying in the background of thinking about law in this tradition were three common assumptions. First, it was assumed that common to laws of all kinds was the fact that laws "pertain to" intelligent beings, and order their behavior;[11] correlatively, law orders behavior in a way appropriate to such beings. The proximate aim of such directives, we might say, is the ordering of their behavior in this distinctive way. Laws have a characteristic *modus operandi*, and an anticipated outcome of this operation is that the behavior and interactions of free intelligent beings will manifest a certain order. Thus, it was widely assumed that the juridical was a department of the practical, that inquiry into the nature of law was part of the more general inquiry into the domain of practical life: the philosophical task was to explain law's ordering of intelligent human action.

Second, the thetic tradition rested on a strong assumption about the nature of beings subject to law. Laws, it was assumed, do not merely characterize or describe an ordering, either real or ideal; neither do they merely create, sustain, or "cause" that ordering. Laws direct the conduct of free beings and through such direction that order is achieved. Although it was important to explain how law could be productive of behavior, the manner in which law sought to be productive, on this view, was determined by the nature of the beings whose behavior it governed. The characteristic response sought from a law-subject by law was not that of the snake to its charmer.[12] To be sure, laws and sanctions sometimes do influence behavior of

[11] See, e.g., Suarez, *On Laws and God the Lawgiver* (1612), G.L. Williams, A. Brown, J. Waldron, trans. (Oxford: Oxford University Press, 1944), I.1.1–2, I.3.2–3, 8. At OL I.4.2 Suarez wrote: "properly speaking, only those who have the use of intellect and reason are governed by law, or are capable of being so governed."

[12] "One may succumb to the policeman's voice or bearing not from any considerations, but like the snake obeying its charmer." W.D. Falk, "Goading and Guiding," in Falk, *Ought, Reasons, and Morality* (Ithaca: Cornell University Press, 1986), 51. Falk says that such "direct pleading" is "the continuation

rational agents in this way—they may merely succumb to the policeman's voice or bearing, as David Falk pointed out—but when law has this effect it does not influence them *qua* free beings. A defining fact about law, in this tradition, is that it pertains to—it is addressed to—free, intelligent beings. It articulates a normative order addressed to free agents.

This freedom of free agents was understood to involve, at the most fundamental level, a degree of understanding of oneself, one's actions, and the world in which one acts, and a capacity based on this understanding to direct one's actions according to a rule or norm, or according to the reasons available to one.[13] Joseph Raz captured this assumption concerning the nature of law-subject in his exploration of normativity. Persons have a "capacity to perceive and understand how things are, and what response is appropriate to them" and an "ability to respond appropriately," he wrote. They can direct their lives "in accordance with their appreciation of themselves and their environment, and of the reasons with which, given how they are, the world presents them."[14] Some command theorists insist, further, that freedom involves what is now called freedom of alternative possibilities, that is, an ability to do or not do an act as one wills.[15]

Law, then, was said to "pertain to" its subjects regarded as free, self-directing beings. They pertain to them not merely in the sense of being *concerned with* them or their behavior, as, for example, rules for the care of pet turtles pertain to turtles, but in the stronger sense of being *addressed to* them in their capacity as free self-directing beings. Law addresses rules, norms, and requirements to them; it bestows on them powers and entitlements. In doing so, it assumes that they are capable of grasping the rules and norms and acting in accord with them based on this understanding, and expects them to behave in certain ways because they exercise these capacities effectively. On this view, it is an essential feature of laws that they seek to play a special role in the practical reasoning of those to whom they are addressed.

Third, it was assumed that the law's mode of ordering was distinctive. In this tradition, law was distinguished from evaluative judgments, standards of instrumental rationality, and even judgments of moral right and wrong by the fact that law alone imposes *binding obligations*. A law, Suarez argued, is not merely a rule or

of violence by other means. It is coercive in the sense of controlling others while bypassing, if not paralyzing, any voluntary contribution to their own behavior."

[13] Pufendorf maintained that law operates by creating and imposing *obligations*, but one is subject to law and legal obligations, he argued, only if (*inter alia*) (1) one is *free*—one "has a will that can turn either way," (2) one has the ability to understand one's self (and so can understand one's situation and one's action relative to it), and, accordingly, (3) one is capable of making one's actions accord with a rule or norm. See Samuel Pufendorf, *On the Law of Nature and of Nations*, in *The Political Writings of Samuel Pufendorf*, C. L. Carr, ed., M. J. Seidler, trans. (Oxford: Oxford University Press, 1994), I.1.7, I.6.8, and Pufendorf, *On the Duty of Man and Citizen* (1673), John Tully, ed., Michael Silverthorne, trans. (Cambridge: Cambridge University Press, 1991), I.2.4. See also Suarez, OL I.3.2.

[14] Joseph Raz, *Engaging Reason* (Oxford: Oxford University Press, 1999), 67.

[15] See, e.g., Pufendorf, DMC 1.2.4; OLN I.4.2, and I.6.8.

measure of action; it is a binding precept (OL I.1.5–7). Thus, "the will of God," for example, "assumes in the actions themselves [that it commands or forbids] some necessary rightness or wrongness, and *joins to them* a special obligation of law" (OL II.6.11, emphasis added).[16] Hobbes, too, recognized the practical force of "dictates of reason" (his "laws" of nature), but distinguished them from laws proper, which was thought to have a special binding force that is best modeled by a command (*Lev* 111, 185). Law is not merely normative; it is a distinct *species* of the normative. What this tradition sought to explain with the model of command is not normativity *in general*, but law's *specific kind* of normativity.

NORMATIVITY OF LAW IN THE THETIC TRADITION

I propose to take a closer look at the model of command as it was developed especially by seventeenth-century legal philosophers. This model was built out of three basic concepts: will, unequal social relations, and generality. These concepts provide the terms in which the special conception of normative guidance attributed to law was expressed.

Will. The concept of will bears the largest part of the explanatory burden. Writers in this tradition sought to model several important features of law's normativity with the help of this notion. First, will was typically understood to be the faculty that is most nearly proximate to rational action. Will, Suarez wrote, is "the principle that moves and brings one to the performance of an action" (OL I.5.15). Hobbes, famously defined will as "the last Appetite, or Aversion, immediately adhaering to the action, or to the omission thereof" (*Lev* 127). Pufendorf called will "a determinative principle."[17] According to this tradition, will is a rational faculty in the sense that it is responsive to reasons and judgment, but its job is strictly *executive*. It is, in Pufendorf's word, the "internal directress of [one's] action" (OLN I.4.1); Suarez called it "the executory power" (OL I.4.11). Will is "the starting point of voluntary actions," wrote Hobbes, "hence it is not capable of deliberation and agreements."[18]

[16] Suarez adds, "this law prohibits a given thing because that thing is evil; and therefore prior to the existence of the said law, there exists the obligation of avoiding such evil" (OL II.9.4). This comment is uncharacteristic of Suarez, who typically restricts the term "obligation" to that which is imposed by law (note however, that he says here that the obligation in question is an "intrinsic natural obligation"). A more characteristic formulation of the point can be found at Suarez, OL I.5.21, where he admits (in accord with his attempt to reconcile the intellectualist and voluntarist wings of the natural-law tradition) that insofar as law directs us to that which is in fact good and necessary (for our well-being) law has a certain "moving force," the appreciation of which is due to the intellect. However, the "moving force" in law that "makes an action obligatory" lies in an act of will of the prince. Both passages underscore my point that for Suarez, a *special kind* of normativity characterizes law.

[17] Pufendorf, *Elements of Universal Jurisprudence* in Carr and Seidler, *The Political Writings of Samuel Pufendorf*, 49.

[18] Hobbes, *On the Citizen*, Richard Tuck, ed. (Cambridge: Cambridge University Press, 1998), Chapter 5.8.

The nature of self-directed action (that is, *imperium*—command) was a contested issue in Scholastic philosophy.[19] Aquinas, for example, insisted that *imperium* was an act of intelligence—the product of deliberation and decision—that sets the decided-upon course of action before one proceeds.[20] Suarez accepted that in order for the command of the lawmaker to direct the action of the subject the subject must bring the command "before and into direct contact with" his will, which is an act of judgment or the intellect (OL I.4.5). However, with respect to self-chosen, freely willed action, Suarez thought that Aquinas's *imperium* was a fiction. In his view, Aquinas had introduced an unnecessary step in his account of the process of intelligent movement from deliberation to action; indeed, he declared that such an act of the intellect was impossible (OL I.4.11). Will or command, as Suarez saw it, was precisely that which "moves" the subject to action (OL I.4.10–12, I.5.6). However, it is clear that in this debate all parties assumed that will (and hence command) appears only at the stage of *executing* deliberative resolution.[21] As Suarez put it, "To the will pertains the subsequent application of the other power in actual use"—including judgment or the intellect (OL I.4.11). With the concept of will, the thetic tradition captured the *executive* nature of commands (and hence of law).

Second, not only is will the faculty by which one moves *oneself* to action; it is equally the faculty by which one "moves" another to act.[22] Will, we might say, is *transitive*; it somehow communicates its "motion." A decree does not remain in the mind and will of the person who makes it, says Pufendorf; rather, "it is instilled into a subject's mind in such a way as to make him understand the necessity of conforming himself to it" (OLN I.6.4). Suarez even maintained at one point that no act of will by the law-subject to accept the prince's command is necessary for it to do its action-guiding work, "unless it be on account of some defect of power in the lawmaker" (OL I.4.5). This "transitive" aspect of the will and commands was used to capture what theorists in this tradition took to be a salient feature of law: law was *active* and *productive*, in the sense that its commands are oriented to producing behavior of some sort.

However, third, the tradition's understanding of the "power" and "moving" involved in commanding the behavior of another person was subtle. The way

[19] On this debate, see John Finnis, *Natural Law and Natural Rights* (Oxford: Clarendon Press, 1980), Chapter XI.8.

[20] Aquinas, ST IaIIae 17 a.1.

[21] Finnis puts Aquinas's view this way: "The important thing is that the expressed *imperium*, the promulgated 'intention of the legislator', represents to the subject an intelligible determinate pattern of action, which, having been chosen by the lawgiver to be obligatory, can actually *be* obligatory in the eyes of a reasonable subject because the ruler's *imperium* can (for the sake of the common good) be reasonably treated by the subject as if it were his own *imperium*" (*Natural Law and Natural Rights*, 341).

[22] Law involves by its nature an act of will, says Suarez, because a "characteristic condition requisite for law ... [consists in] moving and bringing of the subject to performance of an action" (OL I.5.15). At OL II.6.22 he says, that law-generated obligation is a certain kind of "moral moving," and the lawgiver move another to act through an act of the will (OL I.6.15, II.6.1).

commands, and hence laws, direct action, according to this tradition, respects the fact that the beings that the commander seeks to move are free, self-directing beings. As we have seen, a straightforward, mechanically causal account of this directing was ruled out from the start. Writers in this tradition would have agreed with Peter Railton's characterization of normative guidance as involving a "peculiar mix of force and freedom."[23] The force of one's will on another is not "physical," but "moral," as Suarez put it.[24] Obligation, he says, "is a certain kind of moral moving [of someone] to act."[25] The commander addresses the will of the other person; he does not manipulate the body, or even the motivations, of his subject. The moral force ("moral moving") necessitates in a way that is consistent with freedom; the mode of address is obligation. Suarez goes so far as to maintain that the commander wills not the action of his subject, but rather wills *to bind* his subject (OL I.4.8).[26] The will's power is not causal, but normative. It "moves" by addressing the moral capacities of agents.

Pufendorf was even clearer on this score. In *On the Duties of Man and Citizen* he wrote that law is a "decree by which a superior obliges anyone who is subject to him." The command creates an obligation, "a bond of right by which we are constrained by the necessity of making some performance" (DMC I.2.2–3). Yet, the necessity of conforming one's action to obligation rooted in command never compromises the subject's freedom to act or refrain from acting.[27] Obligation, he maintained, "contains sufficient force to bend the will," but it does so "morally." Unlike coercion, which "shakes the will in an external fashion only and impels it to select an unwelcome thing solely through the awareness of an impending evil," obligation "farther engage[s] the Person."[28] One both "understands the necessity of conforming himself to it" (OLN I.6.4) and one is disposed to judge his own behavior in light of the obligation-imposing norm. The will is imbued "with a special internal

[23] Peter Railton, "Normative Force and Normative Freedom," in Jonathan Dancy, ed., *Normativity* (Oxford: Blackwell, 2000), 7.

[24] "God, in establishing law, does not impel one physically toward the act prescribed by law, but merely imposes an obligation which is of a moral nature and cannot thus be brought about" (Suarez, OL I.5.7). At OL I.4.9 Suarez wrote, "the object of the efficacious will of the legislator" is "moral rather than physical."

[25] "[O]*bligatio est motio quaedam moralis ad agendum*" (Suarez, OL II.6.22). I follow a reading suggested by T.H. Irwin in "Obligation, Rightness, and Natural Law: Suarez and Some Critics," in *Interpreting Suarez: Critical Essays*, D. Schwartz, ed. (Cambridge: Cambridge University Press, 2012), 149–52.

[26] Suarez's motivation was at least partly theological. He wanted to claim that God commands us to comply with natural law and divine law, but if commands by their nature determine (in the sense of efficiently cause) their subject's behavior, then we could never obey God *freely*, since the will of an omnipotent God is literally irresistible. God's command would utterly eradicate our freedom.

[27] In his *Elements of Universal Jurisprudence*, Pufendorf wrote, "obligation throws a kind of moral bridle over our freedom of action, as it were, so that we cannot rightly proceed in any other direction than the one in which it leads; although the natural efficacy of no obligation so constrains the natural freedom of our will that it cannot in fact turn toward other things" (EUJ 50). See also Pufendorf, OLN I.6.5.

[28] Pufendorf, OLN I.6.5; the phrase, "farther engage[s] the Person," is Basil Kennet's English rendering of the passage in *De jure naturae et gentium* (London, 1769), 58.

sense that compels it to censure its own actions and deem itself blameworthy if it has not conformed itself to the prescribed norm" (OLN I.6.5; see also DMC I.2.3).

Fourth, will expressed in commands is thought by writers in this tradition to be, in a certain respect, normatively *creative*. Through the exercise of will obligations are imposed on others, new "moral entities" (as Pufendorf put it) are *created*.[29] The commander addresses the will, not the intellect, of the subject. Recognizing the risk of distorting the views of some contributors to this tradition, we can make their point most clearly using the language of reasons for action. As we have seen, the will is conceived, in this tradition, as a rational—in the sense of reason-responsive—faculty, and the reasons supplied to it by the command of another are not merely the reasons already available, or that already apply, to the agent addressed. This is one important respect in which law is repeatedly said to differ from advice or counsel.[30] One who offers advice or counsel seeks to influence another person's behavior by rehearsing "considerations drawn from the thing itself," as Pufendorf put it (OLN I.6.1). The advisor may issue imperatives, Hobbes wrote, but he only "deduceth his reasons from the benefit that arriveth by it to him to whom he saith it" (*Lev* 303). In contrast, the reasons addressed to the will by command, and hence by law, are in some sense *new*, supplied by the commander, not merely adduced or proffered by him.

Moreover, that new reason has a very definite content, namely the (expression of the) will of the commander, and it alone. The "moving force" in law, according to Suarez, lies in the prince's will (OL I.5.21). Hobbes's formulation of this point in the *Leviathan* is perhaps the most familiar: "Command is, where a man saith, *Doe this*, or *Doe not this*, without expecting other reason than the Will of him that sayes it" (*Lev* 303). Elsewhere Hobbes wrote even more pointedly: "Commanding . . . is that speech by which we signify to another our appetite or desire to have anything done, or left undone, for reasons contained in the will itself: for it is not properly said *Sic volo, sic jubeo*, without the other clause, *Stet pro ratione voluntas*."[31] Pufendorf added, commenting on a parallel passage in Hobbes's *De Cive* (ch. 14.1), "And so laws are obeyed principally because of their prescriber's will and not because of their content" (OLN I.6.1; see also EUJ 58). These reasons are regarded as "content-independent," as we now say. It is the fact of the commander's having issued the command—the commander's "will," they would say—and not anything about the action commanded that is supposed to give sole and sufficient reason to do the commanded action.

[29] Suarez wrote at OL I.5.23 "law is that act of the prince which of itself and by its own force creates an obligation and binds the subject." See also Pufendorf, OLN I.1.4.

[30] It is standard practice for writers in this tradition to distinguish law from advice or counsel. See Suarez, OL I.1.7–8 and esp. I.12.4; Hobbes, DC 14.1; *Lev* Chapter 25, esp. 302–3; Pufendorf OLN, I.6.1; EJU, 58.

[31] Hobbes, *Human Nature*, chapter XIII, para. 6, in *The English Works of Thomas Hobbes*, William Molesworth, ed., (London, 1840), vol. 4, 74–5.

It would seem that this fits nicely into positivist jurisprudence, but not its natural law counterpart, especially as positivism is currently understood, but the matter is more complex than this would suggest. We find Pufendorf explicitly arguing that although a law "should also have its reasons, to be sure," nevertheless, "these are not properly the ground of obedience to it. This lies rather in the authority of the one prescribing the law who, in announcing a decree of his will, obligates a subject to act in complete accord with his prescription" (OLN I.6.1). Suarez, similarly, conceded that, while law directs us to that which is good and necessary, nevertheless, the moving force of law regarded as imposing obligations rests solely in the will of the prince (OL I.5.21). Yet, his explanation of the Augustinian conundrum, "an unjust law is not a law," underscores his commitment to this aspect of the command model (see OL I.9.4). A prince may prescribe unjust things, but his precepts lack validity as law, and hence fail to impose binding obligations on their subjects. This is not due merely to the fact that they are inconsistent with precepts of natural law understood as principles of justice. It is due rather to the fact that natural law is commanded by God, the proper (and only) superior of the prince, and no inferior can create or impose an obligation contrary to the will of his superior. The unjust precept is strictly void, it is formally invalid we might say, because "it is not possible that men should be bound, at one and the same time, to do and to abstain from doing a given thing" and "no law made by an inferior can annul the obligation imposed by the superior" (OL I.9.4).

Finally, these newly supplied reasons are of a special kind. They are not merely recommendatory, but rather they are categorical. They make the action prescribed *non-optional* in a special way. They "induce" action "by imposing a moral necessity" (Suarez, OL I.1.8–9). They make action "necessary" while at the same time respecting the agent's freedom (Pufendorf, OLN I.6.5, also EUJ 50). Legal obligations "bridle" the will of the parties obliged. The subject is free to act as he wills, but in a key sense he is not free to will. He is deprived of rational choice. He has no choice, not in the physical or metaphysical sense, but rather in the sense that no other rationally appropriate option is open to him. Moreover, he is precluded from considering those options or reasons for them.[32] The commands are peremptory.

This peremptory, deliberation-precluding aspect of commands reinforces the *executory* aspect of commands that we noticed earlier. It leads Pufendorf, for example, to deny that it is possible for one to bind oneself (OLN I.6.6–7), or for the sovereign to make "perfect," that is, binding promises to his subjects (OLN I.1.19 and III.5.6). To take on the nature of commands, these devices must preclude all deliberation, but they are unable to do so. "Even after he has made a final

[32] Pufendorf, OLN I.6.1; Hobbes, *Lev* 303. Joseph Raz, of course, denies that peremptory reasons preclude consideration of excluded reasons, but only *action on* them (*Practical Reason and Norms*, Princeton: Princeton University Press, 1990), 184.) However, to Hobbes this is likely to appear to be a distinction without a difference, in view of the close connection he finds between deliberation and action.

determination and firmly committed himself to something, the force of his decision (insofar as it stems from his will) is not so strong as to prevent him from changing or abrogating it at his own pleasure ... unless, that is, external considerations prohibit him from altering his will once it has been determined and declared" (OLN I.6.6). Perhaps it was a similar thought that actually led Hobbes to his famous definition of will as the last appetite before action. For until the action takes place, there was, in his view, still room for further deliberation.

Social relations. According to the seventeenth-century thetic tradition, commands presuppose the existence of a certain kind of relationship between the commander and the subject addressed. The key difference between *counsel* and *law* is consistently characterized by the difference in the relationships between the parties. While counsel is guidance addressed by one rational agent to *an equal*, petition and command presuppose inequalities between the parties. Petitions are addressed to a superior, Suarez observed, while commands are addressed to an inferior (OL I.12.4). To this standard Scholastic point, Hobbes and Pufendorf added that law must also be distinguished from covenant or pact, again on the ground that the latter involve exchange of promises among equals, while command presupposes superiority.[33] The exchange of promises yields *obligations*, they maintain, but not obligations *of law*, unless sovereignty is involved.[34]

Commands create new, peremptory constraints, as we have seen, but judgments of counsel or advice are not able to create such constraints. This is because the reasons are not new, and because the reason they offer are not peremptory. To explain this distinctive feature of commands, the tradition appealed to the inequality of the relationship between the parties. Command entails the subordination of the will of one person to that of another.

I hasten to add that, for writers in this seventeenth-century thetic tradition, this unequal social relationship is never portrayed as simply a matter of inequality of sheer physical power, the subjection of one person to the physical power of another. Rather, law's distinctive normative force arises from, and is an expression of an unequal social relationship that is a normatively charged. This is clearly the case for the religious tradition on which the command theory draws. For God's authority to command was always seen to be rooted in, and an expression of, the covenant relationship between God and His people. (This covenantal context was especially important in the sixteenth century to voluntarists in the Calvinist Protestant camp.) Some writers in the thetic tradition, Suarez, for example, explained our subjection to God in terms of our status as *creatures* of the creator (OL I.3.3). But this relationship is itself characterized in moral terms, not merely factual ones. The Creator is, in virtue of being creator, the trustee and guardian of His creation, and

[33] Hobbes, DC Chapter 14.2; Pufendorf, OLN I.6.2 and VII.4.9; EUJ 58–9.
[34] Hobbes, *Lev* Chapter 14; Pufendorf, OLN VII.4.9 and EUJ 59.

we acknowledge His superior authority out of gratitude for His continued superintendence.[35] In this tradition, Hobbes came closest to treating the relationship as one of sheer power. Commands, by definition, are addressed to those who are "formerly obliged to obey him," he maintained (*Lev* 312), but God's commands rest ultimately on God's "irresistible power" (DC, ch. 15.5). It is not clear whether that power alone gives God sovereignty, or whether it still requires as well (possibly coerced, but, for Hobbes, no less voluntary) acceptance of His creatures. Pufendorf (OLN I.6.10) argued at length against Hobbes's "irresistible power" thesis, taking it to mean nothing more than God's power to physically compel action and hence obedience. Against Hobbes, he insisted that this logically cannot ground our obligation to obey because "compulsion and obligation are different" (OLN I.6.10); and he argued at length that the *potestas* to command rests neither on superior strength or sheer ability to compel, nor on any other measure of "natural eminence" (OLN I.6.9–12). (Hobbes, for his part, insisted that our obligation to obey God consists not in God's power but our voluntary submission.) Still, for all that, the relation between commander and subject, for all theorists in this tradition, is, necessarily, a matter of *subordination* of one will to another will. The inequality, whatever its ground, consists in or entails, the subordination of one will to another.

This allows us to put sharply into perspective the role of coercive sanctions in law according to the thetic tradition. Sanctions are logically, not just pragmatically, necessary to the command relationship, yet they are thought to provide neither the primary motivation for compliance nor the ground of the superiority of the commander over the subject. Sanctions supply useful, indeed indispensable, auxiliary motives, but the primary impelling reason from the point of view of law, is acknowledgement of the will of the superior (OLN I.6.12). Coercion is always "external" and supplementary to the law's norm; obligation is the "internal" reflection of the law's normativity, it "engages the person" (OLN I.6.5). Because the fear of coercive sanction is always external to the norm, and contingent upon the particular circumstances in which agents find themselves, it cannot explain the normative force of law, which claims to persist despite these contingencies. "It is true," Pufendorf wrote, "that strength alone can set me against my own inclination, so that I prefer temporarily to obey another's will instead of experiencing his power. But once my fear is gone, there is nothing to prevent me from acting more according to my discretion than according to his" (OLN I.6.9).

Yet, the ability to back up commands with credible sanctions is (logically) necessary to command authority, according to a substantial part of this tradition. For, as

[35] This is especially clear in Pufendorf, see OLN I.6.11–12. At DMC I.2.5, he says "When a [superior] has signified his will, fear tempered by respect [*reverentia*] must arise in a man's mind [*animus*]—fear from power, respect from reflection on the reason which ought to induce one to accept his will even apart from fear." The latter reasons include "if [the superior] has conferred exceptional benefits on him" and "if it is evident that he wishes the other well and can look out for him better than he can for himself" (see also OLN I.6.9, 12).

Pufendorf put it, "it is vain to prescribe something that can be neglected with impunity" (EUJ 59) and "one who can be disregarded with impunity rules only by the indulgence of others" (OLN I.6.12). That is, while power to coerce is not the *ground* of the commander's authority (as we saw above), it is a *necessary mark and component* of that authority.[36] To lack the power to coerce, and the title to exercise that power, is to lack the requisite superiority. To rule "only by the indulgence of others" is not to command.

Hence, on this view, the relation between commands and sanctions is logical, not merely empirical or instrumental. That is, the relationship between command and punishment, on this view, is not like that of a threat of retaliation between rival political powers. The logic of law, on this view, is very different from the logic of threats. This may be what lies at the root of retributivist intuitions about punishment, but we must keep in mind that this notion has nothing to do with justice. On this way of thinking, punishment is normatively required for the simple conceptual reason that it is part of what is involved in subordination of the will of another. To fail to punish disobedience is like refusing to draw the conclusion *q*, although one believed *p* and *p logically implies q*. In the latter case, one is forced on pain of inconsistency to abandon either the belief that *p* or the belief that *p logically implies q*. So, too, upon pain of inconsistency, one is forced to abandon one's claim to dominion over the will of the other. It is consistency (consistency of willing, we might say), and not justice, on this view, that demands punishment.

Thus, according to this tradition, law is an expression of *dominion*, the power of one will over another will. Suarez wrote, "Lawmaking is an act of jurisdiction and of superior power ... Consequently, it is ... the use of a form of dominion" (OL I.5.15). Similarly, Pufendorf argued, "the faculty of enjoining something in the manner of a law or precept implies superiority, just as the obligation to obey proves that we are inferior to one who is able to prescribe to us" (EJU 59). Subordination of the will is the mode in which intelligent, free beings are *necessitated*. Subjects retain the *ability* to will, and so do, otherwise—therein lies their "freedom." Yet they are not *free to will* to do otherwise. Law (that is, the law-giver) imposes constraints on an inferior's willing. Disobedience is possible, of course, but in that case dominion is expressed in punishment, the imposition of suffering designed to humble the disobedient will. Hence, punishment upon disobedience is not something *added to* the command to motivate behavior in accord with it; rather, punishment is simply another form in which the subordination of the will of the inferior to the superior is expressed. Moreover, dominion is a defining feature of law—of any kind of law, of

[36] This view also seems to have been held by Richard Cumberland. By definition, law includes sanctions, he argued, but the sanction does not generate the obligation. Rather, it serves two other functions: (1) as a motivational supplement, and (2) as evidence of the sanctioned action's having been commanded. See Richard Cumberland, *A Treatise of the Laws of Nature* (1672), John Maxwell, tr. (London, 1727), Chapter 5, para. xxii, in Jerome B. Schneewind, ed., *Moral Philosophy from Montaigne to Kant* (Cambridge: Cambridge University Press, 1990), vol.1, 151–2.

anything that purports to be law. According to this tradition, dominion expresses the special kind of normativity of law.

It is interesting to note that Sir Matthew Hale, writing squarely within the English common-law tradition, also adopted a *thetic* conception of law and accepted much of this philosophical framework, but he did not accept the view that command-generated obligations constitute deliberation-blocking reasons for action. Neither did he hold that to be under obligation is to be subject to another's will. Rather, to be under obligation is to participate in a certain kind of normative relationship, that of being liable to being held to account by another.[37] But, for Hale, this accountability did not necessarily involve liability to punishment. Even our allegiance to God is grounded not his God's absolute and irresistible power, but rather in the relationship of love and divine caring, rooted in the fundamental commitment of the Giver of life who has chosen to link His good with ours.[38]

Generality. Implicit in the discussion thus far, according to our writers, is the fact that the commands that lawmakers give are necessarily characterized by generality (or at least most laws will take this form).[39] This is thought to follow from the nature of law, not from the nature of commands, and so it is, strictly speaking, an addition to the concept of command. Law is a *species* of commands. The necessary generality is of broadly two kinds: the law's commands are addressed to classes of persons, not to specific individuals, and direct them to types of actions. These conditions put a strain on the command model.[40] The fact that law's commands are addressed not merely to a plurality of persons but to *classes* of persons introduces a degree of impersonalism into a relationship that is otherwise portrayed as personal in nature. The personal nature is suggested by the characterization of the social relation between superior and inferior, and the idea, especially strong in Suarez, that it is an act of mind of the sovereign lawgiver that communicates its motion to the minds of his subjects. Suarez, however, admitted that the tension exists and actually identified a further one. He argued for the necessary generality of law in part on the ground that it is a direct consequence of the necessary "perpetual" nature (Hart would call it "persistence") of the law. But this requires, he recognized, that "it is inherent in the nature of law that it shall not depend on the life of the lawmaker."[41]

[37] See Matthew Hale, "Treatise of the Nature of Laws in General and Touching Upon the Law of Nature," in Matthew Hale, *On the Law of Nature, Reason, and Common Law: Selected Jurisprudential Writings*, Gerald J. Postema, ed. (Oxford: Oxford University Press, 2017), 9, 64–5 and "Editor's Introduction," xxiii, xxxii–xxxiii.

[38] See "Editor's Introduction" to Hale, *On the Law of Nature, Reason, and Common Law*, l–li, and references given there.

[39] Suarez, OL I.6, especially paras. 8–17; John Austin, *The Province of Jurisprudence Determined*, H.L.A. Hart, ed. (London: Weidenfeld and Nicolson, 1955), 18–24.

[40] Hart exploited this strain in his critique of Austin's deployment of the model; see H.L.A. Hart, *The Concept of Law*, 2nd edn, Penelope A. Bulloch and Joseph Raz, eds. (Oxford: Clarendon Press, 1994), Chapters 2–4.

[41] Suarez, OL I.6.12; see Hart, *Concept of Law*, 61–6.

It might be argued that the fact that law commands (often broad) *types* of actions also qualifies its strictly *executive* and deliberation-precluding properties. This is partly correct. Since legal norms direct subjects to types of action, those subjects must exercise their judgment at least insofar as it is necessary to identify a concrete action open to them as a token of the type (or rather, a more specific sub-type, since such judgment always works with representations of actions considered *ex ante*). Yet, on this view, deliberation is still strongly channeled. For subjects are required only to ask whether the action falls under the norm, not to determine whether the action is in some broader view good, right, or wise, or whether norm meets certain standards of rationality (or justice). Thus, command model does not preclude practical reasoning on the part law-subjects, but it does strongly tend to represent this practical reasoning, and so to characterize the reasoning proper to law, as deductive in form, or at least as a matter of applying pre-established general norms to concrete facts. In this respect, the command model remains faithful to its basic intuition that law represents to those who fall under its authority the *result* of deliberation carried on elsewhere, expecting them to *execute* the deliberative decision of the lawgiver. The normativity of law, we might say, is still distinctively executory. So, subjects addressed by law are expected to hold the pattern of action defined by the norm before their minds' eye and act in accord with it.[42] Thus, some deliberation, or at least interpretation, is typically required, but it is still ratiocination at the executive stage of practical deliberation.

In sum, the command model assumes that law, *qua law*, creates new, categorical reasons for acting that are intended to operate at the executive stage of practical deliberation. They are imposed by directives to rational agents and they have their moral or practical force in virtue of the special relationship that exists between lawgiver and subject. It is possible to see now why this model might be attractive to both natural law and positivist legal philosophers. Because it focuses exclusively on the executive stage of deliberate action, it can be silent about whether, and what kind, of reasons must lie behind it. It is possible to debate whether, *in addition*, law's directives must meet conditions of justice or reasonableness in order to be valid. But that dispute is about how best to characterize law as depicted by this model. That is, this dispute does not challenge the model, and both sides can in fact presuppose it as common ground. The model structures that dispute. The dispute turns in part on whether the model alone adequately captures certain abstract beliefs we have about law and its mode of operation in practical reasoning and on possibly conflicting ideas about the tasks or functions of law.

Hobbes developed this tradition in an important way, arguing for it on explicitly normative grounds. He argued that, in the absence of a common authority (that is, in the state of nature), we lack common standards and are forced to make

[42] Recall that Suarez thought that an act of judgment was necessary if a subject is to grasp the prince's command and bring it before his will (OL I.4.5).

private judgments of good and evil, right and wrong, and mine and thine, as well as judgments of our own best interest and the common interest. Certain demonstrable "laws" of nature and equity are available to the natural reason of each of us, he argued, but they bind only on the condition that we can reasonably expect others to comply with them as well, a condition that is manifestly unmet in the state of nature. We are likely, then, to suffer regular, persistent, and disastrous conflicts of interest and of principle, which can be avoided, he argued, only by putting full and unlimited authority in the hands of a sovereign. However, to solve this problem, the sovereign is charged with minimizing such disastrous conflicts by defining for us and enforcing common public standards to govern our interactions. That is, the sovereign is expected to exercise authority *through law*. In his *Dialogue*, Hobbes wrote, "A Law is the Command of him, or them, that have the Soveraign Power, given to those that be his or their Subjects, declaring Publickly, and plainly what every of them may do and what they must forbear to do" (*Dialogue* 31). He looked to law to make clear, decisive, and determinate standards by which people can be expected to govern their actions in the polity. Law is not like philosophy "and other disputable Arts," he argued, but rather is a matter of explicit, public, manifestly authentic commands (*Dialogue* 29). This brings to mind Aquinas's view of the primary task of law, except that Hobbes insisted further that, for this purpose, the standing of a norm as valid and binding must not depend in any way on its judgments of its justice or reasonableness. "It is not Wisdom," he argued, "but Authority [alone] that makes a Law" (*Dialogue* 10). Hobbes acknowledged that law is (the expression of) reason, but the reason he had in view is only the fallible, utterly ordinary "natural reason" of the sovereign, which is *deemed* by law-subjects to be *public reason*, that is, reason that is meant to take the place of their individual, private reason and judgment. The law of the sovereign "is all the right reason we have."[43] To achieve this purpose, the sovereign's commands, the authenticity of which are public and undisputed (*Lev* 189), must displace the private deliberation and judgment of each citizen. Law, conceived on the command model, is an essential part of the solution to the problem of privacy of judgment which in his view bedevils public life.

BENTHAM'S RECEPTION AND REVISION OF THE THETIC TRADITION

We saw in Chapter 7 that Bentham was a tireless and penetrating critic of the practice of English law, arguing that its devices, pretenses and modes of thought forced it to lurch unpredictably between absurd rigidity and unconstrained flexibility. The constructed rules of common-law jurisprudence, he argued, are nothing more than

[43] Hobbes, *English Works*, V, 194.

private conjectures. Yet, what we demand of law are "common standard[s] which all men acknowledge, and all men are ready to resort to" (UC 69.188). Private conjectures, no matter how clever, or how accurately they capture the import of a line of cases, cannot serve as law. Law, he assumed (and thought that common-law jurists assumed), is necessarily a matter of common *public* standards and can only perform characteristic tasks of law if it meets the test of publicity. Common-law rules failed as law, because their alleged general and authoritative rules systematically failed the fundamental test of publicity law. This, he charged, made it radically unsuited to serve the fundamental tasks of law, which are to secure expectations and coordinate the complex interactions characteristic of modern social life.

Bentham's criticism of common law confirmed for him that, if law is to be understood, and its potential for both good and evil appreciated fully, it must be seen as *a set of laws authoritatively posited and systematically ordered*. The thought orienting his jurisprudential reflections was that *law* is a system of authoritatively posited *laws* (IPML 294, 299). To articulate and elaborate this orienting thought he sought to construct a "new model" for law (*Corr.* I, 367). Ironically, for this purpose he turned to the ancient thetic model of law. Bentham thought that the command model was best suited to the demand of publicity and he offered a definition of law tailored to this model (UC 69.69–76; UC 70a.3–6). This model called for laws to wear unmistakable marks of their authenticity and to make their content manifest in canonical language; and it linked the directive aspect of law to its prominent coercive aspect in a natural way. All of this, as Hobbes had been keen to argue, was to be done in a way that promised to provide common, public standards for people struggling to make their way through the dangerous network of social interaction.

Bentham developed the most comprehensive, systematic and sophisticated theory of law in the positivist tradition before the mid-twentieth century. Yet his boundless intellectual energy could not be contained within any paradigm and his restless drive to reform legal thought and practice led him to large-scale revisions of received ideas even as he explicitly endorsed them. In the remainder of this chapter, I propose to sketch the main outlines of Bentham's universal jurisprudence, highlighting his revisions of the core doctrines of the broad jurisprudential tradition described in earlier in this chapter.

Early Thoughts

Bentham began in his early work (in the mid- to late-1770s) with an orthodox understanding of the command model. The idea of "[l]aw was invented to denote a General Command of Public Government" (UC 69.142), he wrote. In his essay "What a Law Is" (UC 70a. 3–6), he developed this thought. A command, he wrote, is the verbal expression of the wish of a superior addressed to an inferior that the latter act in a certain way. In expressing this wish, the superior seeks to produce this conduct in the inferior, and for this to occur two ideas must be communicated: an idea of the type of action he has in mind and an idea of his wish or volition. This volition of the commander is meant to furnish the requisite motive to perform the action (UC 69.71). Petitions, requests, and commands are all expressions of volition aimed at producing conduct in others; they differ only with respect to the social relations between the parties: requests are made of equals, petitions of superiors, commands to inferiors.

The inequality Bentham had in mind in these early manuscripts was primarily, but not exclusively inequality of physical power—that is, differential ability to inflict suffering on a person. But he was keenly aware, especially in the next decade (for example, in *Limits*), that physical power was not of the right kind to explain what we called earlier the special normativity of law. He distinguished sharply between "the power of contrectation"—the power of physically affecting bodies—and "the power of imperation"—power to command (*Limits* 103, 148–50 n. b). The power of imperation depends often (but not exclusively) on the power of contrectation, but it is fundamentally different from it. The power of imperation is a power over the "active faculties" of persons whereas the power of contrectation is power over their "passive faculties." Like the earlier thetic tradition, Bentham recognized that law depends on a normative relation. It is a mistake, I believe, to think that Bentham sought conceptually to reduce law to strictly factual relations, like those of sheer physical power.

Finally, Bentham observed that, in virtue of being general, the effects of commands can be seen in certain regularities of behavior. This, he argued, has led many to confuse law properly so-called with other phenomena or fictions regarding them (UC 69.142–3). Law must not be confused with a mere regularity of behavior of inanimate or animate beings. Law, he wrote, "came to be considered as a cause of uniformity among such acts . . . Looking forward from the Law [i.e., juridical law], men observed an uniformity produced by it: and looking backwards from an assemblage of uniform actions, saw them resulting by a law" (UC 69.142). However, he insisted that law is not merely any regularity, nor merely any cause of such regularity. Law is a matter of command, and legal order is an order produced by such commands. Hence, he argued, it is a mistake to think of customs or laws of nature as proper *laws*, in virtue of some regularity of behavior (ideal or real) associated with them. Similarly, he argued that law is not utility or a dictate of utility. For utility is a fact that operates as a reason for action (or law), but it is not a law; neither is a "dictate of utility" a law. It is just an opinion about utility (UC 69.72). Law, in contrast, is a command, an *act of will*, not an act of the understanding. Law is the expression of the will of one person communicated to the will of another. Furthermore, laws are *general* commands. Hence, common-law decisions, while they may produce some degree of uniformity of behavior, appear to have "somewhat of the effect of general laws" only "in virtue of the more extensive interpretation which people are disposed to put upon" those commands (*Limits* 161). Common law is not law, we saw in Chapter 7, because insofar as it involves commands they are particular, and insofar as it pretends to be general (as represented in propositions inferred or "abstracted" from particular decisions) it fails to take the form of commands.

Thus far, Bentham seems to have walked a familiar jurisprudential path (albeit begging important questions along the way). Yet, even in these very early manuscripts, he departed from the orthodox command model in one respect. He held that sanctions may be needed for the law to be "effectual," but he was willing to concede that they are not logically required by the concept of command, or even the concept of law (UC 70(a).5). Sanctions play a key role in law, but they are not logically necessary elements of law. From the beginning of his career, Bentham argued that laws typically have a complex command structure: a "primary" law addresses individual law subjects and commands a certain action (or refraining), while a "secondary" law commands a third party (an official, for example) to punish disobedience of the primary law (UC 69.74). Sometimes the secondary law is not needed, or is replaced by promise of reward, or ambient reasons are sufficient to provide addressees with reasons to comply.

The Command Model Revised

Very early in his career, Bentham discovered that, for his purposes, the received command model was limited in several ways.[44] The model could not capture key features of law. Unlike later critics of the command model,[45] Bentham thought these serious defects called for the model to be refined rather than abandoned. Still, his refinements dramatically transformed the model. Bentham's continued use of the simple model throughout his life, where context did not demand a more nuanced concept, masked the extent of this transformation from his contemporaries and from admirers and critics alike well into the twentieth century. I will mention a few of the most important revisions of the thetic model. In Chapter 13, I will link these revisions to Bentham's underlying conviction regarding the public nature of law.

The first revision resulted from the mode of analysis of law that Bentham developed. This mode of analysis proceeded on two levels simultaneously. One focused on the logical form of laws, the elemental components of (a system of) law; the other focused on the fundamental social–political tasks of law. The former proceeded from the assumption (familiar in the thetic tradition) that the most basic mode of operation of law is that of directing the actions of individual rational agents; the latter from the assumption that law's fundamental task is the

[44] For further discussion of this topic see Chapter 13, 291–4.

[45] See Gerald J. Postema, *Legal Philosophy in the Twentieth Century: The Common-Law World* (Dordrecht: Springer, 2011), Chapters 1 and 7.

ordering or structuring of social and political life, thereby promoting the "security" of every member (BCLT ch. 5). Viewed from the former analytic perspective, the *directive* and *coercive* ("penal") aspects of law appear primary, but viewed from the latter perspective the *constitutive* aspect of law, defining social and political relationships and putting them into coherent order, is more salient. Bentham called the latter aspect the "distributive" dimension of law. It has two complementary parts: civil law ("*droit distributif privè*") and constitutional law ("*droit distributif politique*") (UC 99. 34; UC 32.130). Law not only structures horizontal relationships among citizens, enabling coordination of social interaction, but it also structures political power, enabling it to do its governing with a claim to legitimacy, and defining institutions for holding governing power publicly accountable. Thus, from a logical point of view, the "penal" aspects of law appear primary and "civil" or "distributive" aspects only secondary, as handmaidens to the penal; however, viewed from a practical and functional point of view it is the "distributive" aspect that provides the focus and the "penal" (especially the coercive-sanctioning) aspect underwriters, facilitates of the primary work of law. "With relation to the civil code" Bentham wrote, "the matter of the penal code is but a means" (CC (B) 12).

Although Bentham sustained the view throughout his vast writings that the proper model of the logical structure of a single law is that of command—with two major parts: a punitory and an expository part—he gave the definitional and expository elements greater emphasis. From time to time, he even toyed with the idea of trying to capture the entirety of the law in (or from the point of view of) the civil code (B iii. 161; CC (B) 12). Law is not, or not merely, a means of "inducing" behavior, he believed; it is also, and more importantly, a means of making known to citizens what each person's property is, what relationships each bears to others, and the like (CC (B) 12). Law plays a key epistemic role in society, defining and, for legal and public purposes, constituting social and political relationships. Law's *epistemic* role in society, Bentham thought, is at least as important as its *directive* role. Bentham came to realize that in large part law does its practical, directing, action-guiding work indirectly, through this expository, constituting work. He was especially keen to analyze and map this constitutive dimension of law.

Through its comprehensive and systematic character, Bentham argued, law seeks to relate and integrate the activities and patterns of interaction of citizens across the whole community. "Law provides a general rule covering the whole field of action" (UC 30.60). Law seeks to structure all fundamental social relationships and recurring forms of interaction. It links together people and transactions across the community both synchronically and diachronically, and brings actions and solutions of areas distant in space or time to bear on immediate problems. Effective public knowledge of this linkage is essential for a society which is too large for its members to interact on an intimate, face-to-face basis, but which is nevertheless pervasively interdependent.

In this way, "definitional" or "distributive" law supplements the penal law in its motivational task, by redefining the practical situations that parties face. What might appear to the parties to be an isolated conflict, can be seen through the lens of law to have wider public significance, and the web which the law attempts to spin provides a context of sufficient breadth to make reasonable the adoption and maintenance of a sense of common interest.

Second, Bentham recognized that many laws do not function as directives for action—some issue permissions, defining liberties rather than duties, some set out conditions for legal recognition of contracts or transfers of property or of explicit law-making activities, some define the legal status of persons rather than directing their actions. In view of the defects of the simple command model, Bentham structured his logical analysis of laws around an "imperational" theory of law.[46] His empiricist–pragmatist ontology (see Chapter 1), combined with his keen sense of the essentially public character of law, led Bentham to take verbally expressed volitions as the ultimate unit of analysis of legal norms. "A law may be defined [in part] as an assemblage of signs declarative of a volition conceived or adopted by the sovereign in a state" (*Limits* 24). From a logical point of view, laws are a species of linguistically formulated propositions which express volitions of certain persons. Canonical linguistic formulations of the laws is as essential to this picture as the volitions they publicly express. Moreover, these propositions are attributed to persons either directly or indirectly (by "adoption" via other norms). Since volitions are always the volitions *of someone*, laws must be traced ultimately to the declarations or adoptions of persons authorized to make them. From this starting point, Bentham was able to distinguish several various kinds of "imperations" (prohibitions, prescriptions, countermands, permissions) and work out an impressive, if rudimentary, deontic logic ("logic of imperation").[47] Also, crucial for his larger project was his analysis of the way in which components of the propositions can restrict or qualify other parts, imposing conditions on them, limiting their scope or application (*Limits* §12). Within this single conceptual framework, Bentham sought to give an account of the variety of legal norms, including what we, after Hart,[48] call power-conferring rules. Like Kelsen a century later, Bentham tried to capture legal powers for conceptual purposes as "parts" of larger, more complicated units of analysis of which a volitional element was also a part.[49] But, as we have seen, this was not because he took the basic social function of law to be penal control.

Third, Bentham's imperational theory has implications for his understanding of law which depart significantly from other uses of the command model in the

[46] David B. Lyons, *In the Interest of the Governed*. Oxford: Clarendon Press 1973 (revised 1991), Chapters 6–7.

[47] *Limits* §12; see Lyons, *In the Interest of the Governed*, Chapter 6.

[48] Hart, *Concept of Law*, Chapter 3.1.

[49] H.L.A. Hart, "Bentham on Legal Powers," *Yale Law Journal* 81 (1972), 799–822.

thetic tradition. Bentham recognized that typically law *supplies* reasons for compliance with law's directives. But even in this respect Bentham's account departs from the simpler Hobbes-Austin model of commands. The sanction, on Bentham's view, may be either negative (penalty) or positive (reward). And, more surprisingly, he held that whether a sanction is attached to a legal directive is a contingent matter, a matter to be determined by the law-maker, on practical grounds. Sometimes, law-makers do not make any special provision for sanctions, leaving the motivation for compliance either to the judgment of those subject to the laws, or to existing extra-legal forces (the "moral" or "religious" sanction). In Bentham's view, norms or directives do not fail *as laws* just by lacking specifically legal means of enforcement. Thus, Bentham treated constitutional constraints on the power of the sovereign—he called them "laws *in principem*"—as matters of *legal duty*, even though he recognized that sovereign commitments will not, and probably cannot, be legally enforced against the sovereign (see Chapter 12, 279–81). They impose legal duties, nevertheless, by virtue of their enforcement by the social or "moral" sanction of public opinion (*Limits* 86–93).

Moreover, sanctions are not properly understood as *likely* consequences of non-compliance (or of compliance, in the case of rewards), they are consequences that *ought* by law to occur, and this *normative* relationship between the directive and the sanction is grounded in secondary legal norms, directives addressed to officials to *see to it* that the primary laws are enforced; which directives themselves rest on further directives to other officials, or ultimately on the judgments of the public which hold officials to their legal responsibilities.[50] Thus, on Bentham's view, coercion is not law-defining, but rather is one element of multi-part institutional-cum-informal structure for securing the effectiveness of the law's system of norms.

Fourth, with respect to the obligative laws—proper "commands"—Bentham rejected Hobbes's view that law's directives are *peremptory*, meant to displace the judgment of those addressed with the judgment of the authority who "conceives or adopts" it. Sovereign commands, or imperations more generally, publicly mark certain types of actions for special attention, but reasons for behaving in accord with them lie not in the imperations themselves. Moreover, the commands must not replace the exercise by law's subjects of their judgment with respect to so acting. Law requires submission of conduct, he insisted, but not submission of judgment (*Com.* 346); and those who demand such submission, defeat their claim to authority. "Those who are able to convince men, will treat them like men," he wrote, "those who only command, avow their inability to convince" and lose their right to command (B i. 160). The reasons for compliance might not always come from the reasonableness of the laws themselves, but from their ability to focus expectations

[50] *Limits* §13; see Guillaume Tusseau, "An Old English Tale? Bentham's Theory of the Force of a Law," in *The Legal Philosophy and Influence of Jeremy Bentham*, Guillaume Tusseau, ed. (London: Routledge, 2014), 86–9.

of people in such a way to enable the coordination of their actions and thus make compliance with the law the thing, on balance, that it is most reasonable to do. This led Bentham later in his career to insist that the publicly articulated and promulgated codes of law always include a "perpetual commentary of reasons" (LW 121 n. a; see also Chapter 13).

This leads us to one final significant modification by Bentham of the thetic model of law. In Bentham's view, the idea of command brought forward the necessity of formal "marks" of authenticity, for what we now call the "validity" of a law was strictly a matter of its issuing from an authorized source in a prescribed manner (Bentham UC 70(a).5). But this formal notion of validity did not exhaust Bentham's view of the essential constituents of law. Laws may be conceived as commands, but "[a] law . . . is a command," he wrote, only "when it is entire" (B iii. 217). The concept he sought to articulate throughout his career—the focal point of his "universal jurisprudence"—was the concept of *a law*, and of *the law*, understood as "the sum total of . . . individual laws taken together" (IPML 294). The first and most fundamental question of this jurisprudential investigation, therefore, is: What is *a law*—a complete, whole, "entire but single law" (UC 70(a).5, 8; IPML 299). And he was very clear about the fact that what he sought was "the logical, the ideal, the intellectual whole, not the physical one: the *law* not the *statute*" (IPML 301). Law in this "integral sense" is to statutes as the whole muscle dissected by an anatomist is to the steak cut by a butcher (*Limits* 35). Invariably, enacted rules are "fractional," that is, fragmentary or portions of some number of complete laws (B iii. 217). Thus, Bentham's core concept of law is rational rather than empirical, the idea of an indispensable fictitious entity—not the idea of *ideal law*, of good or just law, but of law *properly understood*.[51] And, in Bentham's view, law properly understood includes not only conditions of validity (marks of authenticity), but also condition of completeness.

At the core of Bentham's model of a complete law is the idea of a complete directive for action, one which includes in it "everything necessary for adequate direction" (*Limits* 176–8; B iii. 217), including all the qualifications, limitations, elaborations that apply to it and all the institutional and procedural conditions of its implementation and enforcement (UC 70(a).8; IPML 164–5).[52] Of course, none of this expository, elaborative, and qualificative material is *uniquely* tied to a single (complete) law; indeed, a vast amount of it will be shared by a large number of laws. Laws are like pyramids represented as standing on one base (IPML 234). A law is complete, then, when all its necessary elements are connected and this is made explicit by "juxtaposition" or "reference" (*Limits* 171–2). Thus, laws are systematically interconnected, not only in their logical relations, but in their shared substance,

[51] See Bentham's letter to Lord Ashburton, OLG 310; see also *Limits* 222–3.

[52] "Leaning on his elbow, in an attitude of profound and solemn meditation, '*What a multitude of things there are*' (exclaimed the dancing-master Marcel), '*in a minuet*?'—May we now add? *and in a law*" (IPML 311).

and this implies that the idea of a complete law *presupposes* the idea of a complete body of law:

> [T]he idea of a law, meaning one single but entire law, is in a manner inseparably connected with that of a complete body of laws; so that what is a law and what are the contents of a complete body of the laws are questions of which neither can well be answered without the other. A body of laws is a vast and complicated piece of mechanism, of which no part can be fully explained without the rest. To understand the functions of a balance-wheel you must take to pieces the whole watch: to understand the nature of a law you must take to pieces the whole code (IPML 299).

To explicate the concept of law, we must explicate the notion of *a* (complete) *law*, but that is not possible without recognizing, and putting at the center of our explication, the *systematic substantive* relationships among laws. This insight, which structured all of Bentham's vast writings on "universal jurisprudence," follows from his conviction that law, necessarily (by its nature), directs and orders action of rational agents and it can do so only if it is public and accessible.

Publicity is an essential feature and requirement of law, according to Bentham, a characteristic any given law or body of laws is likely to have only to some degree. But it is not merely a good-making property of law; rather, it is a characteristic without which law would be inconceivable, pointless. In this respect, Bentham followed Hobbes, but he departed from him in his view of what this implies for law and the conditions under which law can hope to do its work with a modicum of effectiveness. Bentham presupposed, what Hobbes was very keen to deny, that there is a language of practical reasons that is sufficiently public such that it can support and underwrite the law's project of coordinating social interaction and holding governing power accountable. Hobbes looked to law to *create* a language of public reasons; Bentham looked to law to *facilitate* and enhance a language already available. In Chapter 13 we will trace the importance of publicity in Bentham's moral and political philosophy as well as his jurisprudence.

9

Facts, Fictions, and Law

Foundations of the Law of Evidence

Bentham's writings on evidence in law represent an impressive intellectual achievement.* Already in the early 1770s, Bentham sketched the outlines of his theory,[1] but the largest part of the work was written between 1802 and 1812.[2] From the great mass of manuscripts, James Mill in 1809–11 gathered together work eventually published in the Bowring edition of Bentham's *Works* as *An Introductory View of the Rationale of Evidence* (B vi. 1–187). Dumont composed *Traité des peuves judiciares* from Bentham's manuscripts and published it in French in 1823 (later published in English as *A Treatise on Judicial Evidence* in 1825). And John Stuart Mill, in a Herculean effort, edited *Rationale of Judicial Evidence* in five volumes in 1827 (published in Bowring at B vi. 188–595 and B vii. 1–600). In this work, Bentham combined an impressive command of the English law of evidence and treatises on it and infinite patience for detailed analysis and critique of its "technical system" with his mature epistemology and theory of language, and a refined utilitarian theory of law and legislation.

Bentham's theory of evidence was part of a larger blueprint for legal procedure and that in turn was part of his general theory of adjudication. The principle of utility defined the ultimate aim of this institutional engineering and the general practical frame for the analysis of the law of evidence. The influence of his work on universal jurisprudence, as represented in, for example, *Limits of the Penal Branch of Jurisprudence*, is also apparent, but somewhat less so. Prominent in many of the more philosophically interesting portions of these massive texts are his general philosophical theories of language, judgment, and belief, which we explored in Chapter 1.

Bentham's analysis of the probative force of evidence appears to be skeptical and relativist. His theory is rooted in a deep skepticism regarding the possibility of

* Adapted with permission from G.J. Postema: "Fact, Fictions and Law: Bentham on the Foundations of Evidence," in *Facts in Law, Proceedings Durham 1982*, W. Twining, ed. (Wiesbaden: Steiner, 1983), 45–54.

[1] See UC 51a.1–35 (1772?), UC 46.1–55 (1780–85).

[2] For an account of the history of Bentham's work on evidence see A.D.E. Lewis, "The Background to Bentham on Evidence," *Utilitas* 2 (1990), 195–219; William Twining, *Theories of Evidence: Bentham and Wigmore* (Stanford: Stanford University Press, 1985), 18–27, and Twining, "Bentham's Writings on Evidence," *Bentham Newsletter* 10 (1986), 34–40. In *Theories of Evidence* (27–47), Twining offers a useful précis of Bentham's *Rationale of Judicial Evidence*.

constructing adequate rules for assessing the admissibility, reliability, and weight of evidence.[3] Bentham was convinced that in all aspects of the judicial assessment of evidence, there was no place for formal, rule-bound reasoning, and it is tempting to trace this rule-skepticism to a deeper epistemological skepticism. One might imagine Bentham arguing that it is impossible to construct useful or adequate rules for the admission or exclusion of evidence, or for assessing its weight or reliability, precisely because there is no objective basis for making such assessments and judgments, and consequently any such rules could only be entirely arbitrary.

Bentham's discussions of the notions of the weight of evidence and of its "probative force" sometimes suggest this explanation. For example, he insisted that judging the "degree of connexion" between a principal fact and an alleged evidentiary fact is strictly an "instinctive operation" (RJE vi. 216). Not only is the strength of evidence for a conclusion likely to be different from one occasion to another, but, he often insisted, this degree of strength *just is* the extent to which one feels persuaded of the truth of a proposition given the evidence, and that, of course, is something that can vary from person to person. "In the case of circumstantial evidence," he wrote, "the probative force of the evidentiary fact, considered as indicative of the existence of the principal fact (which is as much as to say the strength of the persuasion produced by it), is susceptible of every variety of degree in the bosom of the judge" (RJE vi. 224). This seems to commit Bentham to a skeptical view of evidence and inference in juridical contexts. Yet his monumental *Rationale of Judicial Evidence* shows few signs of this epistemologically skeptical foundation. Rather, seen in light of his theory of language and fictitious entities, the empiricist, quasi-pragmatist elements of his theory become clear.

In this chapter, I shall argue that Bentham was no skeptic or radical subjectivist regarding the evaluation of evidence. Statements of probability, or of the persuasive force of some piece of evidence, on Bentham's view, are subject to rational assessment. Judgments of the probative value of evidence, like moral judgments, are *expressions* of the speaker's state of mind; they express degrees of conviction of the speaker, which are subject to the discipline of rational method. To be sure, Bentham was a subjectivist regarding probability statements, but, I shall argue, he was a subjectivist with a difference—a difference which is, I believe, historically and philosophically significant. Although Bentham was primarily concerned with the ontology or semantics, rather than the syntax, of probability statements, his semantic views have important implications for our understanding of the syntax of probability statements. Thus, discussion of his views adds a historical voice to the chorus in recent debates over the logic of probability in its primary juridical uses. The evidence from Bentham's texts is not unambiguous, and Bentham himself did not view the issues in quite the sharply defined terms of the debate between

[3] See Twining, *Theories of Evidence* 66–72 for discussion of Bentham's "anti-nomian thesis."

Pascalian/Bayesians and Baconians;[4] nevertheless the preponderance of evidence suggests that, if he were forced to choose, he would side with the Baconians. This is of historical interest, of course, but more interesting from a philosophical point of view is his attempt to ground this Baconian interpretation of probability in juridical contexts on a sophisticated subjectivist foundation.

BENTHAM'S SUBJECTIVIST ACCOUNT OF PROBABILITY

Correct adjudicative decisions must be based on particular propositions of law and particular statements of fact. The former are inferred from general propositions of law, the latter are grounded on other particular statements of fact—that is, on evidence. Evidence, according to Bentham, is some matter of fact (or statement regarding some matter of fact) which is presented to the judge (fact-finder) for the purpose of producing in the judge's mind persuasion of some other material fact necessary for the judge's decision (IRE 7–8). Evidentiary facts persuade fact-finders of the existence of principal facts in virtue of their "probative force." Evidentiary facts "prove," or at least "probabilize" or "disprobabilize," principal facts to some degree (RJE vii. 4). The account thus far set out has two noteworthy implications. (a) Probative force comes in degrees. In its highest degree, probative force is conclusive of some proposition (makes it "practically certain," in Bentham's phrase); in some lesser degree it is said to make the proposition more (or less) probable. (b) Probative force is not a property of single facts—either evidentiary or principal—rather it is a property of an evidentiary fact *E* only insofar as *E* is evidence of principal fact *P*. More precisely, it is a *relation between* sets of facts or propositions. *P* is "probabilized" *by E* and it is probable *relative to E*. Thus, the probability of *P* cannot logically be detached from *E*. There is no "absolute" or without-qualifications probability of *P*, unless by this one refers to the probability of *P* given *all* there is to know.[5]

[4] The so-called Baconian attack on the standard Pascalian/Bayesian understanding of probability was led by L. Jonathan Cohen in several papers and especially his book, *The Probable and the Provable* (Oxford: Clarendon Press, 1977). On the American side of the Atlantic, the cause was taken up by, among others, Lea Brilmayer and Lewis Kornhauser, "Review: Quantitative Methods and Legal Decisions," *University of Chicago Law Review* 46 (1978), 116. The Pascalian case has been made by Richard Eggleston in his *Evidence, Proof, and Probability* (London: Weidenfeld and Nicolson, 1978), and carried forward against Cohen by Glanville Williams, "The Mathematics of Proof," *Criminal Law Review* (1979), 297, 340 and *Criminal Law Review* (1980), 678. See also Cohen's reply "The Logic of Proof," *Criminal Law Review* (1980), and 747. For the growing literature in American legal journals see David Kaye, "The Laws of Probability and the Law of the Land," *University of Chicago Law Review* 47 (1979), 34. Note: this essay was initially written in the early 1980s. I have made no attempt to relate the discussion here to more recent developments in the philosophical literature on foundations of probability.

[5] This is the clear implication of Bentham's claim that to say without qualification that some proposition P is impossible or improbable is to assume omniscience (B viii, 211).

The central logical and epistemic questions at the foundations of the law of evidence concern this notion of probability or probative force of evidence. However, in Bentham's view, our investigation of these questions is faced immediately with a difficulty concerning the semantics of the language of probability that threatens the entire enterprise. First, following Locke, we might distinguish between the probability of a proposition and the degree of assurance we attach to the proposition.[6] This would incline us to regard probability as an objective property of the facts themselves—existing with them "in nature." However, this cannot be, Bentham insisted. Consider a pair of facts such that *P* is probable to some degree given (i.e., relative to) *E*. No matter how hard we look, he argued, we will not be able to find among the sensible properties of *P* or *E* the property of *P's* probability given *E*.[7] Moreover, "be the fact what it may, between its existence and non-existence … there is no medium: and thence it is that, ascribed to facts themselves, *probability* and *improbability*, with their infinity of degrees are mere figments of imagination."[8] That is, facts either exist, or they do not; there is no such thing as a probable fact. Existing as a fact does not come in degrees, but probability does admit of degrees; therefore, probability cannot be a fact or quality of facts in nature.[9] "Upon examination," he concluded, "this quality … is a purely fictitious one" (RJE vii. 77). But if the probability of an event is not an objective property of the event as the surface language of probability leads us to believe, then either we are talking sheer nonsense, or a different semantic interpretation of the language of probability must be given. For Bentham, this semantic or ontological question must be answered before the epistemic issues underlying the concept of evidence and proof in law can be addressed.

[6] Locke, *Essay Concerning Human Understanding*, P.H. Nidditch, ed. (Oxford: Oxford University Press, 1975), IV, 20, 16.

[7] Compare Hume's famous argument regarding moral properties in THN III, I, i.

[8] IRE 46. See the parallel passage at RJE vii. 78–9 where he goes on to say: "the matter of fact being, at the time in question, either in existence or not in existence, … neither the evidence nor the persuasion [is] capable of making any the slightest change in it."

[9] John Venn, half a century later, drew the opposite conclusion from almost the same argument:

> I am about to toss one [penny] up, and I therefore half believe … that it will give head. Now it seems to be overlooked that if we appeal to the event, … our belief must inevitably be wrong, and therefore the test above mentioned will fail. For the thing must either happen or not happen: i.e., in this case the penny must either give head or not give it; there is no third alternative. But whichever way it occurs, our half-belief, so far as such a state of mind admits of interpretation, must be wrong. If head does come, I am wrong in not having expected it enough; for I only half believed in its occurrence. If it does not happen, I am equally wrong in having expected it too much; for I half believed in its occurrence, when in fact it did not occur at all … The two states of belief and disbelief correspond admirably to the two results of the event happening and not happening respectively, … but to partial belief there is nothing corresponding in the result, for the event cannot partially happen in such cases as we are concerned with.

John Venn, *The Logic of Chance* (1866), Chapter VI, reprinted in *Studies in Subjective Probability*, Henry Kyburg and Howard Smokler, eds. (New York: John Wiley & Sons, 1964), 32, 33. However, Venn ignores, as Bentham to his credit does not, that probability is always relative to evidence.

According to Bentham, the language of probability may be fictitious language, but to say this is not to say that it is language we must, or even can, dispense with. The language of probability is significant, not because it is used to refer to concrete material entities or actual events, but because it expresses or captures an important sort of psychological fact, viz., the degree to which one is persuaded of the truth of a proposition, given the evidence for it. Subjective persuasion of the existence of facts, unlike facts themselves, does admit of degrees and, thus, naturally fits our concepts of probability better than any objective fact or property.

> Probative force, and closeness of connexion as between fact and fact, having not more than apparent and relative existence (relative, viz. relation being had to him by whom the facts are contemplated in his view) nothing more can be truly indicated by them [i.e., "probative force" and "closeness of connexion"] than strength of persuasion on his part.[10]

That is, since probability is not an objective property of facts, and since probability is relative to the assessor of evidence, it must be just the degree of his persuasion of the principal fact which he expresses when he attributes the quality of probability to that fact.

However, the argument implicit in these remarks seems to rest on a confusion of two ways in which probability assessments may be said to be relative to the assessor. For, from the fact that the probability of an event can be determined only with respect to a body of evidence, it follows that if John claims that it is likely to rain today, then there must be some body of John's beliefs that constitutes the evidence on the basis of which John makes his claim. The logic of probability warrants relativizing John's assertion to some set of beliefs that John presumably holds. But it does not follow from this that John's claim indicates nothing more than John's degree of persuasion of the truth of the statement "It will rain today." It does not follow that probability is relative to John's *persuasion* of *P* given *E*, though it does follow that it is relative to *E*, which John believes.

This confusion not only affects the validity of Bentham's implicit argument, it also raises some doubt about the precise character of the account of probability he wished to advance. It might be helpful to contrast two sharply different accounts of probability that take seriously the relativity of probability to evidence and then ask which of them have greater affinity to Bentham's account.

The first might be associated with Leibniz,[11] whose views on probability, like Bentham's, were much influenced by reflection on juridical evidence and

[10] RJE vii. 64; see also B viii. 211.

[11] Leibniz seems to have sketched a prototype of the modern logical theory associated with Keynes, Carnap, and others. My discussion of Leibniz follows Ian Hacking, *The Emergence of Probability* (Cambridge: Cambridge University Press, 1975), Chapters 10 and 15.

proof.[12] All juridical inference, he observed, is relative to the evidence set before the court, and thus, all probability conclusions are "*ex datis*"; that is, conditional on, and proportional to, what we know. He noted further that evidence seldom conclusively establishes a proposition, but that it can warrant our inferences. This warrant is due, in Leibniz's view, to a *logical* relation obtaining between *propositions*, independent of anyone's beliefs about them. On this view, there might be different assessments of the weight of evidence, but there is only one correct assessment, the correctness of which is due to the logical relation between the propositions in question and is entirely independent of any personal opinion about it.

Sharply contrasting with this Leibnizian view is what I shall call the "Humean" subjectivist view, which holds that probability is *nothing more* than the degree of assurance which a person feels in the truth of some proposition after considering a body of evidence. This degree of persuasion is simply the *product* of the impact of the evidence on the mind of the assessor. "Inferences" drawn from evidence, then, are not open to rational assessment; such inferences neither have nor need objective warrant. Inference is merely a matter of moving from evidence to conclusion in a way paved by association or custom.[13]

Now, neither his rejection of the notion of probable facts, nor his recognition of the relativity of the probability of a proposition to evidence, forced Bentham to adopt one or the other of these two views. Yet, what we have seen of Bentham's positive view seems to commit him to something very close to the Humean view. He seems to have held that probative force of *E* regarding *P just is* the intensity of one's persuasion of *P* given *E*. "To say that the probative force of the evidence is at such or such a degree, is to say that, in the bosom of the judge, intensity of persuasion is at that degree" (IRE 18 n.). The language of probability, he suggested, is restricted to the two functions of (a) expressing degrees of confidence, or lack of it, in statements of fact, and (b) inducing similar attitudes toward such statements of fact in others.[14] Why, then, ascribe the qualities of probability, certainty, etc. (wrongly) to

[12] He called the theory of probability "natural jurisprudence," and regarded juridical argument as the model of reasoning and deliberation about contingencies, as mathematics was regarded as the model of reasoning about necessary truths.

[13] Hume wrote,

> Thus, all probable reasoning is nothing but a species of sensation. Tis not solely in poetry and music, we must follow our taste and sentiment, but likewise in philosophy. When I am convinc'd of any principle, 'tis only an idea, which strikes more strongly upon me. When I give the preference to one set of arguments above another, I do nothing but decide from my feeling concerning the superiority of their influence. Objects have no discoverable connexion together; nor is it from any other principle but custom operating upon the imagination, that we can draw any inference from the appearance of one to the existence of another (THN I, III, viii).

It is a question of some complexity whether Hume himself was a "Humean" subjectivist. See John A. Passmore, "Hume and the Ethics of Belief," in *David Hume: Bicentenary Papers*, G.P. Morice, ed. (Edinburgh: Edinburgh University Press, 1977), 77–92.

[14] Probative force is a fictitious quality, "a quality, having nothing of the reality connected with it but the *persuasion* ... as it hath place in the mind of him, by whom, for the more convenient expression of it, or for the more effectual spreading of the like persuasion, the fictitious quality in question is thus

the facts themselves? For the sake of convenience, Bentham replied, and because it is rhetorically effective, since one is more likely to convince another of the truth of the claim one makes if one can disguise one's own role in the "probabilizing" of it.

However, like contemporary subjectivist theories of probability, which it anticipates, this view faces several serious difficulties. First, we should note that, unlike Ramsey and other subjectivists, Bentham fashioned his account strictly in terms of degrees of persuasion, rather than degree of *belief*. This avoids the difficulties many have found in the notion of degrees of belief and it retains the focus of the analysis of probability on the context of argument and proof. Still, one might doubt whether there are discrete degrees of persuasion. We might grant that it is possible roughly and qualitatively to grade confidence in a proposition, but insist that, nevertheless, it is quite another thing to hold that persuasion comes in qualitatively measurable degrees, such that talk of degrees of persuasion can qualify as an interpretation of the formal mathematical calculus of probability.[15]

However, as we will see later in this chapter, there is good reason to believe that Bentham did not intend his account of probability to provide a semantics of the Pascalian probability calculus. Thus, his account may need no more precision than the terms that he relies on allow. Still, Bentham would not have been content to leave the matter here, for he thought it made good sense to talk of discrete and measurable degrees of persuasion, and he sought to demonstrate this. Anticipating Ramsey and others,[16] he argued that the practice of wagering provides both the *proof of* the fact that persuasion admits of, and exists in, degrees of strength, and an adequate *measure* of the probability one assigns to a proposition.[17] This argument, however, is persuasive for the general conclusion that confidence does sometimes come in measurable quantities, but there are serious questions about its general applicability in juridical contexts. Dumont, for example, questioned the intelligibility of the notion of wagers in this context. The analogy with wagers, he argued, is mistaken because "Testimony turns on past events: wagers turn on future events: as a witness, I know, I believe, or I doubt; as a wagerer, I know nothing, but I conjecture, I calculate probabilities" (RJE vi. 235; editor's note). But this does not put the objection very clearly. The key difference is not between future and past, but between wagers on which there is a clear, uncontroversially determinable outcome (which,

attributed to ... that fact itself" (IRE 46). See also RJE vii. 91–2, 78–9. The parallel of this analysis of probative force with the emotivist analysis of moral language is striking.

---

[15] See Venn, in Kyburg and Smokler, *Studies in Subjective Probability*, 21.

[16] Frank P. Ramsey, "Truth and Probability"; Bruno de Finetti, "Foresight: Its Logical Laws, Its Subjective Sources;" and Leonard Savage, "The Foundations of Statistics Reconsidered;" all in Kyburg and Smokler, *Studies in Subjective Probability*.

[17] RJE vi. 223. It must be noted that this device serves for Bentham, as a measure of the degree of persuasion which has, in his view, independent existence as a psychological fact. In this respect, Bentham differs from some recent subjectivists who tend to take a more behaviorist approach to the wager-measure.

of course, will not be known at the time of the wager) and a wager on matters which are in principle unsettlable. In the latter case, accepting reasonable odds may have no rational basis,[18] and those are just the sorts of cases which figure prominently in law.

A second, more important, objection can be raised to the subjectivist account. If the probability of a proposition is just the degree of confidence one feels in the proposition, then either such probability statements make no assertion at all (they lose all cognitive context and cannot bear truth value), or they are merely statements about the state of mind of the speaker. In either case disputes over probability assignments are rendered unintelligible. If the first is true, there is nothing to dispute about, and if the second is true disputes are reduced to disagreements in attitude, or even worse to disagreements about the accuracy of certain psychological descriptions. Rational assessment of probability assignments is completely ruled out; and this leaves their ability to warrant decisions made on the basis of them a complete mystery. Recent probability subjectivists, in order to insure that a system of wagers conforms to the standard axioms of the probability calculus, insist on coherence of the system,[19] and in this way they countenance at least one normative constraint on probability assignments.[20] But this constraint is very weak; it gives us no guarantee that such assignments will be even minimally reasonable.[21] The coherence requirement represents a step back from radical Humean subjectivism, but it still allows that there may be more than one assignment of probability given some body of evidence, and that there is no rational basis for assessing any assignment as unreasonable. Surely, some probability assignments are more reasonable than others, one might protest; and in the juridical context we want to guarantee that fact-finders make the most reasonable assignments of the probative force of evidence. After all, justice depends on it.

Finally, Humean subjectivism, even under the constraint of coherence, finds no place for the rational exercise of *judgment* in the *formation* of beliefs. It pays attention only to the outcome of the process of "assessment" of evidence; it ignores

[18] On this problem see Clark Glymour, *Theory and Evidence* (Princeton: Princeton University Press, 1980), 70; and Cohen, *Probable and Provable*, 89–91. This problem afflicts attempts to apply the wager notion to capture probabilities in *general* theoretic statements (see Henry Kyburg, *Probability and the Logic of Rational Belief* (Middleton, Con.: Wesleyan University Press, 1964), 35). But it also afflicts probability statements regarding singular events in the past, which are the most common sort of facts that need to be proven in a court of law.

[19] A system of wagers is coherent, in the current usage, if a "Dutch Book" cannot be made against the wagerer, i.e., his system of wagers does not guarantee that he will lose.

[20] See Kyburg and Smokler, *Studies in Subjective Probability*, 10–11.

[21] Bayesians argue that intersubjective convergence regarding probability assignments will eventually be achieved if persons are exposed to the same data and they are required to "learn from experience," revising initial probability assignments upon consideration of new data through repeated applications of Bayes' Theorem and the Inverse Probability Theorem. This prospect may relieve the burden of the above objection, if our concern is with assignments of probability in scientific reasoning. But for determination of probative force of evidence in juridical contexts the reply is lame, since there is no time or opportunity to carry out the "learning" process.

the fact that one attempts (more or less rationally) to *draw* this conclusion, and that one may wish to use the same evidence to construct an *argument* to persuade others of the truth or likelihood of the conclusion. Clark Glymour rightly points out that:

> To ascribe to me degrees of belief that make my slide from my premises to my conclusion a plausible one fails to explain anything ... because, even if it is a correct assignment of my degrees of belief, it does not explain why what I am doing is *arguing*—why, that is, what I say should have the least influence on others, or why I might hope it should.[22]

And the shift from talk of degrees of belief to degrees of persuasion does not avoid this problem. But surely, in law as in science, the objective of presenting evidence to fact-finders is to present reasons—that is, considerations in argument—for drawing the conclusion from this evidence.

These are powerful objections against Humean subjectivism, and Bentham was sensitive to them, especially the last one. He sought an account of probability which avoided the unacceptable ontological commitments of objectivism (and of the Leibnizian view), while leaving substantial room for the rational assessment of probability assignments. I shall argue in the remainder of this chapter that despite appearances to the contrary, the view suggested above, when properly understood against the background of Bentham's general philosophical views, explored in Chapter 1, falls between the Humean and Leibnizian extremes. Bentham sketched a sophisticated version of subjectivism that goes some distance toward meeting the above objections.

In light of what we have already seen of Bentham's discussion of evidence, it should be no surprise that one can find a short outline of the central claims of his theory of the language of fictitious entities prefacing early work on juridical evidence (UC 46.18–22). And his mature theory of evidence clearly shows the marks of the maturing of his theory of fictitious language. That theory, which we explored in Chapter 1, provides the key to understanding his view of the foundations of the law of evidence.

LANGUAGE AND FICTITIOUS ENTITIES

Bentham maintained that probability, necessity, possibility, and like modal terms are names of "ontological fictions" (B viii. 120), i.e., fictions concerned with existence. Indeed, he regarded existence itself as a fictitious entity, a quality predicated

[22] Glymour, *Theory and Evidence*, 75.

properly of real entities or events, and predicated of fictitious entities in a manner of speaking (B viii. 210). Unlike other fictitious entities, however, ontological fictions are doubly fictitious; they are, he says, "fictitious qualities."

> Quality itself is but a fictitious entity, but these are all of them so many fictitious qualities. They do not, as real qualities, —they do not, like gravity, solidity, roundness, hardness, belong to the objects themselves to which they are ascribed, —in the character of attributes of the objects to which they are ascribed (B viii. 211).

Bentham's point is not merely that probability and its kin are qualities of qualities (i.e., second- or higher-order fictitious entities), for, as we saw in Chapter 1, many kinds of fictitious entities can be regarded in this way. Rather, the point is that although all qualities are fictitiously said to exist (directly or indirectly) *in* real entities, these qualities are fictitiously ascribed *to events or facts*, whereas in fact they are qualities of experiences or beliefs about events or facts. Probability and its kin signify a modification of belief: "a disposition, a persuasion of the mind ... in relation to the state of things, or the event or events to which these qualities are ascribed" (*ibid.*). To understand Bentham's argument for his subjectivist interpretation of probability, we must recall some things we learned about his theory of language in Chapter 1.

According to Bentham, language is not merely a set of labels conventionally adopted to denote objects in the external world. Rather, language is the indispensable expression or embodiment of human thought, the instrument with which we shape our conceptions of ourselves and the external world. Terms in this language sometimes actually denote real entities (material or mental), but often they express ideas for which there is no real entity referent. It is important, he maintained, to distinguish between the *immediate* subject of communication and the indirect or *ulterior* subject. The only immediate subject of communication, he claimed, is some belief, conviction, attitude, or feeling of the speaker (B viii. 330). But such thoughts, because they involve judgments, point beyond themselves; they always have secondary subjects as well, viz., actual events, states of affairs, or real entities in the world (B viii. 321, 330–1, 333, 336, 187). We talk about the world, Bentham maintained, but only by way of making known, "signifying," contents of the mind. To *signify* some content in the speaker's mind, for Bentham, is not to denote it, but to express it, and thereby to convey the speaker's thought to another person.

Bentham held that the immediate subject of language about real entities is a *thought* or *idea* about the real entity in question—language expresses that thought. The ulterior subject is the real entity itself—it refers to or denotes that entity. This is simple enough; but the matter gets more complicated when we turn to language ostensibly referring to fictitious entities, especially ontological fictions. His view seems to be that the immediate subjects of language using fictitious terms are, again, thoughts or ideas, which are products of the mind (or language). Because this language develops on the patterns established for communicating about real entities, it appears to refer to real entities too, that is, to material objects in the external world; but it does not. There are no real entities (not even ideas) which are the ulterior subjects of such discourse. Such talk is not nonsense, nor is it incapable of validation. However, validation of the use of names of fictitious entities must be carried out by tracing the fictitious entity back to the real entities from which it was constructed or abstracted and assessing the process by which it was fashioned (i.e., by definition via archetypation, phraseoplerosis, and paraphrasis). Since the mind in the exercise of its active powers is governed by rational principles, the fictitious reference can be regarded as legitimate if the (rational) process through which it was created was properly followed.

All language, on Bentham's view, is expressive of (signifies) ideas. This is not a feature peculiar to discourse about morality or probability, and this fact does not preclude rational assessment of judgments, although the methods of testing them will vary according to the nature of the ideas or thoughts involved. Thus, the following picture of Bentham's view of the relations obtaining among reality, thought, and language emerges. It is only through creation of abstract ideas with the aid of names of fictitious entities that the advances of thought of which the human mind is capable can be achieved. Through the exercise of its rational faculties, utilizing the technologies of thought it has devised, the human mind fashions a framework for understanding and manipulating the world around it. This framework is embodied, imperfectly, in language. Language directly signifies our thought and ideas; it does not (cannot) mirror the actual structure of the external world. Language does not provide us with a picture of reality, but with the tools needed to grasp and manipulate reality to our own purposes. On this view, we have sensory access to the external world to some extent, but the structure of reality *as we know it* is the artificial product of the human intellect. This conceptual apparatus is determined, not by *a priori* principles or categories, but by the needs, interests, and purposes of human beings and the strategies they develop to meet their needs and advance their purposes.

THE LANGUAGE OF PROBABILITY

Bentham's argument for his subjectivist interpretation of probability now becomes clearer. Noting correctly that probability was not an ordinary natural property of events, his lean ontology led him to regard probability language as expressive of certain ideas without direct reference to real entities. His theory of language encouraged this move and suggested to him the most plausible alternative analysis.

From his distinction between the immediate and ulterior subjects of discourse Bentham inferred his doctrine of elliptical expression, a doctrine which leads naturally to regarding probability language as expressive of degrees of persuasion.

In his view, my utterance "Eurybiades struck Themistocles" must be regarded as elliptical, since the expression inside the quotation marks does not capture and display all that is conveyed by my utterance. It leaves out the fact that I *expressed* my belief in the event's having taken place. Thus, Bentham argued, if the matter were to fully be expressed, the representation of my utterance should read: "It is my belief that Eurybiades struck Themistocles."[23] Now, accepting this doctrine for the time being, consider the utterance "Eurybiades probably struck Themistocles." How should this be understood? One might try: "It is my belief that Eurybiades probably struck Themistocles." But that would locate the probability as a property of the event and that has already been ruled out. A more natural analysis would be: "I am reasonably confident that Eurybiades struck Themistocles." For we say, for example, "I know Eurybiades struck Themistocles," or "I think Eurybiades struck Themistocles." And in each case the qualifier modifies the opinion, not the fact. To say, "I know that Eurybiades struck Themistocles" is, among other things, to say quite emphatically "Eurybiades struck Themistocles." To do so in no way changes the event referred to; rather, it qualifies the speaker's relationship to the statement referring to that event. The use of "probably" and its kin naturally fits this pattern.

This, then, is Bentham's argument for his subjectivist account of probability. Despite the evident weaknesses that remain, this argument does not commit Bentham to skeptical Humean subjectivism. We have already seen that he does not believe that expressivist or performative aspect of probability language precludes critical assessment of the ideas thereby expressed. He did insist, insofar as immediate signification is concerned, that the speaker is infallible (since he cannot mistake the contents of his mind), but it does not follow from this that the belief or conviction is true, correct, justified, or reasonable. Neither, does Bentham warrant any such inference. As we have seen, there is nothing in his views generally that precludes rational assessment of such expressions. Indeed, his meta-ethical theory combined an expressivist account of moral judgments with recognition that moral judgments, by their nature, point beyond themselves to something that is in principle available to other moral judgers (see Chapter 3, 60–63). Concerning probability assignments, Bentham seems to have allowed explicitly for rational assessment of them: "to say that such a degree of probative force is *properly belonging* to a mass of evidence in question, is to say that, upon receipt of the same mass of evidence, the same degree of intensity of persuasion is the degree which is *fit and proper* to have place in the bosom of the judge" (IRE 18 n, original emphasis). This is not simply a matter of the "historical or psychological cause," but rather the "justificative cause" (RJE vi. 464).

[23] This does not generate an infinite regress (such that "p" means "I believe that p" which, in turn, means "I believe that I believe that p," etc.) because in Bentham's notation "I believe that . . ." marks the *expression* of the belief; it does not *report that* one believes.

This should come as no surprise considering what we learned from our discussion of Bentham's philosophical foundations. His analysis of probability as a fictitious quality allowed him to put to rest questions regarding the ontological status of probabilities which constantly troubled him, while leaving open crucial epistemological questions. Probabilities are neither objective entities nor events "in nature," nor are they mysterious abstract entities. They are, insofar as they have any reality, psychological facts of a special sort. But Bentham's subjectivism does not stop there. The "ideas" which fictitious terms signify are not merely the products of the impact of material bodies on our senses, or of the association of two or more given ideas. As we saw in Chapter 1, Bentham insisted that human rational faculties play an active role in the formation of such ideas. This is especially true of belief (in all its grades), which, he insisted, is the product of judgment (U.C. 69.133), i.e., of the exercise of the "judicial faculty." And the exercise of these faculties is open to critical assessment. Thus, although the subjective degree of confidence that a person has in a hypothesis is a fact about the state of mind of that person (one which, Bentham held, is capable of being directly apprehended by the person), this degree of confidence is itself subject to rational assessment, through assessment of the exercise of that person's rational faculties that produced the confidence. Such ideas have, or ought to have, a rational basis, and that basis, and the inference from it, are open to critical assessment. Hence, probability statements or assessments of the probative force of evidence (*E*) for some principal fact (*P*) must be seen to involve more than expression of the speaker's current state of mind. They also implicitly appeal to a complex fact about how (or how much) *E would* incline the speaker to embrace *P* when they are both regarded under certain appropriate conditions, and subjected to proper exercise of the judicial faculty. Confidence in the inference from *E* to *P* is open to correction just as perceptual judgments or beliefs may be corrected for distance or perspective.

Direct support for this reading of Bentham's subjectivism comes from several quarters. First, Bentham allowed that it is not uncommon for people to express full confidence in propositions that in fact are self-contradictory (B viii. 211; IRE 47). Such propositions represent impossible states of affairs, and this is so regardless of what people think about the matter. Their confidence is ill-placed; their judgment of probability is just wrong. Their mistake is to be explained, in this type of case, in terms of a failure sufficiently to attend to the meaning of the words in question, which failure results in misdirection of attention to experience and evidence. Thus, he concluded, those who seriously entertain such propositions are simply mistaken—not about their degree of confidence, but about the warrant available for that confidence.

Second, immediately after asserting forcefully that probability and improbability are not real qualities inhering in facts themselves, but only fictitious qualities expressing degrees of persuasion, Bentham turned to the question of justification. What are the causes, that is, *grounds*, of this persuasion? he asked:

> It having been shown that improbability and impossibility, applied to a matter of fact, are merely terms expressing a certain strength of persuasion of the non-existence of that fact—what remains is, to show what are the grounds on which such a persuasion is liable to be entertained: to show, in other words, in what consists the improbability or impossibility of any alleged fact.[24]

Bentham here was not content to locate the psychological source of probability claims; he thought it necessary to give an account of how such persuasion can be justified. Confidence, on his view, is not a brute datum; it calls for explanation and justification.

Rational assessments of probability, in Bentham's tentative account, proceeds in two stages. The first stage concerns judgments of improbability, defining conditions under which claims may properly be disbelieved with full confidence. The primary test is whether the proposition or alleged fact conforms, or fails to conform, to "the established course of nature," as understood or judged by the speaker.[25] The judgment of the improbability of an event is based on a judgment of failure of conformity between the alleged event's occurring and what the speaker knows about the regular causal relations that obtain in nature. Bentham made clear that this is a potentially complex judgment of the overall fit (or lack of it) of the alleged fact with the rest of our beliefs about nature gained from extensive experience. The process involved is akin to inference to the best explanation of a large body of our beliefs. The judgment of improbability, then, will be relative to the assessor's beliefs about the established course of nature, and his best explanatory account of his beliefs, but this is still a rational assessment based on experience, and not simply the immediate response of the mind to the appearance in his field of awareness of the piece of evidence in close proximity to the principal fact in question.

Bentham emphatically rejected the view that belief or persuasion is formed simply as a brute or intuitive response to experience. He called this "nonsense psychology" or "nonsense *pisteutics*," and lumped this heresy together with "nonsense ethics" (moral sense and moral sentiments theories), which he excoriated in Chapter 2 of the *Introduction to the Principles of Morals and Legislation*. He attacked Hume for falling into this heresy after seeing the utilitarian light (RJE vi. 240 n*). All of these heresies rest on the irrational "principle of sympathy and antipathy," he argued. The mistake both in ethics and "pisteutics" is that the view short circuits the process of rational formation of judgments in light of experience (and utility). This process takes "thought and talent," he insisted, not mere sentiment or the propensity to believe.

The second stage concerns assessment of the relative degree of probative force of a body of evidence for some principal fact. Bentham called this the method of

[24] RJE vii. 79. See also RJE vii. 83–4; IRE 46.

[25] IRE 45–7; RJE vii. 83–105.

"infirmative suppositions" (RJE vii, 64–5). The method is defined roughly as follows: Suppose that one regards some evidentiary fact *E* as counting in favor of some principal fact *P* to *some* extent or other (in court of law this would be a minimal condition of relevance[26]). To determine the probative force of *E* with regard to *P*, first consider whether there are any facts which are neither impossible nor improbable as defined above, and which, were they to obtain, would be incompatible with the existence of *P* or in virtue of which the existence of *P* would be less probable. We are to think of circumstances (which are themselves, and in combination with *E*, compatible with the course of nature) which when added to *E* would make *P's* obtaining a matter contrary to *E*, given what we know of the course of nature. Now, if *no* such "infirmative suppositions" are, from one's perspective (i.e., given one's overall beliefs), conceivable, then *E* is *conclusive* of *P*. If, however, one or more such infirmative suppositions is conceivable, then the probative force of *E* on *P* falls short of practical certainty, depending on how likely the occurrence of the subject of the infirmative supposition—or perhaps how reasonable it is to entertain the infirmative supposition. The degree of probative force of *E* on *P*, according to Bentham, is then equal to the ratio expressive of practical certainty minus the likelihood of the infirmative supposition's obtaining. And where there is more than one such infirmative supposition (say, I_1, I_2, I_3... I_n) conceivable, the probative force of *E* on *P* is equal to practical certainty minus the likelihood of (I_1, or I_2, or I_3, or ... or I_n) obtaining.[27] The basic idea seems to be that the proper degree of persuasion of *P* given *E* for a given person can be determined by measuring the shortfall from full confidence (practical certainty) produced by doubts put in the way of full confidence, qualified by the seriousness of those doubts. This is likely to be in many cases a complex matter of judgment.

The above proposal for a method of determining the strength of inference from evidentiary to principal facts, despite its sketchy character, reveals clearly Bentham's fundamental approach to the question of assessing probative force of evidence. The radical version of subjectivism is decisively ruled out. Confidence to some degree in *P* is not simply *produced* by reflecting on *E*. The belief is the product of a judgment arrived at by following a rational, evidence-attentive strategy. But, similarly, the strictly logical, Leibnizian view of the relation between evidence and hypothesis is rejected. Nowhere, least of all in his description of the method of infirmative suppositions, does Bentham embrace the view that there is only one objective, logical (though non-deductive) relation between evidence and conclusion such that belief in *P* is rational or justified given *E* just to the degree that that relation holds.[28] The degree of confidence which a person ought to have in a given statement is determined

[26] See Eggleston, *Evidence, Proof, and Probability*, 64–8.

[27] This, I believe is what Bentham means when he speaks of "the sum of their informative forces" (RJE vii. 65).

[28] See for example, John Maynard Keynes, *A Treatise on Probability*, (London: Macmillan, 1921), Chapter 1; Rudolph Carnap, *Logical Foundations of Probability* (Chicago: University of Chicago Press, 1950).

by application of "logical" rules, but these are not rules of logic strictly speaking. They are, rather, strategies for the direction of the mind. They are "procedural" rather than "substantive" logical rules. As we have seen, Bentham's approach to logic was essentially pragmatic. Rejecting what he regarded as the sterile syllogistic logic of the "Aristotelians," he sought to bring Bacon's insights into the scientific process to bear on the whole field of intellectual and practical affairs. He sought a method by the use of which the human mind could learn from and build on observation and experience. The task of such a logic, in his view, is to define strategies for the best use of the rational faculties, where "best use" is defined in terms, ultimately, of successfully advancing human purposes and satisfying human needs and interests.

Thus, Bentham' account of probability, both within and outside the law, is subjectivist and pragmatist. Sharing many features with both modern subjectivism—especially its stress on the essential connection between probability assessments and decisions, choice, and action—and the longer Leibnizian tradition with its stress on rational assessment of assignments of probability, it calls attention to a philosophically interesting middle way. However, the picture I have sketched of Bentham's views of the semantic and epistemological foundations of probability may be too clean, representing Bentham's views as more coherent and well-developed than they in fact are. It is time, now to muddy the waters some.

We may begin by considering the relation between Bentham's modified subjectivism and relativism concerning probability assignments. Unlike modern subjectivists, Bentham sketched a method of assessing the rationality of initial probability assignments. But this account gives no guarantee that rational assignments by different people will be the same. Bentham's sophisticated subjectivism does not rule out a robust interpersonal relativism. It seems that Bentham was willing to accept this, but he attributed it to the relativity of probability assignments to evidence and background beliefs (RJE vii. 80–2, 91–8). (The King of Siam rejected travelers' reports of "hardened water" in northern climates as absurd because they do not fit well with his experience and beliefs about the ordinary course of nature (RJE vii. 95).) But Bentham also fervently believed that, given the same store of background beliefs regarding the ordinary course of nature, people would make the same assignments of probability, provided they follow the procedure faithfully. Thus, in the end, Bentham's account of probability, though subjectivist, is not radically relativist. But we have already seen that this does not follow from anything in the account of rational assessment of probability assignments. Bentham seems to have introduced a contingent assumption here akin to Cohen's assumption of "universal cognitive competence."[29] Bentham never explicitly defended this assumption, but motivation for it, perhaps, can be found in his general enlightenment attitude toward knowledge and human improvement. In his view, a heavy blanket

[29] See L. Jonathan Cohen, "Freedom of Proof," in *Facts in Law*, William Twining, ed. (1983) *Archiv Für Rechts- und Sozialphilosophie* (Beiheft 16).

of ignorance, prejudice, and superstition smothers universal human potential for rational judgment in practical and theoretical affairs. If the blanket is lifted, if obstacles to rational judgment and human progress are eliminated, the clear and pure light of truth will shine through, the same for everyone, just as clearing away ignorance, prejudice, and superstition will reveal a deep and universal commitment to the simple rationality of the principle of utility. But if this was Bentham's motivation, we have uncovered a residual and quite broad objectivism in his view of truth and knowledge that is not entirely consistent with his professed, though sophisticated, subjectivism, nor in his implicit pragmatism.

BENTHAM AND THE PASCALIAN–BACONIAN DEBATE

In closing, a few words remain to be said, regarding the relationship between Bentham's account of the semantics of probability and the debate between Pascalians and Baconians over the syntax of probability statements.[30] It should be clear from the above discussion that there is nothing in Bentham's general account of the semantics of probability that puts him firmly in either camp. But his remarks about the epistemology of probability and the model of rational assessment of probability assignments suggest that he would side with the Baconians if he were forced to choose.

First, we should note that, despite his proposal of the wager as a device for measuring a person's degree of persuasion,[31] Bentham seems to have harbored serious doubts about the Pascalian understanding of probability (the "doctrine of chances"), at least for it use in juridical contexts. He seems to have regarded himself as providing an account not of "mathematical" probability as measured by the doctrine of chances, but of "ordinary" probability.[32] Cohen rightly called attention to Bentham's rejection of the Pascalian calculus,[33] but he drew this correct conclusion from what I believe is the wrong textual evidence. In the passage Cohen cited to support his claim (RJE vi. 224) Bentham rejected what he called the "mathematical" scale for measuring probative force, but what he had in mind in that passage is a scale of measurement that has no upper bound (the "infinite scale") which he links (wrongly?) to the doctrine of chances. He rejected *this* scale not because he believed it to be conceptually mistaken, but only because he thought it infeasible for use in juridical contexts. The criticism rests on the assumption that, strictly speaking, no matter how strong a case has been made for some proposition, the

[30] See note 4 above.

[31] See RJE vi. 223. This passage must not be given too much weight in determining Bentham's general views on probability. The wager, in fact, is not a good device for measuring degrees of *persuasion*—i.e., probative force of *evidence for* a hypothesis—since it measures only one's confidence in the hypothesis (without taking into account the evidence for it). For Bentham's purposes, it measures the wrong thing.

[32] This is not to say that he was averse to searching for a feasible probability scale or measure which could be expressed in quantitative terms. See RJE vi. 223–35.

[33] Cohen, *The Probable and the Provable*, 54.

addition of even more evidence would make that case even stronger: one hundred unimpeachable witnesses to the commission of a crime make the case twice as strong (Bentham held) as fifty such witnesses. But for practical purposes we need to define some upper limit of evidence—practical certainty—and treat probative force as if it were a finitely divisible quantity. This does not commit Bentham to rejection of the Pascalian probability calculus.

However, there is stronger evidence of such a rejection later in the *Rationale of Judicial Evidence* (RJE vi. 240–4). The context of the passage is Bentham's attack on "innatists" who wish to explain our willingness to believe an eye witness to an event, the prior probability of which is extremely small, in terms of an innate propensity to believe testimony of others, even against our judgment of the near impossibility of the event's occurring. This, Bentham objected, would commit us to abandon reason and experience for sentiment, which would be irrational. Belief in the trustworthiness of witnesses, like judgments of probability generally, are based on experience of the normal course of nature. In both cases, one's degree of persuasion is not based on some judgment of relative frequency, but rather on what makes sense of experience in terms of orderly causal relations in nature. Thus, we believe witnesses in the face of mathematically or statistically improbable events because (or when) we judge that the events, though statistically improbable, are *not extraordinary*. As Mill pointed out in his editorial note to this passage (RJE vi. 243–4), Bentham in this passage distinguishes sharply between mathematical improbability and "ordinary" improbability. Mathematically improbable events occur all the time; we do not regard them as improbable because they conform to our views regarding the orderly behavior of nature. Although this argument is not free of confusion, it is reasonably clear that Bentham had in mind a conception of probability not reducible to the standard Pascalian conception.

Second, the model of rational assessment of probability and probative force which Bentham sketched, though admittedly rough and undefended, bears a certain kinship relation to the recently revived Baconian conception of probability. The method of "infirmative suppositions" is Baconian in spirit. It is designed to assess the strength of inferences from a body of facts to another particular fact against the background of already established or accepted (though defeasible) causal generalizations. The initial judgment of relevance of evidence is made on this basis and the inference is challenged by other hypotheses which are themselves established on the same basis. The probability of *P* given *E* is determined by locating relevant circumstances that would defeat the *prime facie* inference from *E* to *P*. This resembles, though it does not reproduce, Cohen's "method of relevant variables" and "the balancing off of favourable and unfavourable circumstances" in the assessment of inductive probabilities.[34]

One might object that Bentham's account of probability is circular and uninformative, since it defines probability of *P* given *E* in terms of the probability of the potential infirmative suppositions, but this is not a serious objection for two

[34] See Cohen, *The Probable and the Provable*, sections 42–4, 58–62.

reasons. (a) Bentham is not *defining* probability or probative force here. That definition, or an approximation to it, was given earlier—the probative force of *E* is the degree to which a person would be persuaded of *P* on the evidence of *E* were he to assess *E* in the appropriate fashion. What Bentham sets out here is the method for properly assessing probative force. (b) According to this process, the inference from *E* to *P* is a function of the strength of other inferences which are themselves based on other inferences. The warrant from any inference is drawn from the web of inferences and beliefs to which it is connected. This is at least plausible, though not uncontroversial, once we recognize the deep pragmatism of Bentham's epistemology.

Problems, of course, remain. One of them concerns the status of the probabilities involved in "infirmative suppositions." Once they are brought into the process two different judgments of probability are required: (a) the probability of the evidence *E plus* the infirmative suppositions yielding the complement of the principal fact *P* (or weakening the probability of *P*) and (b) the probability of the circumstances of the infirmative suppositions *and* those of *E* simultaneously obtaining. Now, clearly Bentham regarded the probability assessment in (a) to be of the same kind as those already discussed. But what is the nature of the judgment in (b)? Is this also to be understood on the same model? Or does this involve a judgment of frequency? And if the latter, how does that affect the overall probative force of *E* on *P*?

Bentham's account of probability, like all his philosophical reflections, was borne out of the need to establish the foundations of a practical discipline. Both the strengths and weaknesses of his account can be traced largely to this point of origin. Its strengths lie in this sensitivity to the complex "subjective" and "objective" dimensions of legal proof—to the roles of both belief, decision and persuasion *and* rational justification in this process. Thus, one often finds passages stressing the rhetorical or expressive uses of probability language alongside other passages pointing out the commitment implicit in such use to rational justification for the assignments of probability made. Out of this appreciation comes a sketch of an account of probability which is of genuine philosophical interest. But at the same time, the account tends to be eclectic, and the tensions between subjective and objective elements are not fully resolved. Perhaps because of the practical origin of the excursion into the theory of probability, perhaps also because of his own philosophical limitations, Bentham did not develop the view in detail once it was sketched out to his immediate satisfaction. Thus, it remains a sketch—suggestive, but wanting fuller, detailed articulation and defense.

No doubt the rule-skepticism running through his theory of evidence is influenced by his epistemology and his conception of the probative force of evidence (although there may be other motivations for it also). However, this is not a skeptic's epistemology. The precise relationship between Bentham's rule-skepticism and his epistemology remains to be worked out, but the initial paradox that motivated our excursion into Bentham's theory of probability is now resolved.

10

In Defense of "French Nonsense"

Fundamental Rights in Constitutional Jurisprudence

> No free government, or the blessings of liberty, can be preserved to any people, but by firm adherence to justice, moderation, temperance, frugality, and virtue, and by frequent recurrence to fundamental principles.
>
> Bill of Rights, Virginia Constitution (1776)

On 26 August 1789, the fledgling National Assembly of France adopted the "Declaration of the Rights of Man and the Citizen," thereby securing a prominent place for the language of rights in modern Western political discourse.* Two years later (1791), the Declaration was prefixed to the Constitution of the French Republic, and the American Republic attached a Bill of Rights to its Federal Constitution, thereby securing a place for the language of rights in the discourse of constitutional jurisprudence. The enduring relevance of the language of rights in constitutional practice and theory to the present day was assured by the emergence of a robust practice of judicial review in the United States in the first decade of the nineteenth century.

Yet from their first appearance in political debate and constitutional jurisprudence, appeals to the glittering declamatory generalities of Natural Right have attracted savage criticism. There has been no more severe or persistent critic of this "pestilential French nonsense" than Jeremy Bentham, who, ironically, began the scorching attack on the French Declaration[1] shortly after the infant French Republic made him an Honorary Citizen.[2] Bentham's critique is intemperate, polemical, tendentious, and perversely unsympathetic. Yet, buried beneath the intemperate rhetoric lies a serious and potentially deep challenge to the jurisprudence of

* Adapted with permission from "In Defense of 'French Nonsense': Fundamental Rights in Constitutional Jurisprudence," in *Enlightenment, Rights, and Revolution*, N. MacCormick and Z. Bankowski, eds. (Aberdeen: Aberdeen University Press, 1989), 107–33.

1 Jeremy Bentham, *Nonsense upon Stilts* in RRR 317–401. Bentham seriously considered the following title for his critique: "No French Nonsense: or a Cross-Buttock for the first Declaration of Rights: together with a kick of the A—for the Second . . . by a practitioner of the Old English Art of Self-Defense." Draft letter to Wm Corbett, 30 June 1801, UC 108.114.

2 The main lines of Bentham's criticism of natural rights, however, can be found already in his criticism of Blackstone in the early and mid-1770s, in his *Comment on the Commentaries* and *Fragment on Government* and his substantial, though unacknowledged, contributions to John Lind's *Answer to the Declaration of the American Congress* (1776). See Bentham, *Comment*, Editors' "Introduction," xxiv–xxviii; and Douglas Long, *Bentham on Liberty* (Toronto: University of Toronto Press, 1977), Chapter 3.

Utility, Publicity, and Law: Essays on Bentham's Moral and Legal Philosophy. Gerald J. Postema.

rights in constitutional adjudication, a challenge which emerged, newly invigorated (and largely unaware of its roots), in American legal and constitutional theory in the late twentieth century.[3] My aim in this essay is to uncover, articulate, and respond to this Benthamite challenge.

Before I turn to Bentham's attack, I will sketch very broadly an understanding of the role of rights in constitutional adjudication which has its roots in the French and American experience in the late eighteenth and early nineteenth centuries.

RIGHTS AND THE DEMOCRATIC CONSTITUTION

The constitutions of the American and French Republics announced the marriage of the ideology of natural rights with an emerging ideology of democratic constitutionalism. Consequent upon this marriage, the notion of fundamental rights took on new political significance and new legal tasks. Of course, there was nothing new in the idea of a "higher law," transcending, yet standing as ground and measure of, positive law. This was the legacy of the natural-law tradition. Neither was it novel to recognize certain rights against government as *legal* rights. This was the legacy of the Magna Carta preserved in British constitutional tradition. However, the notion of rights began a new legal and political career when the American and French peoples, in their sovereign self-constituting acts, declared publicly their commitment to certain rights and incorporated them into their constituting documents.

The political significance of this incorporation was twofold. First, it made respect for fundamental rights a publicly recognized condition of the validity of law and of the legitimate exercise of governmental power. Through incorporation of fundamental rights into the basic law of the constitution, the product of their political self-constituting activity, the people articulated publicly to and for each other the basic conditions of their national political association. What may have been regarded earlier as transcendent principles of political morality or reason-grounded natural law, took concrete shape as the core commitments of the emerging public morality of the new nations. Frequent recourse *by the people* to these public principles, making them the focus of public attention and commitment, the authors of the Virginia Constitution believed, was essential to "free government [and] the

[3] See Duncan Kennedy, "The Structure of Blackstone's Commentaries," *Buffalo Law Review* 28 (1979), 205; Mark Tushnet, "An Essay on Rights," *Texas Law Review* 62 (1984), 1363–403; Tushnet, "Constitutionalism and Critical Legal Studies," in *Constitutionalism: The Philosophical Dimension*, Alan S. Rosenbaum, ed. (New York: Greenwood Press, 1988), 150–66; Paul Brest, "The Fundamental Rights Controversy: The Essential Contradictions of Normative Constitutional Scholarship," *Yale Law Journal* 90 (1981), 1063–109; Frank Michelman, "Justification (and Justifiability) of Law in a Contradictory World, in *Justification, NOMOS, XXVIII*, J. Roland Pennock and John W. Chapman, eds. (New York: New York University Press, 1986), 71–99; John Ely, *Democracy and Distrust* (Cambridge, MA.: Harvard University Press, 1980), Chapter 3.

blessings of liberty."[4] With the emergence of the practice of judicial review, an institutional focus for such recourse was provided in the courts.

Second, incorporation of fundamental rights in the enacted constitutional documents represented a substantial limitation by the people on the exercise of their sovereign power, in both the creation and execution of law. How could such limits on the sovereign power be made consistent with the principles of democracy? Some argued that it is not, strictly speaking, consistent with *unqualified* democracy, but represents a substantial, but nevertheless justified limitation of democracy. Others argued that it is consistent with democracy, since these limits define the conditions under which alone truly democratic politics can be pursued. Regardless of the line adopted, it was standardly thought, especially by the Federalists, who became dominant in the American post-revolutionary period, that the aim of constitutional limits was to put certain issues *beyond politics*. Guardianship of such matters was granted to the judiciary, which was to adjudicate such matters on impartial and objective standards of reason which transcend the inevitable short-sighted expediency and interest-driven horse-trading of ordinary politics. The rhetoric of rights, especially natural rights, seemed especially attractive for this purpose. Such rights were thought to demarcate spheres of *private* activity into which government, and the aggregate interests of others must not intrude. They also promised to root political reality in a constant and transcendent moral reality which was, nevertheless, accessible to human reason, although, perhaps, only after submitting it to the special discipline of legal reason.

The immediate target of Bentham's blistering attack was rights constitutionalism rooted in the natural-rights tradition. Natural-rights theory, however, represents only one substantive theory of rights among several, although it was at the time the dominant theory.[5] Yet Bentham's arguments, like those of modern critics, are directed against *any* attempt to incorporate the language of rights into constitutional jurisprudence without regimenting that language to canonically formulated, specific rules of law. We might say, then, that Bentham sought to banish from constitutional jurisprudence not one or another substantive conception of rights, but the very concept of rights.

While I wish to make no brief for reviving natural-rights theory, I believe there are strong reasons for preserving the central role of the concept of rights in our constitutional jurisprudence. It is precisely the discipline and structure which the *concept* of rights brings to constitutional jurisprudence, and not any particular

[4] Section 15 of the Bill of Rights of the Virginia Constitution of 1776. Similar language can be found in several other states of the new American Republic. See C. M. Kenyon, "Constitutionalism in Revolutionary America," in *Constitutionalism, NOMOS, XX*, J. Roland Pennock and John W. Chapman, eds. (New York: New York University Press, 1979), 84–121.

[5] On this theory, rights are: (1) distinctively liberal-individualist in content; (2) pre-social in origin, i.e., the property of human beings entirely apart from their membership in any community; and (3) self-evident.

substantive theory of rights, least of all the liberal–individualist doctrine of natural rights, that I believe is its most valuable contribution. To lay the groundwork for Bentham's criticism and my later qualified defense, I wish first to look at some structural features of the concept of rights. Far from undermining Bentham's criticism, this analytical prelude is likely to make it seem more compelling. I undertake it in order to sharpen the issues between myself and Benthamite critics of rights-constitutionalism.

THE CONCEPT OF RIGHTS

The semantic realm of rights is the realm of practical deliberation and normative argument—the realm of goals and aims, duties and obligations, justification and liability.[6] To understand the language of rights we need to mark out its distinctive place in this complex of fundamental normative notions. Rights assertions are thickly textured normative assertions. Their structure is different and more complex than assertions of value, statements of goals or aims, and propositions ascribing duties to particular agents.[7] Assertions of rights typically take the form:

J has a right to X relative to (or "against") K.

A right is a certain kind of normative relation (or set of such relations) between a *bearer* (J), *respecters* (K), and the *object* of the right (X). The nature of the relation itself is complex, and can vary considerably across the range of rights we claim for ourselves and others. Over the next few pages I will explore this complex texture of rights assertions.

Interests and the Focus of Rights

While the *concept* of rights imposes few limits on the range of objects of rights, it does assume that the objects are linked to certain interests, or components of the good, of bearers.[8] Rights assertions necessarily presuppose that securing the object

[6] The discussion in this section depends heavily on work on the concept of rights in the 1970s and 1980s, in particular work of Neil MacCormick, "Rights in Legislation," in P.M.S. Hacker and Joseph Raz, eds., *Law, Morality, and Society* (Oxford: Clarendon Press, 1977); Joseph Raz, *The Morality of Freedom* (Oxford: Clarendon Press, 1986), Chs. 7, 8, and 10; and Jules Coleman, "Rethinking the Theory of Legal Rights," in Coleman, *Markets, Morals and the Law* (Cambridge: Cambridge University Press, 1988), 28–63.

[7] Carl Wellman, *A Theory of Rights* (Totowa, NJ: Rowman & Alanheld, 1985), 10; Joel Feinberg, "The Nature and Value of Rights," *Journal of Value Inquiry* 4 (1970), 243–57.

[8] This thesis is neutral between the so-called "will theory" of rights and its rival the "benefit theory." They are best understood not as theses about the *concept* of rights, but as *substantive* theories about the components of what I will call bellow the "exercise-respect structure" of all rights. (See Coleman,

to the bearer is good *because* or *insofar* as the object answers to the interest of the bearer, that is, insofar as it is a component of, or means to, the good of the bearer.[9]

It is often said that rights are essentially concerned with securing interests of *individual* human beings.[10] As a claim about the logic of rights this is false, although it may be true on some substantive theories of rights. It is true, however, that rights are "focused" in a way that distinguishes them from other kinds of moral or political aims and marks out the peculiar niche rights occupy in the conceptual environment of normative deliberation and argument. Relative to a class of moral subjects, rights focus on the good of "each and every member severally,"[11] rather than the aggregate or collective good of that class. The logic of rights requires that we distinguish between goods of the class understood *collectively* or *in the aggregate* and goods of the class understood *distributively*, but it does not require that the members of the class be *individual* human beings. There is no conceptual barrier to speaking of rights of groups, classes, states, corporations, nations, or families that are not reducible to rights of members considered apart from their membership in the group. (Of course, some group rights may *indirectly imply*, or give rise to, rights of their members.) It is conceivable, then, that some rights might secure collective goods or interests.

Again, it is often said that the essential "normative function" of rights assertions is to express a compelling demand which ordinarily will defeat considerations of aggregate or collective good.[12] But this seems to confuse a claim about the logic of rights with a substantive claim about their relative weight. From the fact that assertions of rights are logically distinct from statements of collective or aggregate goals, and that these two kinds of normative assertions can come into conflict, nothing *follows* about the weight of either kind of consideration.[13] If rights regularly defeat

"Rethinking," 38.) The will theory, as I understand it, holds the substantive thesis that there is one interest the securing of which is common to all actual rights, viz., the interest of the bearer in autonomy, or control over some area of life (or public recognition of this autonomy).

[9] In some cases, the benefit to a particular bearer of a given right *is imputed* or *assumed* rather than *actual*. This is possible because rights are typically ascribed to members of a *class* of bearers and the ascription of a right will seem appropriate if the object answers to interests of the members of that class generally speaking. See MacCormick, "Rights in Legislation," 202.

[10] MacCormick, "Rights in Legislation," 205; this also seems to be Ronald Dworkin's view in *Taking Rights Seriously* (Cambridge, MA: Harvard University Press, 1978), xi and *passim*.

[11] MacCormick, "Rights in Legislation," 205.

[12] Dworkin, *Taking Rights Seriously*, xi, 92, 191–2; Ronald Dworkin, *A Matter of Principle* (Cambridge MA.: Harvard University Press, 1985), 359; L. W. Sumner, *Moral Foundations of Rights* (Oxford: Clarendon Press, 1986), 15.

[13] Why, then, think this is a defining feature of rights? Because, Dworkin suggests, "[w]e need rights, as a distinct element in political theory, only when some decision that injures some people nevertheless finds *prima facie* support in the claim that it will make the community as a whole better off" (*Matter of Principle*, 371). But this seems false. We need rights as a distinct element in political theory whenever we find it important to recognize *distributively* certain claims of members of a class or group, regardless of the logical character of the competing moral or political considerations. Rights are distinctive normative assertions in virtue of their complex texture. They retain this distinctive character, and have a distinctive impact on practical deliberation as a result, as long as they are capable of competing with other practical considerations, including other rights.

considerations of collective or aggregate good when they conflict, this is so in virtue of their place in a substantive moral or political theory—and in particular, in virtue of the substantive importance of the interests secured by the rights—not in virtue of their logic alone.

The Content of Rights

Rights, then, are normative relations focused around the interests of bearers. We can better appreciate the complex texture of rights if we inquire after the nature of these normative relations. Consider the content of rights.

Rights as grounds. Let us begin with Bentham's positivist analysis of rights. One has a right, says Bentham, *just in case* one is the intended beneficiary of a (regularly enforced) obligation (PF 218).[14] On this analysis, talk of rights is empty except where there are legally (or informal socially) enforced obligations already in place. Moreover, the language of rights becomes entirely dispensable, since everything we want to say about rights can be said equally well with the language of obligation.[15] Bentham was not much bothered by these implications, but they troubled others, including John Stuart Mill.

Mill shifted the focus of Bentham's analysis of rights. To say a person has a right, Mill wrote, is to say:

> that he has a valid claim upon society to protect him in the possession of it, either by force of law or by that of education and opinion. If he has what we consider a sufficient claim, on whatever account, to have something guaranteed him by society, we say he has a right to it. To have a right, then, is, I conceive, to have something that society ought to defend me in the possession of (*Utilitarianism* 250).

Rights, on Mill's view, are not statements about protections actually provided by law or society for certain interests, but rather about *grounds* or reasons of a certain sort *for* these protections.

Joseph Raz proposed a more refined version of this account. X has a right, Raz maintained, if and only if "X can have rights and, other things being equal, an aspect of X's well-being (his interest) is a sufficient reason for holding some other person(s) to be under a duty."[16] This proposal seems vulnerable to Bentham's retort that "reasons for wishing there were such things as rights are not rights … want is not supply—hunger is not bread" (NS 330).[17] But the Mill-Raz thesis is not

[14] See H.L.A Hart, "Natural Rights: Bentham and John Stuart Mill," and "Legal Rights" both in *Essays on Bentham* (Oxford: Clarendon Press, 1982).
[15] Hart, "Legal Rights," 181–2.
[16] Raz, *Morality of Freedom*, 166; see also MacCormick, "Rights in Legislation," 204.
[17] See Chapter 3, 70.

that rights are reasons for rights, which of course is nonsense, but that one has a right to X just in case one's interest in X is sufficient reason for (constitutes "a valid claim upon") society to use its enforcement resources to guarantee or protect one's enjoyment of X.

The nature of rights, I have said, is determined by their role in moral and political deliberation and argument. On the Mill-Raz proposal, the role of assertions of rights is to link certain interests of rights bearers to a network of what Neil MacCormick called "normative protections." The link is provided, specifically, by the assertion that the interest is sufficiently important to *ground* or *justify* these normative protections. Rights, then, should be identified with neither the interests which ought to be protected, nor the protections that are or ought to be provided. Rather, rights assertions are normative bridges between certain interests and certain sets of normative protections.

I have put the Mill-Raz thesis in terms of *normative protections*, rather than just *duties* and *obligations* as Raz (and Mill implicitly) does. I have done this for two reasons. First, the structure and composition of the normative protections can be complex and varied; they can include elements other than duties. These protections consist of a set of normative relations which determine what the bearer may or is *empowered* to do or say relative to certain other parties, and what is *owed to* the bearer by those parties. I shall call this set of relations the "exercise–respect structure" (the E–R structure) of a right,[18] because it determines specifically how the right may be exercised by the bearer and is to be respected by others.[19] Second, the components of the E–R structure (the "content") of rights—whether of some species of rights, or of rights in general—is a matter for substantive rights theory, not formal analysis, to determine.[20] The E–R structure is determined by the weight and importance of the background interest in the circumstances in which the right will be exercised and respected, and so will depend on the E–R structure of other rights, as well as the importance of other competing moral or political considerations. Let me elaborate on each of these points.

The E–R structure of rights. My analysis makes use of the conceptual scheme made familiar in Hohfeld's *Fundamental Legal Conceptions*.[21] Hohfeld's conceptual

[18] Coleman calls this the "transaction structure" of the right ("Rethinking," 35). I follow Coleman here, although my notion is somewhat broader.

[19] This way of conceptualizing rights brings the modern notion back to its roots in pre-imperial Roman law. See Richard Tuck, *Natural Rights Theories* (Cambridge: Cambridge University Press, 1979), 9–10. *Iura* were not *possessions* of an individual over which we had sovereign control, but rather established relations and responsibilities between parties arising from an agreement between them. The modern concept of rights differs from the Roman concept in this respect: whereas *iura* were grounded in agreements between the parties, modern rights are grounded in certain interests of one of the parties. In virtue of this fact, we designate that party the right-*bearer*, even though both bearers and respecters may have liberties, powers, disabilities, etc., relative to each other.

[20] This is effectively argued by Coleman, "Rethinking."

[21] W.N. Hohfeld, "Fundamental Legal Conceptions," *Yale Law Journal* 26 (1917), 710–70. For a discussion and analysis of Hohfeld's contribution to legal philosophy, see Postema, *Legal Philosophy in the Twentieth Century: The Common Law World* (Dordrecht: Springer, 2011), Chapter 3.1.3.

scheme is best understood not as a typology of rights (or discrete legal relationships, as he proposed), but as a typology of components of the E–R structure of rights. If we look around at the rights people tend to claim for themselves or others it will be clear that they involve more or less complex clusters of Hohfeldian elements,[22] that is, sets of Hohfeldian claims, duties and liberties, or sets of powers, immunities, and disabilities, or (more typically) a complex combination of both. For any given right, these relations may be somewhat different for different classes of rights respecters.[23]

Philosophers make much of the "directionality" of duties associated with rights.[24] This is not surprising, since such duties are prominent in the E–R structure of many rights. However, note that the claims, liberties, powers, and disabilities *of bearers* are equally "directed" *toward respecters*. It is not only the relational character of the E–R structure of rights itself that explains the sense that rights are directed to the bearer, but also the fact that the *normative ground* of that E–R structure is an important interest of the bearer.

Similarly, the E–R structure is thought to provide "normative advantages" to the bearer. But this is not because the bearer enjoys liberties, powers, and immunities ("advantages"), and only the respecters suffer constraints on their choices and actions in the form of duties, liabilities, and disabilities ("disadvantages"). For bearers often "suffer" such constraints as well. An "inalienability rule," for example, imposes a disability on the bearer as well as conferring on him or her an immunity. The "normative advantages" enjoyed by the bearer can be explained only in terms of the anticipated effects of the cluster of normative protections defined by the E–R structure on social interactions.

Primary vs Secondary E–R structures. Mill's analysis of rights quoted above is deficient in one important respect.[25] Mill mentions explicitly only one party to whom bearers are related, viz., society, but surely it is possible for one to have rights against individuals, too. Moreover, Mill says that as a right bearer one has a claim to society's protection of one's *rights*, but that seems to commit Mill either to a viciously circular analysis of rights, or to the confusion of rights with arguments for them which Bentham pointed out.

The problem is that Mill failed to recognize that the E–R structure of rights is layered.[26] The *primary* layer of a right's E–R structure consists of the cluster of Hohfeldian elements I described above. The *secondary* layer—which also may include a complex set of claims, duties, powers, immunities, and the like—is designed

[22] See MacCormick, "Rights in Legislation," 205–6; Jeremy Waldron, "Introduction" to his, *Theories of Rights* (Oxford: Oxford University Press, 1984), 10–11.

[23] These relations, *pace* Hohfeld, need not be dyadic; they may well be one-many relations. See MacCormick, 206; and Wellman, *Theory of Rights*, 24, 43.

[24] See, e.g., Feinberg, "Nature and Value of Rights," 247–9, and Sumner, *Moral Foundations*, 42–3.

[25] See Hart, "Natural Rights," 92–3.

[26] The terminology is mine, but the basic distinction was introduced by Coleman, "Rethinking," 34, 36.

to *enforce* the normative relations at the primary level. These Hohfeldian normative elements come into play when the primary elements are violated or improperly invoked. Like the E–R structure, the secondary structure is determined by the weight and importance of the background interests of the bearer in the circumstances in which the right will be exercised and respected. Thus, it will depend on the nature of the primary structure, the need for enforcing it, available means for enforcing it, their costs, and the like.[27]

While the primary E–R structure may define relations between individuals, the secondary structure typically (though not necessarily) involves claims against the community more generally (or government acting as its agent) to underwrite and vindicate the primary structure. Mill's mistake was to focus exclusively on the secondary E–R structure of some rights.

Interests and the E–R Structure of Rights

It is likely that different rights will combine Hohfeldian elements into different E–R structures, some relatively simple, others very complex. The bearer's *focal interest* generates and unifies the bundle of Hohfeldian elements of any given right, and preserves the integrity of the right through changes in its E–R structure.[28] The exact nature of the E–R structure for any given right depends on the nature and moral importance of the right's focal interest and how an interest of that kind and that degree of importance can best be protected in the circumstances in which the bearer and respecters interact.

Furthermore, a right can be said to *exist* only if the focal interest is of the appropriate kind and of sufficient moral weight in the circumstances to justify a specific E–R structure relative to certain bearers and respecters.[29] It must be possible to justify this structure in light of the burdens or restrictions it places on people and the opportunity costs and other costs consequent upon respecting it. As Carl Wellman observes, "any complete justification of the assertion that some specified right exists must have a complexity comparable to the complex structure of the

[27] It is tempting to think of the distinction between the primary and secondary layers in terms of the distinction between moral and legal rights, but this would be a mistake. First, we can find this layering in *both* legal and moral rights. In the former, the distinction between layers parallels roughly the distinction between rights and remedies (if we include in the latter category also certain procedural rights). In the latter, there are informal analogues to the enforcement structure. For example, it would determine those who may and who *are authorized* to make or press the claims defined by the primary structure. Second, while some legal rights may rest on more fundamental and moral rights, other moral rights imply at most that there *ought to be* legal recognition of them, *not that there is* such recognition. Moreover, third, there may be some moral rights, with at least minimal secondary E–R structures, for which legal recognition would be undesirable. Fourth, some legal rights do not rest on moral rights at all, but still have both primary and secondary exercise–respect structures.

[28] Waldron, "Introduction" in *Theories of Rights*, 11.

[29] Raz, *Morality of Freedom*, 181–3.

rights justified . . . the grounds of rights can only be the sorts of reasons that would establish the existence of claims, liberties, powers and immunities."[30]

Thus, the *existence* and *content* of an alleged right depend on the kind of interest it seeks to protect, its moral weight or importance, and the circumstances in which it may be exercised and must be respected. That is to say, they depend on matters for substantive moral–political argument. It has always been recognized that what rights *there are*—that is, *who* has rights to *what*—is a morally and politically substantive matter. It is now clear that *what it is to have or enjoy* any given right is also in large part a morally and politically substantive matter.

Thus, if our view of an alleged right's focal interest changes, or its moral importance relative to other goals or principles changes, so too may our view of the right's content (the E–R structure), or even its existence, change. Even if we keep constant our view of a given right's focal interest, the right can generate new duties, disabilities, and the like, if the circumstances in which bearers and respecters interact change materially. As Raz pointed out, rights have thus a "dynamic aspect." No closed list of duties (or other components of the E–R structure) correspond to any given right.[31] That which preserves continuity of the right through changes in its E–R structure is the right's focal interest.

Raz also correctly observes that it may be possible to recognize that an interest is morally important enough to justify *some* significant E–R structure, without yet identifying in detail all the components of that structure.[32] Rights assertions often take this form, especially in the rhetoric of politics. We must keep in mind, however, that in this form they function as enthymemes in an extended moral-political argument, invitations to more detailed inquiry and argument. Such inquiry and argument would have to extend both "behind" the right to a more careful and detailed accounting of the importance of its focal interest and the place of that interest in a larger moral–political theory, and "ahead" to a more detailed articulation of its E–R structure and its place in the existing network of rights and other social relationships.

Given what we have learned here about the texture of rights assertions and their role in moral–political argument, we should not be surprised to find that rights assertions are contestable. Parties may agree that some right exists, but disagree about the components of the E–R structure that the right is supposed to ground and consequently disagree about the practical implications to be drawn from the existence of the right. This may be due to different general substantive theories of rights, or to disagreements localized to the species of right in question. Disagreement may turn on different characterizations of the focal interest of the right, or different assessments of its weight or importance, or different views of the

[30] Wellman, *Theory of Rights*, 5.
[31] Raz, *Morality of Freedom*, 171.
[32] Raz, *Morality of Freedom*, 184–5.

context of social relationships (actual or ideal) in which the right takes on concrete life, or different views of the best way to protect or promote that interest. Since rights promise to protect key interests from characteristic threats,[33] disagreements may arise regarding the sources or nature of these threats, or the costs of protecting against them.

Thus, rights assertions, especially when they ascribe to bearers relatively abstract rights the *existence* of which we may all grant, are likely to be invitations to extended argument and debate, rather than major premises in a very short practical syllogism. For this reason I am skeptical of Raz's view that the "mediational" role of rights in moral-political argument makes possible "a common culture ... formed round shared intermediate conclusions in spite of a great degree of haziness and disagreement concerning ultimate values."[34] The "shared intermediate conclusions" regarding the existence of certain rights are important for shaping a common culture, but not because they make it possible for us to agree on concrete practical conclusions while disagreeing about fundamentals. Because rights assertions are *bridges between* fundamental ideals and social visions and concrete social life, the disagreements about fundamentals are very likely to emerge in the concrete implications drawn from the "shared intermediate conclusions." They are as likely to generate disagreement as consensus. Their contribution to a common political culture lies in their ability to focus and structure the debate in a distinctive and constructive way, to pose common questions and problems, to bring our conflicting ideals and social visions into contact with common facts about our community's history and future.

BENTHAM'S CRITIQUE OF RIGHTS-CONSTITUTIONALISM

With this understanding of some of the distinctive features of rights claims and the logic of moral-political arguments regarding rights we can return to Bentham's broadside against "French Nonsense." In his *Nonsense upon Stilts* and elsewhere Bentham directed a heavy barrage of critical fire against rights constitutionalism of the sort outlined earlier. From this almost indiscriminate barrage I isolate three connected criticisms, which, I believe, lie at the heart of his attack.

A Conceptual Mistake?

First, Bentham argued that rights constitutionalism rests on a simple conceptual confusion. Rights are supposed to define limits on the exercise of law-making power

33 James Nickel, *Making Sense of Human Rights* (Oxford: Blackwell, 2007), Chapter 5.
34 Raz, *Morality of Freedom*, 181.

such that legislative acts in violation of constitutional rights simply fail to become law. Thus, it is said, law-makers *cannot* make law in violation of these constitutional rights. But to speak this way, Bentham maintained, confuses "cannot" with "ought not" (RRR 187–9; NS 327–8). Surely, law-makers can, and frequently do, succeed in making such laws. Proof of their success lies in the fact that people tend to obey them.

While this criticism may have some force against naïve natural-law claims, it fails against constitutional rights; for, through incorporation in the constitution, rights were made *part of* fundamental law. Bentham himself recognized that the power to make law is created, defined, and vested by a law or norm.[35] This norm authorizes parties to exercise power in certain circumstances, according to certain modes (UC 70(a).5, UC 69.87), and, he recognized, to define normative power is also to define its limits. "On the one hand," Bentham argued, constitutional laws "confer . . . public fiduciary powers: on the other hand, they prescribe limits to those powers narrowing the description of the modes of acting authorized" (UC 69.148). When those limits are exceeded, the agent fails to exercise the power. Whether the limits be substantive or formal, the *logic* of success and failure is the same. If it is a mistake in one case, it is a mistake in the other.

Bentham recognized this in the case of subordinate officials, but he insisted that confusion arises when it is claimed that there are substantive limits on supreme legislative power. But, this "mistake"—if that's what it is—is not a conceptual one. Supremacy of law-making power is not necessarily compromised by normative limits on that power, since normative limits on law-making power can be introduced without subordinating the law-making body to some other law-making body. Of course, we may wish to institutionalize the enforcement of the limits through judicial review of the exercise of legislative power. However, this is not to subordinate one law-making body to another; it is to hold the supreme law-making body accountable to the public through the courts. I suspect that Bentham's worry was not about judicial review *per se*, since even he, presumably, wished to provide for adjudication of charges of formal *ultra vires* legislative action (where formal conditions of authenticity have allegedly been violated). Bentham, then, cannot consistently complain that the idea of constitutional limits on legislative power rests on a conceptual confusion. His objection must have been that there is something about the *language of rights* which makes it an altogether inadequate vehicle for expressing constitutional limits.

Indeterminacy

The political rhetoric of rights, Bentham charged, is not the rhetoric of rational deliberation, but rather from beginning to end it is the rhetoric of bare assertion

[35] See *Constitutional Code*, (CC (B) 9) for the development of Bentham's constitutional thought on this score, see BCLT, Chapter 7.3.

and counter-assertion. "The dictates of reason and utility are the result of circumstances which require genius to discover, strength of mind to weigh, and patience to investigate: the language of natural rights require[s] nothing but a hard front, a hard heart and an unblushing countenance. It is from the beginning to the end so much flat assertion" (*Supply without Burden*, Stark i, 335). Rights rhetoric confuses assertion with proof. Rights partisans "lay down as a fundamental and inviolable principle whatever is in dispute" (*ibid.*; see B viii. 328, and B x. 63). Rather than contribute to rational practical deliberation and push debate toward resolution, they cut off debate and short-cut deliberation. Their remarkable "talent for turning up on both sides of an issue"[36] guarantees that discussion and deliberation will come to an end without bringing the disputants any closer to resolution (SM 23–4). Violence, not rational public discussion, is the legacy of the rhetoric of rights. "When I hear of Natural Rights," Bentham complains, "I always see in the background a cluster of daggers or of pikes introduced into the National Assembly" (*Supply without Burden*, Stark i, 336).

If we ignore the hyperbole, it is hard to deny the force of these objections; and the popular rhetoric of rights has not much improved over the two centuries since Bentham penned these objections.[37] Yet, one is inclined to dismiss them as merely criticisms of the partisan *abuse* of the language of rights (especially natural rights), calling us to a more measured and responsible use, rather than a radical critique of the very notion of rights requiring us to abandon it in political and especially constitutional contexts.

Of course, we are less sanguine than the leaders of the fledgling American and French Republics were two centuries ago about the prospects of anchoring our constitutional rhetoric in self-evident claims of right. Many of us look with a skeptical eye on the project of constructing a moral–political theory on the *basis* of certain rights.[38] Rights-based theories start too far down the theoretical road, we are inclined to say; rights are normatively too complex and presuppose too much to function plausibly as the primitives or basic constituents of a moral–political theory. Rights assertions may be an intelligible and even rationally sound, but they are not self-justifying. Thus, we may be inclined to admit, if reluctantly, that Bentham has correctly exposed the emptiness of natural right-based political discourse.

We might concede Bentham's objections, but resist his denial of rights any role the constitutional context. Suppose we give up rights *naturalism* and agree that rights claims need to be grounded in a deeper moral–political theory. Does this require that we purge talk of fundamental rights from our

[36] Sumner, *Moral Foundation*, 8. See also John Ely, *Democracy and Distrust*, 50.

[37] For contemporary criticism in precisely this vein, see Raymond Geuss, "Human Rights: A Very Bad Idea," *Theoria* 60 (2013), 83–103.

[38] See Sumner, *Moral Foundations*, 111–26; J. L. Mackie, "Can There be a Right-Based Morality?" *Midwest Studies in Philosophy*, vol. 3 (1978). For a defense see Raz, *The Morality of Freedom*, Chapter 8.

constitutional jurisprudence? Bentham thought it would. The virus infecting rights, disabling them from proper use in constitutional jurisprudence, is not, in his view, limited to kin of rights naturalism. To cut off constitutional rights from the natural-rights tradition, and its hope that its rhetoric can be anchored to some objectively discoverable moral facts, is to feed the virus, not to kill it, he feared.

The deeper problem in Bentham's view, we noticed in Chapter 3, is that the language of rights supplies no determinate basis for deciding particular cases.

> Lay out of question the idea of *law*, and all you get by the use of the word *right*, is a sound to dispute about. I say I have a right: I say you have no such right. Men keep talking on at that rate till they are exhausted with vociferation and rage, and, when they have done be no nearer to the coming to a mutual conception and agreement they were before (SM 23).

Only the precisely defined rights of statute and case have "any determinate and intelligible meaning" (B iii. 218). Deprived of this content all that is left "is a sound to dispute about." The language of fundamental political rights, no less than that of natural rights, is criterionless and appeals to such rights in constitutional argument inevitably result in unsettleable disputes.[39] Trading assertions of rights is more likely to bring disputants to blows than to agreement.[40]

Objectivity, Publicity, and Legal Justification

In the view of modern critics, indeterminacy of rights language undermines the alleged *objectivity* of judicial decision-making.[41] To accept the fact of indeterminacy is to acknowledge that our pious assertions that ours is a system "of law" rather than "of men" is a fraud.[42] Bentham saw clearly, however, it is not *objectivity*—in the sense of a decision's being ideally correct, or rationally preferred when seen "from nowhere"—but rather *publicity* that is threatened by indeterminacy. He recognized that, when it comes to law, the advantages of "objectivity" come not from actually *being correct*, but from being able to communicate the grounds of one's

[39] Hart, "Natural Rights," 82.

[40] Discussions of rights are coherent, a contemporary critic of rights constitutionalism maintains, "only so long as the participants agree not to raise questions about the measure of value, the level of generality [of rights claims], or descriptions of background. But as soon as a rights-claimant sees that her claim is likely to be rejected if the discussion proceeds, the claimant ought to raise these questions. At that point coherence disappears and the shouting beings." Tushnet, "Essay on Rights," 1371.

[41] For example, see Brest, "Fundamental Rights," 1096; Robert M. Unger, *The Critical Legal Studies Movement* (Cambridge, MA: Harvard University Press, 1986), 1–14. For a defense of the "objectivity" of adjudication, see Owen Fiss, "Objectivity and Interpretation," *Stanford Law Review* 34 (1982), 739–63.

[42] See Tushnet, "Constitutionalism and Critical Legal Studies," 163–4.

decision.[43] A judge's sense of the rightness of her decision may well *be* veridical (if we may speak this way for the moment), but if this sense is ineffable, if the grounds for the judgment cannot be publicly stated, then it will be impossible for anyone else (and perhaps even for the judge herself) to distinguish a veridical judgment from a lucky guess or the expression of taste or feeling.

Judicial decisions must be *defended*, we insist, and the justification must be *principled* and *public*. That is, it must proceed from general considerations that transcend both the unique circumstances of the individual case and the personal point of view of the decider.[44] Bentham agreed. As we saw in Chapter 3, Bentham insisted that practical justification in "point of right" is justification "by a person addressing himself to the community" (IPML 28; see also UC 69.238–9). Especially in the case of law, the "catechism of reasons is worthless if it cannot be made the catechism of the people" (B i. 163). For Bentham, legal justification is always addressed by a defender to others. Justification is public if the normative resources—reasons, standards, and methods of argument—it draws on are public, i.e., they transcend the private and personal point of view of the defender and are held in common by defenders and those whom they address. Reasons given in justification must be accessible *to each*, and assessable *by each*, reasonable and normatively competent member of the community in question, *independently* of the defender's word, opinion, or judgment.[45] Justification is public relative to a real historical community of agents who have available to them a fund of mutual knowledge of normative resources defining for them a public practical point of view.[46]

Thus, Bentham argued that the indeterminacy of rights language is a fundamental threat to the rule of law, because it undermines conditions of genuine public justification. The language of rights provides no public standards for evaluating rights assertions. On the contrary, appeals to rights, like appeals to the "Law of Nature" or to "Reason," merely express private opinions or sentiments *disguised* as appeals to public standards. "What is called the Law of Nature is neither a Precept nor a Sanction, but the mere opinion of men self-constituted into Legislators" (UC 69.190). "When a man disapproves of a mode of conduct considered independently of any actual System of Jurisprudence he says there is a Law of Nature against it ... If he cannot tell why he disapproves of it he begins talking of a Rule of

[43] We learned in Chapter 7 that in an early MS (UC 63.49; see UC 69.239–9), Bentham worried that a judge's direct utilitarian reasoning may be, in one sense correct, and yet fail to meet standards of legal justification because it is insufficiently public.

[44] Michelman, "Justification," 73.

[45] Challenging Blackstone, Bentham wrote, "Had our Author again instead of reason said utility, he would have said something. He would have referred us for a foundation for our judgment, to something distinct from that judgment itself" (*Com.* 199).

[46] Public justification differs from contractualist, hypothetical justification as it is now commonly conceived. The "agreement" or concurrence sought is *actual* agreement or concurrence from a *public* point of view actually available to members of the community, rather than hypothetical agreement which we surmise *would* arise *were* rational beings to take up some ideally rational and impartial point of view.

Right ... or some other imaginary standard which howsoever varied in description, is from first to last nothing but his own private opinion in disguise" (UC 69.102).[47]

Due to their indeterminacy, statements of rights fail to "stand for something that is fixed and certain, and that all men are agree about" (*Com.* 159). It is simply not possible, he maintained, to determine "by certain indications independent of opinion" whether a given course of conduct respects or violates an alleged right.[48] Without such public standards, each assertion of a fundamental right or argument based on it amounts to no more than private conjecture, which, if it coincides or converges with the conjectures of others, does so only by accident. Rights, then, even when enshrined magisterially in a constitutional document, cannot provide the resources for genuine public justification; on the contrary they undermine it.[49]

Publicity and Demonstrability

The pivotal assumption of Bentham's argument is that considerations are sufficiently public only if they "stand for something that is fixed and certain, and that all men are agreed about (*Com.* 159). I will call this the *demonstrability thesis.*[50] According to this thesis, an action, decision, or standard is publicly justifiable only if it can be grounded in arguments that *any* competent member of the community in question would accept as conclusive support for it. Public justification, on this understanding, amounts to showing that one's decision or action follows directly and indisputably from standards already agreed upon. The indeterminacy of constitutional rights language poses a serious threat to public justification, as Bentham conceived it, because it makes demonstrability unachievable.

Demonstrability is an interpretation of the demand of publicity. This interpretation can be traced to two roots in Bentham's jurisprudence: (a) his conception of the nature and fundamental tasks of law; and (b) his convictions regarding what we might call the conditions of legitimacy of authority. I will here consider only the latter because they bring us back to the central concerns of democratic constitutionalism with which we opened this essay.

Bentham's "legitimacy" argument for publicity was twofold. First, he argued that publicity is essential for fully adequate public accountability of the exercise of

[47] Compare this argument with Bentham's attack on the "principle of sympathy and antipathy" in IPML II.

[48] The immediate target of his attack at *Com.* 159 is the *criterionless* use of terms like "reason" and "reasonable," but the argument is clearly applicable to problems Bentham later finds with the rhetorical use of "rights."

[49] This argument parallels Bentham's critique of common-law theory. See Chapter 7.

[50] This is not the demonstrability thesis Dworkin attacks in *Matter of Principle*, 137–45. Dworkin's thesis makes demonstrability a condition of *truth* of propositions of law; Bentham makes it a condition of adequate public justification.

governmental power.[51] Indeterminacy, he argued, shields officials from effective public scrutiny leaving them free to act as they please.[52] The currency of public justification is thereby debased because indeterminacy denies us any sure, public means of distinguishing between good faith argument and cynical manipulation of available legal materials.

Second, Bentham argued that publicity is a fundamental condition of what we might call "rational autonomy" under law.[53] Deeply committed to the Enlightenment ideal of liberating individual judgment from the bondage of ignorance and authority, Bentham argued that law could legitimately require submission of *conduct*, but never submission of *judgment*.[54] Every citizen, he maintained, has "the right . . . of having the reasons publicly assigned and canvassed of every act of power that is exerted over him" (FG IV.24). Only through recognizing that right does law succeed in treating citizens "like men" rather than beasts (B i. 160).

As his political views matured, these two conditions—full official accountability to the public and engagement of the rational judgment of each citizen—became pillars of Bentham's conception of a democratic constitutional order. But publicity was not only a fundamental condition of *de jure* democratic legitimacy for Bentham; it was also a condition of *de facto* legitimacy. For, he argued, law is effective, and stable over time only if allegiance is based on conviction. "Power gives existence to a law for the moment, but it is upon reason that it must depend for its stability" (B iv. 310).

This brings us round to the concerns of democratic constitutionalism which motivated the founders of the American and French Republics to introduce into their fundamental law broad statements of basic rights. The core issue between them and Bentham has finally to be joined. They introduced rights into their constitutional law in order publicly to establish and preserve the conditions of "free government." This strategy, Bentham argued, was self-defeating: far from securing the conditions of democratic legitimacy, they introduced a serious threat to them. Democratic legitimacy, he argued, requires publicity and publicity demands demonstrability of legal standards. But bills of rights succeed only in giving birth to interminable disputes about the fundamental conditions of association, disputes which divide the citizenry and liberate government officials from public accountability.

[51] In his extended critical response to the National Assembly's proposed reform of the French judiciary Bentham wrote, "Publicity is the very soul of justice. It is the keenest spur to extortion, and the surest of all guards against improbity" (*Judicial Establishment in France*, B iv. 316). See Chapter 12.

[52] "Such is the case where, within his reach, [the judge] sees two opposite sources of decision, from either of which he can draw at pleasure" (B v. 478; see BCLT 278–9). A leading spokesman for the CLS movement expresses the same idea: "The Archimedean principle of constitutional law is 'Give a judge an example of a justified invalidation of a statute, and an explanation of why it is justified, and he or she will be able to do anything he/she wants'" (Tushnet, "Constitutionalism and Critical Legal Studies," 163).

[53] See Chapter 13 and BCLT, 269, 271, 310–12, 355–63.

[54] "Submission in behaviour . . . is the mother of peace: but submission of judgement . . . is the mother of stupidity" (*Com.* 346, n. 1). The root of tyranny, he argued, is the denial of the "right of private judgment," the "basis of everything that an Englishman holds dear" (FG 406).

This is an important challenge to the tradition of rights constitutionalism borne over two hundred years ago. It deserves a reply. One possible line of defense would be to deny the indeterminacy of constitutional rights assertions. Justice Iredell of the U.S. Supreme Court, for example, held in 1798 that the writers of the American Bill of Rights had succeeded in transforming broad and indeterminate standards of natural law into precisely defined precepts and settled rules.[55] But this view was hardly plausible then and the experience of two centuries did not lend it any more credibility. Our earlier investigations of some features of the logic of rights suggest that this is no accident. It is no more plausible to think that determinacy is possible by tying the interpretation of rights language in the Constitution to historical facts about the intentions and beliefs of the Founders.

The key to a plausible defense of rights constitutionalism, I believe, is not to deny the indeterminacy of constitutional rights language, but rather to deny Bentham's demonstrability thesis. Public justification requisite for a genuinely democratic policy, I believe, does not require demonstrability, but can accommodate, even to an extent welcome, indeterminacy of the sort that worried Bentham so greatly.

DEMOCRACY AND THE INDETERMINACY OF CONSTITUTIONAL RIGHTS

Bentham was correct, I believe, to have insisted upon the importance of publicity in a democratic constitutional order. However, he mistakenly assumed that public justification is possible only if the conditions of his demonstrability thesis are met. I propose to now sketch a defense of constitutional rights jurisprudence that seeks to answer Bentham's critique. I will outline an alternative conception of public justification and argue that public justification understood in this way is not threatened by indeterminacy.[56] I will then argue that a practice of constitutional rights jurisprudence could meet the conditions of this conception of public justification. Such a practice, I will argue, will greatly enhance the vitality of a democratic polity. I will not argue, however, that any existing society meets the conditions of public justification that I outline. In fact, at the end of my remarks I will mention at least one reason for thinking we are not yet able to make such a demonstration. My argument, then, will be a qualified defense of constitutional rights, a defense of the *possibility* of a democratic practice of constitutional rights jurisprudence.

[55] Instead of permitting judicial appeal to "ideas of natural justice [which] are regulated by no fixed standard," he wrote, "it has been the policy . . . of the people of the United States, when they framed the Federal Constitution, to define with precision the objects of the legislative power, and to restrain its exercise within marked and settled boundaries." *Calder* v. *Bull*, 3 U.S. (3 Dall.) 386, 399 (1798).

[56] For a broader defense of the view outlined here, see Gerald J. Postema, "Objectivity Fit for Law," in *Objectivity in Morality and Law*, B. Leiter, ed. (Cambridge: Cambridge University Press, 2000), 99–143.

Public Justification as Common Discourse

Bentham assumed that public practical reasoning must take the form of *demonstration*, that is, it must secure rationally the concurrence of all competent members of a society by appeal to already shared principles and rules. This assimilates public practical reasoning to practices of counting and measuring, which are marked by constancy in results. Many games, also, tolerate very little indeterminacy of results, and explicitly provide for prompt resolution when it does arise. But we do not demand such a high degree of determinacy in *all* our deliberative or interpretative practices. Indeed, in some of them a degree of indeterminacy is even regarded as desirable, a sign of the vitality of the practice.[57] There is room, it seems, for a notion of public justification—of reasoning in and for a public—which demands less constancy and determinacy.

There is available to us, I believe, a form of public justification characterized more by common discourse, including interdependence and explanatory exchange, than by demonstration, more by commitment to a common past and common task, than by consensus on specific norms or values. I take the term "common discourse" from Aristotle's discussion of commonality among friends. His discussion supplies my point of departure.[58] Aristotle argued that friendship is sustained, not so much by consensus as by common discourse and thought.[59] This is especially true of "political friendship"—the relationship among members of a *polis* (public)—since *diversity* is essential to the nature and vitality of the *polis*.[60] Common deliberation has its roots, according to Aristotle, in living together, in a common history and shared activities. "He must, then, perceive his friend's being together [with his own], and he will do this when they live together and share conversation and thought," Aristotle argues. "For in the case of human beings what seems to count as living together is this sharing of conversation and thought, not sharing the same pasture, as in the case of grazing animals."[61] Such common deliberation, which gives human shape to life together, seems to have two important effects, according to Aristotle. First, members come to see themselves *as members*. They come to think in terms of *we* rather than *me*. Second, through this ongoing process of common deliberation, and the mutual choices that issue from it, the *community* speaks and acts.

[57] Different traditions of theological reflection or scriptural interpretation, for example, vary in the degree of tolerance they are willing to show to indeterminacy. See Gerald J. Postema, "Sweet Dissonance: Conflict, Consensus, and the Rule of Law," *The Harvard Review of Philosophy*, Issue XVII (2010), 36–55.

[58] This section draws on my critical discussion of Dworkin's theory of interpretation in Postema, "'Protestant' Interpretation and Social Practice," *Law and Philosophy* 6 (1987), 308–17.

[59] Aristotle, *Nicomachean Ethics*, Terence Irwin, tr. (Indianapolis: Hackett Publishing, 1985), 1170b 9–12.

[60] Aristotle, *Politics*, C.D.C. Reeve, tr. (Indianapolis: Hackett Publishing, 1998), II.2; but see *Nicomachean Ethics*, 1167a 22–b4, where concord plays a more prominent role in political friendship.

[61] *Nicomachean Ethics*, 1170b 10–12.

Public justification, we have seen, is justification from a public point of view. Following Aristotle, we can say that this point of view must be rooted in a public marked by extensive interaction and interdependence amongst members in their daily lives, which interaction gives rise to common practice, with a common history and a common future. Through this practice the community acts, and through the deliberations of its members, when they deliberate as members (from the public point of view), the community deliberates. Moreover, since the practice has a history, and the specific shape of the aims and commitments of the practice at any point in this history is constituted by common deliberation and reflection on it, members will have the sense that they are joining an argument already underway. Thus, insofar as members regard themselves as acting as members, this practice is normative for them. The aims and commitments embodied in this historical practice are the aims and commitments of this public or community—"they are *our* aims and commitments," members are inclined to say.

If the practice is reflective, and especially if it deals with matters of serious import, and if the public is to some degree philosophically or ideologically heterogeneous, then the aims and commitments of the practice are likely to be some degree controversial. Nevertheless, common deliberation in such a context is possible, not only regarding matters on which there is consensus, but also regarding the proper understanding of the basic aims and commitments of the practice. Such deliberation is public if it involves argument and deliberation *from* this public point of view, and if it takes this common practice and its history as the point of reference of its argument. Let me elaborate these two conditions.

First, deliberations will take the form of proposals regarding the aims and principles to which "we," the community, are committed. This public point of view, then, is "our" point of view, as they would put it. Second, since the community in question exists in and through its practice, that practice must be the point of departure for all such arguments, and that to which proposals must repair when challenged. What the members have in common—the material for their common deliberation—is not a detailed, articulated understanding of the aims or underlying values of the practice, for these may be in dispute, but rather a mastery (to some degree) of the discipline of the shared and collectively meaningful activity. Third, the reflective, deliberative activity of member will be essentially interpretative, in Dworkin's sense.[62] Each member will bring their evaluative and moral convictions to bear on the task of articulating the aims and commitments of the community in virtue of its common practice.

Finally, this interpretative activity will be essentially interactive. This is so in two respects. First, deliberation is common—justification is public—in virtue of the fact that the aims an individual member puts forward, the reasons she cites, and the intentions she forms on this basis, are her proposals regarding aims, reasons,

[62] Ronald Dworkin, *Law's Empire* (Cambridge, MA: Harvard University Press, 1986), Chapter 2.

and intentions of the community—*of "us."*[63] But, then, the formulations of other participants represents more than just a threat to the hegemony of her formulations; those formulations are *defeasible*, logically open to challenge from other participants. Their proposals constitute perspectives on their common practice. She must meet the challenge they pose; she must provide reasons, drawn from the same sources from which they draw, to persuade them that her understanding is correct.

This interpretative activity is interactive in a second, deeper sense. Because the practice is constituted by the purposive activity of participants, activity guided at least in part by members' reflective understanding of their practice and its aims, no interpretative account of the community's commitments can ignore the interpretive activity of other participants. Their individual interpretative efforts will be interdependent. In their deliberations, each must not simply hope for eventual convergence of understanding, each must attempt to anticipate the interpretation which other participants will put on the practice—which includes the self-conscious, reflective part of others in it. (As Alice put it, "He was part of my dream, of course—but then I was part of his dream too!"[64]) To illustrate this point, permit me to extend, as I have done on another occasion, Dworkin's example of a chain novel.[65]

Imagine a group of writers undertaking to produce a novel together, each novelist writing a new chapter after having been given the chapters completed by others earlier in the chain. Each novelist wants to do her part in producing the best novel possible, but must continue from the point where the previous writer left off. This forces each novelist to interpret what has been written, and in continuing the story to develop the themes uncovered from the work up to that point. Note, however, that each contributor must recognize that the adequacy of her interpretation depends on the success of the chapter she writes based on that interpretation. But the success of that chapter, in consequence of the success of the interpretation, depends in part on the interpretative activities of other contributors. The chain novelist must view the writing of the novel as a collective project to which she will contribute, the meaning and success of which is a product of the interaction (in both interpreting and writing) of all the contributions. She must shape her interpretation and her chapter in light of the interpretations she attributes to writers earlier in the chain, and in anticipation of the interpretations and contributions of others to come. Actual practices are likely to be even more complex than this simple model of the chain novel, because this deliberative-interpretative interaction can

[63] Of course, she may formulate reasons, and on their basis express intentions for her to act, but in such cases these reasons and intentions are derivative, following from her essentially intersubjective intentions by means of premises in which she identifies herself as a member of the community in question. See Wilfrid Sellars, "Objectivity, Intersubjectivity and the Moral Point of View," in Sellars, *Science and Metaphysics* (London: Routledge and Kegan Paul, 1968), 217–22; and Jay F. Rosenberg, *One World and Our Knowledge of It* (Dordrecht: Reidel, 1980), Chapter VII.

[64] Lewis Carroll, *Through the Looking Glass* (1871), (New York: Random House, 1965), 165.

[65] The following paragraph reproduces part of my discussion in "'Protestant' Interpretation," 311–12.

extend synchronically as well as diachronically, but the point is clear enough. Each contributor must propose and act on an interpretation of the ongoing common work, but since the work is common, she cannot ignore the interpretative activity of other contributors without jeopardizing the success of her contribution and the integrity of the work as a whole.

Practical reasoning that meets the above conditions is public in a rich sense. It is practical reasoning *in a public*, from *a public point of view*. It is reasoning which is not so much demonstrative as interactively deliberative. Its reasons and arguments are drawn from common experience. They invite the participation, affirmation, and challenges of other members. Disputes over competing articulations of fundamental aims or commitments ("indeterminacy") need not be a sign of the breakdown of the practice; indeed, it may be a sign of its vitality. Indeterminacy, then, is not threat to public justification of this sort. Consensus understood as explicit agreement on articulations of the aims and commitments of this practice, is not necessary, nor is consensus always the immediate and overriding aim of this sort of public practical reasoning. What *is* necessary is participation in an ongoing common activity and the shared assumption that this activity and its history are normative for participants in virtue of the fact that they regard themselves as engaged in a common work. Thus, consensus is a kind of regulative ideal expressed in the recognition on the part of each member that she is a participant in a common activity with others and in their commitment to view practical problems that arise for them from the public point of view that it defines.

Constitutional Rights and Public Justification

The activity of formulating and articulating the rights incorporated in the text of a constitution is often controversial, and arguments for contested formulations seldom meet conditions of determinacy and demonstrability. We should not expect more given what we have learned about the concept of rights earlier in this chapter. Nevertheless, constitutional practice (at least American constitutional practice) provides the substance and framework for genuine public practical deliberation understood not as demonstration but as common discourse. Benthamite critics too easily overlook the resources of genuine public discourse available in constitutional practice.

First, rights language itself imposes a discipline on public argument. While frequently contestable, rights claims are not unavoidably arbitrary or empty, as Bentham charged. On the contrary, as we have seen, they are richly textured. Rights assertions link convictions regarding ultimate values with concrete circumstances and social environments. The language of rights brings ultimate values and broad social visions to bear on concrete situations and the structure of social relationships. Far from licensing flat assertion, as Bentham charged, it *presupposes*, and in virtue of this presupposition *demands*, argument and defense. It imposes a distinctive structure and discipline on that argument. Rights claims do not close off argument, they invite it, and set the agenda for extensive practical deliberation. The language of rights, of course, can be used irresponsibly and exploited rhetorically, but this is true of all normative language, especially when it touches our deepest convictions and engages significant moral visions.

Second, incorporating this richly textured language into the fundamental laws of the land further enhances its contribution to genuine public discourse. First, incorporation sets the problem and context for deliberation about constitutional rights. As we noted at the opening of our discussion, through incorporation of rights into a constitution the question of the fundamental ground rules—the basic conditions of legitimacy—of our political association was institutionalized, and thereby made a permanent part of our public morality. Rights language, then, structures the public debate over the fundamental conditions of association. Secondly, rights were not just incorporated into a text, they were put at the center of a historically continuous common practice of deliberation and argument. Constitutional practice may meet all the conditions of "common discourse" outlined above. The argument structured by formal rights language is anchored in the concrete history of this ongoing practice. Here conflicting social visions and conceptions of ultimate value can meet on the common ground of a shared history and a common future.

Thus, constitutional rights discourse and argument, while inevitably political (since it engages potentially competing social visions), nevertheless, is neither arbitrary nor merely a matter of bargaining for greatest satisfaction of private or narrow group interests. It is *argument of principle about public matters*, disciplined by both the abstract structure of rights language and the concrete focus of constitutional history. Constitutional rights jurisprudence, then, is foundational, because it addresses the question of the basic conditions of legitimacy within our polity; yet, it is concrete, because through it general and comprehensive moral theories or social visions must come to terms with the common history of our public debate over these conditions and focus on the concrete present and future of our common political life. I conclude, then, that constitutional rights, while it can never meet the conditions of publicity as demonstration, can serve the cause of public justification understood as a practice of common discourse. This is essential, I believe, to a democratic polity.

Constitutional Rights and Democratic Legitimacy

The writers of the Virginia Constitution of 1776 may have understood the importance of such practice for their fledgling democracy. Although they sought to articulate in broad terms the basic conditions of legitimacy, they clearly realized that guarantees of "free government" were ultimately rooted not in a text or statement of rights, but in the spirit of a people, in their continued commitment to "justice, moderation, temperance, frugality, and virtue." Essential to keeping this commitment vital, they believed, was "frequent recurrence to fundamental principles." The Bill of Rights was designed to provide them the opportunity and structure for such "frequent recurrence." In a pluralistic democratic polity such recurrence is inevitably "political" in the sense of engaging our most deeply held and potentially conflicting convictions and social visions. Because such matters deal with the foundations of ordinary democratic politics—politics of interest and legislative bargaining—there is good reason to set them above such politics. But in a democratic polity it is neither feasible nor desirable to set the matters entirely above politics.

First, consider the feasibility of such a strategy. To remove such matters from the political agenda, while still preserving their relevance as fundamental political standards, we must have available a determinate formulation of the rights and principles in question, one which is clear to all and which yields unique results. Consistency with conditions of democratic legitimacy requires that this formulation of fundamental be accepted or regarded by citizens as appropriate foundations for their political association.

However, in a pluralistic democratic community, it is unlikely that any substantive conception of such rights can achieve the requisite degree of determinacy *and* command wide consensus. I argued earlier against Raz that it is precisely because of their intermediary, "bridging" role in political reasoning, that rights assertions are likely to attract consensus only when broadly formulated, and that the apparent consensus will dissolve as the E–R structures of the rights are made more concrete. To expect substantial consensus around a relatively determinate substantive conception of these rights is unrealistic.

The alternative is to seek consensus around some "neutral" or "formally realizable" articulation of the rights, that is, a formulation in evaluatively neutral and empirically determinate terms. However, the more successful we are in formulating such a "neutral" conception, the greater the distance there is between it and valued features of our social life and recognizable aims that can claim our allegiance, and hence the more likely it is to appear arbitrary. Thus, the more successfully neutral the formulation is, the less appropriate it will be as a formulation of the fundamental conditions of our political association.

Secondly, it is not desirable to set such matters entirely beyond political debate. The demand for determinacy at the level of constitutional doctrine, like the Founders' attempt to take certain foundational matters permanently off the political agenda, rests on the assumption that the basic terms of political association in a democratic polity can be settled once and for all by some extra-political act. This is a mistake, I believe. But it is understandable, because to reject this assumption is to embrace something of a paradox. If enduring legitimacy of a democratic constitutional regime depends on the willing allegiance of its citizens to the fundamental terms of association it defines, then not only our commitment to these terms, but the nature and scope of these terms, must be constantly open to reformulation. Precisely because of the overriding political importance and pervasive influence of these terms of association, their precise determination and contemporary significance cannot be entrusted to others, either our political ancestors or some contemporary élite. These matters are as vital to us as to the Founders, and our participation in their determination is essential to the enduring legitimacy of the constitutional order.

The paradox in this idea lies in the fact that according to it the very terms (preconditions) of democratic association and so of democratic politics are to be settled by democratic politics. Yet, there is not an alternative, consistent with our commitment democratic self-government in a pluralistic community. The sting of the paradox, however, can be pulled, not by locating the source of our fundamental terms of association in transcendent principles of natural right, or in evaluatively neutral facts about intentions and beliefs of the Founders, but by submitting political debate over terms of association to the discipline of principled pubic deliberation. We need a forum and a structured form of argument in which foundational issues can be publicly addressed, articulated, debated, and resolved, if only temporarily. The practice of constitutional jurisprudence focused by a shared concept of rights can provide such a forum. The principled politics of constitutional rights makes possible the continual re-articulation of a community's public conception of morality.

The indeterminacy and lack of closure of this form of public justification is, in this instance, not a defect, but a virtue. For determination in detail of the terms of association at any particular time occurs through fully public deliberation, argument addressed to and engaging the community. It does not assume full substantive consensus will be achieved, but it makes possible temporary resolution without full consensus, while providing the opportunity, the forum, and the focus for reflective, public reconsideration. The practice of constitutional rights jurisprudence, then, is not a threat to democratic polity, but an important, indeed essential, component of it. The constitution can retain its legitimacy in a democratic polity only to the extent that such a forum for the politics of principle is available to its members.

While rights constitutionalism puts foundational matters beyond the politics of interest bargaining, it cannot put them beyond the politics of principle. This is as it should be in a democratic polity. We can say, then, in response to the philosopher of Queen's Square Place, that rights play an indispensable role in a democratic constitutional polity. At the same time, we must admit that it does so in a way that some Founders of the French and American Republics may not have fully understood.

CONCLUSION

I conclude this defense of "French nonsense" with a remark about the limits of my argument. The greatest threat to democracy posed by constitutional practice as I have portrayed it lies not in its indeterminacy and lack of closure, but two other conditions. One such threat lies in limitations on access to this process of public political debate. Rights language in the adjudicative forum, I have argued, is capable of focusing and encouraging genuinely public deliberation about fundamental conditions of our common life, but by no means does it guarantee it. The process and access to it need to be democratically structured.

What does democratic structure of this process look like? Unfortunately, this is not entirely clear. At the core of the notion of democratic politics that I have relied on is the principle of equal political power, equal participation. However, while we are relatively clear that equality of participation in electoral political requires respect for the principle of one person one vote and majority rule, it is not clear what equality means when it comes to constitutional politics of the sort I have described. But because this is not entirely clear, it is difficult to say whether democratizing the process of constitutional politics will enhance or threaten to undermine conditions needed to maintain the principled character of the debate.

The second condition is that participants in the deliberative process, the democratic citizenry, must be committed to participate sincerely, without cant, cynicism, and prevarication. The process of democratic deliberation has only as much integrity as the integrity its participants bring to it. Such integrity requires respect for truth, respect for facts, respect for principles and principled argument, and most fundamentally respect for other participants. Open and democratic processes of deliberation cannot guarantee that its participants will engage in them with integrity; and, sadly, they are especially vulnerable to people, especially people with resources and power, who lack such integrity, or even worse, regard integrity as a kind of weakness.

Democratic institutions ultimately are only as strong as the people willing to fight for them. Until we can guarantee genuine public deliberation, I am forced to regard my argument as only a qualified defense of "French Nonsense."

11
Utilitarian International Order

> If a man be gracious and courteous to strangers, it shews he is a citizen of the world, and that his heart is no island cut off from other lands, but a continent that joins to them.
>
> Francis Bacon

CITIZEN OF THE WORLD

Bentham was fond of referring to himself as "an Englishman by birth," but "a citizen of the world by naturalization" and "in affection."[1] He claimed "the Globe" as his "field of Dominion" (UC 25.26), and intended the scope of his utilitarian principle to be universal, applying *mutatis mutandis* to all peoples and all times. What he called the "empire" of his theoretical ambition encompassed "the whole human race . . . in all habitable places of the earth, at all future time. . . . Limits it has no other than those of the earth."[2] His foundational work in jurisprudence also was meant to have universal scope, although he acknowledged that if his "Pannomion" is to be workably determinate, it would need to take into account the peculiar circumstances, cultures and histories specific societies.[3]

His ambition was also global in another sense. From very early in his life, he took his theoretical remit to include considering the implications of his moral–political and jurisprudential theories for the international and transnational order. One can find reflections on the law of nations and world order scattered among his writings starting from the very beginning of his career. By the early 1780s his ambitious legisprudential project explicitly incorporated a plan for international law and world order, alongside plans for domestic penal, civil, procedural, and constitutional

[1] *Corr.* vol. 7, 565; *Col.* 204. See also *Corr.* vol. 4, 132 n. 1 and CC (B) ix. 537. The epigraph comes from Francis Bacon, "Of Goodness and the Goodness of Nature," in *The Essays or Counsels Civil and Moral* (1625) in Bacon, *The Major Works*, Brian Vickers, ed. (Oxford: Oxford University Press, 1996), 364. I am grateful to Philip Bourcier for directing me to this passage.

[2] "Bentham Memorandum Book" (entry dated February 16, 1831) in B xi. 72. Bentham argued that his proposals for peace were designed to serve "the cause of humanity" (UC 25.20). However, as we shall see presently, Bentham's theory of global political morality adopts a constrained cosmopolitanism, unlike present-day utilitarian theories, because it accords states a dominant role in the global order.

[3] See, generally, Bentham, "Of the Influence of Time and Place in Matters of Legislation" (B i. 169–94), newly edited by Philip Schofield and Stephen Engelmann, "Place and Time," in *Jeremy Bentham: Selected Writings*, Stephen Engelmann, ed. (New Haven: Yale University Press, 2011), 152–219; and Jennifer Pitts, "Jeremy Bentham: Legislator of the World?" in Pitts, *A Turn to Empire* (Princeton: Princeton University Press, 2005).

Utility, Publicity, and Law: Essays on Bentham's Moral and Legal Philosophy. Gerald J. Postema.

law, for all of which he intended to provide theoretical foundations. In drafts of work produced in 1780s and early 1790s, he sketched two related projects, "*Projet Forme—Entregens*" and "*Projet Matiere—Entregens*," concerned with the form and substance of law between nations (UC 25.2–4, 81–82). Decades later, John Bowring and Richard Smith stitched together these sketches to form four essays published as "Principles of International Law."[4] In his *Introduction to the Principles of Morals and Legislation*, published in 1789 but composed in the early 1780s, Bentham announced that the principles defended in that work apply equally to "international" and "internal" law (IPML 6, 296). He briefly returned to theoretical consideration of the topic in the last five years of his life (IL (1827) 120–5). The global focus of his theoretical and practical attention is also evident in several of his works written in the long interim period, including *Securities against Misrule* (SM) and the writings included in *Colonies, Commerce and Constitutional Law—Rid Yourselves of Ultramaria* (*Col.*).

Law of Nations vs International Law

Bentham was skeptical of talk of the "law of nations"—no nation has ever made such a law, he argued (UC 25.64)—and he never discussed and rarely even referred to masters of early modern *ius genium*, like Grotius or Vattel. His reasons are familiar. He complained that talk of the law of nations tended to draw on or be confused with the law of nature, which, of course, was a phantom in his view (*Com.* 35–6; UC 69.124). Appeals to the law of nations, like appeals to natural law, only masqueraded as real argument. "There is no such thing as an offense against laws of nations; for there is no law of nations" (UC 69.122). In place of the term "law of nations" (*ius gentium/droit des gens*), he proposed "international law" (*ius inter gentes/droit entre les gens*)—a term he coined—because it avoided confusion with natural law and better captured the subject matter he wished to address (IPML 296 n. x). "Law of nations," when not used vacuously or mendaciously, suggested to Bentham law internal to specific nations ("internal law"). In contrast, he was concerned with law as it pertains to the relations between nations. Some scholars have charged that Bentham's neologism distorted the field of transnational law of the eighteenth century, because it focused attention only on inter-state relations, ignoring global principles that were thought to apply to all nations and peoples regardless of how they were politically organized.[5] However, Bentham did not set out to give a general exposition of the international law of his day; rather, he sought

[4] PIL, 535–60. Written about the same time, his "General View of a Complete Code of Laws" includes a sketch of a "Plan of the International Code" (Gen. View, 200–1).

[5] Mark Weston Janis, "Blackstone and Bentham: The Law of *Nations* and *International Law*," in Janis, *America and the Law of Nations, 1776–1939* (Oxford: Oxford University Press, 2010), 13–14.

to articulate what he took to be a more adequate theoretical framework for global legal order. As we will see, he assumed that a citizen of the world, tasked with constructing a code of law for this world, must start with the fact, as he saw it, that the world is divided into largely independent states. Law for this world could only be international—inter-state—law, *droit entre les gens*.

Bentham's perspective on international law was that of a legislator, an engineer of global order, not that of expositor or theorist of the existing law.[6] His is a theory of international legislation—global legisprudence. He was neither a positive theorist of international law or the law of nations, nor a positive theorist of the international relations. Still, he worked from general assumptions about the nature of international relations, drawn from his general theory of human motivation and social psychology. This, he thought, was entirely appropriate, since the main players in the global arena are sovereign rulers, who are either individuals or ruling elites. He also had a general idea of what in his view passed as the existing law between nations. Insofar as there was nascent law in this global domain, it was made up of treaties between states and usage or custom of nations (*Com.* 36; UC 69.122; UC 25.118; PIL 540). He styled the usage and custom of nations as law "as it is supposed to be"—not law as it *ought to be*, but as it is *taken* to be *by supposition* or "conjecture."[7] This is not to say, there is no law, but rather that "all the matter of law in the law of nations [is] acts of will" issuing in actions constituting and following usage. Usage is not nothing, for it can generate and focus expectations, and, since defeating expectations causes "the pain of disappointment," there may be good reason to follow usage. But following usage always involves some conjecture or "abstraction" from the resemblance of acts one to another. Prior to the articulation and enactment of a code of international law, the law consists only in a collection of treaties and "the common law of nations" abstracted from usage.[8]

At times, Bentham expressed reservations regarding international law that seem to anticipate Austin's well-known objections.[9] He maintained that international law is "incomplete" and "unwritten," that is, it is not backed up by formal enforcement mechanisms (Gen. View 162) and largely a matter of usage or

[6] In his *Introduction to the Principles of Moral and Legislation*, Bentham recognized the possibility of "expository jurisprudence" of international law, but his efforts are almost entirely constructive, "censorial" (IPML XVII. 24–5).

[7] In a letter to Jabez Henry (15 January 1830), whom Bentham sought to enlist in his international law project, Bentham wrote: the law discussed in your *Foreign Law* "is law as *it is*, including what it is supposed to be. Of inter-national law *as it is* the principal part of the matter is composed of treaties between State and State: of what it is *supposed to be* the matter is composed of deductions from those same *written instruments*; and from the operations of the several States in relation to each other" (BL Add MSS 30,151.19; original emphasis). I am grateful to Chris Riley of the Bentham Project for making a transcript of this manuscript available to me.

[8] This, of course, echoes Bentham's understanding of English common law; see Chapter 7 and BCLT, Chapter 8.3.

[9] John Austin, *The Province of Jurisprudence Determined*, H.L.A. Hart, ed. (London: Weidenfeld and Nicolson, 1955), 141–2, 201.

custom; hence, it was uncertain and vulnerable to manipulation. However, these concerns did not prevent him from thinking of international law as proper, albeit atypical, law. He did not treat its incompleteness as a reason to dismiss it (as he did English common law); rather, he devoted much energy to devising a code of law for the international order. War, he argued, has among its most important causes, uncertainty of state rights and duties; and an important means of prevention of war is "homologation" (digestion, codification) of "unwritten laws which are considered as established by custom" (PIL 539–40; UC 25.118v). By this effort, something real (a written code) would replace the fictitious "unwritten law" (IL (1827) 120).

The "incompleteness" of international law, Bentham argued, is analogous to the "incompleteness" of what he called "laws *in principem*" (Gen. View 162).[10] Laws *in principem* are constitutional norms and arrangements that bind the sovereign, although the sovereign is not subject to ordinary legal sanctions (*Limits* 86–93). The sanctions underwriting them are "moral" rather than "legal." Nevertheless, Bentham refused to dismiss such constitutional arrangements as merely "positive morality," as Austin later would do. He adopted the same view of international law. Properly codified, international law, like constitutional law, could do its work as a species of law. Bentham rejected common law because by nature it was unsystematic and "conjectural," and hence *uncertain*. The law of nations, similar in nature to common law, also is irreparably uncertain, in Bentham's view. It is a "fictitious entity." But his solution was not to consign the global order to custom and "positive morality," but to replace the law of nations with a carefully drafted, systematic, rational and publicly accessible code. Such a code, even if not enacted and enforced by a global sovereign, could do the work he expected law to do. Codified international law could be sufficiently law-like for Bentham's theoretical purposes, even though it does not (and must not) have a sovereign law-maker or coercive law-enforcer (IL (1827) 124).[11]

This underlines an important feature of Bentham's jurisprudential method. Austin and later Austinians, observing a manifest difference between municipal and international law, exiled international law from the province of jurisprudence. Bentham, in contrast, observing the same difference, brought international law within his wider jurisprudential domain, addressed it and its distinctive features, and found a role for it to play in a world order governed by utilitarian principles.

[10] See Chapter 8, 198 and Chapter 12, 279–81.

[11] Bentham says little about who the agents of this codification would be, but we must assume that they are the states themselves (or, rather, those who rule them), because they are the only agents populating the world order. Regarding the enforcing of international law, he proposed a "common tribunal," but denied it coercive power (see below, 320–1).

FOUNDATIONS OF INTERNATIONAL LAW

At several points in his career, Bentham took up his ambitious project of global legisprudence. Although he never developed his theory of international law to the extent that he did his theory of penal or constitutional law, nevertheless his sketches are detailed and nuanced. They raise several questions about the relationship between this theoretical endeavor and his more familiar work on politics and morals. To understand his substantive proposals, we must first get a sense of the focus and scope of his project and of the principle on which it is built.

The Domain of International Law

Our first task is to delimit as precisely as we can the domain of Bentham's global legisprudence. Bentham never left any doubt that the principle of utility, requiring maximization of human well-being, is the guiding star of the project, but he maintained consistently throughout his career that the "subjects" of his international law code are exclusively state sovereigns. Law at the global level is inter-national, or rather inter-state; it concerns the actions of rulers of sovereign states and transactions between one sovereign state and another. Bentham spent a good bit of time working out what or who the proper subjects (i.e., objects of attention and concern) of actors in the international domain are (PIL 540–4), but he was very clear from the outset that the only such actors are states—more accurately, those who exercise ruling power in sovereign states. This apparent narrowing of the focus of utilitarian concern is a bit surprising and perhaps puzzling. It requires an explanation.

We start on the trail of an explanation by considering Bentham's division of "ethics" (or "deontology") into three branches. According to Bentham, the fundamental concern of ethics is to determine and indicate that action which "on each occasion" most conduces to its single end—maximal well-being (*Deont.* 331). But, he conceded, this immediately prompts the question "whose well-being?" The answer to that question is determined by the "field" of ethics in which our inquiry is engaged (*Deont.* 331–3). Boundaries of a given "field" in which an agent might act are determined by two factors: (i) the persons[12] whose interests or well-being the agent takes into account; and (ii) the capacities and resources the agent has available to affect their well-being or interests. An agent might consider only his own "purely personal interest" ("private ethics") or he might consider the effects of his actions on others not considered within the scope of his personal interest ("public ethics"). In the latter case, his attention, concern and interest can focus narrowly on a single individual, or a small group of them (e.g., his family), or expand outward

[12] Of course, Bentham held that utilitarian concern should extend to all sentient beings (*Limits* 4–5, n. a), but for present purposes we can restrict our attention to human persons.

to include members of his neighborhood, his whole community, or nation, members of other societies or nations, even to all human beings ("mankind at large," (UC 25.20)). In principle, his concern and interest can take any of these objects. Two factors determine the scope of his concern: the extent of his sympathy (aided, perhaps, by the encouragements of moral, legal, or religious sanctions) and his capacity to act in ways that materially affect their well-being. Although in principle, "public ethics" has an indefinite number of groups of individuals on which it could focus concern, Bentham singled out the national and universal groups for his theoretical attention. Thus, the main branches of ethics, in Bentham's view, are *private ethics*, *internal politics* and *international politics* (*Deont.* 331–3; IPML 296; *Chrest.* 204).

Thus, it is nearly correct to say that the concern of private ethics is restricted to the well-being of the individual agent herself, while the concern internal or national ethics is the well-being of the (national) community, and the concern of international ethics is the global "community." However, this is not quite what Bentham has in mind, although he sometimes says things that suggest this thought. There are two problems with this summary. First, Bentham's fundamental normative principle, the principle of utility, requires that on each occasion each agent, whatever his or her circumstances, office or station, must perform that action which serves the well-bring of all human beings, regardless of their relationship to the agent. This implies that a private individual must consider the well-being of all those who might be affected by his actions, not merely his own well-being. Likewise, lawmakers for a national community must not ignore the effects of their laws on people beyond their national boundaries. Secondly, and for the same reason, it would seem that in the global domain, agents, whether sovereign authorities or non-governmental entities or individuals should act with the entire membership of the global community in mind, and not focus solely on sovereign-to-sovereign relations.

Some years ago, David Lyons argued that Bentham's principle of utility was not a single principle, but rather a set of principles, members of which apply to different agents depending on the range of those who are under their control or governance. Hence, the private individual must maximize his own well-being and the legislator of a given national community must focus solely on the community for which he is responsible.[13] I agree with H.L.A. Hart that the textual evidence strongly argues against Lyons' interpretation and strongly supports reading the principle of utility as unitary and universalistic,[14] but I think, nevertheless, Lyons called attention to

[13] David B. Lyons, *In the Interest of the Governed* (Oxford: Oxford University Press, 1973). For criticism of Lyons' revisionist interpretation of Bentham's Principle of Utility, see John R. Dinwiddy, "Bentham on Private Ethics and the Principle of Utility," *Revue International de Philosophie* 36 (1982), 278–300.

[14] H.L.A. Hart, "Bentham's Principle of Utility and Theory of Penal Law," in IPML xciv–xcvi.

one of two features of Bentham's theoretical approach to "ethics" that we must attend to in order to solve the problems mentioned above.

First, Lyons was right to suggest that the principle of utility is sensitive to the various positions, offices, and circumstances in which moral agents find themselves. Bentham's utilitarian theories of morality and politics are fundamentally sensitive to the variability of facts and circumstances. Moreover, for various purposes, especially when engineering major social and political institutions and arrangements, he thought it was entirely appropriate for agents, who are guided ultimately by the principle of utility, to focus their practical attention on the most widely occurring range of facts and circumstances. Thus, we might expect a heuristic formulation of the principle to provide targeted agents a more focused orientation of their institution-building efforts and exercises of judgment within the institution, once the principle is put into operation.

Second, Bentham tended to think of "ethics" in two different but not incompatible ways. Understood in one way, "ethics" is the activity of determining for each agent, "on every occasion," what act is morally optimal to perform. The familiar and typical way to understand Bentham's project puts this casuistic dimension of ethics in the foreground. But Bentham often—one might say, predominantly—conceived of ethics on an advisory or engineering model, as the task of someone charged with providing agents within the scope of their influence with the resources—including information, perspective, and motivation—needed to act in ways that serve the greatest happiness. "Ethics," as Bentham conceived it, combines casuistry with engineering—knowledge and guidance of judgment with technique. These two elements are not in conflict, as Hart thought;[15] rather, they are interdependent. The advising or engineering part of the project depends on casuistry for the target of its efforts; and the casuistry is without force until the demands of utilitarian morality are brought home to agents governed by it—providing them with the insight, judgment, and motivation needed to do what utility requires of them.

But then, the "deontologist" engaging in "private ethics" will do all he can to show his advisee that the advisee's interests (very broadly construed to include the well-being of others) call for actions which are, in fact, required by the principle of utility.[16] Among his tools, will be the "moral sanction," calling his advisee's attention to the likely judgments of the "public opinion tribunal" (*Deont.* 334–6, 338). This, also, explains why Bentham considers the remaining two branches of "ethics" to be domains of "politics." The focus of "internal [i.e., national] politics" is on *government*, that is, on arrangements and institutions designed to secure behavior of citizen and rulers that serves the well-being of the community. Likewise, the focus

[15] Hart, "Bentham's Principle of Utility," IPML xcv. Hart presented what I suppose are two elements of a single understanding of "ethics" as competing interpretations of Bentham's "ethics" project.

[16] This is the theme and focus of Bentham's late work, *Deontology*. See Chapter 3, 49, 56–7.

of "international" politics is international law and governance, on institutions and arrangements that promote human well-being.

Thus, Bentham's view seems to be that the ultimate utilitarian end is best served, if legislators concentrate their efforts on those whose well-being they can most effectively influence.[17] They should not *ignore* effects beyond their borders, but as a useful heuristic, they may for the most part confine their attention to the well-being of the community they are authorized to govern. This heuristic makes sense, of course, only to the extent that certain assumptions about the nature and scope of the capability, power, and authority of national political leaders are true.

With these features of Bentham's general theoretical project in view, we can limn the boundaries of the global domain. The single, universal principle of utility lies behind his enterprise, but his theoretical focus was trained on only the part of the universal domain that falls within the concern of that principle. Without explicit argument or assessment, he assumed, or took as a fixed fact, that the global domain was carved into independent sovereign states, and that the agents addressed by principles governing the global domain are only the rulers of such states. (Thus, if the fundamental utilitarian principle mandates serving the welfare of mankind at large, it has a distinctively "cosmopolitan" shape; however, the only cosmopolitan agents are rulers of states.)

Bentham also seems to have assumed, without offering any argument to support his assumption, that the well-being of members of the universal community is best served by ordering the relations among these sovereign states, and more particularly by ordering the relations among those who exercise ruling power within those states. How shall we understand this assumption? Perhaps we should regard it as a normative principle of global governance, rather than a descriptive thesis. The following passage from his sketch of guiding articles of his international code suggests as much. "Each Government," Bentham wrote,

> can not but be considered as regarding its own form [of government] as being in a higher degree than any other conducive to the greatest happiness of the whole number of the members of the community of which it is the government: but it means not to pass condemnation on any other, or to put into dispute its fitness for the community of which it is the government (IL (1827) 125).

This passage expresses a statist analogue of the principle, "the individual is the best judge of his own interest." In a global order of roughly equal and interdependent states, it involves a concession and a demand. It concedes recognition of the right to non-interference of other states on condition of their recognition of its demand of non-interference in its own affairs. Read in this way, the principle of universal good governance is the product of a concession to the facts of power and its

[17] See Hart, "Bentham's Principle of Utility," IPML xcvi and n 37.

limits in the global domain. If this is correct, Bentham's view of the global order in late the eighteenth and early nineteenth century falls squarely in line with the "Westphalian" orthodoxy of the period. Also, this argument assumes that there is a significant degree of interaction, indeed interdependence, among sovereign states, and, in consequence, considerable potential for reciprocity (Gen. View 200). The interdependence of action is due, he believed, to the complex interweaving of national interests. He also assumed that the actions of states are to a large degree public, rather than secret. So, the reasoning of agents in the international domain are themselves internally linked (see PIL 538).

Reciprocity is a critical feature of Bentham's account of the circumstances of international order. He believed that effective coercive enforcement of rules is not feasible and institutions designed coercively to enforce the rule must not be contemplated. Rather, rules of international law must be largely self-enforcing, relying at most on the sanction of negative public opinion.

A Principle of Utility for International Law

The "leading principle" of "International Law as it ought to be" is "the Greatest Happiness," Bentham declared to Jabez Henry in 1830 (BL Add MSS 30,151.19). Early in his career he articulated this principle in the following way: the fundamental end to which sovereigns must direct their actions is "the most extended welfare of all nations on earth," "the greatest happiness of all nations taken together" (PIL 538). This, of course, is Bentham's foundational principle, the point of departure for this inquiry, as it is for any inquiry, but here it is addressed to agents who have as their "field" of action the global domain.

At the opening of his essays on international law, Bentham offers a refined version of this principle. The object or end of a "universal international code," he writes, is "the greatest common utility of all nations taken together,"[18] or more precisely: "the [greatest] common and equal utility of all nations," (PIL 538, 537; UC 25.5). Bentham designed this principle, a refinement of his generic principle of utility, specifically for the global domain as he understood it.

This formulation of his foundational principle of utility is striking in three respects. First, it clearly takes *nations*, not individual human beings, as the primary unit of well-being. This is not to say that Bentham ever thought of nations or communities in ontologically collective terms. He always thought of nations as aggregates of individual human beings. He was fond of asking, "What are nations but aggregates of individuals?" (*Col.* 149). Nevertheless, the focus of his ordering

[18] "The common welfare of all civilised nations" (UC 25.36). The guiding aim of "disinterested legislator" in the global domain is "*utilité commune de toutes les nations indistinctement*"—the common utility of all nations [viewed] indiscriminately (UC 25.1).

principle for the global domain is trained on human beings organized into nation-states.[19] Although Bentham thought that the well-being of a given nation-state can only be understood as a direct function of the well-being of its members,[20] his principle addressed the well-being of the aggregated group. Second, the "field" of this principle's concern is universal; it encompasses the utility of *all* nations *taken together*—their *common* utility.[21] Third, and perhaps most striking, the aim set by this standard is the *common* and *equal* utility of all nations—"equity," he called it (PIL 537). The "creed" of the utility-governed sovereign is: "Did it depend on me I would not obtain for my own nation the smallest privilege of which I would not impart in equal measure to every other nation"; for "Equality is Equity: and Equity is the only wisdom" (UC 25.112). Bentham's *Constitutional Code* requires that the legislator pledge to seek or accept no recognition of superiority of his state in relation to any other state (CC (B) 202).

This is, perhaps, the natural and obvious principle for "philosophes" and "philanthropic citizens of the world" (UC 25.1; PIL 537), Bentham conceded, but it hardly expresses the usual perspective of actual sovereigns. When they are not focused on their own private (sinister) interests, they are focused on the exclusive interests and prejudices of their respective nations (UC 25.1). Moreover, the narrower focus of attention on nation's particular interests would seem to be required by each sovereign's overriding obligation to serve the interests of those they govern (PIL 537). Yet, "it is from ignorance and weakness that men deviate from the path of rectitude, more frequently than from selfishness and malevolence." This is no less true of those who govern as of individuals who are governed. Bentham insisted that "information and reason" are capable of defeating error and ignorance (PIL 553), and that it possible to show that the ruler actually serves his sovereign duty, and acts with the requisite virtue of a sovereign, by following the guidance of this foundational principle (PIL 537). Indeed, in his late writings on the constitutional code, Bentham has his legislator pledge, in his dealings with other states, "sincerely and constantly" to direct his endeavours "to the observance of the same strict justice and impartiality" as he would accord to his constituents (CC (B) 202).

The ruler ("legislator") of any particular nation must embrace this principle for two reasons. First, he may follow this universal object because his particular object, viz., to serve the well-being of his nation, is comprised in it (PIL 537). This so in

[19] Yet, in his *Constitutional Code*, he encouraged a focus on individual members of states. In the "Legislator's Inaugural Declaration" sketched there, the Legislator pledges to render "all positive good offices" to "*the subjects* ... of every foreign State," and "*for their sake*" to the constituted authorities of those states (CC (B) 203; emphasis added). In a striking passage in this "Inaugural Declaration," Bentham's focus on individuals is also evident. He has the Legislator pledge that no obstacle will be placed in the way of constituents' migration to other parts of the globe, and equally no obstacle to migration in his country. "In the territory of this State," the Legislator declares, "I behold and asylum to all: a prison to none" (*ibid.*).

[20] IPML I.4–5; see Chapter 3, 59.

[21] "*L'utilité commune & plus grande de toutes les nations prises ensemble*" (UC 25.5).

two respects. (i) The fundamental aim, greatest equal common utility, includes as an essential part the well-being of each nation. It is *common* and *equal* utility: actions and arrangements or laws that serve the common utility serve the well-being of each, equally. The principle articulates a standard of equal, mutual benefit: each party enjoys the benefits of interaction in the global domain and bears its burdens equally. At times, Bentham is inclined to say, extravagantly I believe, that "between the interests of nations there is nowhere any real conflict," that apparent conflicts are due to misunderstanding (UC 25.57). More plausibly, he frequently insists that the aim of actors in the global domain is to seek the "community of interests among nations" (UC 25.133). This is made compatible with seeking the welfare of their respective nations because, as we learn later, (ii) the principle builds in a proviso that permits derogation from arrangements or laws that work greatly to the disadvantage of a given nation. (We will return to this point presently.) At the direction of Bentham's *Constitutional Code*, the legislator-ruler pledges:

> On every favourable occasion—my endeavours shall be employed to the rendering, to the subjects, and for their sake to the constituted Authorities, of every foreign State, all such positive good offices, as can be rendered thereto, without its being at the expense of some other State or States, or against the rightly presumable inclination, as well as at the expense, of the majority of my fellow-countrymen, in this our State (CC (B) 203).

Second, adopting the common-and-equal-utility principle, sovereign rulers can frame their expectations of the behavior of other sovereigns and the demands they can reasonably make on other sovereign rulers.

> The line of common utility once drawn, this would be the direction towards which the conduct of all nations would tend—in which their common efforts would find least resistance—in which they would operate with greatest force—and in which the equilibrium once established, would be maintained with the least difficulty (PIL 537; also UC 25.5).

This argument reminds one of the argument we explored in Chapter 3 in which Bentham argued from publicity for the principle of utility itself. In conditions of extensive interdependence and reciprocity, Bentham here argued, the equal common utility principle (and more specific rules and arrangements manifestly grounded in it) is the only principle that any given sovereign can *publicly* endorse and reasonably hope that others would do so as well. It is the principle that rationally motivated sovereigns, concerned for the well-being of their own nations, but forced to interact with other independent sovereign nations on whom they are dependent, converge on if they are required publicly to endorse a principle for their common governance. Bentham offered an example of this process of convergence:

> Let us take, for example, the famous law with respect to prizes, adopted by so many nations at the suggestion of Catherine II of Russia. How formidable so ever may have been the initiating power, there is no reason to think that it was fear which operated upon so many nations, together so powerful, and some of them so remote: it must have been its equity, that is to say, its common utility, or, what amounts to the same thing, its apparent utility, which determined their acceptance of it (PIL 537).

Bentham here imagines that sovereigns face what we would now call a coordination problem. The equal common utility principle alone, he argues, is "the point of repose ... in which all the forces find their equilibrium, from which the greatest difficulty would be found in making them to depart" (PIL 538). In the absence of effective coercive mechanisms, rules, and arrangements of international law must be self-enforcing.

One important axiom of Bentham's international theory concerns the equality of states. "Equality as between individual and individual, so far as is consistent with subsistence and security—there you have perfection of internal law: equality as between nation and nation—there you have perfection in international law," Bentham maintained in his writings on colonies (*Col.* 148). This axiom, which at times seems to take the form of a descriptive generalization, is better understood as a normative component, or perhaps implication, of his foundational principle. The axiom is explicitly deployed in his late sketch of a code of international law as "Art. 2": The equality of all [states] is hereby recognized by all" (IL (1827) 124). This principle underwrites the next three articles, which are articles of toleration and self-determination:

> Art. 3. Each has its own form of government; each respects the form of government of every other.
>
> Art. 4. Each has its own opinions and enactments on the subject of religion; each respects those of every other.
>
> Art. 5. Each has its own manners, customs and opinions; each respects the manners, customs and opinions of every other. (*ibid.*)

In addition, as we have seen, in Art. 8, the code commits each state to regard the governments of other states, as it regards its own, as the best servant of the greatest happiness of its members. Each state "means not to pass condemnation on any other, or put into dispute its fitness for the community of which it is the government" (IL (1827) 125).

Bentham imagined his code of international law to include both "duties" and "rights" of states (PIL 538). It requires of each state, negatively, to do no injury to other nations, and, positively, to do the greatest good possible for them; it also seeks to secure protection against injury and maximal benefit from other states. These "duties" and "rights" must be consistent with and manifestly serve the principle of equal common utility, so they are subject to a general proviso. The duties bind each state, "saving the regard that is proper to its own well-being"; and the rights impose duties on other states, "saving the regard due to the well-being of these nations" (PIL 538). However, if this proviso is not to consume the original principle and its corollaries, the regard proper to the well-being of each state must be limited to cases in which the principle or its corollaries impose a sacrifice of local well-being beyond that which is required of each, equally. The legislator's duty to render "good offices" to subjects of foreign states is qualified, to be sure, by consideration of expense to his own constituents, but it is qualified equally by consideration of expense to subjects of other states (CC (B) 203). Thus, it appears that Bentham's proviso is not meant to elevate consideration of local or (nationally) particular concerns over transnational concerns, but rather to secure so far as possible equal mutual or common interest of (subjects of) nations. Moreover, in his writings on specific issues in the global domain, Bentham is clear that duties on sovereign nations may well require sacrifice. But he insisted repeatedly that, looking to the long run and considering the great benefit of securing and preserving the cooperation of other nations—not the least in avoiding the immeasurable costs of war—these sacrifices will serve their own greater good as well as that of other nations in the global community.

Bentham's Vision of Utilitarian International Order

Bentham's code of international law was to provide the infrastructure for a global order of "peace ... mutual good-will and consequent mutual good offices" among all the members of the global community (IL (1827) 124). Bentham envisioned an order of solidarity *entregens*, but this order was artificial, not natural. Like the domestic social order among individuals that Bentham sought to construct, it could only be the product of cultivation and carefully engineered international institutions. We observed in Chapter 2 that Bentham believed that individuals can (and must) be educated and motivated to take the point of view of the community, so here he held that nations (or rather their rulers) can (and must) be educated and motivated to take the point of view of the community of nations. International law—the code of rules and the offices and institutions it creates and sustains—were among the most important means by which Bentham sought to urge this ideal order into existence. The "citizen of the world," who finds himself in the position of "legislator" of this new global order, plays a role like that of the utilitarian "deontologist" in private ethics, and even more like the ideal legislator in the field of internal politics. The global legislator, in contrast to these other utilitarian advisor-engineers, addresses sovereign nations and their rulers, rather than individuals. In this respect, the model for the global legislator is the theorist and writer of constitutional law for a nation's government, there being no world-government (and in Bentham's view there ought not to be). Without reservations, Bentham cast himself in this role.

However, Bentham recognized that the problem of managing subjects whose practical focus is dominated by "purely personal interest" has its analogue in the global domain, with a further complication. Sovereign subjects, the primary subjects of his legislative efforts, bear a special responsibility to focus only on the well-being of their constituencies (PIL 537) and thus seem duty-bound to pursue maximal constituency well-being, rather than the equal common utility. Bentham's answer to this objection was familiar. First, he argued, as we saw above, that in the existing global world, characterized as it is by interdependence and the need for reciprocity, a rational and sufficiently enlightened sovereign will recognize that his nation's well-being will be served best in the long run by a public commitment undertaken with sovereigns of the other nations to the principle of equal common utility of all nations. Where reciprocity is possible and mutually rewarding, the interests of the nation are best served by consulting and following the common interest, he argued, and the institutions of the international order are designed to establish these conditions.

Bentham's argument drew upon premises also at work in the private ethics "deontologist's" repertoire. It is important to recall that the deontologist did not set out to show that satisfaction of an individual's purely personal interests are maximized by seeking the well-being of others, but rather to call attention to and in some cases to stimulate or give focus to the individual's other-regarding interests, interests that tied his or her good, broadly considered, to the good of others. Over time and with practice and guidance from the deontologist, an individual will come to feel the motivational force of the common benefit (one's own good being included as an indispensable part), according to Bentham. He believed something like this training was also possible for national ruling elites (PIL 553–4). In circumstances of global interdependence and publicity of national action, there will be many actions that tend to serve common utility of nations, he thought. Bentham's own efforts at advising ruling elites of his day to undertake efforts that appeared to compromise their nation's "purely personal" interests tended to call attention to the nation's commitments to the well-being of related nations or to certain principles in which the nation's interest was invested. His counsels were not restricted to appeals to strictly self-serving ("sinister") interests, but to what he sometimes called a nation's "effective benevolence."[22] These counsels, he was confident, would not fall on entirely deaf ears.[23] "Effective benevolence," as Bentham understood it, was not

[22] Bentham deploys the distinction in SM 254, 263. He explains it (somewhat) in *Deont.* 184, 255–61, 278–9.

[23] Bentham never accepted the international-relations "realist" thesis that national rulers never act for reasons other than narrow national self-interest. In *Limits* he argued that the thesis that sovereigns keep engagement only when convenient is "trite and idle" and no truer of national sovereigns than of private individual (*Limits* 93 n. a).

the calculating, Hobbesian, game-the-system, "enlightened self-interest." Rather, he cast national interest more broadly to include a kind of international solidarity. This is another case in which "by this community of interest is produced a community of sympathy" (FPP 71; see Chapter 2, 45.) Bentham's vision of international order is a vision of a world community dedicated to genuine peace and mutual good will.

All that said, Bentham never conceived of this community as bound to global *altruism*. Requirements on sovereigns to avoid injury and serve the interests of other nations as well as its own were limited by a proviso permitting states to derogate from obligations that imposed undue burdens that were not compensated sufficiently in the long run. Bentham's vision of international order is more Grotian than Hobbesian.

INSTITUTIONS OF INTERNATIONAL ORDER

Utilitarian global order is not a natural condition, as Bentham understood it. It must be engineered and sustained by artificial means, in the first instance at least, by the rules, principles, institutions, and arrangements of international law. This, Bentham argued, required a codified body of legal principles, issued by a "proper legislative authority," interpreted and supported by a common international court (IL (1827) 120).[24] However, unlike Bentham's conception of municipal law, his model of international law rejected centralized authority. Bentham advocated and strongly argued for state pluralism and against world government or a universal republic (*ibid.*). World government is inconsistent with the fundamental axiom of equality of sovereign nations, Bentham argued, as are formal institutions punishment.

In the absence of a centralized coercive power, war was commonly regarded as the instrument of legal punishment, sanctioning violations of international law. It was common to regard war as "a species of procedure by which one nation endeavours to enforce its rights at the expense of another nation" (PIL 538; but see Gen. View 200f). Bentham seems to have accepted this common thought, but with serious reservations. Domestic institutions of punishment are often problematic, he observed, but "international [coercive, punitive] procedure is attended by ills infinitely more painful—in certain respects in point of intensity, commonly in point

[24] In this text, Bentham limited the scope of the code of international law to "all civilized nations: which at present is as much as to say all nations professing the Christian Religion." This significantly narrows the scope of international law as conceived elsewhere, especially in his *Principles of International Law*, written more than forty years earlier. It is not clear why Bentham restricted his code in this way. Perhaps his remarks were directed to a particular (but unspecified) problem or set of circumstances and thus contemplated a temporary restriction. Jennifer Pitts argues persuasively that Bentham did not embrace the narrow parochialism that John Stuart Mill inherited from his father. See Pitts, *A Turn to Empire*, Chapter 4.

of duration, and always in point of extent" (PIL 539). The primary problem is that nearly always the responsible criminal offender is not the whole people, but their national leaders; yet it is the whole people who suffer. "However criminal the aggression may be, there is properly no other criminal than the chief:—individuals are only his innocent and unfortunate instruments" (*ibid.*). Thus, from the point of view of utilitarian theory of punishment (IPML XIII), the vengeance unleashed in war lacks a proper object; punishment is "unnecessary, useless, expensive, and inefficacious"—occasions of war are always cases unmeet for punishment (PIL 539). War is justified, he argued, only in self-defense (CC (B) 202) and only as a last resort, there being no other means of settling disputes, "no arbitrator between [disputing parties] sufficiently strong, absolutely to take from them all hope of resistance" (PIL 538–9).

In the place of war, Bentham insisted on a clear code of the rights and duties of nations and institutions that can to some considerable extent provide for peaceful arbitration of international disputes. For this care must be taken to secure appropriate form and substance of international law.

International Law: Form and Substance

Form. In view of his general jurisprudence, it is not surprising that Bentham insisted that the body of international law must take the form of a carefully drafted, systematic code (Gen. View 200–201). In his view, it must include (i) "existing unwritten laws … established by custom," that are gathered, redrafted, and systematically arranged (subjected to "homologation") and (ii) "new conventions … made upon all points which remain unascertained" (PIL 540). Thus, the rules of international law *as it is* (existing treaties), as *it is supposed to be* (implications drawn from the former and articulations of custom), along with all the provisions that are needed to fill out the body of law, are reduced to writing and made fully public. A complex and insufficiently public fictitious entity is replaced with a systematic real entity (or with at least something that can in principle be traced to real entities[25]). When international law is removed from the the conjectural realm and secured in the province of publicly accessible principle, Bentham argued, the aim of "adjustment and pre-appointed definition of all rights and obligations" would be achieved (IL (1827) 124).

Writing and promulgation would give the provisions of international law the salience to attract the self-enforcing equilibrium they need to order relations among states. In that way, the body of international law, by its form, will serve the common utility of all nations. It will do so in part by undercutting some of the main causes of

[25] IL (1827) 120; see Chapter 1 for an extended discussion of Bentham's theory of real and fictitious entities.

what Bentham called "good faith" wars—wars due to uncertainty over or disputes regarding the respective rights and duties of contending nations (PIL 539f), thus minimizing the occasions of resentment for supposed injuries (IL (1827) 120). Yet, Bentham was realistic. Even the best code will be ineffective against sovereigns who acts *de mauvaise foi* with their minds set on conquest (*ibid.*)

Substance. From the outset of his career, international law and global order were key parts of his general project to "rear the fabric of felicity by the hands of reason and law" (IPML 11). Yet, unlike his penal theory and constitutional theory, he left his international law theory in an embryonic state. He delimited its domain and articulated its foundational principles, as we have seen, but he never worked out the substance of his code of international law beyond its rudiments. He identified some of the topics that the code must address, for example, the definition of the subjects of sovereigns (citizenship), the boundaries of states and rights of possession of territory, regulation of trade on the seas, the relations of states to members of other nations (PIL 540–4; IL (1827) 120–1). His foundational principles of equality of states and universal tolerance and respect imply a general presumption of self-determination and a presumption against intervention, especially military intervention, in the internal affairs of other nations. Two of four essays included in his "Principles of International Law" are devoted to war and a plan for universal peace, but the essays are short and narrowly focused. It is difficult to draw firm conclusions even about this core topic of international law. In general, Bentham was wary of war: "war is mischief upon the largest scale" (PIL 544), he wrote at the opening of his essay on the causes and consequences of war. He believed defensive war to be justified, as one would expect from his realism about the ability of international law to prevent "bad faith," i.e., unjust aggressive war; and he insisted that efforts must to taken to restrict the inevitable destruction, loss, and suffering of war to those driving the nation to war, so far as that is possible. Also, in his writings on specific historical topics, he appears to endorse some military intervention for humanitarian purposes and perhaps even for what we now call "regime change."[26] But, as we have seen, he rejected out of hand war as a means of enforcing the duties and rights of international law. War, in the absence of a common tribunal, may be the only option, but this "concession to notorious injustice invites fresh injustice," he insisted. When the code of international rights and duties is clear and public and a common tribunal is available to try disputes, "the necessity for war no longer follows from difference of opinion. Just or unjust, the decision of the arbiters will save the credit, the honour of the contending party" (PIL 552).

[26] See Bentham's letter to United States' President, John Quincy Adams, urging him to give military support to Bentham's plan for intervention in Tripoli (SM 145–52). Bentham's proposals for intervention in Tripoli and Greece are discussed in Lorenzo Cello, *Jeremy Bentham's Ethics of Intervention: The Utilitarian 'Moral Casuistry' of a Cosmopolitan* (University of Queensland, PhD Thesis), Chapter 5. I am grateful to Dr. Cello for permitting me to read portions of his thesis.

Enactment and Enforcement of International Law

We look in vain to Bentham, then, for an articulation of the rights and duties of states vis-à-vis other states or individual persons, but he had some important, albeit only lightly sketched, thoughts about core institutions of his new utilitarian international order. He built his new order around three key institutions: a legislative assembly, a common court of judicature and the "Public Opinion Tribunal." These institutions provided the infrastructure of the international order defined by a code of international law.

The code of international law must not only be competently drafted, it also must be authoritatively enacted and promulgated. But, because fundamental principles of this order rule out a centralized government, this task must be assigned to a representative body of all the states. Bentham envisioned a diet or congress of nations, composed of representatives from each independent state, akin to the German Diet or Swiss League (PIL 552; IL (1827) 120). This body, being representative of each of the equal sovereign states, would enjoy authority sufficient to enact the code, which by virtue of that authoritative enactment would bind all the member states. This law, he assumed, would be incorporated into the domestic law of each member state. Bentham called it the "the universal code." Particular codes, articulating the agreements and arrangements between individual states that do not depend on the legislative activity of the congress, would be included in the domestic law of the respective states alongside this universal code (Gen. View 200). Since the congress of nations is given no executive or administrative powers, one might have thought that the congress would go out of existence once the code was enacted. However, Bentham assigned a continuing judicial task to the congress. In his design, the congress defined and empowered a common adjudicative institution—an kind of international court of justice—and constituted itself as "a sort of Appellate Judicatory" (IL (1827) 120; PIL 552, 554).

Primary judicial activity was to be performed by the ordinary judicatory. It was to be empowered to exercise most recognized adjudicative functions, including hearing evidence and arguments of counsel from the contending states and issuing judgments on disputed matters, based on that evidence and those arguments and the prevailing international law. It was to have power to issue judgments and circulate them as widely as possible. Its decisions and its argument in support of them were to be made "universally notorious" (IL (1827) 120; PIL 554), aided by freedom of the press in every state. However, neither this common tribunal, nor the appellate judicatory of the international congress is empowered, in Bentham's design, to exercise coercive (or "imperative") power. "Under a system of international law the imperative [function] could not be exercised by any authority: not even by the international congress" (IL (1827) 120).

Bentham left enforcement of the decisions of the international judicatory, and, by extension, of the law that it seeks to execute, entirely to the operation of the "moral sanction" as applied by the Public Opinion Tribunal.[27] In this respect, as we noted earlier, international law is, in Bentham's jurisprudence, on a par with that part of constitutional law he called "laws *in principem*." The international court, regarded as an impartial arbiter and thus enjoying the trust of all the parties, mobilizes the opinion and good offices of states not involved in the disputes and use this public pressure to secure compliance of the contending parties with its decision. In his discussion of laws *in principem*, Bentham recognized two quarters from which can stem public pressure (the moral sanction) on the sovereign to conform to "express covenants": from subjects of the sovereign and from foreign states (*Limits* 92–3). The Public Opinion Tribunal consists of other states and the subjects of the several states whose opinion contending states may honor and whose good will they may wish to preserve. In an early draft of material for his essays on international law entitled "International Protest," Bentham criticized the British people for deferring to their rulers when it comes to international affairs. This, he complained, is "a natural error" but nevertheless "a very unfortunate one" (UC 25.110). The problem, however, was not that the moral sanction was ineffective when applied to rulers, but that the people were insufficiently vigilant and excessively deferential (UC 25.51). He also recognized that rulers were complicit in this silence, by keeping as much of their activity from the public as possible. In his constitutional writing, as well as his early writings on international law (for example in manuscripts headed "Cabinet No Secresy," UC 25.50ff), he sought to make the operations of government, including foreign affairs, as transparent as possible (CC (B) 210), although he recognized the need at times for *temporary* secrecy (CC (B) 165). Publicity, we see again, was a critical precondition of effective exercise of power, in Bentham's view. He thought this form of what we now call "soft power" was ultimately more effective than military intervention, because it enjoys the credibility of impartiality and law-based, reasoned argument. Moreover, he thought, it is less dangerous than war because it is less likely to escalate into cycles of recrimination, creating fresh injustices in response to the first.

CONCLUSION

International politics was integral to Bentham's comprehensive theoretical project. Although he never developed his theory of international politics to any substantial degree, he offered a sketch of a global order and its grounding principles that enriches our understanding of his larger jurisprudential project. He articulated a distinctive (quasi-) cosmopolitan principle for the governance of a state-pluralist global order. This state-pluralism was, for him, a settled fact for which there was

[27] For an extended discussion of the constitution and the *modus operandi* of the Public Opinion Tribunal, see Chapter 12.

support in his normative theory. Rejecting any form of a unified universal republic, he insisted on the normative equality of all independent states.

This was the only structure, he argued, that could adequately serve the sole ultimate end of international law and global order, namely, the greatest equal common utility of all nations taken together. This formulation of the utilitarian cosmopolitan principle is remarkable when viewed from the point of view of twenty-first century utilitarianism. But it is not all that remarkable seen in light of Bentham's mature political–constitutional theory, as discussed in Chapters 5. In his view, the greatest equal utility of human beings of all nations and races is best served by establishing and securing global institutions that serve the greatest equal common utility of all nations. Although the "fields" of internal and international politics are distinct domains of action, as Bentham conceived of them, they are also in key ways complementary. Agents working in each have distinct but related responsibilities. Those working in the field of international politics are responsible for securing the equal common utility of nations and those working in internal politics are responsible for securing equal utility so far as possible within their respective nations.

Although he rejected a universal republic, Bentham envisioned the global order as a kind of loose affiliation of states, each of which participates on an equal basis in a common congress accorded legislative authority through their participation. They are also subject to the jurisdiction of this congress sitting as an appellate court and to a system of lower courts created and supported by the congress. Bentham's ultimate solution to the problem of war was threefold: (i) the unwritten, customary law was to be put on a clear, authoritative and fully public basis in a carefully drafted and systematic code; (ii) all disputes arising in international relations were to be directed to this code and the common judicatory, empowered to resolve the disputes in an impartial way, based on hearing and responding to arguments taking the code as their primary text; and (iii) all international institutions were to operate in a fully transparent manner—all activities of the common judicatory, especially, were to be fully public, open to a freely operating press and relying ultimately on the power of public opinion, of nations and individuals, to secure compliance with its decisions.

The central themes of his theory of international politics, announced but never fully developed, resonate with and to a degree underline themes more fully developed elsewhere in his moral–political theory.

12
The Soul of Justice
Bentham on Publicity, Law, and the Rule of Law

Publicity is a central concept of Bentham's theory of law and governing.* In Bentham's view, security of society and its individual members is the focal aim and fundamental task of law (BCLT Ch. 5). Yet, law must be made, administered, adjudicated, and enforced; so if law is introduced into a political community, human beings must be entrusted with making, applying, and enforcing that law. Law is the primary mode or instrument of governing, but it governs only through the efforts of those who govern with it. Although law is given the task of securing us against the abuse of power, it also creates new opportunities and resources for such abuse. Thus, law introduces a new and especially worrisome form of political insecurity arising from the potential for abuse of the power that entrusted to governing officials. In Bentham's view, the only effective solution to this problem lay in publicity, the most robust and comprehensive system of public oversight of public power in all its forms. "Publicity is the very soul of justice [i.e., law] ... through publicity alone justice is the mother of security" (B iv. 316, 317).

The *rule of law* is that state or condition of a political community in which *law effectively rules*. When the rule of law is robust in a political community, when law effectively rules in that community, members of the community are protected against the arbitrary exercise of power by public officials as well as by fellow members (both individual and corporate).[1] Law rules, we might say, when law is not just an instrument in the hands of those who govern, but also guides, directs, and controls those who govern with it. However, at this point an ancient and still troubling question arises: how can *law* rule if, as Plato taught, only *men* rule? The ancient answer is that law can rule only when those entrusted to rule with law submit to its governance, commit to be guided and controlled by it.[2]

* Adapted with permission from "The Soul of Justice: Bentham on Publicity, Law and the Rule of Law," in *Bentham's Theory of Law and Public Opinion*, Xiaobo Zhai and Michael Quinn, eds. (Cambridge: Cambridge University Press, 2014), 40–62.

[1] I argue that this captures the core of the ideal of the rule of law in "Law's Rule: Reflexivity, Mutual Accountability, and the Rule of Law," in Xiaobo Zhai and Michael Quinn, *Bentham's Theory of Law and Public Opinion* (Cambridge: Cambridge University Press, 2014), 10–14.

[2] This answer finds classic expression in Roman law: "It is a statement worth of the majesty of a ruler for the prince to profess himself bound by the laws. So much does our authority depend on the authority of the law. And indeed it is greater for the imperium to submit the principate to the laws" (*Codex*, 1.14.4). See Brian Tierney, " 'The Prince is Not Bound.' Accursius and the Origins of the Modern State," *Comparative Studies in Society and History* 5 (1963), 378–400.

Utility, Publicity, and Law: Essays on Bentham's Moral and Legal Philosophy. Gerald J. Postema.

Arguably, that commitment is not personal but political and thus law can rule only when there is among officials and law-subjects a rich *ethos* of reciprocal responsibilities and commitments to holding each other accountably under that law.[3] However, one might reasonably argue that that answer is at best incomplete. It speaks only of attitudes and activities, of internalized responsibilities, but nothing of their necessary social conditions and nothing of institutions that enable and empower this practice of accountability holding, that give it focus and power. We need an account of the infrastructure of the rule of law.

At this point, Bentham's reflections on publicity promise to offer something of value to the long tradition of thinking about the rule of law. Yet, this is not obvious from his massive writing on the merits of publicity. It is not surprising, of course, that he never used the term "the rule of law," since it is of more recent vintage; but also some features of his jurisprudence might suggest that he would be hostile to its use. One might ask, then, does Bentham offer us an elaborated *conception of* the rule of law, or at least the resources for constructing a deeper and more comprehensive conception of the rule of law; or does he offer an *alternative to* the idea and ideology of the rule of law? The answer to this question is complex and nuanced. I will return to it at the conclusion of this chapter. To address it we must first explore the role that the notion and manifold devices of publicity play in Bentham's theory of law and governing.

PUBLICITY AND ITS PROGENY

Security against Misrule

Two strategies for securing ordinary law-subjects against the arbitrary exercise of power at the hands of ruling officials have commonly been deployed in the western rule-of-law tradition: one involves entrenching fundamental rights in the constitution; the other involves sharply separating the powers of government, especially securing the independence and supremacy of the judiciary empowered to hold the other branches of government to exercises of power within their respective constitutional limits. Bentham rejected both strategies out of hand. Notoriously, he rejected the idea of natural rights as nonsense, and, as we have seen in Chapter 10, he rejected the strategy of American and French constitution-writers to incorporate fundamental natural rights into their respective constitutions.

His objections were many and detailed, but the most important and most familiar were twofold. (1) He argued that the notions to which such constitutional provisions appealed are hopelessly vague, and they are made no more concrete or

[3] See Postema, "Law's Rule," 18–20, 26–9, and Postema, "Fidelity in Law's Commonwealth," in *Private Law and the Rule of Law*, Dennis Klimchuk, ed. (Oxford: Oxford University Press, 2014), 21, 30–6.

publicly accessible by being entrenched in the nation's basic law (SM 231). (2) By making the validity of an exercise of legislative power depend on meeting some standard of fundamental rights constitutional constraints have the effect of transferring legislative power to the judiciary. This was, in Bentham's view, a recipe for tyranny (FG 485–8). Bentham had no difficulty distinguishing between legal duties and legal limits on its power (Hohfeldian *disabilities*); he simply objected to subjecting the legislative branch of government to such disabilities, because, by limiting legislative power in this way, untrammeled power was put in the hands of judges. A similar objection lay at the core of his rejection of Montesquieu's constitutional doctrine of the separation of powers. He argued that it was a fundamental mistake of government institution-building to limit the powers of government institutions and to subject them to competition and constraint by the others. The more rational and effective strategy, he argued repeatedly, was to give government institutions all the power they needed to be effective, but, at the same time, to subject them to comprehensive, relentless, and unavoidable *public* oversight—he called it "full responsibility."

Rather than relying on appeals to natural rights, or embedding them in a system's basic or constitutional law, or designing an elaborate scheme for the separation of powers, Bentham proposed a carefully engineered system of "securities against misrule" to counteract the pervasive real threat of abuse of power by officials. *Security against misrule* was his mantra and his singular aim; publicity was his most powerful tool.

Moral Aptitude

In Bentham's view, political rule can misfire in three different ways, corresponding to the failures of three components of "official aptitude": (1) failure of intellectual aptitude—of knowledge or (non-normative) judgment; (2) failure of active aptitude—of attendance and attention; (3) failure of moral aptitude—of moral or legal judgment and, more fundamentally, of motivation to act on right judgment. By far the most important concern, on which Bentham spent most of his energy in his numerous writings on the topic, was failure of moral aptitude on the part of governing officials. The "misrule" he primarily sought to secure against was failure of moral aptitude, which he linked directly with the abuse of power or arbitrary exercise of power,[4] driven by what he called "sinister sacrifice"—that is, sacrifice of the public interest to the private interests of those in power. His overarching aim was to engineer institutional devices that would "maximize official moral aptitude."[5]

[4] "Of the quality correspondent and opposite to appropriate moral aptitude, the most mischievous effect is—disposition to exercise arbitrary power" (B v. 556).

[5] See FP 13–76, 270–324; OAM 21–38; and SM generally.

Bentham understood "moral aptitude" in terms of the judgment-shaping and motivating *interests* of agents—their private or personal interests and their universal or public interests.[6] When an individual's interests lead her to act in a way that is likely to work against the interests of others, and especially against the public interest generally, Bentham called such private interests "sinister." Accordingly, Bentham characterized moral aptitude, first, in a negative mode as the *absence* of a certain characteristic disposition, namely, "a certain propensity universal in human nature ... to sacrifice all other interests to that which at each moment appears to him to be his own preponderant interest" (FP 13). In the political context, Bentham thought that the contrary of "appropriate moral aptitude" is the "disposition to exercise arbitrary power" (B v. 556).

It is possible to counteract the sinister interests of officials, and thereby encourage or enable moral aptitude in them, in two ways, according to Bentham: it can be done either by providing them with weighty considerations of public interest or by denying them opportunities to act on their conflicting private interests (FP 236). The former is feasible only if social regard and a kind of sympathy is a naturally predominant motive of officials such that they are willing to sacrifice their own happiness for the happiness of others. Bentham thought this was possible but rare. So he thought that it would be a grave mistake to rely on that sort of public spirit when planning legal and political institutions. The only safe institutional design strategy is to assume that, given the opportunity, officials will make the sinister sacrifice.[7] The wiser course, then, is to "render [officials] unable to do wrong, yet sufficiently able to do right" (FP 15). This is done by making the "wrong" unavailable (FP 236; CC (B) 100; BCLT 383–4), or by making it ineligible (because too personally costly), that is, by "bringing ... the particular interest of rulers into accordance with the universal interest" (FP 235).

What motive remains when desire is denied hope and an official's private interest no longer stands opposed to the public interest? Sometimes Bentham says that the "sinister" dimension of the official's private interest can be neutralized by aligning private and public interests (that is, by giving the official sufficient personal incentive to act in the public interest). However, at other times he suggests that when an official's private interest has been denied hope of fulfillment, what drives his action is his concern for the public interest (of which, he recognizes, his interest constitutes an integral part). Having thereby been "virtually divested of all such sinister interest," Bentham argued, there "remains as the only interest whereby his conduct can be determined, his right and proper interest, which is to say that interest which is in accordance with the universal interest taken in the aggregate" (FP 236). Thus, Bentham seems to have recognized that the "moral aptitude" has a *positive*

[6] On Bentham's distinction between universal and particular (private or personal) interests, as well as the related notions of public interests and sinister interests, see Chapter 6.

[7] FP 15, 234. On Bentham's "strategic egoism," see Chapter 2, 47–50 and BCLT 11.4.

aspect: the disposition of a person to act in the public interest (at least insofar as he recognizes that his own interest is an integral part of the public interest and claims a part of it).[8] On the whole, Bentham tended to focus his attention on the negative characterization, but at times he sought to mobilize this positive dimension as well. His account of the "moral sanction," we shall see below, seems to rely in part on more than merely the addition of extrinsic disincentives to outweigh countervailing, potentially sinister, personal or private interests.

Publicity

To maximize official moral aptitude, Bentham proposed a number of institutional devices, including, for example, minimizing the amount of money at an official's disposal and, where feasible, subjecting officials to legal punishment for violation of their official duties (FP 30–73). But, by far the most important device, in Bentham's view, was *publicity*. Indeed, in *Securities Against Misrule*, he insisted that publicity is the *only* effective check on official power: "Those who desire to see any check whatsoever to the power of the government under which they live, or limit to their sufferings under it, must look for such check and limit to the power of the Public Opinion Tribunal . . . to this place of refuge or to none."[9] At other times, Bentham allowed that other devices might also be useful, but publicity remained, in his view, the indispensable condition of the success of any other institutional strategy for control of official exercise of power. "Without publicity, all other checks are fruitless; in comparison of publicity, all other checks are of small account."[10] "Mischief which you do not know of, you can not controul" (UC 25.50).

Bentham sought to subject governmental action of every sort—legislative, administrative, enforcement, and judicial—to (nearly unlimited[11]) publicity. He enlisted every kind of device and facility he could imagine for this purpose. Laws requiring all kinds of openness and disclosure of governmental actions were among these devices, but he also thought equally about the physical and social

[8] For a fuller discussion of these two understandings of the moral aptitude and their relationship to "the moral sanction," see Chapter 2, 50–1, and BCLT 11.3, 11.5.

[9] SM 125; see also FP 241, PT 29 and the following: "To the pernicious exercise of the power of government [public opinion] is the only check; to the beneficial, an indispensable supplement" (CC (CW) vol. 1, 36). "The state of the *law* being given—for every practical purpose, appropriate *moral* aptitude [of judges] must be considered as exactly proportioned to the strictness of his dependence upon *public* opinion" (B v. 555, author's emphasis).

[10] B iv. 317; B vi. 355. "Without publicity, no good is permanent: under the auspices of publicity, no evil can continue" (PT 37).

[11] There is an extended discussion of the necessary limits of publicity in adjudication, at least regarding the taking of evidence, in Bentham's *Rationale of Judicial Evidence* (RJE vi. 352–65). In manuscripts from the 1780s, Bentham argued against secrecy even in cases of deliberations concerning going to war (UC 25.50). He conceded that the threat of punishment for entering a war is unlikely to deter ministers, because the people are unlikely to carry out the threat in the middle of the conflict. Nevertheless, Bentham insisted that such deliberations must still be open to the public.

structures of public spaces and of buildings and rooms where public matters were debated and public affairs were transacted. He was an *engineer* of publicity and even more an *architect* of publicity. Publicity is important, Bentham argued, because it gives force to the law and mobilizes the Public Opinion Tribunal; it is the key "instrument of security for appropriate aptitude on the part of all public functionaries" (CC (B) 210).

He also sought to design formal and informal institutions that provided opportunities for and promoted public inquiries into public affairs, public activities, and the activities of public officials. Among the most important of these quasi-formal institutions were the free press and what he called the "quasi-jury." The quasi-jury, as he conceived it, was an institution like the jury familiar to English law, but it lacked the responsibility or power to decide particular cases (B ii. 141–61, CC (B) 41, 554–67). The primary task of the quasi-jury was to oversee the judge's oversight of civil and criminal trials. Publicity "keeps the judge himself, while trying, under trial ... [U]nder the auspices of publicity, the original cause in the court of law and the appeal to the court of public opinion, are going on at the same time" (RJE vi. 355). Bentham sought not merely to make governmental actions of all kinds transparent, but also to encourage, enable, educate, and empower the Public Opinion Tribunal's oversight of governmental actions. Public opinion, he thought, was "more powerful than all other tribunals" (PT 29).

Public Opinion Tribunal

The *public* whose opinion Bentham sought to mobilize through deploying these devices of publicity is the indeterminate aggregate of "unassignable" individuals regarded as a kind of unofficial and informal tribunal (although in his constitutional writings, he gave it official status, treating it as a "committee" of the "supreme constitutive" power). Bentham admitted that the Public Opinion Tribunal, strictly speaking, is fictional or "imaginary" (SM 212), at least insofar as we are inclined to view the "whole aggregate" of the public as if it were a formally constituted body, exercising conferred powers ("with the formalities of a Judge") (SM 28). But he insisted that it is a harmless and useful fiction, indeed a necessary one (FP 70; CC (B) 41; SM 28, 121). And he thought the fiction can be largely avoided by focusing on the subset of members who take an active role in public matters, even more so when a subset of the whole is given a specific quasi-legal function and institutionalization, like his proposed "quasi-jury." Thus, while the relevant *public* consists of all members of the community, Bentham took the membership of the Public Opinion Tribunal proper—that "quasi-judicial" body—to consist of all those who take cognizance of public matters. He liked to think of them as a kind of "committee of the whole," i.e., a determinate but not officially determined subset of the whole which takes upon itself the task of doing the work of the whole (SM 121).

Membership in the Public Opinion Tribunal, as Bentham conceived it, was not limited to members of the enfranchised "supreme constitutive"; rather, all adult members of the community, including women, were eligible. Those who can write and publish play a major role, but so too can those who participate through reading, and even the illiterate are eligible, as long as they can observe and scrutinize the actions of public officials, and on the basis of observation form and express opinions, and join others in sharing views on public matters. Bentham even opened this "public sphere" to persons outside the community who may also take cognizance of such matters and engage actively in discussion of them (SM 28, 57–8, 121; FP 57, 283; CC (B) 41; CC (CW) vol. 1, 35). A free press was, in Bentham's view, essential for vigor and vitality of this wide-open public sphere.

The primary function of Public Opinion Tribunal was "censorial," its aim was to "maximize [the] responsibility" of government officials of all kinds (FP 28). The many devices of publicity were designed in various ways to enable, promote, and underwrite this activity. An important secondary function was educational. Public access to and oversight of legislative and judicial activities offered the general public a "school of justice." Through publicity, courts become schools of justice, where the most important concerns of morality are held up, discussed, and enforced (RJE vi. 355; B ii. 143, 148, 149–50; PT 31). Observing argument and debate, people learn that the primary currency of public discourse is not that of private (sinister) interests, but rather the public or universal interest—not the interests of the community that stand *opposed to* interests of individuals, but rather those interests of the community in which individual members have a significant stake (B ii. 144; see Chapter 6).

Maximize Responsibility

Bentham's view of the "educational" role of publicity is rarely acknowledged and worth extended discussion, but I will focus attention here rather on the disciplinary function of publicity. The central aim of this disciplinary function was what he called "responsibility." "For security against breach of trust, the sole apt remedy is ... constant responsibility ... on every occasion and at all times, the strictest and most absolute dependence" on the public (CC (B) 62). Bentham regarded this responsibility in two complementary ways:[12] (1) as *accountability*, i.e., subjection to the legitimate demand for explicit, public accounting of the reasons for actions taken or proposed; and (2) as *liability* to punishment, i.e., subjection to the moral sanction on analogy to legal liability (CC (CW) vol.1, 24; CC (B) 50–1, 151–2; B ii. 31). Because he often closely associated responsibility (and obligation)

[12] See BCLT 359–60.

with sanctions, it is easy to overlook the accountability dimension and with it the subtlety of Bentham's notion of official responsibility.

The primary leverage used by the moral sanction was reputation or esteem. The "Judge is a man of honour: he has a rich fund of reputation to preserve and to improve" (UC 57.9). Public condemnation threatens an official's reputation. This dimension of Bentham's account of official responsibility is underlined in the "Legislator's Inaugural Declaration," which Bentham included in his model constitutional code (CC (B) 198–204). The Legislator declares publicly his personal commitment to a "moral code" that "maps" guidelines for the whole field of the official's activity. The code is no less demanding for being articulated in terms of very general principles and submitted to the continued judgment of the Public Opinion Tribunal. The code, intentionally, is not formulated in formal terms that lend themselves to assessment by the legal process, but rather articulates the deeper values that underlie the formal constitutional code and give it its vitality and normative force. It is very clear that Bentham took pains to make this declaration a model for the *personal commitment* of officials. They are to pledge to keep themselves free of the influence of sinister interest, corruption, and "factitious respect," and to seek only for "pre-eminent respect at the hands of the community at large" (CC (B) 200). Indeed, the legislator is publicly to acknowledge that he "is accessory to every injury, against which he withholds protection, as well as to every injury to which he gives or leaves facility ... that he is the accomplice to every oppressor and every depredator, into whose hands he thus puts an instrument of injury" (CC (B) 202). This he acknowledges to the members of the Public Opinion Tribunal, and invites them to hold him accountable not only to the law, but more fundamentally to the values and principles on which it is founded.

Moreover, Bentham observed that public opinion typically involves more than mere opinion. It also engages the good or ill offices of the public (CC (B) 41). He recognized and welcomed the fact that such "ill offices" might extend beyond condemnation to withdrawal of obedience and even collective opposition to and obstruction of official action (FG 485). Indeed, Bentham argued that a free government should "cherish," encourage, and enable the popular disposition to resistance.[13] Does this not make the system of public responsibility nothing more

[13] Bentham, *On the Liberty of the Press and Public Discussion and other Legal and Political Writings for Spain and Portugal*, Philip Schofield and Catherine Pease-Watkin, eds. (Oxford: Oxford University Press, 2012), 30. The whole passage reads as follows: "Of a government that is not despotic, it is therefore the essential character, even to *cherish* the disposition to eventual resistance.... Instruments necessary to the existence of such a disposition [of resistance], in a state adequate to the production of the effect, are *instruction, excitation, correspondence*. To the understanding applies instruction; to the will, excitation: both are necessary to appropriate action and correspondent effect; instruction and excitation, in the case of each individual taken separately; correspondence for the sake of concert amongst the number of individuals requisite and sufficient for the production of the ultimate effect. Co-extensive with the instruction and excitation must be the correspondence ... When, to a national purpose, exertions on a national scale are necessary, exertions made without concert (need it be said) are made without effect. By instruction, excitation, and faculty of correspondence—by these three instruments in conjunction, and not by any one or two of them alone—can the national mind be kept in a state of

than "a system of *distrust*"? Bentham asked. Yes, indeed, he replied, but "every good political institution is founded upon this base," for "whom ought we to distrust, if not those to whom is committed great authority, with great temptations to abuse it?" (PT 37).[14] In *Fragment on Government*, Bentham unfurled his jurisprudential banner: *obey punctually and censure freely* (FG 399), but, as his thoughts about the devices necessary for security against misrule developed, the Public Opinion Tribunal, the "tribunal of free criticism" (FP 98), took and even more active role. Criticism could and sometimes must qualify obedience.

Bentham thought the effects of publicity on the behavior of public officials worked in more subtle ways as well. The judge, after all, is a man of honor, so he internalizes judgments of the public. He anticipates the unexpressed judgment entertained by the people (CC (B) 42), which in turn engages his self-esteem. This forces the official to find language in which he can articulate the grounds for his actions. This drive for vindication in the eyes of the public engages the second mode of responsibility—accountability, i.e., liability to the demand for an accounting in the language of public reasons of actions taken in the name of the public. In Bentham's vision, the moral sanction, when mobilized for this legal-political function involves an essential discursive, reasons-demanding and reasons-assessing dimension.

One of the most salutary consequences of full and unconstrained publicity of "judicature," in Bentham's view, was that it forced the judge to seek publicly to explain and justify each decision and action. To avoid the impression that he has taken advantage of obscurity in the law or the evidence presented in court, or complexity of legal arguments made at trial, the judge has a strong incentive to "state, in the presence of the [observers] ... the considerations—reasons—by the force of which the decision so pronounced by him has been made to assume its actual shape, in preference to any other that may have been contended for." Thus, publicity has the "natural and in experience customary"—if not necessary—consequence of forcing the judge into "the habit of giving reasons from the bench." "Specifying reasons is an operation, to the performance of which, under the auspices of publicity, the nature of his situation will ... naturally dispose him to have recourse" (B vi. 357).[15] In this way, the unjust decision exposed, but also "the injustice of it is to a certain degree manifest ... [T]he exposure is in this case effected either by the utter absence

appropriate preparation—a state of preparation for eventual resistance. It is by the conjunct application of all these instruments, that minds are put and kept in a proper state of discipline, as bodies are by the military exercise."

[14] For a general discussion of Bentham's "strategy of distrust," and the rule of trust in maintaining a robust rule of law in a polity, see Gerald J. Postema, "Trust, Distrust, and the Rule of Law," in Matthew Harding and Paul B. Miller, eds. (Cambridge: Cambridge University Press, forthcoming)..

[15] "By the power given to the jury, the judge finds himself under the necessity of addressing his discourse to them explanatory of the nature of the case and of the ground on which his advice and recommendation, if any is given them, has been founded" (CC (B) 141–2; also 147).

of all attempt at exhibiting reasons, or by what may be still better, the weakness and absurdity of his reasons" (B ii. 147). While this necessity is not (and Bentham thought must not be) a matter of *legal* obligation (that is, liable to punishment by law), it is nevertheless a *moral* obligation, enforced by the moral sanction (B vi. 357; CC (B) 147; 555).

This is equally important in other institutional contexts in which government officials must act in the full light of publicity. "In legislation, in judicature, in every line of human action in which the agent is or ought to be accountable to the public or any part of it—giving reasons is, in relation to rectitude of conduct a test, a standard, a security, a source of interpretation" (RJE vi. 357). Already in *Fragment on Government*, Bentham insisted that the *responsibility* of governors consisted in the "right which a subject has of having the reasons publicly assigned and canvassed of every act of power that is exercised over him" (FG 485). Bentham directly linked this demand of public reason-giving accountability with constraints on arbitrary power. "That which constitutes *arbitrary power* in judicature is . . . exemption from the controul of a superior—from the obligation of assigning *reasons* for his acts—and from the superintending scrutiny of the public eye" (B v. 556). One of the key means of securing "responsibility" of officials was for the public to expect and demand an accounting of the grounds for any exercises of power. Full and comprehensive publicity makes such accountability possible and provides the public the tools needed to bridle the power of those who govern.

Public Reasons and Law

Public reason-giving lies at the core of Bentham's view of law's proper functioning. Governing through law is, according to Bentham, sharply distinguished from the exercise of brute force which elicits compliance out of fear. Law involves the public expression of will (of the sovereign), but it does not involve only that, according to Bentham. Law's typical mode of governing, in his view, is to *address* clear, public, systematically organized directives to a people capable of understanding and applying them to their own situations. This is not a matter of one will imposing itself on another, but rather of the understanding of the law-maker and law-applier addressing the understanding of their constituents (UC 126.1; B iv. 539; BCLT 360). "Power gives existence to a law for the moment," Bentham wrote in *Judicial Establishment in France*, "but it is upon reason that it must depend for its stability" (B iv. 310). Governing by will alone inevitably is power answering only to sinister interest. As a mode of governing, it cannot function in the full light of publicity, Bentham believed, because a rational, aware, and informed public will not willingly comply with its commands. Rejecting the authoritarian motto *sic volo, sic jubeo, stat pro ratione voluntas* (B i. 159), Bentham insisted that law governs not by substituting will for reason but rather by conjoining expressions of will (law's commands) with public articulation of the rational grounds of the directives publicly announced. "Those who are able to convince men, will treat them like men; those who only command, avow their inability to convince," and lose their legitimate claim to command (B i. 160). One of his most devastating criticisms of eighteenth-century common-law practice was that it had lost its legitimacy for just this reason. It was "dog-law," imposing penalties with no warning and no public rationale, treating citizens like creatures who understand only the lash (B v. 235; BCLT 269–71).

With this understanding of Bentham's notion of publicity and its role in law we can return to the question I posed at the opening of this essay: Does Bentham offer us a distinctive conception of the rule of law, or does he offer rather a distinctive alternative to that ideal?

PUBLICITY AND THE RULE OF LAW

The Rule of Law

The Rule of Law (ROL) is a complex ideal. It includes formal and procedural standards that apply to legal norms and institutions.[16] If law is to rule in a political community, it must not only be a tool that public officials use to manage that community, but law must also rule those who propose to rule with it. We might call this the *reflexive* dimension of the rule of law. Those in power as well as those subject to that power must be subject to the law. The rule of law is not robust in a community—law does not effectively rule there—if some of those who wield political power and hold others accountable to the law are not themselves accountable under law. The question is whether Bentham's views regarding "securities against misrule" and the central role of publicity in law offer resources for a robust notion of the rule of law, and in particular whether it has room for this reflexive dimension of the rule of law.

I think the answer is yes. In his extended discussion of securities against misrule we have a sustained, articulated exploration of the necessary infrastructure of the rule of law. Other theorists have contributed greatly to our understanding of the formal and procedural elements of the rule of law, but to my knowledge no major legal theorist has contributed more to our understanding of its informal infrastructure. He analyzed the background conditions and engineered the supporting institutions needed for a comprehensive and effective architecture of accountability.

However, this conclusion may seem implausible in view of the well-known fact that Bentham himself argued that, while there may be limits on the legislative or

[16] See, for example, Jeremy Waldron, "The Concept and the Rule of Law," *Georgia Law Review* 43 (2008), 1–61.

executive powers of the sovereign, they are not and cannot be *legal* limits. Early in *On the Limits of the Penal Branch of Jurisprudence*, shortly after offering his definition of law as command of a sovereign, he wrote,

> The mandate of the sovereign, be it what it will, can not be illegal: it may be impolitic; it may even be unconstitutional: but it can not be illegal. It may be unconstitutional, for instance by being repugnant to any privileges that may have been conceded to the people whom it affects: but it would be perverting language and confounding ideas to call it *illegal* (*Limits* 38; original emphasis).

Alleged limits on sovereign law-making (like limits on sovereign exercises of power) may rest on matters of political fact (popular obedience always has its limits) and attempts to transgress them may be "impolitic." Or they may rest on what Austin would later call "positive morality," social rules or customs enforced by the "moral sanction." But they cannot be legal limits enforced by the "political" or "legal" (i.e., law-warranted coercive) sanction. Legal limits on sovereign power, on this view, are not merely unwise, they are impossible. If this was his view, then, whatever we say about Bentham's discussions of "accountability," we must conclude that his theory of law has no room for the idea of *law* limiting or ruling those with sovereign power. We might say that in the place of a robust theory of the infrastructure of the rule of law, Bentham offers a politically realistic alternative to the ideal of the rule of law. However, I believe this conclusion does not do justice to Bentham's view of the nature of law or to his view of role of the "moral sanction" and "popular opinion" in the ordinary, proper, and legitimate functioning of law.

Bentham's reluctance to regard "constitutional" constraints as legal seems to follow directly from his command model of law. However, soon after setting out his command model in *Limits*, he began to back away from it.[17] First, he relaxed (or enhanced and reshaped) his notion of what constitutes an individual law, qualifying his command model. Much of *Limits*, his first major work in jurisprudence, was devoted to working out the logical and conceptual resources needed to construct a complete and integral body of law. Sovereign commands are discrete historical events with canonical linguistic formulations, but laws, on Bentham's considered view, are ideal wholes. A law—as opposed to a statutory instrument enacted by a law-maker—is a part of an integrated system of laws. "The idea of a law, meaning one simple but entire law, is in a manner inseparably connected with that of a compleat body of laws: so that what is a law and what are the contents of a compleat body of the laws are questions of which neither can well be answer'd without the other" (*Limits* 21, n. a). By taking as his central concept that of a *complete law*, Bentham left behind any simple understanding of his command model.

[17] See Chapter 8, 196–201, and Chapter 13, 291–4.

Likewise, although Bentham distinguished *legal* sanctions from *moral* sanctions, he gave moral sanctions an integral role to play in the ordinary and proper functioning of law. Early on, he recognized the possibility of divided sovereignty in a polity, where supreme legislative and executive power (and all but supreme judicial power as well) is located in one body and the power to hold that body accountable is located in another.[18] And he elaborated that idea in subsequent work as he developed the role of the Public Opinion Tribunal in securing official responsibility. Much of what we have seen about the reliance of law on the operation of the public opinion and the moral sanction makes clear that Bentham thought that political power could not be exercised in a distinctively law-like and law-governed way unless it engaged public opinion in the right way in its ordinary operations. Public opinion was, in Bentham's view, integral to law; no jurisprudential inquiry into the foundations of law could ignore the role of the public in law's ordinary functioning.

This close interdependence of law and public opinion is especially clear in his discussion of constitutional constraints on sovereign ruling power in *Of the Limits of the Penal Branch of Jurisprudence*. In the recent new edition of Bentham's early jurisprudential manuscripts (published earlier under the title *Of Laws in General*), Philip Schofield points out that in a marginal comment on the passage quoted above (in which Bentham says limits on the sovereign can be political or constitutional, *but not legal*), Bentham wrote, "Alter. These are laws not *in populum* indeed, but *in principem*" (*Limits*, introduction xxi). Since writing the passage, Bentham had significantly refined his thoughts on the status of sovereign-guiding, sovereign-limiting constitutional norms.[19] He had developed a more nuanced view of the nature and force of such constrains. He began, where Roman and Canon Law theorists had traditionally begun,[20] by thinking of such constitutional constraints as self-imposed, that is, as sovereign commitments to respect certain rights or limits on its power. Yet these commitments were understood to be not merely personal policies or self-addressed commands, but rather, in some way, engage parties beyond the sovereign itself and empower them to judge the actions of the sovereign. What he had earlier styled mere "concessions" (*Limits* 38; see also SM 138), he here calls them "laws *in principem*." They are *laws*, to be sure, albeit "transcendent" ones (*Limits* 86), transcendent because they "prescribe to the sovereign what *he* shall do: what mandates *he* may or may not address to *them* [subjects]; and, in general, how he shall or may conduct himself towards them" (*Limits* 86). He was inclined to think of these commitments on analogy with promises or "covenants" (*Limits* 87; see also SM 138–41), but he realized that the promise model itself was limiting. It

[18] *Limits* 91 n. b. Strictly speaking, he noted, we should say that in that case sovereignty is held jointly although most of us would be inclined to say that the former is *the* sovereign.

[19] The discussion can be found in *Limits* 85–93. For a discussion of the concept of laws *in principem* and the development of Bentham's concept of sovereignty, see BCLT 244–50.

[20] In commentary on *Codex* I.14.4; see above note 2.

restricted the scope of the commitment to the promise-issuing sovereign, while the constitutional limitations he had in mind typically bound successive rulers over time. So, he thought of such sovereign acts of commitment as having two (possibly implicit) aspects: at the same time the sovereign engages himself through entering a covenant and commits his successors through addressing to them, as it were, a "recommendatory mandate" (*Limits* 87). Both commitments have the status as law in virtue of both issuing from the sovereign and engaging the public in holding the sovereigns to them (*Limits* 90).

This way of conceptualizing constitutional limits on otherwise ruling power was not original with Bentham, of course, but if we set this strategy in the context of his principle of publicity and the foundational jurisprudential role he assigns to public opinion, we can better appreciate its jurisprudential significance. First, Bentham asks, what sense can we give to the idea that these constitutional limits are self-imposed—how can one impose an obligation upon himself? (*Limits* 90). He answered that there is no more difficulty in this kind of case than in a case in which a subject binds himself to another subject. In the latter case, this is possible just when there is some party or force to hold him accountable, and the same is true in the former case. The *law*, strictly speaking, is the work of both the covenanter and the guarantor of the covenant. The guarantor in the latter case is public opinion, exercising the moral sanction, and that "public" may include not only subjects of the sovereign, but also foreign states (*Limits* 92; SM 139–40).

Second, Bentham's explanation (at *Limits* 88–9) of the binding force of recommendatory mandates further weakens the promise/covenant analogy and integrates his account of laws *in principem* into his larger theory of the foundations of law. He argues that sovereign covenants, motivated initially by considerations of political expediency, tend to shape the expectations of law-subjects to such an extent that, when a change in sovereign takes place, the new sovereign will be custom-bound to adopt the same covenants. Indeed, it will not be necessary for the new sovereign explicitly to adopt the previous sovereign's covenants, for he will simply be held to have done so (*Limits* 89). Thus, while historically specific constitutional limitations on sovereign power may have originated in some concession or promise of a sovereign, their present status and force do not depend on that origin, but rather on present-day custom, rooted in subjects' expectations, that is binding on the sovereign. Moreover, Bentham adds, the expectation of compliance with such covenants will over time become integrated into the law-constituting, law-grounding convention ("habit") of obedience. "This expectation may even become so strong," he wrote, "as to equal the expectation which is entertained of the prevalence of that disposition to obedience on the part of the people by which the sovereignty *de facto* is constituted: insomuch that the observance of the covenant on the one part shall be looked upon as a condition *sine quâ non* to the obedience that is to be paid on the other" (*Limits* 89).

The expectations and opinions underwriting and enforcing laws *in principem* are all of a piece with expectations at the foundations of law. These expectations are "constitutional" in the literal sense of being law-constituting—i.e., constituting the system or body of law as a whole—because, on Bentham's view, the existence and unity of any legal system depends on the law-making (and executing and adjudicating) efforts of the sovereign and the sovereign has such power just in virtue of the coordinated expectations of law-subjects in the jurisdiction to recognize that power and to tender their compliance with those efforts. Law exists just in virtue of the "habit of obedience" of subjects, but this "habit" is not a thoughtless, rote, or strictly singular responsiveness to commands, but rather a coordinated collective response to the efforts of those in power.[21] It depends on a kind of convention or "custom," the content and shape of which is determined by the collected and uttered opinions of the public. At one point, Bentham was even willing to say explicitly that the rules and standards issuing from firm expectations of public opinion themselves constitute a kind of *law*. "Public Opinion may be considered as a system of law, emanating from the body of the people," he wrote at the opening of his *Constitutional Code*.[22] Its rules may have no explicitly articulated, canonical formulations, "no individually assignable form of words," but in this respect it is no different from English common law, except that, since it issues from the people rather than from a part of the ruling elite, it is not subject to the kind of abuse which was endemic to common law. The customs at the foundations of law, customs that shape and give nuance to the law-constituting dispositions to obedience of law-subjects, are no less law and no less obligations for resting ultimately on the moral sanction of public opinion, that is, on the willingness of law subjects to hold sovereign power accountable.

CONCLUSION

Thus, unlike Hobbes and Austin, Bentham did not think it impossible for law to bind a sovereign. Law, properly understood, binds not only its immediate subjects, but also those entrusted to make, administer, and enforce it. Bentham integrated his account of jurisprudentially necessary constraints on legally authorized officials, and the devices and institutions that make it possible for these officials to be held accountable, into his account of the foundations of law. His analysis of the conditions for the existence of law at the same time, and in his view necessarily, was an analysis of the conditions of *law's ruling* in a political community. Moreover,

[21] For a general discussion of Bentham's expectation-based, "interactional" understanding of the "habit of obedience," see BCLT 227–32.

[22] CC (CW) vol. 1, 36. Although this is the only passage of which I am aware in which Bentham makes this point explicitly, it is hard to dismiss as a slip of the pen, since, it appears in a very prominent part near the opening of his *Constitutional Code*.

this analysis led him to the conclusion that for law to rule—for there to be adequate security against misrule—the sovereign's self-limiting commitments must be matched by an equal commitment on the part of those subject to the sovereign's rule. In Bentham's view, the law's ruling ultimately "depends upon the spirit, the intelligence, the vigilance, the alertness, the intrepidity, the energy, the perseverance, of those of whose opinions Public Opinion is composed" (SM 139). Public opinion can work its constraining magic only if at every point the exercise of governmental power is public. As he said, publicity is the soul of the law and through publicity alone law becomes the mother of security.

13
Bentham
Theorist of Publicity

Publicity is a pervasive theme running through all of Bentham's moral, political, and legal theory.* Publicity is foundational to his thought. Bentham was one of the first theorists of publicity of the modern era, surely its most thorough. He knitted together a systematic theory of what we would now call public reason, integrating utility and law into a complex framework for public reasoning, with a detailed architecture of public space, articulating key institutions and incentives for public accountability and public deliberation. However, despite its fundamental role in Bentham's thought, publicity has rarely been the focus of critical discussion of his work. This may be due to the fact that Bentham highlighted publicity only relatively late in his career and much of his early work in which publicity plays a critical role is as yet unpublished.

At crucial points in the preceding chapters, Bentham's concern for publicity surfaced to play a critical role in his arguments. In this chapter, I bring together the most important occurrences of the idea of publicity, documenting Bentham's reliance on it throughout his career and demonstrating its centrality to his moral, legal, and political thought.

UTILITY AS PUBLIC REASON

Bentham maintained resolutely throughout his life that the principle of utility is the foundation of all moral judgment, the principle by which every action, practice, law, institution, code, and constitution is to be judged. This *ruler* and *decider* of all things (UC 96.73) sets the only right and proper (ultimate) end of government,[1] underwrites and guides the analysis and construction of law (*Limits* 224), and provides the sole measure of moral right and wrong.[2] It "furnishes us with that

* Adapted from *Public Reason in Political Philosophy: Classic Sources and Contemporary Commentaries* by Taylor & Francis. Reproduced with permission of Taylor & Francis in the format Book via Copyright Clearance Center.

[1] FP 3, 234–5; CC vol. 1, 136; CC (B) 5; PF 211.
[2] FG 393, 440n, 446n; IPML 13; B vi. 238.

Utility, Publicity, and Law: Essays on Bentham's Moral and Legal Philosophy. Gerald J. Postema.

reason, which alone depends not upon any higher reason, but which is itself the sole and all-sufficient reason for every point of practice whatsoever" (FG 448, original emphasis).

Bentham recognized that this "principium generalissimum" (UC 96.75) cannot be defended directly, but he frequently offered a telling indirect argument for it (IPML Ch. 2). He observed, to begin, that moral judgments express the sentiments of approbation or disapprobation (B viii, 93) of persons making the judgments, just as empirical judgments express beliefs. Moreover, moral judgments are not "mere averment[s] of one's unfounded sentiments" (IPML 14), or "mere opinion of men self-constituted into Legislators" (UC 69.190); rather, they purport to direct attention to something beyond the sentiment or opinion of the appraiser. Appraisers disapprove of some act or object, "conceiving at the same time that it will be alike disapproved of by most others," because they appreciate or respond to the same judgment-independent ground. They appeal beyond the sentiment of the appraiser to "something that is fixed and certain, and that all men are agreed about, and that it could be told by certain indications independent of opinion, whether a given course of conduct was reasonable [good, right, or ought to be done] or otherwise" (*Com.* 159). Moral judgments claim to be appraiser-transcendent and point to something in the world on which the appraiser's judgment rests, something others could access and assess. In the absence of such appraiser-transcending grounds, expressions of sentiments of approbation and disapprobation are arbitrary, a matter of the appraiser's whim or caprice. As such, they can only be either "despotical" (because one imposes one's idiosyncratic sentiments on everyone else without allowing them the same privilege) or "anarchical" (allowing as many standards as there are appraisers) (IPML 11, 14, 15).

In the absence of such appraiser-transcendent grounds, moral justification of actions would be impossible, for, on Bentham's view. Justification has a public, discursive dimension: justification is a matter of "a person addressing himself to the community" (IPML 28n) with *reasons* that can be communicated to and assessable by others (FG 492). In the public rhetoric of his day, people offer principles that fail to make good on this promise, Bentham argued. Appeals to "reason," "natural law," "natural rights," "moral sense," and the like fail to offer anything beyond themselves as grounds for their assertions.[3] They back their assertions, opinions, or judgments by nothing more than *ipse dixit*: it is so, because I say it is (TSA 24, 26, 304–5; LW 255).

[3] Appeals to "natural law," Bentham argued, are "from first to last nothing but [one's] own private opinion in disguise" (UC 69.102). "To say that a thing ought not to be done because there is a law of nature against it's being done, is an obscure and roundabout way of saying one of two things. 'It ought not to be done, because it would be mischievous or dangerous to the community'; or else 2ndly. 'It ought not to be done, because I say it ought not.' The grand mischief of the expression is that most commonly when examined into, the only meaning which it is found to cover is the latter" (UC 69.106). See also UC 127.483–4; RRR 186–7; SM 23–4n.

However, Bentham insisted that the principle of utility provides just what the public character of moral judgments demands. "Pains and pleasures ... are the only clear sources of ideas in moral. These ideas may be rendered familiar to all the world" (B i. 163). Had theorists appealed to utility, rather than "reason" or "natural law," they "would have said something. [They] would have referred us for a foundation of our judgment, to something distinct from that judgment itself" (*Com.* 199). The principle of utility rests every dispute on matters of fact (FG 491); those to whom a moral judgment is addressed are directed to matters of fact publicly available, matters of common experience:

> In morals, as in legislation, the *principle of utility* is that which holds up to view, as the only sources and tests of right and wrong, human suffering and enjoyment—pain and pleasure. It is by experience, and by that alone, that the tendency of human conduct, in all its modifications, to give birth to pain and pleasure, is brought to view. It is by reference to experience, and to that standard alone, that the tendency of any such modifications to produce more pleasure than pain, and consequently to be *right*—or more pain than pleasure, and consequently to be *wrong*—is made known and demonstrated. In this view of the matter, morality, as well as policy, is always a matter of account (B vi. 238–9).[4]

Guided by the principle of utility, expressing and sharing moral judgments engages us in the business of publicly offering reasons and arguments. Disagreement is still possible, of course, but it is genuine. Controversy does not immediately disintegrate into "childish altercation," but disputing parties "have a plain and open road ... to present reconcilement: at worst to an intelligible and explicit issue" and some reasonable hope for agreement in the future (FG 492).

Reading the passages above, Philip Schofield concludes that Bentham's view was that the principle of utility alone met an essential ontological condition of moral judgments, viz., that they be anchored to "real entities" in the physical world.[5] However, I think Bentham's philosophical motivations were different. He did not offer his analysis of moral language or his critique of "the principle of sympathy and antipathy" as a contribution to the metaphysics of morals. His fundamental concern was publicity, not ontology; rational public discourse, not metaphysics. His forays into logical and metaphysical analysis, including his analysis of "real"

[4] Nearly forty years earlier Bentham wrote that, when I appeal to utility, "I put in issue a set of facts, and call in experience to witness. I allege the existence of certain pains and pleasures ... pains and pleasures such as men have felt in themselves, or recognized in others ... pains and pleasure felt ... by the old stock of senses, such as all men have, and all men know of. Of this sort are a man's *reasons*, if he has any" (UC 69. 72–3 n. i).

[5] Philip Schofield, *Utility and Democracy: The Political Thought of Jeremy Bentham* (Oxford: Oxford University Press, 2006), 28, 47; Philip Schofield, "A Defense of Jeremy Bentham's Critique of Natural Rights," in *Bentham's Theory of Law and Public Opinion*, Xiaobo Zhai and Michael Quinn, eds. (Cambridge: Cambridge University Press, 2014), 216–17.

and "fictitious entities," were meant to serve the over-arching aim to "rear the fabric of felicity by the hands of reason and law" (IPML 11). Thus, it is the unique capability (as Bentham saw it) of the language of utility to answer to the demands for public argument and justification that recommends it as the sole rational ground of moral and political judgments and the sole ultimate end of government and law.

Moreover, he argued, this necessary public function of the principle determines its general shape: publicity necessitates impartiality with regard to the happiness of all those in the community. "On what ground, in the eyes of a common guardian, can any one man's happiness be shown to have any stronger or less strong claim to regard than any others?" (LW 250). No case for partiality to some individual or subgroup can succeed if it must be made to each member of the community. Thus, only the "Greatest Happiness Principle" answers to the demands of impartiality and hence publicity. "In the eyes of every impartial arbiter ... having exactly the same regard for the happiness of every member of the community in question as for that of every other, the greatest happiness of the greatest number of the members of that same community can not but be recognized in the character of the right and proper, and so right and proper, end of government" (FP 235).

The Limits of Utility

Utility—understood as the composite of the pleasures and pains of all members of the community impartially considered—recommended itself to Bentham because of its public accessibility. The utility-effects of actions, policies, or institutions are matters of common knowledge, because they are matters of common experience. Bentham never abandoned this familiar characterization of utility, but early on he recognized its limitations, limits of the public accessibility of the empirical facts regarding these experiences.

First, he acknowledged that, although the duration or extent of pleasures or pains can be measured, the quality or intensity of pleasures are not "ponderable or measureable": "weight, extent, heat, light—for quantities of these articles, we have perceptible and expressible measures: unhappily or happily, for quantities of pleasure or pain, we have no such measures" (LW 253). Moreover, while each person has direct access to his or her own pleasurable or painful experiences, "to no man, can the quality of sensibility in the breast of any other man be made known by anything like equally probative and unfallacious evidence" (*Deont.* 131). Interpersonal access to and comparison of such sensibilities, thus, is limited; moreover, individuals face a like problem regarding *their own* future selves (*Deont.*195). The immediate felt quality of a pleasurable experience is present to one's mind, but when pleasures are considered in prospect, one's access is more akin to that of an observer: "Like a third person his future contingent individual pleasure and pain can not be judged of by him otherwise than from the species it belongs to"(*Deont.*

195). The discrete felt qualities of pleasures and pains are largely inaccessible (across persons and across time), so to make practical judgments of utility we are forced to take a more public point of view, to look to sensibilities or experiences "in their species," that is, those we tend to share with others and come to know through participating with others in daily life.

This refinement gave Bentham's notion of utility-relevant pleasures and pains a more public dimension, which was important for public decision-makers, e.g., judges. The primary utility focus for judges in a legal dispute, Bentham insisted, must be on expectations of the parties to the lawsuit and of the public.[6] So, for example, property title should go to the party whose expectation, seconded by the expectations of the public, is greatest (and thus for whom the pain of disappointment would be greatest) (UC 69.238; OAM 353–7). However, there is no reliable direct means for determining such expectations, and parties have an incentive to exaggerate their disappointment when explicitly asked. The only reliable method for doing so, Bentham conceded, is for the judge to put himself in the place of both parties and the public and to observe from that perspective where the balance of expectations lies.[7] The judge does not seek to uncover the idiosyncratic disappointment-sensibility of the parties affected, not because they are inaccessible to the intuition of judge, but because it would not be possible for the judge to communicate effectively to the public the ground of his assessment:

> The reasons which a man could find for supposing one man's temperament more sanguine than another's must be founded on ocular inspection, or at least in presence, and that in a variety of situations and for a length of time. Such reasons are in their nature uncommunicable in words... These appearances then being indescribable, the Judge could have no means of satisfying the public of the existence of them (UC 69.238–9).

The problem is not fundamentally ontological—that there is no fact of the matter regarding a person's particular sensibility—nor is it narrowly epistemic—that judges cannot in principle know where the expectations, and hence balance of utilities, lie—but rather the problem is that judges are not able to make the grounds of their decisions fully public. The public accessibility of the grounds of decision is, for Bentham's utilitarian purposes, is of decisive importance.

Later in his career, Bentham's favored articulation of his notion of utility took on an even more prominent public character: in place of happiness or pleasure, which still may have provided the psychic ("real entity") anchor of the notion (TSA 5–7, 76,

[6] For Bentham's notion of expectation-utilities, see UC 70a.20; UC 96.74; UC 72.1; *Com.* 231; for the special weight and importance Bentham assigns to expectations, see UC 69.239; UC 70(a).20; *Civ. Code* 308; and Chapter 4, 78–9, Chapter 5, 107–8, Chapter 7, 151–2, and BCLT 155–8.

[7] *Com.* 197 n. c; UC 69.238; OAM 355; B iii. 212; B iv. 312, 388; UC 86.39; UC 81.124–5; UC 114.222, 236.

98–9), Bentham tended to focus on interests.[8] "Interest" identified publicly accessible species of utility. Individuals, in Bentham's understanding, tend to have a special stake in the objects of their interests, yet those objects tend to be widely recognizable and shared. Talk of interests allows us to bracket the immediate quality of the experience and focus attention on the objects of people's interests and to think about how they fit together with other objects into intelligible and easily recognized packages.

Moreover, the language of interests allowed Bentham to articulate a notion of the aggregate good or welfare of the community as a whole. The principle of utility called on policy-makers, legislators, officials, and individuals alike to promote the "universal interest"—"that interest which is common to [oneself] and every other member of the community" (CC (B) 127; see FP 234). While Bentham often speaks of the universal interest as the "aggregate of individual interests" (FP 133, 192), it appears he has in mind the convergence or intersection of such interests, rather than their universal sum. The universal interest is defined in opposition to and excludes the "private" or "sinister" interests of individuals and groups.[9] It embraces the most pressing and important interests of each member, interests that converge with the interests of all the others. An *individual's* public interest is his or her share in the common interest of the community as a whole (B ii. 475; *Col.* 290). *The* public interest—or universal interest—is that set of interests held in common by all members of the community in the realization of which each member has a distinct and positive share (FP 192; *Col.* 290). These interests typically involve projects in which one can reasonably hope to enlist the community at large. "Each separate and sinister interest, finds a bar, and that an insuperable one, in every other separate and sinister interest," Bentham argued, "but each man's share in the universal interest finds an ally and coadjutor in every other man's share in the universal interest" (SM 266; see also SM 56).

The most important of these interests are those served by what Bentham identified as the four immediately subordinate ends of utility: security, subsistence, abundance, and equality (*Civ. Code* 301–13). These goods are the most fundamental constituents of the universal interest—they are primary, public goods that promote the good of all and of each. Utility so understood promises to meet the demands of publicity to which the principle of utility uniquely answered.

LAW: SECURITY, SOVEREIGNTY, AND SYSTEM

Securing Expectations

The only proper end of government, according to Bentham, is the greatest happiness of all members of the community (FP 232) or the "universal interest" (B iii.

[8] For a general defense of the thesis of this paragraph, see Chapter 6.

[9] The universal interest and rival particular interests stand in a relationship of "implacable hostility" (OAM 43; see SM 252–3; FP 192; *Col.* 290); see Chapter 6, 134–6.

453; FP 234), but *security*, the immediate subordinate end and primary component of the universal interest, is "the unrivalled work of law," the principle object of law in general and in every branch (UC 69.44, CC (B) 11; see BCLT Chapter 5.3). Law's task is to secure the community against the arbitrary power ("misrule") of officials and fellow citizens, and to secure expectations by respecting and protecting existing expectations and by focusing and fixing new expectations. While "penal law" is primarily responsible for directing and regulating behavior and protecting existing expectations, "distributive law" (civil and constitutional law) is responsible for fixing expectations. Law organizes and structures social and political institutions, it defines and constitutes social relations of all sorts. Indeed, in Bentham's view, the constitutive or "civil" aspect of law was more fundamental than its regulative or "penal" aspect.[10]

Law pursues this complex task by addressing directive and constitutive norms to the community as a whole. For this purpose, Bentham recognized, it is important that individual members are able to grasp the import of the norms for their behavior, but it is equally important that they are assured that others in the community with whom they interact also grasp them and are likely to follow them.

The importance of this public dimension of regulative and constitutive norms was evident to Bentham already early in his career. In an early manuscript, he argued that in novel cases, although judges must ultimately decide in accord with the dictates of utility (including both "original" and "expectation-utilities"), judges should base their decisions on analogies to established rules and past decisions, rather than on direct appeal to utility. The reason for this indirection is that analogy "is more easily agreed upon" than utility: "to judge whether such a rule which is proposed as being like another rule, is so, a man has but to compare the rules themselves. To judge whether it be in itself right, he has a variety of other circumstances to consider, which presenting themselves in different numbers and differently upon different persons ... make this a task much more difficult" (UC 63.49). The problem is not that judges are likely to get the utility calculations wrong, but that their determinations could not be anticipated with sufficient confidence by members of the community at large (UC 63.49). The rules which were to govern their interactions and hence the determinations of judges assessing those interactions would not be sufficiently public. Analogies drawn from established rules and past decisions, Bentham argued (at this point in his career), were more likely to focus expectations on a recognizable pattern of behavior than directs appeals to utility.

Bentham relied on a similar argument in his critique of Blackstone's natural-law and social-contract accounts of the limits of obedience to law (FG 483–4; see BCLT 238–44). Neither natural law nor social contract provides a sufficiently public standard by which individual citizens can judge when disobedience and resistance

[10] See Chapter 8, 196–7, and BCLT 171–8.

to existing law is justified. The principle of utility promises such a standard, but utility also is inadequate for this purpose, not because appeals to utility are empty or do not point beyond themselves to accessible facts, but because each individual's persuasion regarding the balance of utilities cannot serve the purpose of coordinating their actions with others, which is necessary for successful, utility-serving resistance. The principle of utility can define for each man in particular the limit of his obedience (FG 484), but the point at which resistance is justified must not only be accessible to each, it must be public, available to all. However, an "express convention" regarding the limits of ruling authority can provide the necessary "common signal alike conspicuous and perceptible to all" (FG 484). Constitutional conventions—laws *in principem* Bentham called them—provide the needed common signal (*Limits* 38, 85–93).

Bentham's view, forged early in his career, was that law can successfully secure the community against all forms of depredation and structure social and political relations only if its norms can themselves focus the expectations, and hence the deliberations and actions, of members of the community. Only a system of publicly acknowledged, publicly authenticated, and publicly articulated norms can do this job. In contrast, the form of law practiced and praised in Bentham's England was radically unsuited for law's primary task: "As a system of general [and public] rules, the Common Law is a thing merely imaginary," he boldly charged (*Com.* 119).

Common law, Bentham argued, was radically uncertain and unpredictable, dependent on the arbitrary and unaccountable judgment of judges. According to common-law theory, judges are authorized to decide particular cases, but all formulations of rules grounding their decisions, including those offered by deciding judges themselves, are open to challenge and reformulation. Something akin to rules emerge from this practice; lawyers may be able to construct rules that "appear to be the just expression of the judicial practice in like cases" (UC 100.98). Indeed, judicial decisions, "in virtue of the more extensive interpretation which the people are disposed to put upon them, have somewhat the effect of general laws" (*Limits* 161). However, such customary rules cannot do the fundamental work of law: "From a set of *data* like these, a law is to be extracted by every man who can fancy that he is able: by each man, perhaps a different law: and these, then, are the *monades* which, meeting together, constitute rules which, taken together, constitute . . . the common or customary law" (*Limits* 195). Common law turns individuals in the community loose "into the wilds of perpetual conjecture" (*Com.* 95). Common-law rules are nothing more than "the idea that *you* have formed of the act in question, the idea that *I* have formed of it, the idea that *Titus* has formed of it" (UC 69.151)—merely "inferential entities," private conjectures, which converge only by accident and cannot provide "common standard[s] which all men acknowledge, and all men are ready to resort to" (UC 69.188). They cannot serve *as law,* because they lack the necessary public character.

Law and the Problem of the Privacy of Reason

We can better appreciate the role Bentham assigns to publicity in his jurisprudence by first considering Hobbes's familiar conception of law. The fundamental problem at the heart of Hobbes' political and legal theory is that, in the state of nature, absent a common power, there are no common standards to which human beings can regiment their judgments of good and evil, right and wrong, or by which they can order their social interactions. "Right reason" and the language of moral judgments call for public standards, but no such standards are naturally available (*Dialogue* 26; DC 163). Individual rational agents are forced to rely solely on their private judgments; and private reason, rather than uniting human beings, puts them in deadly opposition. We might call this the problem of the privacy of reason. The only solution is for contending parties to "set up for right Reason, the Reason of some Arbitrator, or Judge," which, "though his Reason be but the Reason of one Man, yet it is set up to supply the place of... Universal Reason" (*Lev* 32–3; *Dialogue*, 26). The practical reason and judgment of each individual must be supplanted, replaced with the reason and judgment of a sovereign expressed in and through law.

Law plays a critical role in Hobbes's solution to the problem of the privacy of judgment. And he was naturally drawn to the age-old *thetic* conception of law.[11] The defining property of law, on this view is not (cannot be), *wisdom*, which is open to assessment and challenge, but *authority* (*Dialogue* 10, 29). Law consists of the commands of one to whom others are antecedently obliged to obey, declaring publicly what one may or must do or forbear to do (*Lev* 183; *Dialogue* 31). The judgment and will of the sovereign displaces the judgment of the law subject, *stat pro ratione voluntas*. Sovereign commands must take the form of law, for the root problem of the state of nature—the problem of the privacy of judgment—lies in the absence of common public standards, not merely the absence of centralized power. "Law is all the Right Reason we have,"[12] and *law*, not merely the will of the sovereign, constitutes right—i.e., public—reason. Thus, if law is to serve its fundamental purpose, it must be general, clearly and publicly declared, intelligible, and manifestly authentic (carrying the marks of the sovereign's authority) (*Lev* 187–9, 239–40, 246). Moreover, if they are to serve this function, the law's standing and validity cannot depend on extra-legal matters of right or good, or justice, or the common good. They must be identifiable independently of all such considerations.

Like Hobbes, and for similar reasons, Bentham found the *thetic* model of law initially attractive; the statute, not rules inferred or constructed from judicial decision, was his paradigm. When he found it necessary, Bentham typically defined *a law* in familiar terms of the expression of will of someone related to persons

[11] By "*thetic*" I refer to that family of conceptions of law that understand law as explicitly and intentionally made and imposed on law-subjects, the ruling metaphor of which is command; see Chapter 8.

[12] Hobbes, *Questions regarding Liberty and Necessity* in *English Works of Thomas Hobbes*, William Molesworth, ed. (London, 1841), vol. v, 194.

addressed via power or authority.[13] But the thetic model required more of law than that it be a (general) command of someone in authority. Most importantly, the command must be articulated in canonical, public language[14] and must be formally "authentic," expressing the "will of the accustomed law-giver or law-givers [and] expressed with the accustomed formalities" (UC 69.87; see UC 70(a).51). The requirement of formal authentication insured that the rules would be publicly articulated and publicly validated. Laws on this thetic model aimed to meet the demands of publicity, shaping and focusing expectations even better than conventions, although conventions supplied the "accustomed formalities" and authorized the "accustomed law-giver."

Bentham called the community-wide practice underlying the formalities, the "habit of obedience"; however, it is clear that this "habit" was not the bare disposition of the members severally to respond to commands from certain discrete sources.[15] Rather, Bentham conceived it as a convention-like interactive practice (BCLT Chapter 7.1–7.2). Likewise, the "obedience" Bentham had in mind was not merely passive or reactive; it always had an active, critical dimension. The limits of this habit of obedience, viewed from one perspective, might be seen as a matter of political fact: a disposition of the people to comply only with laws regarding certain matters issuing from certain authorities (*Limits* 42–3 and nn.). But these dispositions are shaped by common understandings of the proper limits of the authority and the point at which non-compliance and even resistance could be justified (FG 484; *Limits* 88–9, 92). Although Bentham insisted that citizens "obey promptly," he also urged them to "censure freely" (FG 399–400). He regarded the two activities as interdependent. The critical dimension of his notion of the habit of obedience, nascent in his early jurisprudential writing, became increasingly prominent in his constitutional and political writings later in his career, culminating, as we shall see in the next section, in the central role he assigned to the "Public Opinion Tribunal"—the "tribunal of free criticism" (LW 98).

Stretching the Thetic Model of Law[16]

Although Bentham never abandoned the metaphor of command as a convenient model for thinking about law, almost immediately after offering his definition of law as expression of will of a sovereign in his signal work of analytical jurisprudence,

[13] Early on, Bentham wrote boldly, "law is a command" (UC 69. 71), but a little later, when he more carefully articulated his definition of law, he used broader language of "expression of will" (*Limits* 24; *Chrest.* 205n.).

[14] Law, Bentham insisted, must always be "a [piece of] discourse—conceived mostly in *general*, and always in *determinate* words" (*Chrest.* 205n); see also *Com.* 259 n. a; B vi. 552.

[15] As Austin (on Hart's interpretation) portrayed it; see H.L.A. Hart, *The Concept of Law*, Chapter 4.

[16] See also the discussion of this topic in Chapter 8, 196–201.

Of the Limits of the Penal Branch of Law, he began to massage, stretch, and reshape it, and in later work he pushed his revisions further. I will mention several such extensions or revisions that indicate the nature and influence of the idea of publicity in Bentham's jurisprudence.

Following Hobbes (and a long tradition before him[17]), Bentham used the command as a model of law, but he departed from Hobbes's understanding of law in several respects. First, juridical "expressions of will" might include not only imperatives but also permissions and countermands. More generally, Bentham argued that much of law is not immediately *directive*, but rather is *constitutive*, defining and structuring private, public, and political relations. This law is not best understood on the model of commands, although Bentham stretched and pulled the model to fit them, conceiving of this vast body of constitutive law as shared and presupposed parts of a variety of "penal" laws.

Second, even with respect to commands he resisted the view that law's commands entail coercive sanctions. Law-makers typically and prudently attach sanctions to their directives, but they are not properly understood as *likely consequences* of non-compliance. Rather, sanctions are consequences that *ought by law* to occur.[18] This *normative* relationship between the directive and the sanction is grounded in secondary legal norms, directives addressed to officials to *see to it* that the primary laws are enforced. These directives in turn rest on more "remote" directives to other officials backing up the proximate one, etc. (*Limits* 151–2). Ultimately, this series of subsidiary laws bottoms out in the judgments of the public which holds officials to their legal responsibilities (*Limits* 86–92). Thus, on JB's view, coercion plays an important role in law, but as one part of multi-part institutional-cum-informal structure for securing the effectiveness of the law's system of norms as a whole. Moreover, law-makers may decide not to attach, or may find it impossible to attach, legal sanctions to some directives. Constitutional limits on ruling power were typically of the latter kind, in Bentham's view, enforced not in courts of law, but in the court of public opinion (the Public Opinion Tribunal), exercising the "moral sanction."

Further, in an important break with the Hobbesian conception of law, Bentham rejected the view that laws are meant to be *peremptory*. Hobbes wrote that "command is when a man saith do this or do not do this yet without expecting any other reason than the will of him that sayes it" (*Lev* 176). This model fit well the law in view of the task Hobbes assigned to it. It displaced judgment from the law-subject to the commanding sovereign. But, unlike Hobbes, Bentham was clear from the outset that although law requires submission of conduct, it does not submission of

[17] Including natural-law theorists like Suarez and even committed common-law jurists like Matthew Hale; see Chapter 8.

[18] On Bentham's view, every law consists of a "directive" and a "sanctional" part, the former "bids" the latter "prophecies" or "predicts"; however, that prediction is underwritten by a "subsidiary" which bids others (primarily judges) to fulfill the prediction (*Com.* 72; *Limits* 146, 150).

judgment (*Com.* 346). Law does not require law-subjects to abandon their critical and deliberative powers, or only to engage them off-line, as it were. Any attempt to do so would amount to intolerable manipulation of will by will, in his view; rather, law must seek to direct understanding by understanding (UC 126.1; B iv. 539). Law inevitably and unavoidably limits liberty and offers primarily negative incentives to comply (as a complement to their directives), but it is meant to address, and can only function properly when it addresses, the understanding and not (only) the will of law-subjects.

Third, Bentham further stretched the idea of commands, or expressions of will, to incorporate what he took to be law's essential *systemic* character. A law "is a command," that is to say, is a practically determinate directive for action, only "when it is entire" (PF 217), Bentham wrote:

> The idea of a law, meaning one single but entire law, is in a manner inseparably connected with that of a compleat body of laws; so that what is a law and what are the contents of a compleat body of the laws are questions of which neither can well be answer'd without the other. A body of laws is a vast and complicated piece of mechanism of which no part can be fully explained without the rest (*Limits* 21).

The law, on Bentham's view, is not merely an aggregate of discrete and individual *laws*, all traceable to a common source, but an interconnected *system* of laws, each of which is individuated, not by being traced to some discrete, observable public event (some expressing of volition), but by locating it in the system. What is *a law*—a complete, whole, "entire but single law" (IPML 299)—is determined by examining a complete system of law and locating the individual practically determinate directives in it.

Thus, at bottom, Bentham's concept of law is of a complex rational, not an empirical, entity, although it must ultimately be tethered to empirical facts ("real entities"). It is, in one sense of the word, an ideal concept. His researches in *Limits* were meant to uncover and articulate "the logical, ideal, the intellectual whole, not the physical one: the *law* not the *statute*" (IPML 301). Law is abstract, statute concrete; "statutes are such as we find them, laws are such as we may conceive them" (UC 96.85). At the core of Bentham's model of a complete law is the idea of a directive for action that includes in it everything necessary for adequate public guidance of behavior, including all the qualifications, limitations, elaborations that apply to it, and all the institutional and procedural conditions of its implementation and enforcement (*Limits* §16). Of course, none of this expository, elaborative and qualificative material is uniquely tied to a single (complete) law; indeed, a vast amount of it will be shared by a large number of laws. A law is complete, then, when all its necessary elements are linked and this is made explicit by "juxtaposition" or "reference" (*Limits* 171–2).

Laws are systematically interconnected, not only in their logical relations, but in their shared substance. This implies that the idea of a complete law presupposes the idea of a complete body of law. To explicate the concept of law, we must explicate the notion of *a* (complete) *law*, but that is not possible without recognizing, and putting at the center of our explication, the *substantive* relationships that inevitably exist among laws. This insight, which structured all of Bentham's vast writings on universal jurisprudence, follows from his conviction that law by its nature directs and informs actions of rational agents and it can do so only if it is public and accessible. For Bentham, the systematically ordered code of law—the "pannomion"—was designed to meet the demands of publicity. Publicity not only demands that marks of the authenticity of laws be clear, but also that all directives are clearly articulated, and that all the material that qualifies a simple directive is accessible. That puts any given legal directive in a complex network of relations of substance with much of the rest of the law bearing these same marks of authenticity.

Manifested Reasonableness

Further, Bentham held that publicity demands in addition to formal authenticity and completeness the *manifested reasonableness* of the law's systematically structured directives (LW, 121 n. a, 141, 168). Reasons alone address only the understanding, he argued, but bare commands without manifested reasons address only the will. Both are essential, Bentham maintained, if law is to operate in its characteristic mode (LW, 101, 143–4; B i. 159–60). Yet, he observed that for "the crowd of lawmakers," giving reasons is "*hors d'œuvre choses de surabondance*" (UC 25.118)—a trifling extravagance. To *give* reasons, one must *have* some, he insisted, but legislators are governed only by instinct. Even "the great Bacon" advised against offering reasons, on the ground that they foster disputes (*ibid.*); however, the test of reasons is the real ordeal of the legislator ("*l'épreuve aux raisons se seroit la vraie ordalie des législateur*")—to this test he submitted himself and his code (*ibid.*).

On Bentham's view, the manifested reasonableness of the law is an essential requirement of good law: "The greatest advantage" of the manifested reasonableness of the law, "is that which results from conciliating the approbation of all minds, by satisfying the public judgment" (B i. 161). More importantly, it is a necessary condition of law's doing its job fixing and securing expectations by means of public norms. If law subjects are to apply authoritative directives to their specific circumstances, mindful of the likely reason-governed actions of others with whom they must interact, they must exercise intelligent judgment (a product of "the understanding"); however, without manifest reasons of the directives to guide them, they cannot proceed with confidence (B i. 160–1; LW, 45–6). To do this, the law must offer reasons that are publicly accessible. "The catechism of reasons is worthless, if it cannot be the catechism of the people," Bentham argued (B i. 163), and, as we have learned, the only catechism of the people, the only language of reasons fit to do the work, is the language of utility. "To give a reason for a law, is to show that it is conformable to the principle of utility" (B i.163; see LW 101, 121). Thus, unlike Hobbes, Bentham held that the mode of public reason offered by law itself depends on its manifested reasonableness, where that reasonableness is articulated in terms of universal, public interests of members of the community. Publicly articulated and authenticated law and the public language of utility complement each other.[19]

In Bentham's system, the reasonableness of law is manifested primarily in two ways. First, the law is systematically ordered on a principle of "natural arrangement" (FG 415–8; *Limits* 224; B i. 171–2). A natural arrangement "takes such properties to characterize [the laws] by, as men in general are, by common construction of man's nature, disposed to attend to" (FG 415). A natural arrangement of the laws is "best adapted for the generality of the people" (B iii. 161), one that "*naturally*, that is readily, engage[s], and firmly fix[es] the attention of any one" who examined it (IPML 272). The structure of the law, following the principle of natural arrangement, directly "points out the reason of the law" (FG 416–17; see IPML 273–4), which must be reasons of public utility. Bentham's pannomion was designed to focus attention on publicly salient social harms and threats to the universal interest, and organize its directives around such "offences" (see IPML XVI). For Bentham, the "notoriety" or "cognoscibility" of law, its "being present to the mind"(LW 8), depends on its textual clarity, on careful legislative drafting, but his insistence on "natural arrangement" of the law reflects his understanding that genuine clarity of language is possible only if it achieves what John Gardner calls "moral clarity."[20] Law achieves moral clarity when it uses distinctions and terms that reflect the public meanings of actions and engage the public's moral imagination. Bentham's "natural arrangement" sought to do just that. It defined categories and distinctions, relying on the language of universal public interests, because it had the best chance of being a public moral language, available to each member severally and to all publicly.

Bentham's second device to secure the manifest reasonableness of the law was the "perpetual commentary of reasons" drawn from the principle of utility which, in Bentham's plan, was to accompany the publicly articulated code of law.[21] Moreover,

[19] In BCLT and "Bentham and the Public Character of Law," *Utilitas* 1 (1989), 41–61, I did not fully appreciate the importance for Bentham's jurisprudence of the condition of systematicity, or the requirement of "manifested reasonableness." Thus, in those works I presented Bentham's jurisprudence as more closely approximating contemporary "exclusive positivism" than I now believe is true of it. Insofar as it is "positivist," his jurisprudence is a strikingly revisionist version of the currently popular view. See Afterword of BCLT, 2nd edition.

[20] John Gardner, *Offences and Defences: Selected Essays in the Philosophy of Criminal Law* (Oxford: Oxford University Press, 2007), 45–7.

[21] "In a body of law . . . it being in its fabric *reasonable*, the *reasonableness* is manifested by a correspondent and perpetual accompaniment of *reasons*, these reasons being deduced from the universally prevalent and universally recognized principles of human nature . . . [which] will of themselves help to lodge, and serve to

he insisted that the reasons themselves must be manifestly interconnected, thereby underwriting the systemic character of the body of law:

> An isolated reason is a mere trifle: the reasons for the laws, if they are good, are so connected, that unless they have been prepared for the whole body, they cannot with certainty be given for any part. Hence, in order to present in the most advantageous manner the reason for a single law, it is necessary that the plan of a system of reasons for all the laws should have been formed (B i. 163).

Bentham insisted further that the commentary of reasons be interwoven into the text of the publicly promulgated law. "There must be therefore not one system only, but two parallel and connected systems, running on together, the one of legislative provisions, the other of political reasons, each affording to the other correction and support" (IPML 9). He showed how this was to be done in his *Constitutional Code* of 1830 (LW 257 and CC (CW) vol. 1 generally).

The commentary of reasons enables law-makers or judges to justify their exercise of ruling power to the public (LW 45, 141ff). This is not just shrewd ruling practice; for Bentham it was critical to law's performing its proper function. *Reasons* "alone are addressed from understanding to understanding. *Ordinances* without reasons, are but manifestations of will—of the will of the mighty, exacting obedience from the helpless" (LW 100). Without the accompanying commentary of reasons, the exercise of law-making power is nothing more than an expression of will, a bare exercise of political power, not an attempt to address the understanding of law subjects (LW 7–8, 78–9, 143; B i. 161). Law designed according to these principles promised three additional key benefits, Bentham argued.

First, the interpretation of the law, by officials and citizens alike, are directed to a publicly accessible and publicly meaningful source (LW 141, 248; B i. 160–1). Bentham realized that the need for interpretation is inevitable, but the publicly and systematically articulated code, drafted in readily accessible terms, accompanied by a matching systematic account of its underlying principles, serves as a guide for and a hence tether on "liberal interpretation" of judges and officials (*Limits* 174–5, 228–9); it also serves as a common source of understanding for citizens, and hence a basis for anticipating the interpretations of the laws by officials and fellow citizens.

Second, this "rationalized" pannomion supplies a "bridle" with which the public can control "constituted authorities." The rationale provides "a preservative" against "blind routine" and "a restraint to everything arbitrary." Under a "rationalized body of law ... the reign of arbitrary power will be at an end," Bentham optimistically

keep, in the mind those portions of the matter of law, of which the *Main Text* will require to be composed" (LW 121 n. a, original emphasis). See also LW 7–8, 45–6, 79, 101, 248–50, 260; B i. 160–1.

predicted.[22] The system of law, to which all officials must appeal to demonstrate warrant for and justification of their actions, provides a "torch" exposing all official acts of oppression to the critical scrutiny of the Public Opinion Tribunal (SM 121). "In his capacity as censor, every citizen will be enabled to act ... calling to account this or that member of the legislative body, in respect of the code" (LW 270).

Third, it provides a focus for criticism of the law (LW 10–11). "By rendering the law a fully known and comprehensible entity," Lieberman writes, "the *Pannomion* stood exposed to public comment and criticism. This made the Code a fully public resource: an institution of power that utilized methods which enabled the public to monitor and critique the exercise of that power."[23] This, in turn, offered a more general framework of public debate and deliberation. In the early 1780s, Bentham tentatively expressed a hope that giving power to courts to review legislation would provide a framework and discipline for "a public and authorized debate on the propriety of law... The artillery of the tongue is [thereby] played off against the law under the cover of the law itself" (FG 488 n.1). In 1820s Bentham gave the Public Opinion Tribunal a major role in control of governing power. His publicly articulated and authenticated, reasons-manifesting pannomion promised a framework for such general criticism.

THE POLITICAL ROLE OF PUBLICITY

The principle of utility, properly refined and focused, promised to provide a language of public reason; law, properly structured and focused, promised the same. Neither, Bentham came to realize, could do so on their own, but in partnership they could make good on their promises. Bentham saw them as complementary, mutually supportive, the strengths of each answering the limits of the other (LW 78–9, 143). Law was not, as in Hobbes's view, a surrogate for the practical reason of individuals, but rather an essential supplement, a means by which individual practical reason was focused, facilitated, and enhanced. At the same time, Bentham regarded law as a joint product of authority and reason, of authentically public norms integrated into a rationally compelling systematic structure, the reasons for which are manifest.

To this partnership Bentham added an essential third party: an informed, empowered, and active public. Although already implicit in his early jurisprudential work (especially in his reliance on the "moral sanction" at the foundations of law), the political role of publicity became central to his political and constitutional work in the last his last two decades. Since the sole ultimate aim of government is

[22] LW 269, 248–9; B i. 161, UC 80.36; see also LW 141.

[23] David Lieberman, "Bentham's Jurisprudence and Democratic Theory: An Alternative to Hart's Approach," in *Bentham's Theory of Law and Public Opinion*, Zhai and Quinn, eds. (Cambridge: Cambridge University Press, 2014), 139.

the greatest happiness, or universal interest, of the community, the fundamental task of the engineer of political arrangements, he argued, is to define and distribute ruling power so as to achieve this goal. This involves securing the "moral, intellectual, and active aptitude" of all political functionaries, and, most importantly, preventing the "sinister sacrifice" of the universal interest to the private interest of those wielding political power. The first task, then, was to define, structure, and fund devices for "security against misrule." To this end, Bentham rejected the familiar liberal devices of imposing legal limits on the exercise of power through entrenching "natural rights" in some fundamental law or separating powers and putting them in competition (SM 23–4n). Rather, he insisted on "constant responsibility," "the strictest and most absolute dependence" on the public (CC (B) 62; see B iv. 362). "Maximum publicity" was not seen just "a necessary condition to the maximum appropriate attitude" (OAM 26), it was, in Bentham's view, the only effective means to this end.[24] Bentham argued that popular control must never be limited to the exercise of the "locative" and "dislocative" power of the electorate. It must be continuous, not episodic. For this purpose, publicity was essential.

The demand for publicity took two interrelated forms: a demand for *transparency* which mobilized a public discipline of accountability-holding, and a demand for *reasons* which mobilized public deliberation. First, "sinister interest and evil in every shape," Bentham argued, breeds "in the darkness of secrecy" (CC (B) 493). Publicity's harsh light exposes oppression and misrule to searching public scrutiny. In a variety of works, Bentham designed an extraordinary array of formal and informal devices to secure transparency of all governmental activities. He designed public institutions, public buildings, and public spaces in which officials could be observed, interrogated, and judged by members of the Public Opinion Tribunal. These devices exposed official actions to scrutiny and they enabled, encouraged and educated the public's exercise of governmental oversight. Bentham's aim was to subject official actions to the "superintendence" of the public via its exercise of the "moral sanction."[25] Bentham thought that the moral sanction exerts control primarily through officials' concern for reputation or esteem (UC 57.9). "The eye of the public makes the statesman virtuous," he argued (B x. 145). When opportunities to serve sinister interests are limited, concern for the good opinion of others will motivate most officials to behave in accord with common standards, that is, perceived universal interests.

Bentham realized that the public has an even more powerful weapon in its disciplinary arsenal: withdrawal of obedience and even active resistance (SM 123). Bentham held that resistance was justified not only at the extreme limit of government dysfunction, but as a regular "disposition" of the public, which should be encouraged by explicit constitutional arrangements. Free

[24] SM 125; UC 51(b), 378; B iv. 310, 317–18; RRR 202; PT 37; B ii. 8; FP 241.
[25] PT 29–30; CC vol. 1, 24; CC (B) 50–1, 151–2; B ii. 31.

governments should "cherish the disposition to eventual resistance," and take steps to keep "the national mind . . . in a state of appropriate preparation . . . for eventual resistance (B ii. 287). Key to such preparation, Bentham's argued, was a vigorous free press.

Second, Bentham argued that publicity enables and empowers public *accountability*, which mobilizes an effective demand on officials to give reasons to the public for their actions and policies. In *Fragment on Government*, Bentham equated "the responsibility of governors" with "the right which a subject has of having the reasons publicly assigned and canvassed of every act of power that is exerted over him" (FG 485). Likewise, later he tied "superintendency of the public" to the official's "obligation of assigning reasons for his acts" (B v. 556), reasons appealing to the legal or political principles warranting them and the political goals driving them.[26] Publicity not only exposes an unjust action to public view, but it makes its injustice manifest (B ii. 141, 147); similarly, the manner in which just actions serve universal interests is manifested.

In this way, the evaluation and censure of, and possible resistance to, governmental misrule over time is increasingly better informed and more likely to be articulate and securely focused on the universal interest. The public "may err," but, freed from the distorting influences of the "aristocratical class," and participating in public discussion, "it continually tends to become enlightened" (PT 29). "In proportion as [the public] becomes more and more mature," Bentham optimistically believed, it "becomes more and more favorable to the universal interest" (CC (B) 45, 158). Thus, when subject to the demands of publicity and the institutional structures that seek to meet them, law and its administration provide a *school* for public political morality.[27] By observing the giving and assessing of reasons by officials in public, and eventually participating in the process themselves, citizens, "impressed with their own sense of dignity" (B ii. 127), come to develop "a habit of reasoning and discussion" that focuses more on their common or universal interests than on their particular sinister interests, and their "passions, accustomed to a public struggle, will learn reciprocally to restrain themselves" (PT 31; CC (B) 100). The order of debate and deliberation which the public can observe when the business of a community's political assemblies are fully open to view, will "form by imitation the national spirit," which order, in turn, "will be reproduced in clubs and inferior assemblies" (PT 31). Through participation in debates at the local level, members of the community come to recognize the public dimensions of their concern to secure themselves against depredation or oppression and their individual part in that universal interest, and at the same time come to understand the difficulty of enlisting the cooperation of others to advance their private, "sinister" interests. This more informed and disciplined practice of small-scale public discussion

[26] B ii. 141–2, 147; CC (B) 535, 555; B vi. 356.

[27] B vi. 355, 360; B ii. 127, 143, 148, 149–50; PT 31.

enables the community more articulately and effectively to exercise control over government officials and the larger public assemblies.

Of course, Bentham realized that not everyone in this school earns high marks, and blinkered views of the facts, particular passions, and narrowly focused interests can still influence public opinion (CC (B) 42). Nevertheless, Bentham put his faith in publicity: the only effective remedy for the defects of publicity, he thought, is more publicity, more public involvement in public assessment of and debate over the actions and policies of government and the laws which determine the boundaries and directions of the exercise of political power.

Bentham's optimism rested ultimately on his faith in the educative capacity of the continued and widest spread of public discussion in which members of the Public Opinion Tribunal were actively engaged. They were not, on his model, merely passive observers, mobilized when needed to punish governmental misrule; rather, officials directed to them arguments for laws, policies, and official actions, engaging them in the assessment of those reasons, forming and giving expression to judgments, and acting on them (SM 61). Their capacities were developed, resourced, and enriched in this "tribunal of free criticism." Bentham's "public sphere" was meant to be richly and broadly deliberative.

CONCLUSION

Bentham's work on publicity knitted together a systematic theory of public reason, integrating utility and law into a complex framework for public reasoning, with a detailed architecture of public space, and constructing a network of key institutions and incentives for public accountability and public deliberation. He designed these institutions to secure the transparency of every exercise of ruling power and to encourage, educate, and empower the public in their critical task of holding officials to their responsibilities under the law. The law itself was designed to provide fully public—accessible, assessable, and manifestly reasonable—standards for public as well as private actions. This required, on Bentham's account, explicitly articulated, formally enacted, and fully authenticated legal norms that are internally and systematically related according to a plan that made content of the norms and their reasonableness manifest to all members of the political community. Law constructed on this model would provide guidance to all, and hence to each, guidance that addresses their understanding rather than manipulated their wills. The ultimate principle that secured this public reasonableness was, for Bentham, the principle of utility, the only principle, in his view, that met the fundamental demand in the moral as well as political domain for a truly public, rational basis for judgment and action.

Viewed through this lens, Bentham's jurisprudential theory—his thetic conception of law—appears continuous with his moral and his political theories, constituting a systematic whole. Quasi- (or revisionist) positivist in its main outlines this theory may be, but Bentham never succumbed to the methodological ambition of latter-day positivism to construct a theory of law beholden to no moral or political commitments. His moral, political, and legal theories are interdependent and mutually supporting.

Index

Note: For the benefit of digital users, indexed terms that span two pages (e.g., 52–53) may, on occasion, appear on only one of those pages.